D1084844

At the Forefront of Lee's Invasion

CIVIL WAR SOLDIERS AND STRATEGIES
Brian S. Wills, Series Editor

At the Forefront of Lee's Invasion

Retribution, Plunder, and Clashing Cultures on Richard S. Ewell's Road to Gettysburg

Robert J. Wynstra

THE KENT STATE UNIVERSITY PRESS

KENT, OHIO

Library of Congress Catalog Number 2018008734
ISBN 978-1-60635-354-7
Manufactured in the United States of America

LIBRARY OF CONGRESS CATALOGING-IN-PUBLICATION DATA
Names: Wynstra, Robert J., author.
Title: At the forefront of Lee's invasion : retribution, plunder, and clashing cultures on
    Richard S. Ewell's road to Gettysburg / Robert J. Wynstra.
Description: Kent, Ohio : The Kent State University Press, [2018] | Series: Civil War soldiers
    and strategies | Includes bibliographical references and index.
Identifiers: LCCN 2018008734 | ISBN 9781606353547 (hardcover ; alk. paper)
Subjects: LCSH: Gettysburg Campaign, 1863. | United States--History--Civil War,
    1861-1865--Campaigns. | Ewell, Richard Stoddert, 1817-1872.
Classification: LCC E475.51 .W96 2018 | DDC 973.7/349--dc23
LC record available at https://lccn.loc.gov/2018008734

22 21 20 19 18   5 4 3 2 1

Contents

Acknowledgments

This book would not have been possible without kind assistance from numerous people, who shared my enthusiasm for the project. I would especially like to acknowledge prolific author and researcher Scott Mingus Sr., who was kind enough to review my manuscript and contribute from his treasure trove of knowledge about Maj. Gen. Jubal Early's activities in York County, Pennsylvania. His earlier classic book on the Confederate advance to York and Wrightsville, Pennsylvania, served as one of the primary inspirations for my interest in this topic. Without his help and encouragement, my task would have been much more difficult.

Author Steve French generously reviewed many versions of the manuscript and contributed several valuable documents. He has long been a kind friend and source of vital information on wartime activities in the Shenandoah Valley. Most important, I thank him for putting me in touch with Kent State University Press, which ultimately made this book possible.

The young prodigy Cooper Wingert repeatedly provided me with some elusive documents that I could not have obtained or even known about without his kind help. Author Gregory White also went the extra distance to supply me with several newspaper accounts and other important documents from his home state of Georgia. Seasonal ranger and author Charles Teague graciously helped me obtain several important items from the Gettysburg Military Park Library. He also joined me in walking the field at Gettysburg and provided invaluable insights on the terrain and its influence on the battle. Most of all, his enthusiasm and support for my projects over the years are greatly appreciated.

Credit is also due to Thomas L. Elmore, who reviewed my manuscript and contributed several vital documents, diaries, and letters. Benjamin Hoover II provided me with an invaluable family letter for use in my research. Howard Land allowed me to quote from his relative's Civil War diary. The late John Chapla kindly gave me access to several important letters regarding the activities of the Forty-Second Virginia. Fred Ray as always willing shared from his vast storehouse of information on Maj. Eugene Blackford and the sharpshooters in Rodes's Division.

My appreciation extends to prolific author Eric Wittenberg for his early interest in my various projects and his kind assistance over the years. J. David Petruzzi also deserves special recognition for his encouragement and help. Without exception, the staffs from the numerous public and private archives and other institutions that provided source material and photographs for this book were remarkably helpful. From large to small, they provided the kind of dedicated service that makes my research so enjoyable. Thanks are also due to Phil Laino for his superb maps, which so greatly enhance this publication.

Of course, this book would not have been possible without the support from acquisitions editor William Underwood and the staff at Kent State University Press, which well deserves its reputation as one of the premier Civil War publishers in the country. Their enthusiasm and unmatched professionalism made every step in the publishing process remarkably easy. Without them, this book would have been impossible. Thanks are also due to copyeditor Kevin Brock, who patiently guided me through the many baffling intricacies of the *Chicago Manual of Style*. Without his expert help, my efforts would have fallen well short of the mark.

Lastly, I would like to thank Anita Povich for her constant help. Every time I faltered she was there to pick me up and prod me to move forward. Many times she showed more faith in my ability to pull off this project than I did. Without her support and encouragement, I certainly would still be struggling to finish this book.

Introduction

"We Have Our Wishes Gratified"

After clearing the Shenandoah Valley of Federal troops, Gen. Robert E. Lee's bold invasion into the North reached the Maryland shore of the Potomac River on June 15, 1863. A week later the Confederate infantry crossed into lower Pennsylvania, where they had their first sustained interactions with the civilian population of a solidly pro-Union state, laying bare the enormous cultural gulf that separated the two sides in the war. Most of these initial encounters in the lush Cumberland Valley and adjacent regions of Pennsylvania involved the men from the Army of Northern Virginia's famed Second Corps, leading the way as Lee's veteran soldiers advanced north toward their eventual showdown with the Union Army of the Potomac at the crossroads town of Gettysburg.

Lt. Gen. Richard S. Ewell had assumed command of this newly reorganized corps on June 1 as the successor to Lt. Gen. Thomas J. "Stonewall" Jackson, who succumbed on May 10 to complications from the accidental wounds he suffered eight days earlier at Chancellorsville. Ewell, who had finally recovered from the loss of his left leg less than a year before, returned to the army on May 29, arriving in the Fredericksburg area early that day on a train from Richmond. At the age of forty-six, Ewell now ranked as third in command of the army, behind only Lee and Lt. Gen. James Longstreet. His corps included the three divisions commanded by Maj. Gens. Jubal A. Early, Edward "Old Allegheny" Johnson, and Robert E. Rodes.[1]

Ewell's background gave every indication that he was well qualified for his new position. He was a native of Virginia and grew up on a farm near Manassas. After graduating from West Point in 1840 ranked thirteenth in his class, he fought in the Mexican War under Maj. Gen. Winfield Scott and was cited for gallantry during the fighting at Contreras and Churubusco. Ewell continued to serve in the U.S. Army after the war as an officer in the dragoons on the western frontier, eventually rising to the rank of captain. Baldheaded with bulging eyes and a distinct lisp to his speech, he remained a bachelor at the time that he joined the Confederate service in early 1861.

After briefly serving as a regimental commander, Ewell earned promotion to brigadier general in June of that year. As an experienced military man, he quickly rose to command a division under Stonewall Jackson. During the Shenandoah Valley Campaign in the spring of 1862, Ewell emerged as one of the leader's most trusted subordinates, playing a key role in the major victories at Winchester (May 25) and Cross Keys (June 8). He again performed brilliantly during the subsequent fighting at Gaines's Mill (June 27) and Malvern Hill (July 1) during the crucial Seven Days' Campaign.

His service with Jackson was cut short when Ewell suffered a severe leg wound at Groveton during the Second Manassas Campaign that August. While recuperating from the amputation of his limb, the general courted and finally married his cousin, Lizinka Campbell Brown, the widow of a wealthy plantation owner from Mississippi. During his extended absence, Ewell wholeheartedly supported the promotion of General Early to take over his former division. Although he remained without a command of his own, Ewell had largely recovered from his injuries by early May 1863 and was ready to rejoin the army.[2]

The situation suddenly changed on the night of May 2, when some of Brig. Gen. James H. Lane's North Carolina troops accidentally wounded Stonewall Jackson while he carried out a hurried reconnaissance along their front lines at Chancellorsville. Other shooting in the darkness subsequently injured Maj. Gen. Ambrose Powell Hill. "Jackson's left arm was broken and A. P. Hill wounded in the leg (left) by the firing of our own troops," an officer from Rodes's Division lamented in his diary. He noted that the men "fired on nothing—for several minutes our troops cut each other to pieces." The fabled leader died from his injuries little more than a week later.[3]

That devastating loss opened the way for some sweeping changes in the makeup of the Confederate army. With Jackson gone, Lee moved ahead with his plans for reorganizing his force into three infantry corps, each of which would be more manageable in size. He eventually selected Ewell to take over the vaunted Second Corps, which was slightly reduced in numbers, and turned to A. P. Hill, who had commanded the Light Division in Jackson's corps, as the leader of the newly created Third Corps. Lieutenant General Longstreet continued as the head of the First Corps.

Because of Ewell's lengthy association with Jackson, nearly all the officers who had been closest to the fallen general greeted his selection with outright enthusiasm. "We have our wishes gratified here in having Gen. Ewell to command the old army of Gen. Jackson," Capt. Jedediah Hotchkiss, who had served as Jackson's chief topographer, proclaimed in a letter to his wife. "As much of the ardor as could possibly be transferred to any man has been transferred by this corps to Gen. Ewell." Maj. Alexander S. "Sandie" Pendleton, who was Jackson's former assistant adjutant general, described Ewell to his fiancée as "the old hero, friend and fellow soldier & sufferer, comrade in battle and on the march and a fellow mourner with each one of us."[4]

Lt. Gen. Richard S. Ewell. Courtesy Library of Congress.

Most of the soldiers in Early's and Johnson's divisions also knew their new commander well and openly supported his appointment. "The old confidence in Jackson has found a new birth in our faith in Ewell," Col. Clement A. Evans of the Thirty-First Georgia in the Virginian's former division remarked to his wife soon after the general's promotion. "Always a favorite with his division, he is now the idol of his corps." Even the men outside the corps generally held him in high esteem. "Ewell is considered as Jackson's equal, even in dash, and by many persons as his superior in ability," an admiring Georgian officer in Longstreet's First Corps reported to his fiancée. "I am satisfied he will sustain himself and the reputation of the army."[5]

Ewell proved so popular that the troops from the Louisiana brigade in his former division turned out in force to greet him on his return. "Gen. Hays' Louisiana Brigade was present in martial review to receive him, and claimed the honor of escorting their former and favorite commander to this temporary abode," one soldier effused in a letter to a Richmond newspaper. "Amidst deafening cheers and the rolling sounds of martial music, he was once more ushered into active service." The ecstatic troops heaped kind wishes on their triumphant hero from all sides. "May an all-wise Providence shield him, and give victory to the cause of which he is so glorious a champion," the soldier declared.[6]

The men in Rodes's Division remained less familiar with their new corps commander. For many of them, the most telling point in his favor was the widespread rumor that on his deathbed Jackson had requested Ewell as his replacement. "I have also seen it, in print, that it was Jackson's wish that it should fall on Gen Ewell, speaking of him in the highest terms, but as yet, I have heard nothing definite as to his successor," a private from the Twenty-Third North Carolina commented to his sister just prior to the general's appointment.[7]

Ewell further solidified his credentials as Jackson's successor by appointing most of the fallen commander's closest associates to his own staff. He selected Pendleton as assistant adjutant general and soon afterward elevated him to chief of staff. Dr. Hunter H. McGuire continued as the medical director for the Second Corps. Jed Hotchkiss stayed in place as the chief mapmaker for the new leader. Rev. Beverly Tucker Lacy, who was Jackson's favorite preacher, also remained with the corps to provide needed spiritual guidance. One of the few newcomers to the staff was Ewell's stepson and close confidant, Maj. George Campbell Brown, who took a position as assistant adjutant general.[8]

Yet even some of Ewell's supporters in the Second Corps worried that his recent marriage had tamed the once-profane and hard-fighting bachelor. "General Ewell arrived in camp with his wife—a new acquisition—and with one leg less than when I saw him last," quipped Lt. Randolph McKim, who had served with the general throughout much of the war. "From a military point of view the addition of the wife did not compensate for the loss of the leg." He admitted, "we were of the opinion that Ewell was not the same soldier he had been when he was a whole man—and a single one."[9]

Others remained concerned that their corps commander had not yet fully recovered from the amputation of his leg. One soldier from Ewell's former division commented in his diary that the general was "looking quite badly" when he arrived in camp. Lt. Col. Thomas H. Carter, who headed one of the artillery battalions in the corps, had a more mixed reaction to the sight of the new commander. "I saw Genl Ewell yesterday," he wrote to his wife during early June. "The old fellow looks thin & pale but rides with ease & on horse back no one can tell the wooden leg." Even so, Carter continued to worry about his condition. "I hope his health may last, but he looks feeble," the artilleryman admitted.[10]

General Lee also harbored some gnawing doubts about Ewell's fitness for such a demanding position. A close reading of the original endorsement showed only tepid enthusiasm for his selection to head the Second Corps. The army commander noted simply that Ewell "is an honest, brave soldier, who has always done his duty well." In later years Lee acknowledged that he reluctantly moved ahead with Ewell's promotion despite "his faults as a military leader." He especially worried about "his quick alternations from elation to despondency" and "his want of decision &c."[11]

Despite such misgivings about their new leader, most of the troops in the Second Corps hardly wavered at all in their enthusiasm. "Our corps is now commanded by Genrl. Ewell," Col. Francis M. Parker of the Thirtieth North Carolina in Rodes's Division remarked to his wife following the appointment. "He is a fine officer; what to us, is a good recommendation, is the known fact that Genl. Jackson had a very high opinion of him." Like so many others throughout the army, the veteran officer held out high hope that Ewell would "fill the place, made vacant by the loss of the great, the noble Jackson."[12]

Most important, the appointment of someone so close to Stonewall signaled to many of the men that the time had finally arrived to break the stalemate along the Rappahannock River, which had existed since their defensive victory at Fredericksburg during December 1862. Following their stunning triumph at Chancellorsville in May 1863, most of them remained convinced that General Lee rather than the Union commander, Maj. Gen. Joseph Hooker, would make the first move. "If there is any forward movement," Maj. Charles C. Blacknall of the Twenty-Third North Carolina in Rodes's Division wrote to his brother-in-law at the beginning of June, "it will no doubt be initiated by Genl. Lee, as our army is now in fine condition & everything looks favorable for an aggressive campaign."[13]

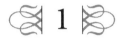

"A Fair Opportunity to Strike a Blow"

The three top leaders in Ewell's new corps comprised a decidedly mixed group. Maj. Gen. Jubal A. Early ranked as the senior division commander. He was born in 1816 and grew up in the hill country of southwestern Virginia. Early graduated from West Point in 1837 and served as a lieutenant in the Third U.S. Artillery during the Second Seminole War (1835–42). Resigning from the army the following year, he returned home and took up the practice of law. Early soon won election to the Virginia legislature, where he served from 1841 to 1843. The former lawmaker then fought during the Mexican War (1846–48) as a major in the First Virginia Volunteers, though he experienced no significant combat.[1]

Returning to Virginia, Early resumed his law career. As a member of the Whig Party, he vehemently opposed leaving the Union during the fractious 1861 Virginia Secession Convention. But the lawyer's principled stance quickly changed once Pres. Abraham Lincoln called on the state to provide troops to put down the rebellion in the Deep South. "I at once recognized my duty to abide the decision of my native State, and to defend her soil against invasion," Early explained years later. When Virginia finally seceded, he tendered his services to the new Confederate army.[2]

Soon after arriving in camp at Lynchburg, Virginia, Early took over as colonel of the Twenty-Fourth Virginia Infantry. He eventually assumed command of a temporary brigade, which he effectively led during the stunning victory at First Manassas in mid-July. Early was promoted to brigadier general soon afterward to rank from the date of that battle. He continued to lead the brigade during the Peninsula Campaign in the fierce fighting on May 5, 1862, at Williamsburg, Virginia, where he suffered a wound to his shoulder but did not leave the field.[3]

While Early recovered from that injury, his troops transferred to other units as part of the army-wide reorganization aimed at putting regiments together in single-state brigades, temporarily leaving him without a command of his own. On June 30

Early took over the brigade formerly headed by Brig. Gen. Arnold Elzey. His new command formed part of Major General Ewell's division in Stonewall Jackson's Second Corps. Early's first combat as leader of that brigade came on the following day at Malvern Hill, near the end of Lee's decisive Seven Days' Campaign.[4]

Early once again led those men during the fierce fighting at Cedar Mountain in early August. The division, however, endured a major blow when Ewell sustained a devastating wound to his left leg at Groveton during this run-up engagement to Second Manassas. Early participated in the fighting at Second Manassas under Brig. Gen. Alexander R. Lawton, who had assumed acting command of the division. Early continued to lead the brigade at Sharpsburg on September 17, during which he took over the division late in the day after Lawton was wounded. He remained as its temporary head during the fighting at Fredericksburg in mid-December.[5]

By early 1863 Early began to vigorously lobby for promotion to permanent command of the division. While no one questioned his fighting abilities, his abrasive manner raised some serious concerns about his fitness for higher command. Prominent staff officer G. Moxley Sorrel complained that Early's "irritable disposition and biting tongue made him anything but popular." John S. Wise, the son of the former governor of Virginia, described the general as "eccentric in appearance, in voice, [and] in manner of speech." He was most put off by his fellow Virginian's constant swearing and utter disrespect for authority. "His opinions were expressed unreservedly, and he was most emphatic and denunciatory, and startlingly profane," Wise explained.[6]

Pvt. James W. Baker from the Thirteenth Virginia echoed the feelings of many in the army when he declared that the general's "cynicism and wickedness were beyond belief." Just as bad was Early's dismissive attitude toward his fellow officers. Brig. Gen. John Brown Gordon, who would later serve under his direct command, recalled that Early "possessed other characteristics peculiarly his own, which were the parents of more or less trouble to him and to those under him: namely, his indisposition to act upon suggestions submitted by subordinates." None of that criticism seemed to bother General Lee, who affectionately referred to Early as his "bad old man."[7]

Despite the brigade commander's prickly personality, Ewell continued to hold a high opinion of his fighting abilities. "General Early is an excellent officer—ought to be Maj. Genl.," he wrote to his future wife a couple of months after suffering the amputation of his leg. By then, Early had become so frustrated with his lack of a promotion that he threatened to transfer to the one of the Confederate armies in the West. Ewell soon made it clear that he would willingly step aside in Early's favor. "When I am fit for duty they may do what they please with me, but I think your claims to the Division, whether length of time or hard service be considered are fully equal, if not superior to mine," he wrote to Early at the beginning of March.[8]

Any lingering concerns about the Virginian's fitness were put aside when Lee promoted Early to major general and head of the division on April 8, 1863, to rank

Maj. Gen. Jubal A. Early. Courtesy Library of Congress.

from January 17. His command included four veteran brigades. Brig. Gen. Harry Hays led a brigade of Louisiana troops, nicknamed the "Louisiana Tigers." Brig. Gen. William "Extra Billy" Smith, who was a former congressman and governor of Virginia, assumed command of Early's old unit. General Gordon, who was one of the heroes of Sharpsburg, led the lone Georgia regiments in the division. Finally, Brig. Gen. Robert Hoke headed a brigade of North Carolina troops.[9]

Early commanded the division at Chancellorsville, where his troops took on the task of holding Marye's Heights around Fredericksburg against a Federal advance. After finally forcing these troops to withdraw, a column from Hooker's army under Maj. Gen. John Sedgwick moved forward against Lee's rear. The Confederates, however, decisively rebuffed this Federal advance at Salem Church on May 4. Early soon redeemed himself by organizing a counterattack that caused Hooker to pull his battered troops across the Rappahannock two days later. General Hoke suffered a severe wound during the fighting, leaving his brigade under the temporary command of Col. Isaac Avery from the Sixth North Carolina.[10]

Early's mixed performance at Chancellorsville apparently did nothing to soften his abrasive personality. "Old Early is the same as ever—neither loving, lovely, or loved," Col. Clement A. Evans from Gordon's Brigade quipped to his wife after watching him during a review by General Lee at the end of May. "I rarely hear him spoken well of." At the same time, Early's reputation as a hard fighter remained largely unaffected. Although having experienced some problems during the recent battle, he still seemed primed to play a key role in what everyone assumed would be an active campaign into the North during the summer of 1863.[11]

Unlike Early, Edward "Old Allegheny" Johnson, who headed Stonewall Jackson's former division, was new to the Army of Northern Virginia. The forty-seven-year-old major general was born in Virginia but grew up in Kentucky. Following his graduation from West Point in 1838, Johnson served as a lieutenant in the Sixth U.S. Infantry. The young officer participated in the campaign against the Seminoles in Florida and later fought under General Scott, earning brevets to captain and major for bravery during the battles around Mexico City. Following the end of that war, he continued to serve in the U.S. Army on the western frontier, rising to the permanent rank of captain.[12]

In the spring of 1861, Johnson resigned his commission and joined the Confederate army as colonel of the Twelfth Georgia. The regiment saw its first action during Lee's failed campaign in the mountains of northwestern Virginia during the late summer of 1861. Soon afterward Johnson assumed command of a brigade-sized force that was grandly dubbed the Army of the Northwest. On December 13, Federal troops under Brig. Gen. Robert H. Milroy launched a determined assault on Johnson's position along the summit of Allegheny Mountain. After a flurry of fierce fighting, the Confederates drove the enemy back in disarray toward their supply base near Cheat Mountain.[13]

Johnson's conduct in this stunning victory won high praise from newspapers throughout the South, earning him the nickname "Old Allegheny" for his gallantry. "Col. Edward Johnson, an old army officer, the commandant of the post, behaved with his usual bravery, and was the hero of the fight," the *Richmond Enquirer* proclaimed. "The letter before us says 'Col. Johnson was *a whale*—he was in the thickest of danger always.'" The *Macon Telegraph* chimed in with the comment that Johnson had "acted most gallantly" during the fighting. According to its colorful account, he boldly led his troops into action "with a musket in one hand and a club in the other."[14]

Some of Johnson's men were just as impressed by what they witnessed during the fighting. Even years later one Virginian in the battle still found his commander's performance beyond reproach. "I remember how I thought Colonel Johnson must be the most wonderful hero in the world, as I saw him at one point, where his men were hard pressed, snatch a musket in one hand and, swinging a big club in the other, he led his line right up among the enemy, driving them headlong down the mountain, killing and wounding many with the bayonet and capturing a large number of prisoners."[15]

But many others had a much different opinion of Johnson's conduct during the battle. Much of this criticism focused on what they regarded as the colonel's cruel behavior toward his troops. One soldier complained that Johnson "displayed great bravery but very poor military skill in the handling of his men." Most troubling were the repeated hard blows that he inflicted on some of the soldiers with his huge walking stick. "Instead of taking a position of observation, he armed himself with a club and mixing himself up with the men went about urging them forward with curses and vaporing of his club," the veteran grumbled.[16]

Johnson's hard-fought victory earned him promotion to brigadier general on February 28, 1862. During the first week of April, his small Army of the Northwest finally moved forward from Allegheny Mountain into the heart of the Shenandoah Valley. On May 6 the troops linked up with Jackson's Army of the Valley near Staunton. Together they engaged Milroy's troops two days later along the heights around McDowell. After enduring a furious onslaught, the Confederate forces eventually forced the Federals to withdraw from the field. Johnson remained amid the action at the head of his troops throughout much of the day.[17]

As darkness approached, Johnson suffered a severe wound that shattered his ankle. Although the injury would require a long period to fully heal, his conduct during the battle made an indelible impression on Jackson. "General Johnson, to whom I had intrusted the management of the troops engaged, proved himself eminently worthy of the confidence reposed in him by the skill, gallantry, and presence of mind which he displayed on the occasion," the commander declared in his official report. After a period of treatment at Staunton, Johnson moved on to Richmond to finish his recuperation.[18]

As a bachelor, Johnson spent much of his time at the capital wooing the single women in the highest circles of society. What attracted the most attention, though, were his many physical quirks. "He had an odd habit of falling into a state of incessant winking as soon as he became the least startled or agitated," Mary Chesnut, whose husband was a top advisor to Pres. Jefferson Davis, wrote in her renowned diary. "In such times he seemed persistently to be winking one eye at you." She was especially put off by the unique appearance of his skull. "His head is strangely shaped, like a cone or an old-fashioned beehive," Chesnut remarked. Her friend Sally Buchanan Preston noted, "there are three tiers of it; it is like a pope's tiara." Not surprisingly, the general's amorous advances went unrequited.[19]

Despite Johnson's failure to find love, Jackson hoped to have him join his corps once the general was ready to return to duty. The position that he eyed for him was the vacancy that came open in early 1863 when Maj. Gen. Daniel Harvey Hill transferred from his division to a command in North Carolina. In February Jackson expressed his strong support for Johnson's promotion in a letter to Richmond. "Gen. Johnson was with me at the Battle of McDowell, when he so distinguished himself as to make me very desirous of securing his services as one of my division commanders," he wrote to Confederate secretary of war James A. Seddon.[20]

While Jackson waited for the opportunity to promote him, Johnson saw his convalescence extend well into the spring. By the time the general was ready to make his return to the army in early May, his prospects for advancement seemed less certain following Jackson's death. Based on Stonewall's dying wishes, Lee selected Robert Rodes to take over D. H. Hill's former division. Luckily for Johnson's advancement, Brig. Gen. Raleigh Colston's lackluster performance while temporarily leading Jackson's former division at Chancellorsville led to his removal, creating a new opening at the top of that command. On May 8 Lee selected Johnson as its permanent head.

Maj. Gen. Edward Johnson. Courtesy
Library of Congress.

Like Johnson, all four of his brigade commanders were new to their positions.
Following Chancellorsville, Lee picked Brig. Gen. George H. "Maryland" Steuart to
lead Colston's mixed command of Tar Heels and Virginians. Brig. Gen. John M. Jones
succeeded John R. Jones, who had disgraced himself by leaving the field amid the
fighting at Chancellorsville. Brig. Gen. James A. Walker assumed leadership of the
famed Stonewall Brigade after its commander, Brig. Gen. Frank Paxton, was killed
during the battle. Col. Jesse M. Williams from the Second Louisiana temporarily
headed the fourth brigade in the absence of Brig. Gen. Francis R. T. Nichols, who on
May 3 had suffered a severe wound in the foot.[21]

Because Johnson was new to the Army of Northern Virginia, most of the troops
based their opinion of him on rumors about his character. Pvt. Ted Barclay from the
Fifth Virginia in the Stonewall Brigade griped that Johnson was "a good general and
a brave man but one of the wickedest men I ever heard of." Lt. Thomas Boatwright
from the Forty-Fourth Virginia in Jones's Brigade complained, "we have such a con-
trary Old General that he will not give passes but seldom." Another soldier described
Johnson as "a brute." Whether the men would ever warm up to their new leader still
remained in doubt as they prepared for the impending move north.[22]

The situation proved much different for Rodes, who commanded the third division of the newly reorganized Second Corps. By the end of the fighting at Chancellorsville, he emerged as one of the rising stars in the Army of Northern Virginia.
While temporarily leading his division, Rodes spearheaded Jackson's brilliant flank
attack in the woods late in the afternoon on May 2. Only impending darkness prevented his troops from completely sweeping the Federal forces from the field. On

the following day his exhausted men endured some of the hardest fighting of the war before finally sealing the Confederate victory in the tangled wilderness just west of Fredericksburg.

More than six feet tall with an imposing sandy mustache, the thirty-four-year-old major general exemplified for many the emerging breed of Confederate warriors. Unlike all others of the same rank in Lee's army, Rodes did not attend West Point. A native of Lynchburg, Virginia, he instead graduated from Virginia Military Institute in 1848. After a brief stint teaching at his alma mater, Rodes moved to Alabama, where he quickly built a thriving career as a civil engineer in the railroad industry. Just prior to the outbreak of war, he accepted appointment as a professor at VMI but never actually served in that position.[23]

Rather than returning to his home state, Rodes stayed in Alabama and organized a volunteer company. Soon after arriving in camp at Montgomery, he won election as colonel of the Fifth Alabama. His regiment reached Virginia just in time for the First Battle of Manassas but took no major part in the fighting. The troops in his command quickly discovered that their colonel was a strict disciplinarian and a proponent of constant drilling. "Rodes I think has the drill-mania, for I think he had rather drill than eat a good dinner," one of the men quipped in his diary during late July 1861. He noted that "the boys grumble considerably."[24]

At the same time, the men found Rodes nearly impossible to dislike. By most accounts, he was a natural-born leader. His stunning good looks and erect military bearing left no doubts with those who met him that he was someone to be reckoned with on the field of battle. Rodes tempered all that with an easy charm that could disarm even his harshest critics. His manner remained the same whether he was dealing with an officer or an enlisted man. One soldier who later served under his command insisted that he had "never met a more just, conscientious and impartial officer."[25]

Rodes's abilities also drew positive notice from General Ewell, who served as his first brigade commander. In late August an officer from Ewell's staff reported to one of his relatives that the colonel was "an able & efficient officer." He added that the general "thinks very highly of him." Rodes finally received promotion to brigadier general in October 1861, when Ewell became commander of Jackson's former brigade. According to the young staffer, General Ewell's "repeated recommendations" played a major role in the selection of Rodes to fill the vacancy.[26]

Rodes's first major action at the head of his new brigade came in late May 1862 at Seven Pines, where he was wounded and cited for bravery. He returned to duty in time to lead his men in the bloody fighting at Gaines's Mill. The general further enhanced his reputation at South Mountain and Sharpsburg during the Maryland Campaign. Despite his enviable record, Rodes failed to earn advancement during the following months. After the transfer of D. H. Hill to North Carolina in early 1863, he assumed temporary command of the division. Even so, Jackson favored the selection of Johnson rather than Rodes as the permanent head. The final decision, however, remained on hold until Johnson was completely healed.[27]

Hill's former division included five brigades with lengthy experience in Lee's army. Brig. Gens. George P. Doles and Alfred H. Colquitt commanded the two Georgia brigades in the division. Col. Edward A. O'Neal from the Twenty-Sixth Alabama temporarily headed Rodes's former brigade (a promotion almost made permanent in June 1863). The division also included two veteran brigades from the Tar Heel State. One served under Brig. Gen. Stephen Dodson Ramseur, who had only recently joined the brigade after recovering from a severe wound to his arm suffered at Malvern Hill. Although he came from Georgia, Brig. Gen. Alfred Holt Iverson commanded the other North Carolina brigade.

Rodes quickly became a favorite among those who dealt with him while he temporarily headed the division. "I like him so much," Lt. James Power Smith from Jackson's staff effused in a letter to his sister during late January 1863. "He is very much admired by all and very popular." Pvt. George Thomas Rust, who served as a courier on the division staff, was equally pleased with his new commander. What stood out most of all was the general's sense of fairness toward those in the ranks. "Genl Rodes is very cordial & treats me as a friend & his equal," Rust gloated in a letter home.[28]

Maj. Eugene Blackford, who was a veteran field officer in the general's former regiment, held him in such high regard that he became indignant over the widespread reports that Johnson instead would "succeed to the command" of the division. "They have missed it much in not making Rodes the commander," he complained to his father. Blackford insisted that Rodes failed to gain this well-deserved promotion largely because he had not graduated from West Point. He lamented that "the prejudice in favour of West Pointers was too strong even for a man of his merit."[29]

The few dissenting opinions about Rodes came mostly among the men from the Twelfth Georgia in Doles's Brigade. Old Allegheny Johnson had served as colonel of the regiment during the early part of the war and remained well respected by the veterans in that command. As a result, many of those troops openly favored his promotion. "It is talked and generally believed that Gen. Ed. Johnson will take command of this division," the Twelfth Georgia's Lt. Irby Goodwin Scott commented to his father during mid-March. "He has been recommended by Lee & Jackson. I hope it may be true. Rodes is not very popular."[30]

Although Johnson's recovery extended well into the spring, Rodes held out little hope that he would be selected as permanent head of the division. Stonewall Jackson certainly gave no hints that he had any intention of changing his original preference for Johnson. Rodes also remained convinced that the first opportunity to fill any other vacancy for a division commander in General Lee's army would go to Brig. Gen. Cadmus M. Wilcox. "As he is a West Point man he will beat me almost to a certainty," he grumbled to Ewell during early spring. "I would prefer being beaten by a baboon but will submit to it quietly, unless they place [him] in command of this Div."[31]

Maj. Gen. Robert E. Rodes.
Courtesy Virginia Military Institute Archives.

The outlook suddenly brightened due to Rodes's brilliant conduct during the fighting at Chancellorsville. "Gen. Rodes distinguished himself much and won a proud name for himself and his division," Maj. Gen. A. P. Hill declared in his official report. General Lee indicated that one of Jackson's "dying messages to me was to the effect that General Rodes should be promoted major general and his promotion should date from May 2." As a result, Lee elevated Rodes to his new rank within days after the battle, while Johnson assumed command of Jackson's former division.[32]

Nearly everyone in the division greeted Rodes's appointment with enthusiasm. Major Blackford, who served under O'Neal's temporary command, reported to his cousin soon after the announcement that the general "well deserved" his promotion. Pvt. W. Davies Tinsley from the Fourth Georgia, which was one of Doles's regiments, described his new division commander in a letter to his mother as "a fine officer." He was especially struck by the youthful appearance of someone in such a high position. "He is a very young man—looks younger than I do," the Georgian declared in amazement.[33]

Most of the troops were even willing to overlook Rodes's well-known reputation for rigid discipline. "We hope he will make a good and efficient officer though some think he will be very Strict with both men and officers, which is all wright in so large a crowd of men," Capt. William B. Haygood from the Forty-Fourth Georgia in Doles's Brigade remarked in a letter home during mid-May. With Rodes in command, he had no doubts that the troops were ready to face whatever test awaited them. Although they had suffered almost 2,900 casualties during the recent fighting, the captain insisted that "our Division is a very efficient corps of men yet and can do good service when ever we are called on."[34]

Despite their success, not everything was positive for the men in the Second Corps following their victory at Chancellorsville. Many of them worried that the recent battle had failed to alter the strategic situation around Fredericksburg. "I fear the grand results of this fight are very few," Pvt. John H. Fain from the Twelfth North Carolina, which was part of Iverson's Brigade, grumbled to his mother. He pointed out that "both armies have taken up their old positions." The Tar Heel laid most of the blame on the huge difference in size between the two armies. He acknowledged that "the smallness of our force kept us from pursuing the enemy."[35]

Others remained convinced that the results of the two days of fierce fighting in the thick wilderness fell far short of justifying the cost. Pvt. Berry Kinney from the Fourteenth North Carolina in Ramseur's Brigade certainly found nothing to support the widely held belief throughout the South that Chancellorsville ranked as the greatest victory of the war. He insisted in a letter home that the huge number of casualties the Army of Northern Virginia had suffered made it pointless to describe the battle as a major triumph. The war-weary soldier argued instead that "it want [sic, won't] take many more such victorys to finish our army."[36]

The loss of Lieutenant General Jackson only added to their woes. Pvt. Allie Clack, who served with the Twenty-Third North Carolina in Iverson's Brigade, reported to his sister that "there is no man's death, just at this time, which has caused such universal sorrow." In Early's Division Lt. Henry E. Handerson from the Ninth Louisiana in Hays's Brigade insisted to his father that "we could have better spared 50000 men." Private Barclay from the Stonewall Brigade admitted in a letter home that "a deep gloom is over our camp over the death of General Jackson."[37]

The massive casualties the Confederates suffered in the recent fighting were even more devastating for the Tar Heel troops in Ewell's corps than the death of Jackson. Within days hundreds of them began yielding to the temptation of returning home. The upsurge in desertions that followed Chancellorsville quickly became a major point of friction between Gov. Zebulon Vance and the Richmond authorities. "I do not believe that one case in a hundred is caused by disloyalty—have no apprehensions on that score," the governor protested in a letter to President Davis. "Home sickness, fatigue, hard fare &c have of course much to do with it."[38]

The continued reduction of rations in the weeks following their victory emerged as another major concern for Ewell's troops. Colonel Evans griped to his wife during late May that the army was "living on a pound and three fourths of Bacon *per week* to the man." He insisted that even "the Negroes" at home "get twice as much." Such problems even extended to obtaining enough fodder for the vast number of horses, which were essential for transporting both artillery and the supply wagons. "Generally speaking our horses are much inferior to those of the enemy, and not half so well fed," Sgt. William S. White from the Third Richmond (Virginia) How-itzers in one of the Corps Reserve Artillery battalions grumbled in his diary.[39]

Most of the troops from Rodes's Division were just as frustrated with the shortage of supplies in the weeks following the battle. Private Kinney from Ramseur's Brigade complained in a letter home that he could eat all his daily rations in one sitting "if I had to work and not have half enough." The embittered conscript noted with disgust that "we have flys on our meat." He insisted that "no body can eat much [of] such do-ings as we have." Pvt. John T. Traylor from the Fourth Georgia griped to his wife that "our fair is rough & short" compared to the abundant food that he had access to while on a brief stay in Richmond. The young soldier admitted that he actually dreaded go-ing back to his brigade camp "on account of short rations" on hand there.[40]

A major shakeup occurred during mid-May when Colquitt's Georgians unexpect-edly transferred to North Carolina in exchange for a fresh Tar Heel brigade com-manded by Brig. Gen. Junius Daniel, which only added to the turmoil. That change resulted from Lee's clear dissatisfaction with Colquitt's performance at Chancellors-ville and the badly depleted condition of his brigade. Except for a brief stint with Lee's army during the Seven Days' Campaign, Daniel's troops had served mostly on gar-rison duty near Drewry's Bluff, Virginia, and in North Carolina before transferring to Rodes's Division.[41]

After a grueling trip, the new brigade reached the Fredericksburg area on the eve-ning of May 24. For many of the men, their arrival in Virginia came with a certain amount of trepidation. The biggest risk was that they would soon face some fierce combat for the first time in the war. Pvt. William J. Lowrey, who served in the Forty-Fifth North Carolina, admitted to his mother that "there is more danger of getting in a fight here." Pvt. Hugh Ingram from the Forty-Third North Carolina acknowledged that they would likely endure many hard battles before there was any chance for peace. "I do believe the war to close in my time," he predicted to his brother soon after reaching the Fredericksburg area.[42]

In the end, the opportunity to rejoin the Army of Northern Virginia after a nearly year-long absence outweighed any worries about what they might encounter in any upcoming action. "Tho it is more dangerous, yet I must say I am proud to be able to say I've joined Lee's Army," Sgt. George W. Wills from the Forty-Third North Caro-lina confided to his sister. Lt. Thomas C. Land from the Fifty-Third North Carolina was just as pleased about serving under Rodes, whom he described as "well qualified to fill the position recently tendered him." Despite those comments, one Tar Heel officer from Johnson's Division claimed after visiting "a number of old friends" in Daniel's camp that the new arrivals were "not very anxious to fight," or at least "not more so than the rest of us."[43]

Despite all their hardships, most of the men in Ewell's corps never wavered in their belief that they could not be defeated on the field of battle by Joseph Hooker or any other general who might succeed him. General Ramseur certainly showed no hesitation in predicting another major victory wherever the Federal commander decided to take them on. "No doubt Gen'l Lee will be ready to meet him at any point and with his veteran army so often blessed by our Father in Heaven, and drive him back with loss and disgrace," he bragged in a letter to his fiancée at the end of May.[44]

Capt. Reuben Allen Pierson from the Ninth Louisiana remained convinced that their current commanders were more than up to the task. "With such soldiers and our present leaders our enemies can never accomplish the unholy design which they have designed for our subjugation," he wrote in a letter home. Private Barclay from the Stonewall Brigade regarded Jackson's death as nothing more than a temporary setback. "Though we mourn his loss we still feel that we are not without a leader," he declared. "God is our leader and protector." The Virginian insisted that "he can raise up many a Jackson and will yet deliver us from the power of the enemy."[45]

Most of the men in Rodes's Division also harbored no doubts about General Lee's abilities to lead them to a final victory. "He is an idol with the army, though Jackson was scarcely subordinate in the affections of the soldiers," Musician Jacob Nathaniel "Nat" Raymer from the band of the Fourth North Carolina in Ramseur's Brigade proclaimed in a letter to his hometown newspaper during late May. Not even the devastating loss of General Jackson did anything to change his certainty that their army's commander would always find a way to come out victorious. Raymer pointed out that "when Lee is seen on the battle field nobody has any fears about the result."[46]

Pvt. James Z. Branscomb from the Third Alabama in O'Neal's Brigade echoed those sentiments about their beloved commanding general in a letter home soon after the battle. "You have no idea what confidence this army has in Lee," he declared to his sister. "What ever he says is thought to be alright by all." Col. Francis M. Parker from Ramseur's Brigade well summed up the prevailing mood among the troops when he reported to his wife following their victory at Chancellorsville that "the army has never been whipped, and the men feel as if it can not be; but our losses are terrible sometimes."[47]

The first sign that the start of the summer offensive was imminent came on June 3, when Rodes's men "received orders to cook our rations and be ready to move." Similar directives arrived at about the same time for the rest of the men in the corps. Any lingering doubts were erased a short time later when the Quartermaster Department directed company commanders to requisition a four-month supply of clothing. Despite all that activity, the soldiers still had no indication of exactly where they might be headed. "We have just rec'd orders to prepare for the march, and I expect will be off tonight," General Ramseur reported to his fiancée. "Where or why we go, none but Gen'l Lee & his Lieuts. know."[48]

Even the top commanders in the army only learned the specifics of Lee's plan a few days prior to their departure. After slipping away from the Fredericksburg area, Lee intended to seize the initiative by pushing north through the Shenandoah Valley into the heart of Maryland and Pennsylvania, thereby providing Virginia with weeks, if not months, of relief from rampaging armies. As the Confederates swept forward, he hoped to gather up huge quantities of badly needed supplies. Lee expected that the advance would draw the Federal army away from its supply base and transfer the "the scene of hostilities north of the Potomac." That move also offered him "a fair opportunity to strike a blow at the army then commanded by Gen. Hooker."[49]

Lee explained his thinking in more detail during a later conversation with Maj. Gen. Henry Heth. The army commander admitted to his old friend that "the question of food for this army gives me more trouble than anything else combined." He remained convinced that "an invasion of the enemy's country" was the most effective way to solve his nagging subsistence problems. Lee anticipated that such a bold move would allow his army to "subsist while there" on Northern resources. He believed that "the absence of the army" would also give the citizens of Virginia "an opportunity to collect supplies" for the upcoming months. The general further argued that "the legitimate fruits of a victory, if gained in Pennsylvania, could be more readily reaped than on our own soil."[50]

Most of the men in the ranks viewed the North's acclaimed Cumberland Valley as a particularly tantalizing source of supplies for the army, especially in comparison to the war-ravaged sections of Virginia. "The whole country in the Wilderness and around Chancellorsville, where both Hooker's and Lee's armies had done some foraging, and thence to the Potomac, was well-nigh exhausted," General Gordon explained. He insisted that "the hungry hosts of Israel did not look across Jordan to the vine-clad hills of Canaan with more longing eyes than did Lee's braves contemplate the yellow grain-fields of Pennsylvania beyond the Potomac."[51]

The campaign finally got underway in Ewell's corps well before dawn on June 4, when Rodes's troops departed from the Fredericksburg area. Their initial line of march took them straight south before swinging west past Guineas Station. That attempt at deception was part of an intricate plan that called for the men to move northwest along the back roads to Culpeper Court House, where Lee intended to concentrate his forces before pushing northwest into the fertile Shenandoah Valley. The army commander expected that the long column of troops would take three full days to complete the nearly forty-mile trip.[52]

Ewell's other two divisions joined in the advance early on the following day. Early's veteran troops departed under cover of darkness at 1:00 A.M., while Johnson's men began moving out of camp about an hour later. The soldiers from Maj. Gen. Lafayette McLaws's division, which was the only part of Lieutenant General Longstreet's First Corps in the immediate vicinity of Fredericksburg, had already slipped away from the area on the morning of June 3. Lieutenant General Hill's newly created Third Corps temporarily remained behind along the Rappahannock River to screen their departure from the prying eyes of the Federal army.[53]

From Guineas Station the troops trudged west past Spotsylvania Court House and then swung northwest through Old Verdiersville. Ewell arrived at the front of the column for the first time during the march just as Rodes's men finished crossing the Rapidan River at Somerville Ford on the third day. "We found Rodes well on the road and across the ford," Hotchkiss remarked in his diary. He noted that "the troops soon recognized General Ewell and began to cheer him as had been their habit with General Jackson, thus transferring to him the ardor they felt for their old Commander." In response the corps commander "took off his cap and rode rapidly along the line."[54]

During their trek, the men suffered through some of the worst heat any of them had ever experienced. One soldier from O'Neal's Brigade openly blamed the generals who were leading the advance to Culpeper Court House for their woes. "Gens. Early and Rodes seemed to be ambitious to see who could reach the Court House first, and the consequence was a foot race, which resulted in laming about one-third of the men and dropping a good many by the roadside who otherwise would have been able to keep up," the Alabamian grumbled in a letter to his hometown newspaper.[55]

Rodes's worn-out men finally reached Culpeper Court House about noon on June 7 and halted three miles to the north. By the next day, nearly all the other men from the First and Second Corps had also moved into the surrounding area. McLaws's Division had arrived there on June 6, while Early's and Johnson's Divisions followed Rodes's men into the area on the afternoon of June 8. Maj. Gen. John B. Hood's division from the First Corps had already been in camp for several days. The exception was Maj. Gen. George E. Pickett's First Corps division, which remained on detached duty near Hanover, Virginia, and would not arrive until June 10.[56]

The troops from the Second Corps quickly settled in for a much-needed rest. Major Pendleton, Ewell's assistant adjutant general, had nothing but praise for their new corps commander up to that point in the advance. "The more I see of Gen Ewell the more I am pleased with him," he wrote to his fiancée on the day after their arrival. "He resembles Gen. Jackson very much in some points of his character, particularly his utter disregard of his own personal comforts & his inflexibility of purpose." The staffer reported to his mother that he expected "great things from him and am glad to say that our troops have for him a great deal of the same feeling that they had towards Gen. Jackson."[57]

Their respite came to an abrupt end just before dawn on June 9, when Maj. Gen. Alfred Pleasonton led a large force of Federal cavalry, supported by two infantry brigades, across two fords on the Rappahannock River northeast of Culpeper Court House. This move caught the cavalry pickets along the river by surprise. As they fell back in disarray, Maj. Gen. James Ewell Brown Stuart's entire cavalry division, which had been camped outside of town since May 20, soon became engaged in a fierce battle along a broad and shifting front around nearby Brandy Station.

Ewell's three divisions remained largely hidden in the rear throughout the fighting. Generals Rodes and Ewell spent their time observing the fast-moving cavalry battle from a house located just behind the front lines on the western spur of Fleetwood Ridge. Lee soon joined them there. At one point the action surged so close to their position that it seemed likely that all three generals would be captured. Hotch-kiss noted that Ewell responded to the danger by calling for them to "gather into the house and defend it to the last." The crisis eventually passed as Stuart's troopers rallied along the nearby ridge and forced the Union cavalry to pull back from the field in what amounted to a draw.[58]

During the early evening, Ewell's troops finally received the command to stand down for the day. Even from their position behind the lines, the men had seen enough of the action to realize that Stuart's troopers had endured some significant losses during the fighting. "I don't know the exact extent of damage done to our cavalry, but fear it is considerable," the Fourth Georgia's Lt. John T. Gay remarked in a letter to his wife. "The fight is said to have been the hardest of the war." Stuart's cavalrymen, in fact, had sustained almost five hundred casualties during the fierce action there, which came as a major shock throughout the army.[59]

Despite the threat of additional fighting around Culpeper Court House, the Second Corps resumed the advance to the northwest in the afternoon on June 10. Lee's plan called for the troops to sweep Federal forces out of the nearby Shenandoah Valley and seize the major crossings over the Potomac River. Once that was accomplished, Longstreet's corps would push forward and secure the primary gaps through the Blue Ridge Mountains. Hill's corps would then withdraw from the Fredericksburg area as quietly as possible and move rapidly into the Valley behind Ewell's main force.[60]

Following a two-day tramp, Rodes's bedraggled troops stopped just north of Flint Hill at the threshold of the Shenandoah Valley. Although Early was supposed to lead the advance, his men encountered some major difficulties on their route, which ran west of Richmond Turnpike through Sperryville. As a result, they only made it as far as Gaines's Cross Roads before darkness fell. One soldier from the Thirty-First Virginia in "Extra Billy" Smith's brigade grumbled in his diary that he was "very tired indeed." Johnson's troops lagged even farther behind and went into camp just west of the crossroads.[61]

After conferring with his other two division commanders that night, Ewell hurried forward in his carriage on the morning of June 12 to catch up with Rodes. That trip took longer than expected because Rodes's men had resumed their advance at the first sign of daylight. Ewell finally overtook the major general "on the road between Flint Hill and Sandy Hook." Once Rodes joined him in his carriage, the generals rolled "on in advance of the army." During the ride, the corps commander spelled out his plans now that Rodes's men would be at the front of the advance as the army moved into the Valley.[62]

The troops soon began the steep climb through the Blue Ridge Mountains at Chester Gap. By midmorning they reached Front Royal in the southern part of the Shenandoah. The sight of the soldiers unleashed a frantic outpouring of relief from the town's many Southern sympathizers, who had chafed for months under the threat of frequent raids by General Milroy's forces from the Federal base at nearby Winchester. "We were received most enthusiastically by the fair inhabitants of this town who welcomed us as deliverers from the tyranny of the hated Milroy," Lt. William Calder from the Second North Carolina in Ramseur's Brigade wrote to his mother.[63]

Twenty-year-old Lucy Buck was quickly caught up in the emotion that erupted when the troops marched by her family's home at Bel Air Estate on the outskirts of town. "Oh how the gallant boys cheered and shouted—Ma and I went up on the house and when they saw us they waved and hurrahed to us," she wrote in her diary. "Oh! It was glorious!" She watched in near ecstasy as "column after column filed past with glistening bayonets, flying colors and rolling artillery, while the strain of martial music and their soul burning shouts mingled in one unbroken, soul thrilling volume of sound." The scene proved so stirring that she was left "almost frantic with excitement and delight."[64]

Thomas Ashby, who was a young boy at the time, recalled that the troops "presented a most interesting and impressive sight." He noted that the soldiers all appeared to be "in splendid condition and in high spirits" when they entered the town. "As they passed through the village the men closed up their ranks and the bands played as if on parade," he continued. Another resident, Charles Eckhardt, was especially struck by the sight of the two top generals as their small buggy rumbled into Front Royal at the front of the column. "In the morning passed General Ewell and his staff through town," he penned in his diary. "He rode in a carriage, and had General Rhodes [sic] by his side."[65]

Like Rodes's troops, the men from the other two divisions received a rousing welcome from the people in Front Royal. Sgt. Edmond Stephens, who served in Early's Division with the Ninth Louisiana, reported that "the citizens met the soldiers with milk, pies, and cool water." Despite the jubilant reception, the troops maintained strict discipline. The Forty-Ninth Virginia's Lt. Robert D. Funkhouser noted that "no man was allowed to break ranks." Even Funkhouser, who was a native of the town, could not leave the column to greet his mother, who was watching their arrival from the crowd along the street.[66]

Amid cheering throngs, Rodes's men at the front of the advance pushed on about a mile north of town to the south branch of the Shenandoah River. "The passing of a pontoon train the day before had made the people anticipate our coming and they came out everywhere to welcome us," Jed Hotchkiss remarked in his journal. The long line of soldiers soon reached the main ford along Winchester Road and plunged into the stream. "Our pontoons were on the shore there but Gen. Ewell said it would take too long to put them down, so our advance waded the rivers," the staffer declared. From there they were now ready to move forward into the heart of the Valley.[67]

"A Worthy Successor of Jackson"

While the troops from the other two divisions lined up to cross the Shenandoah River, Rodes halted the front of his column a couple of miles north of Front Royal so that he could attend a meeting with Generals Ewell and Early in the nearby village of Cedarville. During this session on the afternoon of June 12, the corps commander "fully unfolded" his scheme for the upcoming campaign in the Shenandoah Valley. "The main features of the plan were the simultaneous attack of Winchester and Berryville, the subsequent attack of Martinsburg, and the immediate entrance into Maryland, via Williamsport or any other point near there which events indicated as best," Rodes explained in his official report.[1]

As Rodes's men headed off toward Berryville, Ewell moved ahead with the final arrangements for taking Winchester. That heavily fortified bastion had a population of about 4,400. The town, which stood at the junction of six major roads, served as the primary Federal stronghold in the sprawling Valley. From there troops carried out frequent raids into the surrounding countryside as far south as Front Royal—all of which made it a prime target for Ewell's advancing corps. Sgt. Edmond Stephens from Hays's Brigade noted with high anticipation that it was only ten miles from Front Royal "to the city of Winchester where we expected to meet the enemy in their fortifications."[2]

Brigadier General Milroy, who headed a division in the Federal VIII Corps, had assumed command of the forces there following the most recent occupation of the town on Christmas Eve 1862. Early in the following year, he began to enforce the Emancipation Proclamation by freeing the town's slaves. Over the following months Milroy exiled some of the most ardent Confederate sympathizers and arrested many other civilians, including some women and children. He also used secret detectives to spy on the local population and carried out frequent property seizures. His cruelest act was restricting the purchase of food from sources outside the town, which pushed some residents close to starvation.[3]

Although his administration of Winchester was harsh by any standards, some leaders in the North still praised Milroy's policies, which were heavily influenced

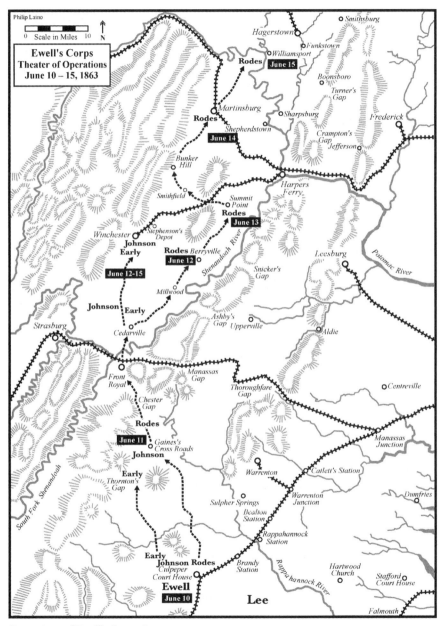

Operations of Ewell's Corps, June 10–15, 1863

by his intense abolitionist beliefs, as necessary to stamp out the scourge of slavery forever and deny aid and comfort to the enemy in prosecuting the war. Gov. Francis Pierpont, who headed the restored Virginia government, insisted that the general's actions were "universally popular" among the most ardent opponents of the South, who "endorse him, while the rebels censure." Another Union official argued that his use of such extreme measures represented the only way to end the "damnable slaveholders' rebellion."[4]

Whether justified or not, his notorious rule made the general one of the most widely hated men in the South and instilled a burning desire among Ewell's troops to see him captured and hanged for what they considered unconscionable behavior. "Milroy, the Yankee general, who commanded at Winchester, was a brutal tyrant, who used to burn the people's plows to prevent them for tilling the ground, stealing niggers, and sending nearly all the Secesh families south," a Georgian from Gordon's Brigade fumed in a letter to his hometown newspaper. A Virginian from the Stonewall Brigade threatened that Milroy "would have fared badly" if he was ever captured.[5]

Planter Marcus Blakemore Buck watched in fascination as a seemingly endless column of Confederate soldiers passed by his house just north of Front Royal along Dickey Ridge. "This morning at 10 o'clock, the head of the column of Ewell's Corps (formerly Jackson's) commenced poking through town and have continued to poke at a quick march during the entire day," he remarked in his diary. The ardent Southern supporter fully expected that those troops would soon rid them of the hated Federal commander. "Milroy is known to have been still in Winchester yesterday morning," Buck exclaimed. "He will soon be made to feel the vengeance of an outraged people, if he is still there."[6]

The troops assigned to push Milroy out of his stronghold included Early's and Johnson's Divisions and the Sixteenth Virginia Cavalry from Brig. Gen. Albert Jenkins's brigade, which had just arrived in camp from the nearby Valley District. Ewell knew that the task would be far from easy. Most worrisome were the three forts guarding the town. "From all the information I could gather, the fortifications of Winchester were only assailable on the west and northwest, from a range of hills which commanded the ridge occupied by their main fortifications," he stated in his official report. "The force there was represented at from 6,000 to 8,000, under General Milroy."[7]

Once the last of his troops finally splashed across the north branch of the Shenandoah River just after dawn on June 13, Ewell ordered Early's Division to proceed north on Front Royal Road toward Winchester. The troops soon veered off onto a dirt road running northwest to Nineveh, where they turned onto the macadamized Valley Turnpike. Lt. William James Kincheloe from the Forty-Ninth Virginia in Smith's Brigade described the Confederate advance in his diary as "a very hot, quick march." To his delight, many of the ladies along the way "had water set out on one side of the road for us."[8]

By then Johnson's Division was also on the move toward Winchester. With the Sixteenth Virginia Cavalry in the lead, the troops pushed north on Front Royal Road to within a couple miles of Milroy's stronghold. After driving in the enemy's cavalry pickets, the troops formed a line of battle southeast of Winchester. Just then they came under intense artillery fire from an enemy battery. Lt. William T. Lambie's section of Capt. John Carpenter's Alleghany (Virginia) Artillery in Johnson's Division opened a vigorous return fire, which soon "put the enemy to precipitate flight upon the town."[9]

While that was going on, Early's men trudged north along the turnpike through the tiny settlement of Newtown, and pushed on past Bartonsville toward Kernstown. At that point the general "found Lieutenant Colonel Herbert of the Maryland line occupying a ridge between the two places with his battalion of infantry, a battery of artillery and a part of a battalion of Maryland cavalry, and engaged in occasional skirmishing with a body of the enemy's troops which had taken position in and near Kernstown." Those Maryland troops had just arrived from the western part of Virginia, where they had been serving under Brig. Gen. William E. "Grumble" Jones.

Early quickly moved his men into place south of Winchester opposite Kernstown, which had been the site of one of Jackson's battles during his 1862 Valley Campaign. From there, he hoped to seize the high ground northwest of the town. Early soon determined that the Federal troops along his front "covered the road which I had to take to get to the west of Winchester." With the way blocked, the general decided to open a path by clearing the enemy forces from around the village. He immediately halted his command and formed "it in line on either side of the turnpike, and proceeded to reconnoiter the ground for the purpose of ascertaining the strength and position of the enemy near Kernstown."[10]

During that time, Johnson's artillery on their right remained busy dueling with the Federal gunners. The exchange became so lively that Johnson shifted his division into a more protected position. He initially deployed Steuart's Brigade and the Stonewall Brigade "in a ravine to the right of the road, out of sight and range of the enemy's guns." Jones's and Williams's brigades took up position on the left of the road in "a body of woods." The troops remained in place outside Winchester for several hours. Later in the day Johnson finally moved the men on the right of the road into "a position nearer the town."[11]

As Johnson's men maneuvered southeast of town, Early determined that the only Federal troops in Kernstown were some cavalry and a few infantry pickets. His reconnaissance further revealed that the enemy had posted a battery just west of there on some high ground known as Pritchard's Hill. While Smith's and Avery's brigades maintained their position along the turnpike, Gordon's and Hays's men shifted to the west along Middle Road to a location where the Federals on the nearby heights "could be attacked with advantage." With those preparations out of the way, Early ordered Hays's troops "to advance and gain possession of Pritchard's Hill."[12]

The Louisianans immediately set up for a direct attack on the hill. Hays initially shifted the troops "about half a mile" to the left. From there he ordered the men from the Ninth Louisiana under Col. Leroy Stafford "to deploy as skirmishers, and drive the enemy from a wooded eminence between my position and the Valley turnpike." The main part of Hays's Brigade quickly took Pritchard's Hill "without opposition, the enemy having withdrawn his battery." As the advance got under-way, the general spotted some Federal troops hidden on his flank and sent a hurried warning to Early that "the enemy had a considerable infantry force" in a strip of woods along a ridge just west of their location.[13]

Early responded to the threat by ordering Gordon's Brigade to clear the troops from the thicket. While the Louisianans secured Pritchard's Hill, the Georgians "swept around" on a dirt lane toward the enemy position on their left. "Gordon ad-vanced handsomely, as directed, encountering a considerable force of infantry, which, in conjunction with a body of skirmishers sent out by Hays, he drove from behind a stone fence, and then swept over the fields beyond the ridge," Early recalled. From there the gritty Confederates chased the startled defenders north across Abram's (Abraham's) Creek toward nearby Bower's Hill on the southern edge of Winchester.[14]

The Federal troops in the woods put up only a brief resistance before giving way. "For a short time the fighting was fast and furious, but the enemy could not stand against charge and yelling, and they broke immediately for the cover of their forti-fications," Pvt. Gordon Bradwell from the Thirty-First Georgia boasted. Lt. W. C. Mathews from the Thirty-Eighth Georgia reported that the enemy soldiers scattered "in every direction, throwing away their guns and everything else." The withdrawal soon turned into a rout. "We shot at them as they ran, and poor devils, we slaugh-tered them like dogs," the Georgian gloated. "I never saw so much running and screaming in my life."[15]

Although most of Milroy's men got away, Gordon's attack succeeded in clearing the area southwest of town. According to Colonel Evans, commanding the Thirty-First Georgia, the Confederates chased the enemy "through woods and fields" to-ward the rear. He insisted that the "Yankees acted cowardly" as they fled in a near panic. A gunner from one of the batteries attached to Early's Division noted that the men pursued the Federals "to within two miles of the town." Even so, their achievement did not come without some significant losses. "In this charge, which was executed with spirit and unchecked at any point, my brigade lost 75 men, in-cluding some efficient officers," Gordon acknowledged.[16]

Milroy's troops soon took up a new defensive position just north of Abram's Creek around Bower's Hill. From there one of their batteries opened up a severe fire on Gordon's advancing troops. About that time Smith's Brigade set up on the far left of the line, directly opposite the hill. Lieutenant Kincheloe griped in his diary that they immediately "came under a considerable fire of shell." Avery's Tar Heels stayed in the rear, where they were assigned to guard the ambulances and

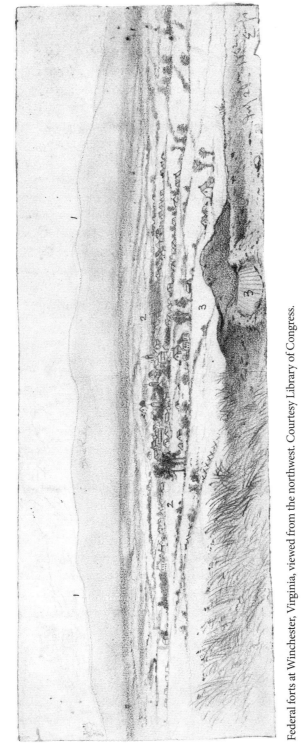

Federal forts at Winchester, Virginia, viewed from the northwest. Courtesy Library of Congress.

ordnance trains. Despite the fierce enemy fire, the main part of the division held in place outside of town, just south and west of Bower's Hill, for "the rest of the day."[17]

Johnson's men on the right continued skirmishing with the Federal troops on the outskirts of Winchester. "When General Early advanced on the left, a body of the enemy's infantry, retreating, became exposed to view," Johnson reported. Two guns from Lambie's section of the Alleghany Artillery immediately opened fire "with good effect, greatly accelerating their speed." The general noted that "this attracted the fire from the fortifications north of the town upon the battery and such portions of the infantry as were necessarily exposed." The enemy continued to lob shells at his position "in desultory manner until nightfall."[18]

The bulk of Milroy's troops hunkered down inside the three massive forts, which provided the primary protection from an enemy attack. The largest of these, which was dubbed Fort Milroy, stood just northwest of town. The newly upgraded West Fort occupied a position on some high ground about 2,000 feet to the west on Flint Ridge. Another, smaller compound, known as the Star Fort, loomed a short distance farther north. These imposing bastions bristled with twenty-four rifled guns. Lt. John M. Steptoe from the Forty-Fourth Virginia in Jones's Brigade described them in a letter home as "the most formidable works that this army has ever encountered."[19]

During the night, the Federal commander pulled most of his troops back from their forward positions into the safety of the forts. "Before morning, the enemy withdrew all their artillery into their fortifications from Bower's Hill and the south and east sides of town," General Ewell reported. Even from the outskirts of town, he could clearly see that Milroy was moving quickly to improve his defenses. "On examining the enemy's fortifications from General Johnson's position, I found they had put up works on the hills I had intended gaining possession of, and were busy strengthening them," Ewell further stated.

Milroy's force was bolstered by the arrival of three regiments and a single battery under Col. Andrew T. McReynolds, which made their way into town after escaping a Confederate attack on nearby Berryville. Those badly needed reinforcements took up position in the Star Fort at about 10:00 P.M. Other troops from Milroy's command remained busy throughout the night further upgrading their formidable defensive lines. Major Brown from Ewell's staff noted that they were "digging like beavers all the time we were there." With all his troops in place, Milroy remained convinced that he could hold out for a day or more until relieved by Hooker's Army of the Potomac.[20]

Despite his apparent confidence, Milroy kept a close watch from inside the main fort on the enemy troops. At one point some soldiers with a block and tackle hoisted the general in a huge wicker basket forty to fifty feet up a flagpole so that he could get a better view of the area surrounding their position. The perch was so high that he remained clearly visible to the men from Johnson's Division on the southeast side of Winchester. Pvt. Samuel Angus Firebaugh from the Tenth Virginia in Steuart's

Brigade looked on in utter disbelief as "old Milroy" ascended "up some 50 feet on the pole in a basket viewing."[21]

Just after daybreak on June 14, General Early moved to consolidate his gains from the previous day. He immediately ordered Gordon and Hays to send a single regiment from each of their brigades across Abram's Creek and "get possession of Bower's Hill, then occupied only by the enemy's skirmishers, as his artillery had been withdrawn during the night." The thin line of troops quickly moved forward and seized the heights after some brief fighting. Early soon shifted the skirmishers from Smith's Brigade into place "across the creek, to the left of those of Hays and Gordon."

About 9:00 A.M. Ewell joined Early at Bower's Hill, where he hoped to get a closer look at the enemy's defenses north and west of the town. The two generals were especially interested in determining whether or not Milroy had fortified the high ground directly overlooking the main fort. Early noted that they proceeded "to reconnoiter the position, and, having gone to the top of Bower's Hill, now occupied by my skirmishers, had a fair view of the enemy's works about Winchester." What they observed appeared far from promising. "From this point we discovered that the hill to the northwest of the enemy's works, which I had been directed to gain, had also been fortified, and was occupied," the division commander acknowledged in his official report.

The situation left him no other choice than to seize West Fort by force. "It became necessary, then to take this hill by assault," Early reported. He quickly "discovered a position to the northwest of it from which it was thought it might be attacked with advantage." The final arrangements called for him to launch the assault from a ridge on Little North Mountain, which directly overlooked the Federal fortifications. "I was directed to move my division around to that position and make the attack, leaving a force where the division then was to amuse the enemy and conceal the movement upon his flank and rear," Early explained.[22]

As part of the plan, Johnson's men would provide an additional distraction during the advance. "About 11 a.m., finding there was no danger of a sortie, and seeing the enemy fortifying a hill north of their main fort, I directed General Johnson to move to the east of the town, and interfere with their work as much as possible, and so divert attention from General Early," Ewell explained. Johnson quickly shifted the Stonewall Brigade into place "between the Millwood and Berryville pikes." From there he deployed a line of skirmishers who "annoyed the enemy so as to force them to leave off work and effectually to engross their attention."[23]

Under pressure from the skirmishers, the Federal troops along their front quickly withdrew to the edge of town. Johnson complained that the enemy "kept up a brisk and continual fire upon our line." A soldier from the Second Virginia in the Stonewall Brigade clearly "heard the bullets whistling over head in a spiteful sort of way." Milroy's men eventually launched a fierce counterattack against the skirmishers, forcing them to fall back. A reserve force from the Fifth Virginia immediately moved forward and drove the Federals from their advanced position. All of that action kept Milroy's left wing well occupied while three of Early's brigades slipped off to the north on the opposite side of the town.[24]

In preparation for the attack, Early moved the remainder of Gordon's Brigade, the Second Maryland Infantry Battalion, and two batteries into place on Bower's Hill. While they held the Federals in check at the south end of town, Early's other brigades and two battalions of artillery tramped west along the Cedar Creek Turnpike, then turned north under cover of some woods. Once the column reached the Romney Road, Early detached the Fifty-Fourth North Carolina from Avery's brigade to picket the entrance into town from the west. The rest of the troops continued north to Pughtown Road, where they formed on "a wooded hill" for an attack on West Fort.

Their long circuitous march left the men completely exhausted. Before launching his assault, Early allowed them to take a much-needed break. "I reached there about 4 p.m., and as the day was excessively hot, and the men had marched a circuit of 8 or 10 miles without meeting with water to drink, and were very much fatigued, I massed them in the woods in rear of the position, and gave them time to blow," the general stated in his official report. While that was going on, he placed his artillery "within easy range of the enemy's works on the hill overlooking his main fort."

As the artillerymen unlimbered their guns, Early shifted Hays's Brigade into position for the attack from a cluster of trees on nearby Apple Pie Ridge. "The men having rested as much as possible under the circumstances, I directed General Hays, whose brigade had been selected to make the assault, to move his brigade near to the edge of the woods facing the enemy's works, and to keep them under cover until the artillery opened," Early explained. The plan called for the Louisiana troops to advance with three regiments in the front line and two more following closely behind.

The division commander soon detached the Fifty-Seventh North Carolina from Avery's brigade as well to protect the artillery from any enemy attempt to move forward in the rear of the Confederates along Pughtown Road. Avery's remaining two regiments formed a second line for the attack. Early placed Smith's men in the rear to provide further support; from there they would be available to exploit any breakthroughs in the enemy's main battle line. With all that maneuvering out of the way, the general was finally primed and ready for action. The main assault would begin once the artillery fire from his two battalions had successfully softened up the Federal defenses.[25]

About 6:00 P.M., the gunners opened a fierce fire on West Fort. Pvt. Thomas Benton Reed from the Ninth Louisiana watched anxiously as the artillerymen unleashed their barrage. "The artillery formed right in front of us, right on the crest of the hill," he recorded in his diary. "They placed thirty-two pieces, and when everything was in readiness we heard the report of a pistol." On that signal the guns instantly erupted with "a deafening noise." Reed noted that the reverberations were so powerful that "it seemed like the hill trembled under those cannon."[26]

The men from the other brigades in Early's Division were just as impressed by what they witnessed that afternoon. "About 5 P.M. suddenly the whole woods and heavens rang with an immense crash of artillery," Lieutenant Kincheloe from Smith's Brigade declared in his diary. "It was perfectly grand, the enemy were caught napping in their quarters." Private Bradwell from Gordon's Brigade, who watched the action from Bower's Hill, described the sound from the cannons as "a great rumbling noise like the sudden moving of many trains." Pvt. John Kerr Walker from the Sixth North Carolina in Avery's brigade called it "the heaviest cannonading that ever was heard."[27]

The barrage sent many of the town's citizens into a panic. One of them declared in her diary that she had "never heard such cannonading in all my life." The gunfire was so intense that she was "afraid our town will yet be blown to atoms." Cornelia Peake McDonald also looked on as the artillery blasted away at the fort. She noted that a wayward shell, which came "crashing through the trees" near her house, soon "reminded us that we were in danger." The woman reacted with terror as the rounds fell all around her. "So they go, whizzing screaming, and coming down with a dreadful thud or crash, and then burst," she penned in her journal. "We hold our breath and cover our eyes till they pass."[28]

The repeated volleys from the massed guns had a devastating effect on the defenders. "Our artillery opened a rapid and well directed fire upon the redoubt," Capt. William Seymour, the assistant adjutant general on Hays's staff, commented in his diary. He reported that "some of the shells explode over the work while others strike the parapet, tearing great holes in it and sending dirt high up in the air." Most impressive of all was the huge number of rounds that belched forth from the cannons. A soldier from the Fifty-Seventh North Carolina informed his wife that "a shell would go over us almost every second." One of the gunners claimed that "the shells were dropping inside at the rate of three a minute."[29]

After about forty-five minutes, Hays's troops prepared to launch the attack down the steep slope along their front. "It was necessary to storm this place, and, as usual, whenever anything daring or dangerous is to be done, the Louisiana Brigade was ordered up," Capt. Samuel H. Chisolm from the Fifth Louisiana boasted in a letter home. "Without letting the men know what was to be done, our gallant Harry Hays called the officers together and in a few words told us what was expected of us." With that out of the way, everyone steeled themselves for action. "We knew that General Hays would lead the charge, and we were willing to follow," Chisolm declared.[30]

Once the artillery finally fell silent, the troops charged forward. The men maintained a perfect alignment as they descended the steep slope. Lt. J. Warren Jackson from the Eighth Louisiana boasted to his brother that "it was the best managed affair Hayes ever had anything to do with." As the men rushed down the ridge, they suddenly encountered the first significant barrier. "On we went and when we were within about one hundred yards of the enemy's breastworks we came to a kind of stockade," Private Reed explained. "This was made of trees fallen or dragged, with the tops of them outward, forming the breastworks and the small ends of the limbs were cut sharp."[31]

That formidable obstacle did little to slow down the Confederates' headlong advance. "At a given signal the well-known voice of Harry sang forth, and at them we pitched over an abatis of fallen timber," Captain Chisolm reported to his brother. As the Louisianans picked their way through the field of sharpened sticks, the enemy opened a ferocious fire from their main redoubt. "Each step we were greeted with showers of Minie balls from the breastworks and the thirteen rifled guns pouring deadly volleys of grape and canister into the ranks of our gallant little brigade," the captain declared. "Whole platoons were swept away."[32]

According to Private Reed, Hays's troops barely hesitated as they pressed on toward their objective. "We had to pass through this mass of stuff before getting to the rifle pits, but this did not stop us," he remarked in his journal. "The Major of the 7th Louisiana regiment was the first man to mount the works, and I was just behind him." An officer from the Thirteenth Virginia in Smith's Brigade watched from the rear as "steel and shot tore through their ranks, but still they pressed onward until within a short distance of the Fort." Captain Seymour from Hays's staff noted that the Federals opened "a brisk fire up on use; but so impetuous was the charge of our men that in a few minutes they were over the breastworks, driving the enemy in great haste and confusion."[33]

Sgt. William Henry Mayo from the Ninth Louisiana boasted in his diary that "our brigade charged the fort" and quickly "drove the enemy from it." Captain Chisolm pointed out that Hays's men did not fire "a shot until within twenty steps of the breastworks, when we gave them a volley and pitched into them with the bayonet." Private Reed claimed that "the Yankees did not know that we were on them until they saw us standing over them." Lieutenant Jackson noted with pride that "we drove the Yankees pell mell from their breastworks." The veteran officer acknowledged, however, that they captured "but few of them as they were rather too nimble for us."[34]

Within moments the entire Federal garrison was in full flight from the fort. "Then you ought to have seen those fellows run, and as they ran down the hill we poured it into them, but they soon scampered away and we were in possession of the breastworks," Reed declared. According to Chisolm, "all those who stood their ground were soon rolling in their own blood and many who ran were shot in the back." As they swarmed through the fort, Hays's men sized six artillery pieces from their gunners. "The Yankee artillerymen, who were regulars, strove hard to save their guns, but by shooting the horses we prevented them from taking away a single piece or caisson," Seymour wrote in his journal.

Despite their success, the captured West Fort remained far from secure. Seymour noted that some of the retreating Federal troops were "seen massing in the valley beyond, apparently with the intention of attempting its recapture." Some volunteers from two of the Louisiana regiments immediately stepped forward in an effort to hold off this counterattack. Sergeant Mayo from the Ninth Louisianan watched in disbelief as impromptu gunners wheeled the captured artillery into place and "turned it" on the enemy. Seymour reported that "a few well directed shots" from the guns soon "drove them [the Federals] back."[35]

While that was going on, the men from Smith's Brigade moved forward from the rear to assist Hays's troops in clearing the fort. Pvt. James W. Baker from the Thirteenth Virginia bragged that "within twenty minutes we had the fort." Pvt. Henry Dedrick from the Fifty-Second Virginia informed his wife that "we charged on them and run them out of their fortifications." Along the way they clambered over some of the Tar Heel troops in the second line, who were moving too slowly. "The North Carolina soldiers had to lay down and let us walk over them," one of the men from the Forty-Ninth Virginia bragged. The soldier noted that the troops rushed ahead with such speed that the enemy "did not have time to kill many of us." He described it as "the fastest double quicking we ever did."[36]

General Early eventually shifted eight additional guns from his artillery reserve into the captured compound, where they began firing on the enemy troops. The gunners in the Star Fort immediately responded with a scattered fire of their own. One of those rounds severely wounded Capt. Charles Thompson, who commanded the Louisiana Guard Artillery. A gunner from his battery reported that Thompson "had his hand shot off & died from want of surgical attendance." Captain Seymour explained that "his wound was in the wrist & comparatively slight, but he would not leave his gun in time to have it properly attended to and consequently died from loss of blood."[37]

Most of the other ninety-four casualties in the attack came in Hays's Brigade, which suffered two officers and ten men killed, and eight officers and fifty-nine men wounded. An officer from the Sixth Louisiana emerged as a major hero in the fight. "After our men had effected an entrance into the redoubt, Adjutant John Orr of the Sixth Regiment, seeing a Yankee color-bearer with a guard of two men carrying off his flag, ran after him to secure it," Captain Seymour wrote in his journal. "Orr seized the standard and with his sword single-handed commenced a fight with the three guardians, and after a short contest was run through the body with a bayonet and the flag carried away." To everyone's relief, the young lieutenant somehow survived his wound.[38]

Many of the men from Orr's regiment received treatment for their injuries in a private home just behind the front lines. The owner's daughters, Elizabeth and Alma Yonley, worked tirelessly tending the wounded troops. Capt. John J. Rivera from that regiment noted that, "not with-standing the bursting shells and the parental admonition to remain in a place of comparative safety," the two young women "went among the stricken soldiers and ministered to their needs in every practical way." He added that the girls remained "zealous in their attentions, and for several weeks they kindly nursed several, the severity of whose wounds did not permit removal."[39]

With the seizure of West Fort, Ewell's rifled guns totally dominated the enemy's position in Fort Milroy to the east. One soldier from Hays's Brigade reported, however, that "when we had captured the works and reformed our line it was deemed too dark to storm the main fort." Although the final attack remained on hold until the following day, the artillery soon began pounding away at the stronghold. A gunner from the reserve artillery noted that he and his comrades "commenced shelling it from every direction." The artilleryman bragged that "the situation of the Yankees was utterly hopeless now, for in the morning we should have torn them to pieces with our artillery."[40]

About 9:00 P.M. Milroy held a war council with his top commanders. He quickly determined that the only hope was for his troops to escape under the cover of darkness. "Our position at Winchester, although affording facilities for defense which would enable an inferior to maintain itself against a superior number for a limited time, could not be successfully defended by the limited means at my command against such an army as surrounded me," the general acknowledged in his official report. Milroy eventually issued an order that his entire force "should march from the forts at 1 o'clock in the morning, carrying with them their arms and the usual supply of ammunition." They had no choice but to leave behind everything else of value.[41]

Ewell, who remained unaware of the Federal evacuation, directed Gordon's Brigade to move forward from Bower's Hill on the following morning in an attempt to seize Fort Milroy, which he assumed would be stoutly defended. "In the dim twilight, with the glimmer of his bayonets and brass howitzers still discernible, I received an order to storm the fortress at daylight the next morning," Gordon recalled. The general was certain that he "had not one chance in a thousand" to live through the attack. As his troops strained up the steep slope just after dawn on June 15, he soon discovered that the huge fortification was empty. "At every moment I expected the storm of shell and ball that would end many a life, my own among them; but on we swept, and into the fort, to find not a soldier there!"[42]

The Georgia troops quickly occupied the abandoned stronghold. "As we entered it, General Gordon came galloping in from somewhere on a large black United States army horse, which we all called 'Old Milroy,' supposing him to belong to the commander of the fort," Private Bradwell recalled. While his men looked on, Gordon turned his attention to removing the Union banner that waved over the bastion. According to Bradwell, the general "rode up to the flag pole in the center of the fort and, hauling down the colors, detached them from the rope and placed one end of them on his saddle."[43]

Sgt. William Beverley Pettit from the Fluvanna (Virginia) Artillery in the Corps Artillery Reserve watched from the high ground overlooking the fort as Gordon's men secured the compound. "Soon afterwards, the flag was hauled down and ours was run up in its place," he reported to his wife. "Soon, too, the firing ceased and we had captured all the forces." Particularly impressive was the huge amount of spoils that Pettit spotted as they joined the Georgians inside the redoubt. The artillery-man noted that "we came on past them, where we saw a good many prisoners and, just this side, were the Yankee wagons, loaded with valuables, standing on the side, while our soldiers went through them."[44]

While all that was going on, Johnson's Division moved north during the middle of the night in an attempt to cut off Milroy's line of retreat. The Confederates soon discovered that "there was a railroad cut masked by a body of woods" about five miles north of Winchester near Stephenson's Depot, along the turnpike on which they expected the enemy to withdraw. Johnson noted that this position "would af-ford excellent shelter for troops in case of an engagement." About 3:30 A.M. his men encountered some Federal cavalry just south of that location near the intersection of Valley Turnpike and Charlestown Road. The general immediately deployed Steuart's Brigade east of the road and ordered the rest of his division forward in support.

While the bulk of Steuart's men settled into place inside the railroad cut, Johnson placed most of his other troops behind a steep embankment to the west. The Loui-sianans from Williams's brigade took up position just to the rear along the ditch. Lt. Charles S. Contee from the First Maryland Artillery set up his guns directly behind a nearby footbridge. A soldier from the Tenth Virginia in Steuart's Brigade described this span as "a narrow wooden bridge spanning a railroad, which bridge was raised and lowered on an artificial approach and abutment." The Maryland gunners quickly unleashed a fierce barrage on the Federal column, drawing an intense return fire.[45]

Milroy's troops launched two major assaults on the Confederate positions around the footbridge to no avail. "After the failure of their first and second frontal attacks on the bridge, they sought to turn our left flank by a force of cavalry and infantry which General Johnson, 'old Alleghany' as he was called, met by forming a line perpendicular to our front line with part of the Louisiana Brigade which had just come up," Lieutenant McKim from Steuart's staff recalled. He looked on with awe as Johnson rode along the front lines, "vehemently giving orders, and waving the big cane which he carried instead of a sword, because of the lameness which resulted from his wound at the battle of Alleghany."

Milroy's men focused their attack on a single gun under Contee, which was posted on the bridge. "That little wooden bridge witnessed one of the most superb displays of dauntless intrepidity that was seen during the whole war," McKim de-clared. "The men serving the piece planted there were fearfully exposed. It was the key of our position, and the fire of the enemy was especially directed to disabling that gun, which had so long held them at bay." He noted that Contee's "men fell around him till all were killed or wounded but himself and one other, but they con-tinued undauntedly serving their piece in its perilous position, unsupported except by a line of bayonets below in the railway cut." Another Marylander boasted that the gritty artillerymen "had practically stopped an army."[46]

Just after dawn, Johnson ordered the late arriving Stonewall Brigade to cut off the enemy's line of retreat along the turnpike running north to Martinsburg. General Walker quickly set up an ambush with his two lead regiments, which succeeded in trapping a large number of Federal prisoners. "The enemy gave way, and retreated back from the pike in disorder at the first fire, returning only a straggling and inaccurate fire," the general explained in his official report. "Pressing them back rapidly to the woods west of the road, they made no stand, but hoisted a white flag, and surrendered to the two regiments before the others came up."[47]

The situation proved just as desperate for the other Federal troops in the rear, who also gave up in droves. To the consternation of Ewell's men, General Milroy slipped away during the height of the fighting and fled northeast to Harpers Ferry. Capt. John Welsh, who served with the Twenty-Seventh Virginia in the Stonewall Brigade, grumbled in a letter home that the Federal commander "got off himself but it was a tight squeeze." Cpl. James Peter Williams from the Chesapeake (Maryland) Artillery in Johnson's Division admitted to his sister that "the only thing I regret is that old Milroy made his escape." Chaplain James Sheeran from the Fourteenth Louisiana in Williams's brigade noted in his diary, "the boys were sorry they had not the opportunity to hang him."[48]

Despite getting away, Milroy lost more than half the men in his command during the fighting around Winchester, including about 4,000 troops taken prisoner. A gunner from the Louisiana Guard Artillery wrote in his diary that he saw "more Yankee prisoners than I have since Harper's Ferry" during the previous year's Maryland Campaign. Federal battle casualties amounted to 95 men killed and another 348 wounded. The toll in Ewell's two divisions proved much lower, with only 47 men killed, 219 wounded, and 3 missing. Sgt. John Garibaldi from the Twenty-Seventh Virginia in the Stonewall Brigade described it to his wife as "the cheapest victory ever achieved."[49]

The massive number of prisoners soon became a major logistical problem for Ewell. On June 17 he assigned the Fifty-Fourth North Carolina from Avery's brigade and the Fifty-Eighth Virginia from Smith's Brigade to escort more than 3,000 captives to Staunton. From there they would send the prisoners on by rail to Richmond. The Thirteenth Virginia, also from Smith's Brigade, remained in Winchester to guard some 750 sick and wounded Federals being held there. Despite their best efforts, all three of those regiments would not rejoin their brigades until after the fighting at Gettysburg was over.[50]

Ewell further seized a huge amount of commissary stores and military supplies that Milroy had abandoned. Pvt. Samuel Hoover from the Second Virginia informed his brother that the wagons were "all loded with valuble things." An engineering officer from Johnson's Division wrote in his diary that "from Winchester to Stephenson the road was strewn with plunder." An artilleryman from one of the Virginia batteries in the reserve artillery reported that "along the roadside were strewn muskets, knapsacks, sutler's wagons, and everything you could think of." Another gunner from the Charlottesville (Virginia) Artillery gloated to his mother that "we took their wagon trains entire, and a large amount of stores."[51]

By any measure, General Lee's plan to gather up supplies on the way to the North was off to a stunning start. Capt. George Bedinger from the Thirty-Third Virginia in the Stonewall Brigade told his sister that the spoils included "over twenty pieces of magnificent cannons, wagons, horses and mules, innumerable stores and plunder of every description to an immense account." Sgt. William S. White from the Third Company of the Richmond Howitzers in the Corps Artillery Reserve noted that the captured wagons were "loaded with everything one could imagine." The contents included "clothing, corn, flour, bacon, boots, shoes, hats, caps, sugar, coffee, tea, raisins, Malaga grapes, maple sugar, and many other items too numerous to mention."[52]

A soldier from the Sixth North Carolina boasted in a letter to his hometown newspaper that they had captured "every species of army equipage." Private Walker from the same regiment informed his parents that "we got a lot of clothing" and "eatables of all kinds." Pvt. William F. Wagner from the Fifty-Seventh North Carolina in the same brigade reported to his wife that he "never saw as many things at one plase in my life." Among the loot scattered along the roadway was "cloathing and rashins and wagons and sugar and coffey." The Tar Heel happily scooped up a number of items for his own use, including "a little pocket full of coffey and a new haver sack and a shirt."[53]

The haul also included luxury goods of almost every description. "Such an abundance of plunder they had never seen before and each man in the regiment was arrayed in style: among other things, linen underwear, patent leather boots, and black slouch hats to cap the climax," one soldier from the Thirteenth Virginia effused. Maj. John Warwick Daniel from Early's staff reported in a letter to his sister that "swords, sashes, fine shirts, collars, boots, shoes, and every article of the toilet" were also present "in bewildering plenty."[54]

The artillery that they captured during the attack consisted of four twenty-pounder Parrotts, two twenty-four-pounder howitzers, and seventeen nearly new three-inch rifled guns. The loot further included about 200,000 rounds of small-arms ammunition. The huge stock of commissary stores that they seized from the sutlers attached to Milroy's command only added to their elation. "We were soon on duty guarding prisoners and captured stores," Pvt. William H. Lyons from the Second Maryland Infantry Battalion of the Maryland Line wrote in his diary. "I was in a sutler's shop soon after we arrived [and] we get plenty of [the] things we needed."[55]

Men throughout the corps heaped numerous accolades on their new commander for what they had accomplished at Winchester. Maj. Henry Kyd Douglas, who served as an assistant adjutant general on Johnson's staff, described Ewell's management of the battle as "quick, skillful and effective—in fact, Jacksonian." Private

Walker declared to his parents that "he is another Jackson." Captain Chisolm from Hays's Brigade was even more vocal in his praise. "That's the way to gain a victory—annihilate the enemy at a blow," the Louisianan effused in a letter home. "The genius shown by Ewell surpasses even the immortal Jackson. He is fast becoming the hero of the whole army, as Jackson was only nine months ago."[56]

Sergeant Pettit from the Fluvanna Artillery in the Corps Artillery Reserve well expressed the feelings of nearly everyone who participated in the battle when he wrote to his wife soon after the end of the fighting. "As it is, General Ewell, who commanded our forces, his corps being here, has shown himself a worthy successor of Jackson," he proudly declared. "With the rapidity of his marches and disposition of his forces, he got Milroy completely in his power, before he was aware of his being this side of the Blue Ridge." In all, it was a triumph almost beyond description. The buoyant artilleryman insisted, in fact, that "there was never a more complete surprise."[57]

While pleased with the results, an officer in Johnson's Division had a somewhat different assessment of what Ewell's men had accomplished at Winchester. "It is certainly a bloodless victory, but we have had some very bloody ones, so this is a desirable change, if it is somewhat tame," Lt. Alfred M. Edgar from the Twenty-Seventh Virginia remarked. Despite their success in the battle, he worried, "we may have more bloody ones in the future, and I greatly fear bloody failures also." Still unknown was which of those outcomes awaited the troops as they continued their bold advance into the North.[58]

3

"Quite a Brilliant Little Affair"

While Ewell attacked Winchester, Major General Rodes implemented the other part of the plan, which called for him to seize Berryville and "then to advance without delay on Martinsburg." He would proceed from there into Maryland and await additional instructions that would follow once Winchester was secured. In order "to carry out this plan the better," the corps commander attached the large cavalry brigade headed by Brig. Gen. Albert G. Jenkins directly to Rodes's command. Jenkins's horsemen would screen the advance through the Shenandoah Valley and seize supplies once the division crossed the Potomac River.[1]

Following the strategy meeting outside Front Royal on the afternoon of June 12, Rodes's men set off along "an unfrequented road" that angled northeast from Cedarville. By the time they halted for the night a few miles north of there, near the small settlement of Stone Bridge, the bulk of the cavalrymen had already linked up with the division. Jenkins's force totaled about 1,600 roughneck troopers, most of whom had no experience operating in coordination with a large infantry force. The horsemen had arrived just after a hard ride from the vicinity of Middletown, Virginia, on Valley Turnpike, a few miles south of Winchester, having earlier operated in the nearby Valley District.

The units assigned to Rodes's command were the Fourteenth, Sixteenth, and Seventeenth Virginia Cavalry and the Thirty-Fourth and Thirty-Sixth Virginia Cavalry Battalions, which had been raised in the rugged western mountains of Virginia; the Sixteenth Virginia Cavalry remained on detached duty for the attack on Winchester. Jenkins's artillery contingent, Capt. William L. Jackson's Charlottesville (Virginia) Horse Artillery, stayed behind at Staunton, Virginia, to finish its reorganization due to the formal exchange of the men from what was then known as the Kanawha Artillery, captured the previous year at Fort Donelson, Tennessee.[2]

Brig. Gen. Albert G. Jenkins. Courtesy Library of Congress.

Jenkins cut a dashing figure, with a long flowing beard that extended below his waist. He was born in 1830 and grew up in northwestern Virginia along the Ohio River. Jenkins attended Jefferson College in Pennsylvania and Harvard Law School. Serving in the U.S. Congress from 1857 to 1861, in the fall of 1861 he won election to the first Confederate Congress. After a brief stint in Richmond, however, he resigned his seat and accepted a commission as brigadier general. His new cavalry command carried out several major raids in the mountains of western Virginia and even into Kentucky and Ohio. Despite its accomplishments in the guerrilla-style warfare along the border, Jenkins's Brigade was widely regarded as being poorly disciplined and ill suited for regular cavalry service.[3]

The first signs of problems were not long in coming. On the morning after Jenkins's arrival, Rodes learned that an enemy patrol had detected the advance on Berryville because of the cavalry's failure to occupy Millwood during the night as Jenkins had been ordered. That mistake left the division commander fuming. He responded to the disheartening news by pushing his troops forward from their camp at 6:00 A.M. "Finding our movements discovered, the division was marched with the utmost celerity through Millwood upon Berryville," Rodes stated in his official report.[4]

The soldiers in the long column were awed by the splendor of the countryside along the road leading north. "On one side there was one of the richest meadows

I have ever seen—covd with the most luxuriant hay grass of some kind, & along a stream running through it were 2 rows of weeping willows—the largest by far and most flourishing I ever saw," Pvt. Samuel Pickens from the Fifth Alabama in O'Neal's Brigade effused in his dairy. He declared, "they must swim in milk and butter all thro' this country." Asst. Surgeon William W. Marston from the Twelfth North Carolina in Iverson's Brigade described it as "the most beautiful country in the sun."[5]

This section of the fertile Shenandoah Valley originally formed part of the five-million-acre estate owned by Lord Thomas Fairfax. As a young man, George Washington carried out several surveys in the region. Members of his family later purchased land near Berryville, and Washington himself frequently visited there. In the late 1700s a large number of land-grant holders moved into the eastern and southern parts of what was then Frederick County from the Tidewater section of the state, bringing with them many slaves and their lavish plantation lifestyle.

An influx of immigrants from Pennsylvania and New Jersey first settled the northern and western parts of the county. Numerous mills and small farms soon filled the area, making that part of Frederick County much less dependent on slave labor than the regions to the south. The differences between the large landowners on the east and south and the German and Scotch-Irish settlers west of Opequon Creek led to the creation of Clarke County in 1836. The portions allotted to the new county came mostly from the eastern and southern sections of Frederick, where slaves made up more than half of the population.[6]

Typical of the rousing reception that Rodes's men received in that solidly pro-Southern part of the valley was the reaction of Matella Page Harrison, who recorded in her diary that it was "one of the brightest days of my life" when the troops passed by her house just south of Millwood. Most startling of all was the huge size of the invading force. "They soon came thick and fast," she wrote. "I ran down through the woods to feast my eyes and oh what a joyful array. Rhodes' [sic] gallant men were marching. Johnston [sic] they said was on the left. Early in the center. There was no escape for Milroy."[7]

As the soldiers made their way into Millwood during midmorning on June 13, many of the jubilant residents crowded onto the roadway handing out all kinds of refreshments. "There were 2 glorious young ladies at a house on the bank of the stream as you enter the place, who worked like trojans bringing buckets of water to the paling for the soldiers," Private Pickens remarked. "It was excellent water, too, cold as ice." The people also informed them that the Federal cavalry "had passed not an hour ahead" of their arrival. The young Alabamian admitted, "we were a little excited to think of being so near the Yanks."[8]

The troops pushed on from Millwood toward Berryville, which served as the seat of government for Clarke County. The town originally sprang up near a crossroads tavern on twenty acres of land owned by Benjamin Berry. Samuel Scollay Moore, who was a young boy at the time the war began, recalled that it "was then a

Turnpike at Millwood, Virginia. Courtesy Clarke County Historical Association.

town of 500 people—most of them professional people, merchants, mechanics, and laborers." After more than two years of repeated Federal occupations, the residents there had hardly wavered at all in their staunch support for the Southern cause.[9]

Although the infantry was closing fast on the enemy, Jenkins's troopers were the first Confederates to reach the town. When Rodes arrived there at about 10:00 A.M., he discovered that the cavalry leader had again let him down. Rather than cutting off the enemy's lines of retreat to the north and west, Jenkins had inexplicably halted his men in front of town, where they were being "held at bay by the Federal artillery." By that point the widespread concerns about the poor quality of the newly arrived cavalrymen appeared to be fully justified. Only time would tell exactly how ineffective they would be.

While far from daunting, the Federal garrison was still larger than the cavalry could handle by itself. The force defending the town totaled about 1,800 men under the command of Col. Andrew T. McReynolds from the First New York (Lincoln) Cavalry. The troops, who formed part of General Milroy's division in the Federal VIII Corps, comprised the Sixth Maryland, the Sixty-Seventh Pennsylvania, the First New York Cavalry, and a four-gun battery of Maryland artillery under the command of Capt. Frederick W. Alexander. Some hastily constructed earthworks blocked the entrance into Berryville from the south.[10]

By most accounts, Colonel McReynolds had displayed little of the despicable behavior attributed to Milroy. A Confederate officer who passed through the area a few days later admitted that McReynolds had earned "an enviable name for moderation; justice and gentlemanly deportment: so far as any one could exercise either who was under the command of that infamous brute, Milroy." He pointed out that the colonel "was an Episcopalean and to this the people in Berryville attribute the fact that the Episcopal church in that village was not appropriated or defaced by the Yankees."[11]

Milroy received the first detailed reports of Ewell's advance in the afternoon of June 12. The general immediately sent a messenger to McReynolds, "notifying him that the enemy was reported to be in force on the Front Royal road, and ordering him to reconnoitre in that direction, to be in readiness to move, and in case of serious attack, to fall back on Winchester." He directed the colonel to hold in place at Berryville until ordered to withdraw and further "arranged that upon the firing of the four large guns in the fort at Winchester he was to march immediately to that place."[12]

On the following morning Milroy finally shot off the cannons as a signal for McReynolds to retreat. The colonel quickly implemented a holding action that would allow his troops to pull back in safety to nearby Winchester. While the bulk of his men prepared to make their escape, he deployed three companies from the Maryland regiment, about 150 troopers from the New York cavalry, and one section of artillery under Lt. H. Eugene Alexander on the south end of town. From there they kept up an active skirmish and artillery fire against the advancing Confederates. With any luck, that action would buy enough time for McReynolds's men to get away.[13]

As Rodes's five infantry brigades began arriving at Berryville just before noon, they suddenly encountered several bursts of fire from the Federal guns posted along the road. After conferring with Jenkins, Rodes observed that the mixed force of infantry, cavalry, and artillery in the town appeared to be making hasty preparations for evacuation. He quickly decided to take some decisive steps before the enemy troops could make good their escape. "I immediately determined to surround them, if possible, and ordered General Jenkins to march to the left of the town, to cut off the enemy toward Winchester," the division commander explained in his official report. "The infantry, save one brigade, without being halted, were ordered to move to the right and left of the place, to unite in the rear."

Within minutes the brigades began shifting into position for an attack on the town. Rodes noted that, just as the flanking maneuver got underway, "it became apparent to me that the enemy was retreating, and I ordered the Alabama brigade, Colonel O'Neal commanding, to advance rapidly upon the town, which was done." O'Neal's troops immediately pushed forward from their position directly in front of Berryville. The colonel reported that once his brigade began its advance, the enemy "precipitately retired, leaving their tents, camps, and a great many valuables in our hands."[14]

According to Private Pickens, the brigade "got to within a mile or 1½ of the place about 1 or 2 P.M. & formed line of battle & expected to have a hard charge to make as the Yanks. had excellent position on an elevated place & we would have been compelled to charge up a slant for nearly a mile, but we were much relieved to see our Brigade file into [the] road & march by flank upon the town." The Alabamian quickly

Berryville, Virginia, looking north on Church Street. Courtesy Clarke County Historical Association.

determined that all "the Yanks had left." On close examination of the enemy fortifications, Pickens discovered that the position they had abandoned consisted of a "splendid redoubt" that was constructed with a "thick bank—planked up on [the] inside."[15]

Many of the defenders were busy preparing their midday meal when the attack finally came. "We cooked our breakfast as usual and had our pots on the fire with beans half cooked, when two guns were taken to the breastworks that we had erected," one of the Federal artillerymen recalled. "Soon their booming was heard." The sounds of an imminent fight sent most of the men scrambling for safety in the rear. The artillerists quickly "dumped the bean soup into the fire, got a few of our tents into a wagon, set fire to the rest and moved on by way of the Martinsburg pike in a round-a-bout way to Winchester, to join the main body of troops under Gen. Milroy."

The sutlers attached to the Federal camp became so frightened that they abandoned immense quantities of scarce supplies during their panicked flight from Berryville. "We passed the camp of the Sixty-Seventh Pennsylvania regiment, where the sutler had taken down his tents and had no time to pack all his goods, so there were barrels of ginger cakes, boxes of lemons, jars of pickels, suspenders, shoe blacking, toilet soap, and many other articles," the artilleryman recalled. Many of the men from the two infantry regiments were also in such a panic to escape that they littered the road with their discarded baggage.[16]

While all that was going on, the troops from Ramseur's Brigade moved into place on the right side of town. Lt. William Calder reported that the men suffered through "a terribly fatiguing march of seven miles" as they attempted to encircle the enemy. "We sharpshooters were deployed to cover the flank and had to walk through wheat waist high and clover knee high over fences and hills until we were completely broken down," he grumbled to his mother. Capt. James I .Harris from the Thirtieth North Carolina also complained that "it was excessively warm and we marched in quick time about 5 miles before we halted . . . within about 600 yards of the town." He admitted, "I don't believe that I ever was so near exhausted before."[17]

Ramseur's men soon found that McReynolds's troops had abandoned their defenses. Lieutenant Calder noted that the brigade "advanced in line of battle until within sight of the town, when we discovered that the enemy had vamoosed leaving his sick and all his camp & garrison equipage and stores." According to Capt. John Gorman from the Second North Carolina, the Confederates "marched in the place about 11 o'clock in line of battle, and the four regiments—composed principally of renegade west Virginians and Marylanders—had hardly got a glimpse of our battle flags across the open fields before they fled in confusion." The Tar Heel veteran added that "not a gun was fired by us, and only some half dozen discharges from a piece of artillery by them."[18]

The troops from Daniel's Brigade, meanwhile, swung around about three miles to the left in order to cut off any escape along Winchester Turnpike. "We then formed in line of battle with sharpshooters in front," Pvt. Louis Leon from the Fifty-Third North Carolina reported. "We gave the Rebel yell and charged. But, when we got to their breastworks the birds had flown." General Daniel quickly determined that the enemy had fled toward Berryville. "I immediately commenced moving in the same direction, when I received notice from Major-General Rodes that the enemy had retreated from the town, and was directed by him to move upon the Martinsburg Pike," he remarked in his official report.[19]

The results were much the same for the men in Iverson's Brigade. Pvt. John Coghill from the Twenty-Third North Carolina noted that the Tar Heels "flanked their breastworks but when we marched up to fight they ware gone." Doles's troops joined in the action from the rear, where they had been assigned to protect the huge supply train. "When in about two miles of Berryville we were ordered to the front," Capt. John H. Harris from the Forty-Fourth Georgia wrote in his diary. As they approached the town, he suddenly "heard a gun or two and thought that the ball would soon open." Harris soon realized that "the Yankees fled, leaving all their company stores, etc., etc." Another Georgian bragged that all this "was accomplished without the firing of a gun."[20]

The arrival of Rodes's men came as a huge relief for the majority of the citizens in Berryville. According to Lt. William Ardrey from the Thirtieth North Carolina, there was "great rejoicing by the citizens to be relieved from the ridicule and insults of our enemy." Among the most ardent Southern sympathizers there was Treadwell Smith, who had lived through nearly two years of Federal occupation. "The Yankees

Treadwell Smith home at Berryville, Virginia. Courtesy Clarke County Historical Association.

left Berryville in a hurry," Smith proudly proclaimed in his diary. He noted with even more delight that "the Confederates came soon after they left."[21]

As the men from Rodes's Division pushed forward into town, they quickly confirmed that almost all the Federal troops were gone. "The cowards had deserted the place and given leg bail, leaving behind over 100 of their sick as prisoners," Capt. James Harris from Ramseur's Brigade explained to a friend. The best part was the huge cache of loot that the enemy soldiers had abandoned as they withdrew. The captain reported that his men "passed on through town and there stood their tents just as they had left them a few minutes before—sutlers tents filled with everything that luxurious living could call for, and officers and privates tents filled with everything that convenience could demand."[22]

Everywhere they looked, the soldiers spotted clear signs of the panic among the Federals. "They left their tents—large white Sibley tents, standing—their clothes and private effects intact, and their dinners cooked ready for eating," Captain Gorman wrote in a letter to a Raleigh newspaper. According to another of Ramseur's officers, the frightened Yankees had abandoned "all their tents, quartermaster's supplies and stores, with dinners on the fire." Pvt. Davies Tinsley, who served in Doles's Brigade, pointed out that the enemy soldiers ran away so quickly that they "left their kettles on the fire, their clothes & many guns—all their tents standing, in fact, taking nothing with them."[23]

While the rest of the troops continued pursuing the enemy, Rodes assigned Private Pickens's company from the Fifth Alabama to guard the huge haul of captured supplies against looting. The men immediately encountered problems with some of the stragglers, who had already begun plundering the camp. "It was as much as we could do to keep them out," he admitted in his diary. "They'd slip in in spite of us." Despite their best efforts, Pickens and his comrades were quickly overwhelmed by a large group of men from Daniel's Brigade, who "came pouring back to the camp" and were "soon all over it."[24]

Within minutes soldiers throughout the division began gathering up their considerable spoils. Lieutenant Calder told his mother that the troops were "allowed to ransack the camps where they found everything you could think that would be most welcome to a needy Confederate." Surgeon John Shaffner, who served with the Fourth North Carolina in Ramseur's Brigade, acknowledged to a friend that the camp "afforded a rich prize to our soldiers." He noted that "coffee, sugar, meat, hard bread abounded plentifully, not to mention other stores." According to Maj. Eugene Blackford from O'Neal's Brigade, the soldiers in his regiment "got everything in the way of eatables & drinkables that one could want."[25]

The men soon discovered that the items available extended far beyond anything they had imaged when they first entered Berryville. One officer from the Fourteenth North Carolina in Ramseur's Brigade found "pots, plenty of pots, full of stewed beef, loaf bread piled in stacks, with other edibles, condiments, etc." He recalled that the troops quickly took the opportunity to eat "all we could, to our entire satisfaction." The massive haul proved just as satisfying for Captain Gorman. The Tar Heel noted in a letter home that "every soldier filled his haversack with the pure bean coffee, sugar and other camp delicacies, which they seemed to have been particularly favored with."[26]

A soldier from one of the division's batteries reported that the most "novel sight" for the men in his command was the "the quantity of Yankee beans" that they uncovered in the camp. "This was a new food to them," he explained, pointing out that "every man supplied himself with a quantity of the beans, as they were among the first to enter the camp and had free access to everything in it." Lt. Col. Wharton J. Green from General Daniel's staff recalled that his share of the loot included "a fine young Newfoundland dog," which he immediately adopted as a pet. They also seized some highly prized Spencer repeating rifles from among the spoils.[27]

The soldiers could hardly believe the extent of the other luxuries available to the Federal troops. "The Yankees lived off the fat of the land, and were well prepared with stoves and cooking utensils, to serve their ration and *extras* up, in the best style," Capt. Joseph B. Reese from the Forty-Fourth Georgia in Doles's Brigade effused in a letter to his hometown newspaper. He insisted that "their quarters were

equal to small carpeted country sitting-rooms." Private Pickens noted that the enemy troops even "had martin boxes fixed up in their Camps."[28]

In the late afternoon Rodes finally assigned some of the men from the Forty-
Fourth Georgia to guard the remaining supplies in Berryville. "We were left with
our company in charge of the camp to destroy tents, &c., and parole the prisoners,"
Capt. James W. Beck reported in a letter home. Despite the widespread looting, the
Georgia troops secured a huge quantity of goods for the division's Quartermaster
and Commissary Departments. They also rounded up about eighty-seven Federal
prisoners, most of whom were sick and had been left behind in a makeshift field
hospital. The only other losses on the Federal side were two men wounded during
the initial skirmishing.[29]

During that time, the division commander remained busy assessing the situation inside the town. Rodes was soon "mortified to learn that the enemy, abandon-
ing his tents, a few stores, &c, had left his cavalry and artillery to keep our cavalry in
check, and had some time before retreated with his infantry toward Charlestown,
without being discovered." Captain Gorman reported in a letter home that, "after a
short rest, the bugle sounded us to our places, and we followed our cavalry who had
gone in pursuit—But neither we nor the cavalry came up with them that night."[30]

Jenkins's troopers initially chased the retreating troops to Summit Point, where
the Federals split their column into two parts. Rather than following the main force
to the west, most of the horsemen galloped off to the north in an attempt to overtake
forty-two supply wagons and several heavily laden sutlers' vehicles that were being
escorted on the road to Martinsburg by Lt. Frank Martindale's company of the First
New York Cavalry and a few men from the Sixty-Seventh Pennsylvania. Along the
way the train linked up with another group of wagons, en route to Berryville with
supplies from Harpers Ferry.[31]

The Confederate cavalrymen quickly closed the gap as they galloped north from
Summit Point. Their first encounter with the wagon train came soon afterward at
the town of Smithfield. With the valuable prize in sight, Jenkins's horsemen moved
into place for an attack aimed at cutting off the enemy's avenue of escape. Lt. Addison A. Smith from the Seventeenth Virginia Cavalry recalled that the general
immediately "ordered a squadron to charge them, which they did successfully, running them about 5 miles, whilst our command followed close to their rear."[32]

With Jenkins's troopers in close pursuit, the long line of wagons sped northwest for a few miles toward Bunker Hill. Despite their overwhelming advantage in
numbers, the inexperienced Confederates remained hesitant to push the attack to a
conclusion. A Federal officer from the Sixth Maryland who was traveling with the
train reported to his hometown newspaper that the small force accompanying the
wagons continued "skirmishing briskly with the enemy." He noted that they held
the enemy "in check, with the loss of one killed and two wounded (one a Captain

of cavalry) on our side and much greater loss to him." They held off their pursuers throughout the morning until they finally reached apparent safety at Bunker Hill.[33]

That tiny village occupied a strategic location at the junction of the main road from Berryville and the turnpike from Winchester. To their relief, the men escorting the wagons found on their arrival that four full companies of infantry from the Federal garrison at Winchester already occupied the town. That force would clearly provide a formidable obstacle to the pursuing rebel cavalrymen. Those troops had strongly fortified the local Presbyterian and Methodist Episcopal churches against a potential attack after being recently assigned there on outpost duty.

As the wagons and their small escort escaped along the road to Martinsburg, men from the Eighty-Seventh Pennsylvania and the One Hundred Sixteenth Ohio under Maj. W. T. Morris hurriedly deployed about three-quarters of a mile east of town between the turnpike and the road from Berryville. The troops formed their main battle line in a hayfield along the crest of a ridge overlooking scenic Mill Creek. Their defenses also included a large barricade that blocked a nearby bridge on the road leading into town, an obstruction Lieutenant Smith from Jenkins's Brigade described as "a heavy fence built across the road." From their position in an "open field," the Federal infantry soon faced an "overwhelming force of the enemy" approaching fast from the opposite side of the creek.

Once his cavalrymen moved into position, Jenkins finally got up enough nerve to make a direct attack on the Federal battle line. Sgt. Isaac Hamilton Brisco from the Seventeenth Virginia Cavalry noted that his company "was in the advance and charged two hundred of them lined up in a field." With the general at the front, the Confederates soon had the enemy in full flight from their position along the creek. "On seeing the enemy fleeing before us, he [Jenkins] led them in a charge, chasing them, whilst we rushed on after them also," Lieutenant Smith from the same regiment explained. "The boys let them have the saber freely."[34]

From the outskirts of Bunker Hill, the bulk of the Federal soldiers scurried for safety toward the center of town. "Their rear guard was overtaken," one of Jenkins's cavalrymen remarked. "Then a running fight commenced, and onward until they were charged upon and driven into their barracks—brick and stone buildings used for the purpose—on Bunker Hill." Several companies of troopers eventually overtook the main enemy force and captured "large squads at the doors" of the churches. The remaining Federals took up positions inside the two main buildings, which were "well provided for defense, with loop-holes and barricades fixed for that purpose."

As the enemy soldiers hunkered down inside the churches, Jenkins sent in local resident John Lamon with a demand for their immediate surrender. Major Morris defiantly replied, "we are not doing that kind of business." The general responded by launching a series of half-hearted attacks against the fortified Federal positions over the course of the late afternoon and early evening. As darkness approached

View across Mill Creek at Bunker Hill, Virginia. Courtesy Library of Congress.

and heavy rain began to fall, Jenkins's nerve failed him again. Rather than press forward, he decided to break off the action for the night. After posting some pickets around the two buildings, the majority of his men settled into camp just outside of town. That decision would turn out to be major blunder.[35]

Although many of them had eluded capture, the Federals had sustained some heavy casualties during the fighting that day. Sergeant Brisco claimed in a letter home that Jenkins's men "killed 16 on the ground and captured sixty-three prisoners." Federal reports listed their losses as seven men killed, thirty-five wounded, and fifty-five captured. At the same time, casualties among the Confederate cavalrymen proved nearly negligible. "Our loss was only two killed and four wounded," one of the troopers reported. "Some four or five of our horses were killed and wounded."[36]

The prisoners included the wife of Capt. William H. Boyd from the First New York Cavalry. Her buggy had overturned in a roadside ditch as the wagon train passed through Bunker Hill, with Jenkins's troopers in close pursuit. Despite suffering a sprained ankle, she attempted to evade capture by scrambling across an open field with her two small children in tow before a squad of galloping horsemen ran her down. After interning her with other civilians at Winchester, the Confederates eventually sent the captain's wife to Richmond, where they released her from custody.[37]

When the Virginia troopers finally returned "just at the dawn" on the following day, they discovered that all of the Federal soldiers hiding in the churches had escaped through a gap in the Confederate lines under the cover of darkness. "We only found the dead, and their camp with tents and plenty of provisions for man and horse, which we feasted on until satisfied," Lieutenant Smith recalled. Another trooper spotted clear indications of the hurried escape by the wagon train, noting that "burned and broken wagons, dead horses, and the strewn articles, of every variety of an army outfit" littered the enemy's route from Bunker Hill.[38]

The escaping column of wagons and their escorts reached nearby Martinsburg without suffering any additional losses. The supply train continued north from there, crossing the Potomac River at Williamsport the following day. After making their escape into Maryland, the escorting troops pushed on as far as north as Pennsylvania, spreading word of the Confederate advance to residents all along their route. The soldiers who had taken refuge in the two churches also made their way to temporary safety with the main Federal force at Winchester.[39]

Although a large portion of the defenders had gotten away, Jenkins's men were buoyed by what they had accomplished at Bunker Hill. "This was the first fight of any importance that our boys ever participated in and every man did his noble duty," Sgt. James Hodam from the Seventeenth Virginia Cavalry gloated. The huge amount of loot that they uncovered, which included "good clothing and brand new blankets, both wool and gum," added to their enjoyment. Despite all that boasting, Jenkins's failure to finish off the enemy only confirmed Rodes's growing concerns that the horsemen lacked the necessary discipline and training in basic cavalry tactics to carry out their duties with any real efficiency.[40]

While all that was going on, Maj. James W. Sweeney's five companies of his Thirty-Sixth Virginia Cavalry Battalion continued to chase McReynolds's main force to the west along the road to Winchester. Their route initially took them north to Summit Point, where they turned west toward Brucetown. Late in the afternoon a squadron of troopers from the First New York Cavalry, two companies from the Sixth Maryland, and a section of two guns under Captain Alexander set up a strong skirmish line at Locke's Ford on Opequon Creek just east of Brucetown to protect the rear of the retreating column from being overtaken by their relentless pursuers.[41]

From there the thin line of Federal troops watched intently for any signs of the fast-approaching cavalrymen from Jenkins's Brigade. The wait for an attack proved much shorter than any of them had anticipated. "I had barely time to make the proper disposition of my troops when, with a fiendish yell, a battalion of rebel cavalry, about 350 strong, under Major Sweeney, dashed down upon me under full charge, with the greatest confidence in their power to 'gobble up' my little command," Maj. Alonzo W. Adams, who temporarily commanded the First New York Cavalry, admitted in his official report.[42]

The Confederate attack came so suddenly that many of the Federal troops faced the real danger of being overrun. The onslaught caught some of them in the middle of seeking much-needed relief from the intense afternoon heat in Opequon Creek. "Here many foot-sore soldiers were refreshing themselves, many bathing their feet, others their heads," one of the men from the Federal artillery recalled. "Up-stream they were refilling their canteens." To his surprise, they suddenly confronted a swarm of enemy cavalrymen. "In this situation the Confederates pounced upon us, emptying their carbines and revolvers from the banks above," the artillerist explained.[43]

The creek bank erupted into a series of fierce clashes that quickly engulfed the entire line. According to one Federal officer, the men "became so mixed up that in the dust that was raised it was for a little while difficult for one to recognize his own comrades." The ferocious hand-to-hand fighting continued until some Federal troopers on the right suddenly opened fire on Sweeney's horsemen with their carbines. Major Adams insisted that this sudden volley succeeded in "emptying many of their saddles, and, for the moment, confused and checked their charge upon us."

When Adams attempted to take advantage of the situation by ordering a counterattack, two of the companies from his regiment failed to join in the advance. The major later protested that the attack fell apart because of deliberate disobedience by some of the company commanders. While no one admitted to ignoring orders, the officers made no secret of their hatred for the major. "The fact was, officers and men had very little confidence in him," one of them confessed. He admitted that Adams "was not wanting in courage, but his effusive and pompous manner and his much talking did not indicate judgment and discretion."

Sweeney's Virginians quickly resumed the offensive and forced the skirmishers back across the creek in disarray. As the Federals withdrew, they eventually set up a new skirmish line in a concealed position near a "short turn" in the road, where they prepared to make a determined stand against the onrushing Confederates. They did not have to wait long. "Taking courage from this movement, and thinking they had me on the skedaddle, the enemy charged over the stream with great impetuosity, screaming and howling like demons," Adams declared.[44]

By that point, however, the two Federal artillery pieces had finally moved into place along the far side of the creek. The attempt to use the guns against the onrushing troopers, however, ran into trouble almost immediately when the carriage for one of the pieces suffered major damage. Lt. Col. William A. McKellip from the Sixth Maryland noted in a letter to a fellow officer, "in the hurry to get the artillery in position, a tongue of one of the caissons broke, and my cavalry being overpowered and driven back, the cannon[s] for the time being were useless."

With the artillery temporarily out of action, Sweeney's horsemen sent the Federal troops scurrying to the rear. "My cavalry retreated from the furious charge of the enemy in disorder behind the guns, leaving them exposed to attack," McKellip acknowledged. He pointed out that the rebel force "came up to within 10 yards and delivered fire from its carbines at the cavalry." This close-quarters fighting continued until some of the Maryland infantrymen suddenly opened fire. "No sooner had they emptied their pieces than I gave them a cross fire from one of my companies right in their faces, and immediately another volley from the other company, with the result that many were killed," McKellip explained.[45]

Major Adams's cavalrymen responded by rushing headlong into the fray. "The rebs gave the charge on our guns, howling at a fearful rate, and ran up to our guns," Pvt. Henry Suydam from the First New York Cavalry explained in a letter home. "Our guns gave it to them hot and heavy, but as they came up to our muzzles, our company was ordered to charge, which saved the guns." Another Federal cavalryman described this sudden foray as "a fearsome onslaught" at a full gallop with sabers drawn. "It was a terrific collision," he insisted. "Adversaries were mingled together." According to one participant, the fighting along the creek "was hand to hand, and blade to blade."

The two sides in the fighting soon became so "mixed that the artillery could not be used" without endangering some of their own men. Captain Alexander responded by limbering up his remaining cannon and moving it "further to the rear." The frustrated artilleryman eventually placed the lone piece "in position at the side of the pike, about 150 yards from the Opequon Creek." Within minutes he issued a command for the Federal troops to pull back "so that the artillery might have a chance." As the men broke off the engagement, the single gun suddenly "opened a terrific fire of canister shot upon the rebel column, carrying death and confusion to their ranks."[46]

The intense barrage quickly forced Sweeney's cavalrymen to withdraw across the creek and end the pursuit. An officer from Adams's regiment boasted that they succeeded in "completely routing the enemy." Federal reports placed Confederate losses at nineteen men killed and forty-seven wounded. The casualties included Major Sweeney, who sustained a severe wound to his arm in the fighting along the creek. The Federals lost two men killed and fifteen wounded. As a result of their determined rearguard stand, McReynolds's entire force safely reached Milroy's stronghold at Winchester.[47]

Although Jenkins's men had failed to capture the bulk of the retreating troops, Lieutenant Calder from Ramseur's Brigade still described the attack on Berryville as "quite a brilliant little affair." At the same time, he readily admitted that the enemy had "about one hour start on us" before the cavalry even began their pursuit. Jenkins's inability to aggressively chase down the Federal troops and keep them from escaping pushed Rodes close to the breaking point. "In the absence of any official report from General Jenkins, I cannot explain why he did not intercept at least a portion of the enemy's force," he declared in exasperation.[48]

Despite the cavalry leader's obvious failures, most of the men found nothing to fault about Rodes's handling of the main attack. One officer from the Thirtieth North Carolina in Ramseur's Brigade was so impressed that he took time to record the details of the victory at Berryville in the regiment's official record of events. "The enemy having fled on our approach and from the quantity of quartermaster and commissary stores left behind together with the Spencers in their camps, tents were struck, rations on the fire cooking, food on the tables ready for eating but not untouched with many other evidences of flight and confusion had a tendency to show that we were not only unwelcome but unexpected visitors," he bragged.[49]

"A Thunderbolt from a Cloudless Sky"

Only hours after attacking Berryville, Rodes's men departed from town along the same route that the enemy troops had used for their hurried escape earlier in the day. The soldiers soon put aside any lingering concerns about Jenkins's shortcomings amid the frenzied reception they received from the crowds of women lining the road in the wake of the Federal retreat. "On we went never failing to be greeted at every house by the wayside by any number of the fair sex who seemed much delighted to see us and who seemed as if they would lose their arms in waving their handkerchiefs," as Capt. James Harris from Ramseur's Brigade described the startling scenes along their march.[1]

After slogging a few miles through a torrential downpour, the Confederates finally settled into camp near Summit Point. Rodes remained determined to continue the advance toward Martinsburg, but he still had not received any news about Ewell's attack against Milroy's main force. "Not having heard anything from Winchester, though I had dispatched several couriers to the lieutenant-general commanding, I hesitated for a few moments between proceeding toward Martinsburg, in accordance with my general instructions, and turning toward Winchester," the division commander explained in his official report.[2]

Despite those concerns, Rodes decided to press ahead toward Martinsburg early on the morning of June 14. Just as on the previous day, residents along the road poured out of their homes to greet the advancing troops. Capt. John Gorman from Ramseur's Brigade noted in a letter home that "maidens fairly paved our pathway with flowers, bright eyes beamed with unalloyed pleasure and delight on our tattered, dusty garments, matrons stood at the gates with pitchers and buckets of cool water and milk, offering freely to our thirsty soldiers, whilst even the little children were in the general joy." The veteran insisted that he "never felt so proud as a soldier before."[3]

As the troops tramped northwest along a secondary road, they soon reached Smithfield, where a huge throng of well-wishers turned out to cheer them on their arrival. According to Quartermaster Sgt. John S. Tucker from the Fifth Alabama in O'Neal's Brigade, every sidewalk in the town was lined with "ladies dispensing Buttered Bread, Milk, Meats, Boquets &c. with lavish hands." Lt. William Ardrey from Ramseur's Brigade reported in his diary that "the ladies were so rejoicing in Smithfield that they crowded the streets with water and all kinds of eatables, and any quantity of bouquets, etc."[4]

From there the men pushed on a few more miles before linking up with Winchester Turnpike at Bunker Hill. Although nearly everyone up to that point had greeted them with enthusiasm, the mood quickly changed as the column moved deeper into Berkeley County. Unlike the areas around Berryville and Front Royal, which owed their character to an influx of plantation owners from the eastern part of Virginia, the early settlers of this area included numerous Quakers and Scotch-Irish Presbyterians from the Mid-Atlantic colonies. Several waves of German immigrants, who established many of the thriving farms in the region, arrived over the following decades. The small-scale agriculturalists who predominated in the county had little need for large numbers of slaves.[5]

Baltimore and Ohio Railroad repair facility at Martinsburg, Virginia, in 1858. Courtesy Baltimore and Ohio Railroad Museum.

Martinsburg, which had a population of 1,400, served as the seat of government for Berkeley County. Adam Stephen built the first home along Tuscarora Creek in the early 1770s. He named the settlement that grew up there after his close friend Thomas Bryan Martin, who was the nephew of the area's largest landholder. Stephen later served as a general under George Washington during the Revolutionary War. Over the following years, Martinsburg became home to numerous prosperous businesses. In 1848 the Baltimore and Ohio Railroad established a huge repair complex in the town.[6]

While the older families of Martinsburg remained overwhelmingly pro-Southern, most of those associated with the railroad industry harbored strong Unionist views. Their influence was never more apparent than during the balloting to approve the secession ordnance for Virginia. More than 1,200 citizens in the county voted against it, while about 400 voted to approve it. Soon afterward, a hostile crowd of railroad workers and local Union sympathizers hooted and jeered a company of Confederate troops drilling in the courthouse square. One Southern soldier who arrived about a month later described Berkeley County as "the meanest Abolition hole on the face of the earth, Martinsburg especially."[7]

As a major transportation center, the town held strategic importance for both sides in the war. In June 1861 Stonewall Jackson's men burned the roundhouse and machine shops at the repair facility and destroyed most of the locomotives and coal cars at the site, using teams of horses to haul about a dozen of the best locomotives to Staunton. The massive destruction from the raid remained visible as late as the following spring. "Forty-four locomotives stand on the track here—all a perfect wreck," a Federal soldier serving in Martinsburg remarked in a letter home. He pointed out that "the workshops have been stripped of all their tools and machinery, and the wonder is that They, too, were not destroyed—even the turntables are all gone."[8]

By the time Rodes's men arrived in June 1863, the county had joined the Restored Virginia Government under Governor Pierpont and would soon become part of the new state of West Virginia. For many of the Confederate soldiers, that move branded the residents as traitors to the cause. "We were now in Berkeley County which voted itself into the Pierpont government, and our reception was not so joyous as before and we passed many houses with doors and windows closed against us," Lieutenant Calder grumbled in a letter to his mother.[9]

The dramatic shift in public sentiment among the people along their route quickly became apparent to nearly everyone in the division. Sgt. George W. Wills from Daniel's Brigade informed his mother that he "found the citizens mostly Unionists" once they departed from Smithfield. He reported, "in fact there are very few rebels in Berkeley County." Another soldier from one of the division's artillery batteries insisted in a letter to his hometown newspaper that "all that part of Virginia, I fear, with very few exceptions, is unsound to the core."[10]

While the infantry brigades proceeded north on Winchester Turnpike, Jenkins's troopers moved into position just outside of Martinsburg. Opposing them were about 1,200 Federal troops under the command of Col. Benjamin F. Smith. That force comprised eight companies from the One Hundred Twenty-Sixth Ohio, another eight companies from the One Hundred Sixth New York, a company of Maryland home-guard cavalry, and a six-gun West Virginia battery commanded by Capt. Thomas A. Maulsby. The New York troops had just arrived in town the previous evening from their encampment at nearby North Mountain Depot. Lieutenant Martindale's company of the First New York Cavalry, which had stayed in town after safely escorting the escaping wagon train from Berryville, provided additional support. Another First New York company, under Capt. William H. Boyd, joined them there after arriving from Winchester about 10:00 A.M. with dispatches from General Milroy indicating that he faced an attack from a large Confederate force. A company of the One Hundred Twenty-Sixth Ohio remained on detached duty about two miles east of Martinsburg, guarding a strategically important railroad bridge over Opequon Creek.[11]

Colonel Smith initially deployed most of his troops about a mile south of town along the turnpike from Winchester, sending out two companies of skirmishers in support of pickets placed farther down the road. Pvt. Lewis H. Fuller from the One Hundred Sixth New York noted that they soon had "quite a brush" with lead elements from the Confederate cavalry. According to one of Jenkins's troopers, the "picket skirmishing was kept up for two hours, in which time they were driven back some two miles, when they opened their artillery fire upon our columns."[12]

The sudden barrage from the guns posted behind some boulders on the top of the ridge sent the cavalrymen scurrying for safety in the rear. One soldier from the One Hundred Twenty-Sixth Ohio noted that "our battery gave them a broadside which caused them to break and run back with our cavalry on their heels whooping them up with barking carbines." According to Pvt. Henry Gaddis from the One Hundred Sixth New York, Jenkins's troopers "scedadled as fast as their horses could carry them." Despite that respite from the attack, the soldiers soon began to see signs that more Confederates were approaching from the south. Another New Yorker recalled that "clouds of dust down the valley" clearly indicated "a big force of Johnnies coming our way."[13]

As the skirmishing escalated in the early afternoon, Smith finally withdrew his men toward town. Most of them moved into position around Shower's Hill, on the southeastern outskirts of Martinsburg, a wooded prominence also known as Union Hill because of the large number of Northern supporters who lived in the surrounding area. From the top of the outcropping, the men in Colonel Smith's command got their first unobstructed look at the size of the Confederate force. What they saw shocked them. "We could see them as thick as hair on a dog," Private Gaddis exclaimed in a letter home.[14]

Smith responded to the looming threat by placing four guns from Captain Mauls-by's battery facing south along a ridge about 150 yards in front of his main battle line. He also pushed the left wing of the One Hundred Sixth New York forward to provide support for the artillerists. Those troops took up position just southeast of the manor house owned by Lt. Col. Charles J. Faulkner, a former U.S. congressman who now served as chief of staff for General Ewell. Another section of two guns from Maulsby's battery set up on the right of the hill to cover the main approaches from the west.

The rest of the infantry remained in the rear, where they began loading up wag-ons in preparation for evacuation. By that point, Captain Boyd's company had al-ready departed from town as an escort for a large wagon train of supplies being sent to safety along the main road north to Williamsport. Capt. William Firey's Maryland company, meanwhile, took a defensive position on the northwest edge of town. Lieutenant Martindale's company from the First New York Cavalry deployed just north of there to protect the lines of retreat along Williamsport Road.[15]

Brig. Gen. Dan Tyler, the commander of the First Division in the Federal VIII Corps, had arrived earlier that day on a "special train" from Baltimore and now supervised the arrangements. He had traveled to the Valley to ensure that proper defenses were in place and to provide support for General Milroy's forces at Win-chester. Tyler carried orders that called for Federal troops to retreat from Martins-burg if they faced an overwhelming enemy force. Now, rather than take over in the middle of the impending attack, the general informed Colonel Smith that he "would not assume command, but would be on the field for advice, if necessary."[16]

While all that was going on, Rodes made his way to Martinsburg, his forces finally arriving on the outskirts of town in midafternoon. The general was frus-trated to find that Jenkins's Brigade had inexplicably halted along the turnpike, where it continued to receive sporadic fire from the Federal artillery. "The enemy's forces were drawn up in line of battle on the right of town, exhibiting infantry, cav-alry, and artillery," the division leader noted in his official report. "General Jenkins, through Captain Harris, of my staff, had summoned the Federal commander to surrender, which he had declined doing."

Jenkins had sent that capitulation demand earlier in the day under a flag of truce. In case of a refusal, he called for Colonel Smith "to notify the inhabitants of the place to remove forthwith to a place of safety." Jenkins gave the Federal com-mander one hour to make his reply before the Confederates would take any further action. "After that, I shall feel at liberty to shell the town, if I see proper," the caval-ryman declared in his note. "Should you refuse to give the necessary notification to the inhabitants, I shall be compelled to hold your command responsible."

Smith defiantly responded that he had no intention of surrendering. "You may commence shelling as soon as you choose," he exclaimed in his brief reply. "I will, however, inform the inhabitants of your threat." Word of the impending attack quickly spread throughout the populace. Local resident Susan Nourse Riddle re-

corded in her diary that there was soon "tremendous excitement" among the people in Martinsburg. She continued watching from the garret of her house as women
and children began "running to our cellars for protection."[17]

Rather than attacking immediately, Rodes decided to wait until all his infantry
had moved into position. In the meantime he ordered Jenkins "to move most of
his force to the left of town, to dismount it, and send it forward as skirmishers, to
endeavor to get possession of the town, thus cutting off the enemy's retreat toward
Hedgesville and Williamsport, and to report to me what force, if any, he discovered
in and to the left of town." One of Jenkins's troopers later reported, however, that
"the enemy, supposing we had no artillery, formed their lines on our left wing, under cover, so as to command a cross fire of musketry and front our men with their
shell, which placed our column in a most perilous position."[18]

The harassing fire from the Federal battery continued as the rest of the troops
in the division finally reached the field in the hours just before sunset. An officer in
Doles's Brigade recalled that "the 'Yanks' threw a couple of shell[s] that passed over
us" as the Georgians approached the town. Colonel O'Neal griped that the enemy
artillery bombarded his brigade "furiously for a few moments." The firing eventually
became so annoying that Rodes directed Lieutenant Colonel Carter to position the
guns from the division's artillery battalion so as "to silence the opposing battery."[19]

Carter, who had just turned thirty-two years old the previous day, came from a
prominent family in King William County, Virginia, and was General Lee's cousin.
He entered military service as captain of the King William (Virginia) Artillery,
which was soon attached to Rodes's Brigade. Carter was promoted to lieutenant
colonel and assigned command of the artillery battalion in what was then D. H.
Hill's division in December 1862. His batteries included the Orange (Virginia) Artillery, the Morris (Virginia) Artillery, the Jeff Davis (Alabama) Artillery, and the King
William Artillery, which was headed by his half-brother, Capt. William P. Carter.[20]

Within minutes of receiving Rodes's orders, Lieutenant Colonel Carter unleashed a fierce barrage with his sixteen guns on the troops around the hill. The
Federal gunners responded with a sporadic fire of their own. "After a few rounds we
were surprised to hear artillery firing and to have shells passing us, a few exploding
uncomfortably close," Cpl. Thomas Catesby Jones from the King William Artillery
recalled. "We now saw a Yankee battery and commenced firing upon it." The cannon
fire soon sent the enemy fleeing for safety. An officer from one of the other Confederate batteries bragged in a letter home that "in the brief time of twenty minutes—
before our infantry could get into position—we had the enemy flying in great haste
from the 'ragged rebels.'"[21]

The artillery fire commenced just as the Federal troops were packing up for
their withdrawal north along Williamsport Road. A New York newspaperman who
had just arrived in town reported that the atmosphere was soon "howling with the
sound of flying shot and the explosion of shells." The rounds hit so close to their

lines that many of the men around the hill broke in confusion toward the rear along the Shepherdstown Road. "Their artillery opened unexpectedly from a position commanding us, ploughing the ground around us with shot and shell and grape," Col. Edward James from the New York regiment informed his mother. "I never knew so hot a fire before. The battery horses, some wounded or killed, became wholly unmanageable."[22]

According to Private Gaddis, the first shot struck "in the face of the hill about a rod" in front of the Federal position. "[The] next volly of shell Bursted above our heads and the fragments flew like vengence in all directions," he wrote in a letter home. Fellow New Yorker Pvt. Darwin Sunderland recalled that the shells soon "began to fall among us like hail." Cpl. David Close from the One Hundred Twenty-Sixth Ohio noted that the artillery rounds "came screaming over our heads some bursting and scattering the pieces all around, others would strike the ground and scatter the earth in every direction." He insisted that he had "never seen Shells look so firy before."[23]

Wild rumors that the Confederates had stuffed their guns with all kinds of scrap iron added to the growing terror among the Ohio troops. Capt. Jonathon McCready complained that "the shells and balls and pieces of rail road iron flew thick and fast over and among us." Another Ohioan claimed that some of the men actually "saw rail-road spikes flying in the air with ties hanging to them." He described the noise from the barrage as so deafening that it "outrivaled the worst prolonged thunder throwing in the explosion of several steam boilers." Pvt. William McVey was struck most of all by the "wild unearthly sound" that the projectiles made as they poured in on the troops around the hill.[24]

This unexpected display of firepower quickly turned the planned withdrawal into a rout. "The surprise came so suddenly upon us that the surroundings did look fearfully, as if our last moment had come," a surgeon from the One Hundred Sixth New York admitted. "Yet, the whole thing did look so ludicrous that one could hardly help laughing while shaking with fear." He recalled that "the pickets were rushing in as fast as their feet could carry them; the infantry leaving the line of battle could be seen hastening to the nearest ravine or ditch, cowering down as close as possible to mother earth."[25]

Despite the intensity of the bombardment, only a few wayward shots from Carter's guns landed inside the town itself. Even those shells caused little or no real damage. "One lit in the street before Mr. Conrad's house and another burst in the garden, tearing off a raspberry bush close to the ground and damaging another," a Confederate officer who rode through Martinsburg a few days later reported after talking to some friends in town. "No further harm was done." He noted that "the family took shelter in the cellar during the danger; which did not last long."[26]

By the time the barrage commenced, four of the brigades from Rodes's Division had already moved into place around Martinsburg. Ramseur's and Iverson's Brigades set up for the attack just south of town along both sides of Winchester Turnpike. The men from Doles's and O'Neal's Brigades took up positions to the east. Most of the troops from Daniel's Brigade remained farther back, guarding the division's massive supply train. Only one regiment from that command was available for the attack, the Fifty-Third North Carolina, which formed directly behind one of Carter's batteries. General Daniel stayed well in the rear with the Forty-Third North Carolina.[27]

The sight of so many troops deployed along their front left Captain McCready with little hope for successfully defending the town. "The Sun was fast sinking in the west when their line of battle came into full view," the Ohioan remarked in a letter to his hometown newspaper. "It was but too evident that we had to contend on unequal terms. Their line of battle must have been near two miles long—long enough to make three or four times around us." The veteran officer estimated that the entire Confederate force "must have numbered from eight to fifteen thousand."[28]

While the artillery continued pounding the Federal positions, Rodes proceeded with his plans for a direct assault. "Before these preparations had been completed, however, the enemy's battery had been nearly silenced, and, fearing he would retreat, I ordered Ramseur's brigade and each of the others in turn to advance with speed upon the enemy's position," the division commander explained in his official report. Ramseur's men on the far left of the line responded to those orders by pushing straight ahead against the troops around the hill.[29]

The swiftness of the attack sent the Federal defenders into a panicked withdrawal. "With a cheer we ascended the hill, and after a few random shots the enemy broke and fled through town," Captain Gorman boasted in a letter to a major Raleigh newspaper. Lieutenant Calder insisted that the Federal troops "had no idea that we had any artillery within ten miles of them until they suddenly found themselves in a perfect hornet's nest, and before they knew that they were about the blamed rebels were within fifteen feet of the battery and they were all prisoners."[30]

Col. Bryan Grimes from the Fourth North Carolina bragged that the men from Ramseur's Brigade were "in advance on the left and charged the enemy driving them pell mell through the town—being a mile or more in advance of all other troops." Although darkness was fast approaching, the Tar Heels continued their headlong rush into the center of Martinsburg. "We captured the town about dark, and pursued the flying Yankees through the streets when there was barely enough daylight to distinguish friend from foe," Lieutenant Calder remarked in a letter to his mother. According to Lt. William Norman from the Second North Carolina, he and the others "did just as General Ramseur wanted us to do, this is, to run right over the enemy."[31]

By then Jenkins's troopers had joined in the attack, with a wild charge from the opposite side of town intended to cut off the Federals' lines of retreat to the north and west. "The musketry fire was fierce for about five minutes," one of the cavalrymen explained. "Then high in the air the signal yell of Gen. Jenkins' Brigade for a charge—the musketry was hushed into silence, and the race frantic; our artillery, in the meantime, entertaining that of the enemy." He reported that "very soon all was silent, save the mighty sounds of the dashing steeds and shouts of those in pursuit."[32]

With Jenkins in the lead, the cavalrymen galloped forward toward Martinsburg. "We were ordered to double quick and charge and on we went, crossing fence after fence, and chasing the enemy from behind them," Lt. Addison A. Smith from the Seventeenth Virginia Cavalry explained. He noted that "many of the boys fell helpless from exhaustion, the charge had been so long duration." The horsemen punctuated the onslaught with the soul-piercing sound of the Rebel yell. One of the Federal defenders described it in a letter home as "one of the d—est yells you ever heard come from human beings."[33]

The attack took the troopers directly into the teeth of the enemy's remaining defenses. "As we went down the street yelling our best there was a sheet of flame on both sides of the street, the balls would come so near that while I had my mouth open yelling one of them passed through my lips doing no injury," Sgt. Isaac Hamilton Brisco, who served in the Seventeenth Virginia Cavalry, claimed in a letter to his family. Sgt. James Hodam from the same regiment boasted that the rampaging horsemen pushed straight ahead "through the town and rode over them scattering them in all directions."[34]

As the men at the front of the advance swarmed through the streets, Captain Harris from Ramseur's Brigade could clearly see "black rows" of Federal troops along the heights beyond the town. "It was their backs however which we saw, for they were getting away as fast as their legs could carry them," he explained. "Our cavalry now charged through town like a streak of lightening and on after the flying wretches. A huge column of smoke now was high in the air & I thought that the rascals had fired the town." To his relief, the Tar Heel quickly determined that the flames were limited to "the long platform at the station on which was piled long rows of corn & hay."[35]

By then most of the Federal troops were fleeing from Martinsburg along the road that ran northeast to Shepherdstown. With Jenkins's troopers in control of the western part of town, that route remained the only safe avenue of escape. Among the men running from the field were the artillerists from a two-gun section in Maulsby's battery commanded by Lt. John S. Herr. After firing a few departing shots, they quickly limbered up their artillery pieces and joined in the evacuation. During the ensuing scramble to get away, one of the guns overturned in a deep gully and had to be abandoned.[36]

The gunners from the other two sections in the battery had even less luck. Ramseur's and Jenkins's men easily overtook them as they attempted to escape north on Williamsport Road and seized their four artillery pieces. "Ramseur's brigade, being in the lead, pursued the enemy at almost a run for 2 miles beyond the town, but, quick as it was, the dismounted cavalry and a squadron or two on horseback, under General Jenkins, were ahead of them, and, after a few shots, compelled the enemy to abandon all his guns," Rodes stated in his report. He bragged that these cannons, along "with their caissons and most of their horses were thus captured."[37]

Capt. James A. Crawford's company from the Seventeenth Virginia Cavalry led the way as they rode down this main part of Maulsby's battery. According to one of the cavalrymen, Pvt. Lucien C. "Cooney" Ricketts remained "far in the lead" during the chase. "This brave young man, only sixteen years of age, pursued the enemy, passing and halting piece after piece of the artillery, until he encountered the captain in person," his fellow trooper reported to a Virginia newspaper. After firing all the chambers in his revolver, the youngster continued fighting "with his empty pistol in hand" against repeated saber blows until they secured the four guns on that part of the field.[38]

Corporal Jones from the King William Artillery was shocked at the sight of the enemy's guns rolling back toward town, though now with Jenkins's cavalrymen astride the caissons. "Seeing a battery very quietly approaching down the same street we hardly knew what to make of it," he recalled. "We were overjoyed to find that Col. Jenkins had cut off the retreat of our very recent antagonist and had captured every gun and caisson." Most startling of all was the high quality of the captured gear. "I never saw such equipment as the North had supplied this Virginia battery," the artilleryman declared in amazement.[39]

While all that was going on, the rest of Rodes's men joined in the main assault on the town. Despite being exhausted from their long march, the troops from the Fifty-Third North Carolina in Daniel's Brigade quickly pressed forward from their position on the far right of the battle line. "We got there about 9 o'clock at night and drove them through the town, and, in fact, we felt like driving the devil out of his stronghold, as this was a very warm day," Pvt. Louis Leon penned in his diary. "We had to march in quick time all day, a distance of twenty-five miles. Therefore we were not in the best of humor."[40]

Although they were also nearly broken down, the soldiers from the other brigades in the division found the attack to be surprisingly easy. Capt. James Beck from the Forty-Fourth Georgia reported to his hometown newspaper that Doles's troops "had a hard march, but reached the town at sundown and again put the Yanks to flight." Pvt. Jeremiah M. Tate from the Fifth Alabama was shocked that the men from O'Neal's Brigade encountered almost no enemy opposition as they swept through the streets of Martinsburg. "The yankes went out at one side of town as we came in at the other," he gloated to his sister.[41]

Iverson's men enjoyed similar success as they charged forward from the left center of the line. According to Pvt. Leonidas Torrence from the Twenty-Third North Carolina, they "had no Fight except for a few Artillery and skirmish shots." Despite the lack of resistance, the situation turned chaotic as Iverson's troops swept through the streets. "Such a terrific yell as was raised simultaneously by all the brigade & such a noise as was caused by charging over the numerous stone fences surrounding the town was never heard before on earth," Maj. Charles Blacknall remarked. "There was such confusion & terror & running to & fro by the Yankees & citizens as I never before witnessed." He further reported that "the Yankees immediately set fire to their army stores & commenced running in every direction."[42]

The Southern supporters in the town greeted Rodes's onrushing troops with ecstatic cheers. "Our reception was all that we could have desired," Captain Harris declared. "The ladies seemed wild with joy." The North Carolinian noted that many of the people along the streets "showered bouquets on us and running out in the street met us, shaking hands." Colonel Grimes sheepishly admitted to his young daughter that "a nice pretty girl about 16 years of age caught hold of me with both hands and really was so glad to see us that I think if I had offered she would have kissed me."[43]

So many frantic well-wishers crowded around the men that some of the troops found it difficult to maneuver through the narrow streets. Col. Risden T. Bennett, who commanded the Fourteenth North Carolina in Ramseur's Brigade, was struck most of all by an encounter with a teenage girl who dashed up to his horse during their advance into town. "As we threaded the streets, by-ways and private lots a young lady of many personal charms, rushing to our head, seized my reins and told me in moving tones of the oppression endured by the citizens," he recalled.[44]

For at least one Southern sympathizer, the arrival of Confederate troops in town was an event almost beyond belief. "The first gray coat road down the hill," Susan Nourse Riddle wrote in her diary that day. "Oh! the joy at seeing it once more—another & another & soon the town is full. Rhodes Division enters the town." To her astonishment, the cavalry continued to pursue "the flying Yankees," capturing all their guns but one. "Such a happy comfortable night we have not spent for six long months," she proclaimed. "May we not forget to 'Bless the Lord': For this happy Sabbath night."[45]

Lieutenant Calder was nearly overwhelmed by the extent of the celebrations. Although the men of Ramseur's Brigade were "all very foot sore and weary," he admitted, they quickly forgot their pains amid the "glad shout of victory" that erupted as the troops passed through the streets. "Old women & young maidens waved their handkerchiefs and bid us good speed," the Tar Heel told his mother. "It is in moments like these that the soldier forgets all the toil, hardship & dangers of his life in the excitement of the moment; and all his labors are repaid in the pleasures of victory."[46]

Yet unlike the towns in the southern Shenandoah Valley, the Confederates' reception in Martinsburg proved far from completely friendly. Asst. Surgeon William Marston from Iverson's Brigade estimated that the town was "about one half Yankees, though we have many strong Southern friends here." Quartermaster Sergeant Tucker also found their greeting to be strangely muted after the "most enthusiastic welcome" they had received everywhere else in the Valley. While conceding that "some of the women & Citizens were delighted to see us," he insisted that the town was "rotten to the Core."[47]

Maj. Eugene Blackford from O'Neal's Brigade was stunned by the hostile reaction they received from some of the ladies who confronted them along the streets. "Most of those we met in this town were violent unionist[s], and the women especially failed not to show us continually," he complained. "I heard here, also, for the first time an oath from a woman's lips, and from quite respectable people apparently." Pvt. Davies Tinsley from Doles's Brigade noted in a letter home that many of the women there "cursed & abused us." He claimed that "even little children" joined in berating the troops.[48]

In a few cases, events threatened to take a more dangerous turn. Colonel Bennett recalled one such instance when "a Dutch woman of strong Union brawn drew a paddling-stick on Captain Gorman" as they entered the town. Only some quick thinking by another officer saved the encounter from getting out of hand. "Gorman's situation was relieved by the arrival of Lieutenant Harney, of the Rough and Ready Guards, who told the woman, with affected severity," the colonel joked, that "if she did not behave herself he would pull every hair out of her head.[49]

While admitting the presence of "many staunch and true Confederates" in Martinsburg, Gorman himself described it as "the foulest Union hole" they had encountered during the advance. "In our race through the streets, some ladies would shout and point which way the Yankees ran," he remarked. "Some with tears in their eyes would seize our hands, and in their transport of joy almost embrace us, while others looked sulky and would scowl at us with snaky hate." He reported that "one young lady, whose Yankee sweetheart had tarried late in bidding her good-bye, actually struck me in madness as I espied him running, when I bade one of my men to shoot him."[50]

Despite their mixed greeting, Major Blacknall insisted that the men from Iverson's Brigade enjoyed "a gay time" as they surged through the streets. "The whole thing was confusion, night had arrived, our troops filled the town & everything was in an uproar," he explained. "I immediately took possession of the Qr. Master & Commissary stores & Provost Marshall office, & found everything that could be desired in abundance." Among the articles he uncovered were several boxes marked as containing twelve dozen Colt repeaters. "But, I found on opening them that they contained each 12 doz. bottles [of] fine French brandy, which I proceeded to capture," the veteran officer slyly remarked.[51]

Many of the soldiers from the other brigades were just as pleased with all the loot they found. Pvt. Sidney J. Richardson of the Fourth Georgia reported to his parents that he secured "as much butter, sugar and coffee as I wanted." Colonel Grimes informed his young daughter that he captured "as my share of the spoils of the Yankee camp a dog & a tame squirrel, which I wish you could get." He noted with obvious affection that the squirrel "is very tame & gentle and is as frolicsome as a kitten—you would be much amused at his pranks."[52]

Some of the most successful foragers came from Jenkins's cavalry brigade. The rugged backwoodsmen uncovered most of the spoils only after a long search that extended well into the late hours of the night. Many of the difficulties that the troopers encountered resulted from the Federal efforts to destroy the abandoned stocks of usable items as they fled in panic from town. "The enemy set fire to most of their supplies and commissary stores before we could secure them," Lieutenant Smith explained. "Yet we got much plunder of various kinds."[53]

In an attempt to restore order, Rodes finally assigned a detachment from the Forty-Fourth Georgia as provost guards for the town. The troops made a thorough search for any enemy soldiers who might be hiding in the homes of the town's pro-Northern families. "Martinsburg is strong for the old Union and several Yankees were found concealed in the houses, even after the owners had sworn none were there," an officer from the division's artillery battalion explained in a letter home. One of O'Neal's soldiers claimed that some later searches even uncovered "horses hid down in the cellars of the citizens."[54]

While the provost guards continued hunting through town, Rodes dispatched two companies from the Forty-Fourth Georgia and one piece of artillery to protect the area directly to the north from any late-arriving enemy forces. Capt. John C. Key recalled that the men from his company were "ordered some distance up the Baltimore & Ohio Railroad to guard against any train coming in with Federal reinforcements." An officer from the other company indicated in his diary that the soldiers under his command were assigned "to watch for a train of cars that were said to be coming down with two thousand troops."[55]

The two companies quickly threw together some temporary defenses along the main railroad line leading into town. "We tore up a little of the track, placed a gun in position so it would bear on the road and posted some of our men on each side of the road," Sgt. Charles Timothy "Tim" Furlow, who served as a courier on Doles's staff, recorded in his journal. Captain Key pointed out that his soldiers also pushed "some large rocks" to the edge of a deep cut in the railroad line. From there, the massive boulders could "be easily rolled down on the tracks." He noted, however, that "no train came, and early next morning, we were ordered back in the town."[56]

The soldiers assigned to the pioneer detachment in the division, meanwhile, pried up several sections of the track and destroyed other parts of the railroad infrastructure in Martinsburg. Their work quickly attracted a large crowd of angry townspeople. Major Blackford complained that many of the citizens "would come down and revile us bitterly" as the Confederates tore down a large railroad bridge in the middle of town. "They were mostly the wives of the workmen employed by the Company," he explained, "who I suppose would be thrown out of employment for some time by this."[57]

During that time, "the appropriate officers" also set to work taking a detailed inventory of the supplies they acquired in Martinsburg. According to Rodes, the stock of goods left behind by the Federals included "some 6,000 bushels of fine grain, some commissary stores, about 400 rounds of rifled artillery ammunition, and small-arms and ammunition in small quantity." He further reported that they "captured two excellent ambulances." Captain Harris from Ramseur's Brigade noted that "some of the finest artillery horse I ever saw also were brought in amid the shouts of our men."[58]

The most valuable items were the five artillery pieces seized from Maulsby's battery, which turned out to be nearly new three-inch rifles. Rodes immediately transferred four of the guns, along with their horses and other equipment, to Capt. William J. Reese's Jeff Davis Artillery. "The old guns of the company, two Rome, Ga., rifles, one bronze Napoleon, and a twelve-pounder howitzer, and the greatly worn equipment, which had been in constant use for about two years, were turned in to the Confederate Ordinance Department," one of the Alabama artillerists recalled.[59]

Rodes even allowed some of the men to go shopping. Private Tinsley from Doles's Brigade reported in a letter home that the general soon ordered the merchants in Martinsburg to open their stores and "forced them to take our money." The soldiers happily purchased molasses, coffee, and various kinds of clothing. According to the young Georgian, they also bought gingham, linen, calicoes, kid gloves, and cavalry boots at cheap prices. "You ought to see the Rebels with Yankee clothes & gloves on," Tinsley boasted to his mother. "They look well."[60]

All those spoils came at the cost of only a handful of casualties, most of which occurred among the troopers from the cavalry brigade. "Our loss, according to the best information, is less than ten, in killed, wounded, and captured, embracing the afternoon skirmishing," one of Jenkins's men reported to a Richmond newspaper. "Our men captured about two hundred prisoners." The only other known casualties came in Capt. Charles Fry's Orange Artillery, which had one gunner killed and another man wounded. According to an artilleryman from the King William Artillery, the gunner died instantly after "being cut almost in two by a shell passing through his body before it exploded."[61]

The losses on the Federal side amounted to 4 men killed, 9 wounded, and 146 captured. The casualties included Captain Maulsby, who suffered a wound to his leg before escaping from town. Jenkins's troopers also captured about 70 men from Capt. Henry C. Yontz's company in the One Hundred Twenty-Sixth Ohio who had been on detached duty guarding a railroad bridge along nearby Opequon Creek. The cavalrymen easily chased them down a few miles outside of Martinsburg as they fled north along Williamsport Turnpike. Only two officers and 13 men from that company managed to get away.[62]

Although the assault on Martinsburg had been remarkably swift, the majority of Federal troops once more eluded capture at the last minute. Rodes conceded that "nothing was seen of the Federal infantry after the attack began, nor was it known for some hours after their retreat that it escaped by the Shepherdstown road, while the cavalry and artillery fled by way of Williamsport." Those results left the division commander far from pleased. Just as at Berryville, Rodes placed the blame directly on the failure of Jenkins's cavalrymen to cut off the enemy's escape routes.[63]

For most of the men in the division, their stunning success in sweeping Federal forces out of the Shenandoah Valley completely overshadowed any failures in hunting down the last of the escaping troops. That was certainly the case for Private Leon from Daniel's Brigade. "Have driven the enemy from the Rapidan to the Potomac, captured prisoners, arms, camps, quartermaster and commissary stores, and the Yankees were any moment as strong in numbers as we, with the advantage of having breastworks to fight behind," the Tar Heel gloated in his diary. "Still they always ran at our appearance."[64]

Together with Ewell's other two divisions, Rodes's men had carried out their commander's plan with near perfection. A gunner from the Morris Artillery boasted in a letter home that "the valley of Va is clear of yankeys now." Major Blacknall from Iverson's Brigade described the Second Corps's advance as nothing less than "a perfect triumphal march." The Tar Heel noted, "we swept the enemy before us & captured everything they had, the result of the campaign being 6000 prisoners, half a dozen towns & cities, villages without number, government stores in great abundance, & all without any loss of consequence."[65]

The speed and audacity with which they had outmaneuvered both Milroy and Hooker reminded many of the men of what they had achieved under the leadership of their fallen hero, Stonewall Jackson. Lt. Col. William Gaston Lewis from the Forty-Third North Carolina in Daniel's Brigade insisted to his fiancée that their accomplishments were "equal to any of Jackson's campaigns, so don't be discouraged at his death for we have other Jacksons living yet." Captain Gorman from Ramseur's Brigade declared that they surprised the enemy so completely that "our coming was as a thunderbolt from a cloudless sky." With the Potomac River only a short distance away, the triumphant soldiers were now ready to strike deep into Union territory.[66]

5

"Cold Indeed Was Our Reception"

During the early hours on June 15, Robert Rodes finally received word that Ewell's other two divisions had captured the bulk of the Federal forces at Winchester. He responded to the news by ordering his own brigades north toward the Potomac River directly opposite Williamsport. While two regiments from O'Neal's Brigade stayed behind as provost guards, the rest of the division hustled out of Martinsburg later in the morning. After securing the river crossing at Williamsport, Rodes's men would await further instructions before moving forward through Maryland and proceeding over the border into Pennsylvania.[1]

Conditions that day proved nearly as daunting as those at the beginning of the advance from Fredericksburg. "It being the latter part of June, and the hottest spell of weather that I have almost ever seen, the troops suffered intensely on the march, fainting in numbers by the roadside," Lt. Col. Wharton J. Green from Daniel's staff recalled. The exhausted men soon fell out of the ranks by the dozens. Rodes described it as "the most trying march we had yet had; most trying because of the intense heat, the character of the road, and the increased number of barefooted men in the command."[2]

The grueling trek from Martinsburg finally ended in the late afternoon, when they reached the south shore of the river. By that point there appeared to be nothing to stand in their way. "Camped in 1/4 mile of the Potomac & in plane view of Williamsport on the other side," Lt. James E. Green from the Fifty-Third North Carolina in Daniel's Brigade wrote in his diary. "It was reported this morning that the Enemy was in our Rear but we came on fearless as to that; we care nothing about the Rear. We are going on. I think it is not so much about them a being in reare of us, no more."[3]

During the waning hours of daylight, the men from Ramseur's, Iverson's, and Doles's Brigades, along with those from three of the division's batteries, finally

Potomac River crossing opposite Williamsport, Maryland. Courtesy Steve French.

waded across the Potomac at nearby Light's Ford. The honor of leading General Lee's infantry into Maryland went to the troops of Ramseur's Brigade. Capt. James Harris acknowledged in a letter to a friend that "this created some jealousy in the other brigades and it was not uncommon to hear the sneering remark 'be bound if there is any advantage given, Ramseur's Brigade will get it.'"[4]

After scrambling onto the north bank, the troops quickly occupied Williamsport. Sgt. Tim Furlow from Doles's staff boasted that the soldiers made their entrance "with as much gusto as if the town was ours." Capt. Joseph Reese from the same brigade noted that they passed through the streets "to the tune of 'Dixie's Land,' which much inspired the troops, as evidenced by their long and continuous cheers." The men from O'Neal's and Daniel's Brigades and the other battery patiently waited on the Virginia side of the Potomac, where they were assigned to guard Martinsburg and the major approaches to the river crossings.[5]

Williamsport, which then had a population of about 1,000 people, stands beside the spot where long and winding Conococheague Creek empties into the broad Potomac. Just beyond the town, the countryside opens up onto the wide expanse of the lush Cumberland Valley. Evan Watkins established a major ferry crossing along that section of the Potomac in 1744. Otho Holland Williams, who served as a general under George Washington, laid out the town that would bear his name in 1787. Soon afterward it received serious consideration as the site for the nation's new capital. But what drew the most attention from Rodes's men in 1863 was the town's strategic location on the upper stretch of the Chesapeake and Ohio Canal.[6]

Just as during the Maryland Campaign, the Confederates found that sentiment in that part of the state tilted strongly toward the Northern cause. Colonel Grimes from Ramseur's Brigade griped to his daughter that "the women and children at this town look very grim and sourly at us." Lt. William Calder from the same brigade complained to his mother that the people were "decidedly Union and our reception somewhat icy." In another letter home the young officer grumbled that the troops remained "in a hotbed of unionism here, hardly a friend to our cause."[7]

The extent of the Northern sympathy became clear from the moment the Southerners entered Williamsport. An officer from one of the batteries observed that "not a soul, save a few boys and [a] scattering of Confederate cavalry graced the scene" as they proceeded along the main street. "All the stores and every house was closed, and every window and even curtain was down, as if the sight of a rebel could not be tolerated," the artilleryman wrote in a letter home. He eventually spotted about "a half dozen young girls" on one corner who "waved their handkerchiefs quite bravely and cheered" as the troops passed nearby. "This we have named secession corner," he quipped.[8]

Despite their chilly greeting, a large group of soldiers soon gathered outside one of the major businesses to celebrate their arrival in Maryland. While bands blared out Southern tunes, the troops who assembled there let loose their pent-up emotions. "The Confederate battle-flag was unfolded to the breeze over the dome of the U.S. Hotel, where cheer after cheer was given for the success of our cause," as Capt. James Beck from Doles's Brigade described the scene in a letter to his hometown newspaper. This was likely a reference to the Taylor House hotel on Potomac Street, which served as Rodes's headquarters. A handful of Southern sympathizers from the town also joined them there.[9]

Most of the men found little to fault about the conduct of the campaign to that point. Pvt. Lucius T. C. Lovelace, who served with the Fourth Georgia in Doles's Brigade, informed his father that "the boys are all cheerful and confident of success, wherever we may strike a blow." He was especially impressed by the leadership abilities of both Rodes and Ewell. Although new to their positions, the two generals had performed brilliantly throughout the advance. "I am better pleased every day with our Maj. & Lieut Generals, both of whom are worthy of the position[s] they occupy," Lovelace declared.[10]

Their accomplishments in making it safely to the Maryland shore of the Potomac even won over some soldiers who had major concerns about taking the war into the North. "I was opposed to invading their lands at first," a Georgian acknowledged in a letter to his parents. "But they have been invading our land so long, I think it is well enough for us to invade their land the same." Their nearly unbroken record of forcing the enemy back with barely a fight provided the best proof that they had made the right decision. He noted with enthusiasm, "I think we are making it pay pretty well so far."[11]

Although many in the ranks remained anxious to continue their advance, Rodes decided that "a halt at Williamsport was absolutely necessary" because of the obvious fatigue among the troops and the large number of men who had no shoes. "Very many of these gallant fellows were still marching in ranks, with feet bruised, bleeding, and swollen, withal so cheerfully as to entitle them to be called the heroes of the Pennsylvania campaign," the division commander declared in his official report. He insisted that "none but the best of soldiers could have made such a march under such circumstances."[12]

Pvt. Henry B. Wood from the Twelfth Alabama in O'Neal's Brigade laid much of the blame for their broken-down condition on the hard surfaces of the macadamized roads they had used for most of the journey. "Traveling on these pike roads is very bad on any ones feet," he grumbled in a letter home. The crushed-stone surfaces were so abrasive that they quickly ripped into shreds the poor-quality shoes that most of the soldiers wore. According to Pvt. Thomas J. Watkins from the Fourteenth North Carolina in Ramseur's Brigade, the result was that "many of the men are now barefooted having worn out their shoes on the rough pike."[13]

As the troops settled in for a much-needed rest, Maj. Charles Blacknall from Iverson's Brigade assumed duties as provost marshal. Once the streets were secured, the men from the division's quartermaster details began searching for any usable goods. "I immediately took possession of all stores, Hotels, Bar rooms, the Bank & all other species of property, put them under guard & selected through the Qr. Master such articles as were needed by the Government," the major bragged in a letter home. He pointed out that "the stocks are very large & goods of all descriptions cheap."[14]

Those efforts reflected the high priority that Lee placed on seizing large stocks of food and war materials compared to the Maryland Campaign, when he remained careful not to force Confederate money on the inhabitants or burden them with heavy demands for supplies. By 1863 the political positions of the people in much of the state had hardened in place. Few expected that a lenient policy would make any difference in whether or not Marylanders would support the Confederate cause. Most important for Lee was the need to sustain his army and draw the enemy into the North for a decisive victory that would hopefully end the war. Everything else remained secondary to fulfilling those essential objectives.[15]

Rodes's men started gathering up the needed goods late on the day of their arrival at Williamsport. The provost guards initially cleared the town of any troops not assigned to the detail. "In the evening, all the men and officers, save the staff officers, were ordered out of town, and the government impressed every thing it wanted paying in Confederate money, and if that was refused paying none at all," one officer assigned to the detail explained. The search parties quickly discovered that "the merchants had concealed their goods in every conceivable place, but a rigid search soon brought them to light."[16]

The results proved so successful that Major Blacknall remained busy for several days "engaged in gathering up our immense stores and sending back to the rear." Rodes was ecstatic over the massive haul of supplies his men obtained there. He noted in his official report that the troops seized more than 5,000 pounds of leather and thirty-five kegs of gunpowder during their stay. They also secured large quantities of foodstuffs and other commissary stores in the town. In addition, Jenkins's cavalry confiscated several hundred head of cattle and dozens of horses from the surrounding countryside.[17]

The loot ready for shipment to Virginia also included some of the "many hundred slaves" that the troops had captured as they moved north. Jenkins's cavalrymen, in particular, had indiscriminately rounded up any runaway slaves and free blacks who were unlucky enough to come within their reach during the march through the Shenandoah Valley. "I have several negroes, free & slave, in my hands but negroes are worth nothing at all," Blacknall reported in a letter home. "No kind of negroes will sell for one hundred dollars." The price was so cheap that he hoped "to make some purchases in that line for southern exportation."[18]

Blacknall eventually issued passes for the remaining soldiers in the division to enter the town so that they could purchase all kinds of scarce goods for themselves and their relatives back home. Rodes ordered the storeowners to sell their merchandise to individual soldiers in exchange for Confederate money. "Of course, articles of every description were immediately advanced—coffee, for instance, at 50 cents per pound, and every other article in like proportions; but no great extortion was allowed," one officer remarked in a letter to his hometown newspaper. He pointed out that "the people say nothing to all this, but you can see that they sell with a very bad grace."[19]

Despite the merchants' reluctance, the troops had no difficulty filling all their needs during their stay. "Encamped at Williamsport, reaped the benefits of the place in the way of luxuries," Lt. William Ardrey from Ramseur's Brigade commented in his diary. He noted that the Confederates "drew rations of whiskey, bought boots, shoes, hats and a great many articles at old prices." Sergeant Furlow happily reported that one of the officers from General Doles's staff "got some excellent boots & I got a pair of trousers—all cheap." Major Blacknall bragged to his wife that he "could get any amount of goods but cannot find means of carrying them on or sending back."[20]

During that time, the pioneers turned their attention to disrupting traffic on the Chesapeake and Ohio Canal. Those soldiers largely focused on damaging the 210-foot aqueduct that spanned Conococheague Creek on the edge of town. The canal superintendent at Williamsport reported that the Confederates tore down the four corners of the massive structure all the way to the bottom. Those assigned to that detail also hurled the stones from the top layer and some of the railings into the creek and made a large breach in one of the three arches. Despite their efforts, the damage to the aqueduct remained largely superficial and was fully repaired by the early part of August.[21]

Nearly everyone in the division engaged in endless speculation about what would happen once their comrades still in Virginia made it safely into Maryland. "We are expecting every day to advance but cannot say what is the programme at this time," Blacknall commented in a letter to his brother-in-law. Capt. Shepherd G. Pryor from the Twelfth Georgia in Doles's Brigade guessed that the army would "perhaps push the war into yankeyland." An officer from Ramseur's Brigade told his mother that he was also "expecting to move very soon and to have a very active campaign."[22]

While all that was going on, Jenkins's troopers rode off on a major raid deep into Pennsylvania's portion of the Cumberland Valley. They initially departed from Martinsburg well before dawn on June 15. Along with the main part of the brigade, the force assigned to the operation included the Sixteenth Virginia Cavalry, which had finally arrived in camp after participating in the attack on Winchester. The cavalrymen first reconnoitered around Dam Number Five on the Potomac River. From there they pushed on to the east and forded the river directly opposite Williamsport. Lt. Addison Smith from the Seventeenth Virginia Cavalry noted that the river "was very low and we had no difficulty in crossing."

After splashing across the Potomac, the troopers briefly halted in Williamsport, where a group of sympathizers provided them with a huge spread of food. As a result of this generosity, Lieutenant Smith reported that the people there were "well disposed toward us," even setting out "long tables along the road well loaded with good eatables, that the hungry soldiers might help themselves." Just as the men from the main part of Rodes's Division would discover later in the day, many other cavalrymen found that the prevailing mood in town remained decidedly mixed or

Jenkins's cavalry crossing the Potomac. From *Frank Leslie's Illustrated Newspaper.*

even hostile. One trooper insisted that the majority of residents displayed only "a smothered expression of sympathy" for the Southern cause.[23]

While Company D, Thirty-Sixth Virginia Cavalry Battalion stayed behind to guard the river crossing, the rest of the brigade soon set off to the north along the turnpike. About noon Jenkins's men passed through nearby Hagerstown, where they received a surprisingly warm reception. Lt. Hermann Schuricht from the Fourteenth Virginia Cavalry noted that the Confederate horsemen "were enthusiastically welcomed by the ladies" in that town. "They made us presents of flowers, and the children shouted, 'Hurrah for Jeff. Davis!'" he wrote in his diary. Another trooper pointed out that the residents were "outspoken and exultant" in their greetings.

Ignoring warnings from the citizens about the presence of Federal troops, the cavalrymen pushed across the state line into Pennsylvania. As they approached nearby Greencastle in the early afternoon, Jenkins hurriedly divided his horsemen into two forces for an attack on a cavalry squad that reportedly occupied the town. "My company belonged to the troops forming the right wing, and pistols and muskets in hand, traversing ditches and fences, we charged and took the town," Schuricht wrote in his diary. The lone disappointment was that "the Federal cavalry escaped, and only one lieutenant was captured."[24]

Jenkins quickly secured the town and began gathering up supplies. According to one area newspaper, he "immediately commenced to empty stables and capture every article within his reach that seemed to fit the fancy of his men." Although the general threatened to "burn and destroy" the town, the only major damage occurred when the Confederates partially burned down the depot for the Cumberland Valley Railroad. Even so, the blaze created quite a stir. "The fire could be seen for miles," one resident reported to a newspaper in New York. "Only three buildings were destroyed, together with some wood and a water tank."

Despite that incident, the officers in charge took great care to keep the men from carrying out any widespread plundering. "Some soldiers broke into one store and were conveying off the goods, when they were observed in this act by one of their own officers," one resident explained. "The officers cleared them out of the place and had the store shut up." He acknowledged that "the soldiers scattered the goods about pretty freely, but did not carry much of value away." After cutting down the telegraph wires, the Confederates finally trotted out of town late in the afternoon toward the north along Valley Turnpike. The newspaper in Greencastle reported that "their stay on this occasion, hardly exceeded an hour."[25]

Following an easy ride, Jenkins's horsemen reached Chambersburg just before midnight on June 15. Within minutes the lead troopers poured into town at the ready for action. "At 11 ½ I heard the clattering of horses hoofs," local resident Rachel Cormany jotted down in her diary. "I hopped out of bed & ran to the front window & sure enough there the Grey backs were going by as fast as their horses could take them down to the Diamond." She found that "it took a long time for them all to pass,

Jenkins's cavalry charge into Chambersburg, Pennsylvania. From *Frank Leslie's Illustrated Newspaper.*

but I could not judge how many there were—not being accustomed to seeing troops in such a body."[26]

Another citizen watched in terror as the "advance guard came into town at full speed, with drawn sabres." One group of riders charged in so recklessly that they were soon far out in front of the main column. As they rushed ahead, two of the troopers suddenly confronted a small group of civilians along the main street. What happened next came as a shocking turnabout. Using a piece of "plastering lath" as a sword, a citizen boldly seized the bridle on one of the horses and demanded the surrender of the cavalryman. Another resident grabbed hold of the other horse. After disarming the startled troopers, two of the men rode off at top speed with the captured horses.

The rest of Jenkins's force soon galloped onto the scene and freed the troopers from their temporary captivity. "Their companions came up just in time to rescue their friends; but they could not recover their horses," one citizen reported to the newspaper in Lancaster, Pennsylvania. The reaction of the cavalrymen made it clear that they would not tolerate any interference from the inhabitants. "This caused a great deal of trouble between the rebels and the citizens," the man explained. "The former were continually threatening to burn the town if we did not return the horses and arms taken from them."[27]

An incident that occurred only moments later added to the growing chaos and confusion. "As the scouts came galloping down Main street, with their carbines cocked and leveled, the darkness prevented them from seeing a mortar-bed and some piles of stone and sand in front of Mr. H. M. White's residence, then in process of building, and one of the horses stumbled and fell, throwing its rider headlong into the mortar-bed," grocery-store owner Jacob Hoke recalled. He noted that "the fall caused his carbine to go off, and he, as well as his comrades, supposed that a citizen had fired upon them."[28]

The troopers reacted to the gunshot with open threats against Chambersburg. "They came back, knocked at the doors and ordered out the citizens in front of whose doors the stones lay, and threatened to burn down their property for not keeping the street clean," a resident recounted to the Lancaster newspaper. "They would not stop to argue the question, but took some of them prisoners and kept them confined until the next day, when they were let off." Cormany watched in terror as some of the troopers rode by her house "with their hands on the gun triggers ready to fire & calling out as they passed along that they would lay the town in ashes if fired on again."[29]

Although a few citizens were temporarily detained for questioning, Jenkins soon had the situation under firm control. A small detachment from the brigade quickly moved into the area surrounding the central square. Jacob Hoke reported that "the larger part passed on down and out by the Harrisburg pike, and after picketing the various roads, encamped about one mile out." According to one of the town's newspapers, the troopers then "threw out their pickets towards Green Village and Scotland, a

Burning railroad bridge at Scotland, Pennsylvania. From *Frank Leslie's Illustrated Newspaper.*

portion of whom proceeded to burn the railroad bridge over the Conococheague, at the latter place, as a precaution against an advance of the federal forces."

This large wood-and-iron bridge served as a vital link on the main Cumberland Valley Railroad line running northeast through Shippensburg and Carlisle to the state capital at Harrisburg. The imposing structure rose high above the rugged creek bed just below. The raging fire damaged many of the timbers but did little to destroy the iron girders that supported much of the main span. Despite repeated attempts, the men assigned to the detail largely failed to knock the bridge out of commission. Following some hasty repairs, railroad workers had the span back in full operation soon after Jenkins's withdrawal.

The brigade commander initially set up his headquarters just outside of town at the home of Col. Alexander K. McClure, a prominent attorney and newspaper owner. Prior to the war, McClure had served as a state senator and head of the Republican State Committee. His wife surprisingly showed open courtesy toward her unexpected rebel guests. Hoke pointed out that Jenkins and his staff were treated to "a bountiful supper prepared for them, the honors of the table being royally done by the colonel's accomplished wife—the colonel himself being prudently absent."[30]

The following morning Jenkins shifted his command post to the Montgomery House Hotel on the town square. "One of his first acts was to summon the burgess and town-council to his head-quarters, when he made a demand for the return of the two horses and equipment taken, and in case of their not being returned, payment for them, and in default of either, he threatened the destruction of the town," Hoke explained. The merchant noted that, "as the captured property was beyond the reach of the council, the matter was adjusted by the payment of $900, and the handing over to him of the same number of pistols taken."[31]

With that matter solved, the general ordered his men to seize a long list of essential supplies from the local merchants. "On Tuesday the Rebels took full possession of the town, and gave us notice that we must open our stores, and permit their soldiers to buy (or steal) what they might fancy, and that any one who refused to take their money or open his store, would have his goods 'confiscated,'" one indignant resident griped to the Lancaster newspaper. "So we opened our stores and in they flocked, and in a short time we were doing a rush business." The extent of the seizures provided a jarring glimpse of what businessmen and farmers throughout this once bucolic valley could expect during the following two weeks.[32]

The troopers methodically searched the major dry-goods, grocery, and drug stores for the required items. Little of possible use to the army escaped their attention. "Each of the four drug stores was placed in charge of a surgeon, who examined the stock on hand, and indicated such articles as they wanted; which articles they packed in boxes and took with them, and for most of which they paid the prices asked in Confederate money," the editor for one of the local newspapers explained. He noted that the town's "dry goods and grocery stores were crowded with customers during their stay; and the rebels generally seemed willing to pay in their own scrip whatever prices the merchants placed upon their goods."[33]

The cavalrymen also made sure to provide for the needs of their hungry mounts. One resident reported that the Confederates "seemed to be particularly desirous of procuring all the forage they could for their horses." Soon after the troopers' arrival, several search parties began the hunt for feed of all kinds throughout the town. "Private stables were relieved of hay and oats, and those articles were taken wherever they were found," the man wrote in a letter to a New York newspaper. He further pointed out that "when the rebels left they carried with them large quantities of this kind of property."[34]

Jenkins's men soon began hauling away huge amounts of loot from all over Chambersburg. Local resident Jemima Cree also witnessed the soldiers stripping the drugstores nearly clean of medical supplies, a sight that she never expected to see in her life. "They took from Jacob Nixon six very large boxes full, valued at about six or eight hundred dollars, about the same from Heyser, and a good many from Spangler and Miller," she fumed to her husband. Cree continued watching as the troopers "placed an armed guard at the doors until they were boxed up and then brought the wagons round and loaded them."[35]

Mary Craig Eyster, who lived in the town, had a similar reaction to all the seizures that day. "[The Confederates] behaved better than we expected—but I dont give them any credit for it—they just did as they pleased, and made us do as they wanted us," she grumbled in a letter to a relative. "They generally paid for what they got, but with confederate scrip." Eyster pointed out that the troopers from the

search parties "got over five hundred dollars worth out of Nixons store." The confiscations hardly went down well with the victims. "I tell you old Mrs. Nixon is mad
at them," the young woman admitted.

One of her relatives had a particularly unsettling confrontation with some of Jenkins's troopers, who were searching for horses on his farm north of town. "Hugh
told them that he had sent his horses away, they said they knew that they were on the
premises and tried to make him tell," she reported. "They made all kinds of threats,
that they would hang him, & shoot him &c and finally told him that they would take
him, that they would rather have him than his horses." The plucky farmer waited for
"his chance and as soon as he had one, made his escape into a wheat field, where he
found uncle Jesse and Davies hid." The raiders finally galloped off without incident
after confiscating the man's saddle and bridle.[36]

On the morning of June 17, Jenkins issued a command for citizens to hand over
all the guns in Chambersburg. The terrified residents meekly gave in to the demand
rather than take the risk that the invaders would plunder or burn their town. Dozens
of them soon lined up at the central square, clutching a huge assortment of out-of-date
weapons. "Many of our citizens complied with this humiliating order, and a committee of our people was appointed to take down the names of all who brought in arms,"
Hoke reported. The merchant acknowledged that "some, of course did not comply,
but enough did so to avoid a general search and probable sacking of the town."[37]

The tedious process of taking in the weapons continued until late morning. Although the haul of guns proved disappointing, the general's attention was suddenly
distracted by reports that a large enemy force was approaching from the north.
"We received about 500 guns of all sorts, sabres, pistols, etc," Lieutenant Schuricht
wrote in his diary. "The useful arms were loaded on wagons and the others were destroyed." He noted that "about 11 o'clock news reached headquarters of the advance
of a strong Yankee force, and consequently we evacuated the city and fell back upon
Hagerstown, Md."[38]

According to one resident, some Federal troopers who had been taken prisoner
just outside of town played a major part in bringing about this withdrawal. "Six of
our cavalry were captured and paraded through the streets," the man reported to a
New York newspaper. Under interrogation, the prisoners falsely informed Jenkins's
men that they were the vanguard of a much larger contingent that was heading in
their direction. "The officers and men talked much of a force of infantry that they
said was near at hand, variously estimated by them at from 10,000 to 40,000, with
a large number of pieces of artillery," he explained.[39]

Despite the stories that a huge Federal army had assembled outside Harrisburg,
claims of major enemy activity around Chambersburg proved unfounded. According to one account, the enemy force that prompted the retreat amounted to nothing
more than a large group of civilians from a nearby village who had come to gawk at
the Southern horsemen. Other stories indicated that the supposed threat consisted

of about forty Federal cavalrymen out on patrol just north of the town of Scotland. Regardless, no real threat existed at this time to Jenkins's Brigade.[40]

Whatever the cause, the Confederates hastily fled from Chambersburg. Their departure did not come without some anxious moments for residents. Merchant Amos Stouffer noted in his diary that one of the troopers "set Oak's and Linn's warehouse on fire" as he galloped off to the south. Only the quick actions of passersby prevented the town from burning to the ground. As another eyewitness reported, "a number of citizens who were standing around succeeded in extinguishing the flames and it is well they did, for if they had not we would have had a large fire, as there were a number of frame buildings and a strawboard manufactory nearby, and wind blowing very high at the time."[41]

Their mad rush to get away failed to stop the cavalrymen from hauling off more than fifty unfortunate African Americans, whom they had captured in the surrounding area. "In their departure, this force of Jenkins carried away a large number of our colored population, old and young, male and female," one of the town's newspapers explained. "Some of these were 'contrabands,' who had come to us from Virginia, but many of them were free and had lived here all their lives." Furthermore, "some of them were very cruelly treated, and the general distress and consternation among them was pitiful to behold."[42]

The slave hunts began almost from the moment Jenkins's men arrived in Chambersburg. Jacob Hoke noted that "many of the soldiers were engaged during Tuesday and Wednesday morning in scouring the fields around the town" for runaway slaves. Although most African American residents had fled the area, the troopers still rounded up a number who had gone into hiding in the fields and cellars. "Many were caught and some, free and slave, were bound and sent under guard South," Hoke recalled. He pointed out in a letter to a New York newspaper that the captives "were driven before the cavalry like cattle, while little helpless children astride the horses clung to their riders to retain their seats."[43]

Rev. Henry Reeves from the Rosedale Female Seminary reported that Jenkins's men made "no distinction in catching Negroes, those born free were taken along with runaway slaves." He insisted that "equal fear seized both free blacks and contrabands." Reeves had recently founded a class for the education of the many former slaves who had escaped north as the war raged in Virginia. The clergyman lamented in a letter to his sister that "some of our Sunday school scholars, as free as you or I am, have gone into perpetual slavery."[44]

The search for runaways extended to every possible hiding place. The newspaper in Lancaster noted that Confederates "went to the part of the town occupied by the colored population, and kidnapped all they could find, from the child in the cradle up to men and women of fifty years of age." According to Jemima Cree, the troopers even grabbed up "little children, whom they had to carry on horseback before them." One of the town's merchants described it as "a sorrowful sight to see the poor

creatures taken away; free and slave alike were taken." He claimed that Jenkins intended to "hold the free ones until exchanged for an equal number of their slaves."[45]

Rachel Cormany was shocked by such cruelty. She watched in utter despair as Jenkins's grim-faced cavalrymen herded the captives "by droves" through the streets of
town. "O! How it grated on our hearts to have to sit quietly & look at such brutal
deeds," Cormany wrote in her diary. "I saw no men among the contrabands—all
women & children. Some of the colored people who were raised here were taken
along—I sat on the front step as they were driven by just like we would drive cattle." She
reported that "some laughed & seemed not to care—but nearly all hung their heads."[46]

Many of the remaining African Americans sought safety with the people who
employed them. Among them were the "contrabands" who worked as domestic
help for Reverend Reeves. To prevent giving away their location to any soldiers who
might attempt to search the house, the women in his family assumed the household
duties while the servants remained hidden away. "Going into the kitchen I found
my wife and two or three of the ladies girded for domestic work and enquiring the
cause learned that all our contrabands had secreted themselves," the minister and
abolitionist educator recounted.[47]

Hoke was astonished to see lifelong Chambersburg resident Esque Hall among
the captives. "A rebel rode past our store with this poor frightened man on behind
him," the merchant recalled. He immediately sought assistance from prominent
minster Benjamin S. Schneck. The clergyman "went to Jenkins' headquarters, and
after assuring Jenkins that Hall was long a resident of this place, and not a fugitive
slave, he was released." The outcome was just as lucky for two other free blacks, who
were snatched up as they arrived in town on a handcar after working on some railroad tracks north of town. "Again Dr. Schneck's services were called for and these
men were released," Hoke reported.[48]

Despite those occasional acts of mercy toward free blacks, most of the cavalrymen considered the rounding up of runaway slaves as being no different than the
confiscation of other movable property, such as horses and cattle. One Southerner
openly boasted in a letter to a major Richmond newspaper that the cavalrymen had
succeeded in "bringing off many 'contrabands' and fine horses" during their foray
into the Pennsylvania countryside. Pvt. Isaac V. Reynolds from the Sixteenth Virginia Cavalry acknowledged to his wife that he spent most of his time at Chambersburg "capturing negroes & horses." Lt. Samuel William Newman Feamster from
the Fourteenth Virginia Cavalry informed his mother that the men in his regiment
grabbed up "several Negroes" during their stay and were "sending them back."[49]

Even so, these slave-catching activities did not always go as the perpetrators anticipated. During the afternoon on June 16, a crowd of angry citizens in Greencastle
freed about thirty African Americans who were being herded through the town by
a chaplain and three or four Confederate soldiers. "As soon as the train with the
negroes came into town the people surrounded it and took the captured ones away,"

one eyewitness to the incident explained. "The negroes were delighted beyond all measure at their fortunate delivery." He was shocked to find that "a large proportion were mere children." The crowd also seized the Confederate soldiers, who were sent as prisoners to nearby Waynesboro.[50]

One of the freed captives later charged that another "contraband" living in Chambersburg had "pointed out her hiding place to the rebels, and induced them to kidnap herself and three children" in an attempt to keep himself from being taken away. On her return to that town, she "had her supposed betrayer arrested." According to an account in a local newspaper, the truth of her story came into question "when she failed to identify him, and the case was accordingly dismissed." The man "then threatened to blow her brains out when he got a chance." Authorities moved to place him under arrest for his threat, but he quickly "plead off" and "said he didn't mean it."[51]

The situation at Greencastle reached a climax on the day after the captives made their escape. Following some hurried negotiations between town officials and "a rebel Colonel," the captured Southerners were "released and brought back" to town. Teenager Mary Clara Forney, who lived in Waynesboro, noted in her diary that "two or three citizens of Greencastle came with a dispatch from the rebel commander saying if we did not have them prisoners returned by the next evening both this place and Greencastle would be laid in ashes." She acknowledged that "in order to save our property we thought best to return them."[52]

Despite the release of the prisoners, the issue of compensation for the loss of the former slaves still remained unresolved. "The Chaplain demanded $50,000 in lieu of the contrabands; and in case this was not complied with, the town should certainly be burned," the newspaper in Greencastle explained. "Two horses were given to make up the money." When that offer was rejected, the citizens feared that Jenkins' men would make good on their threat. Instead of burning the town, the main body of cavalry peacefully passed through later that afternoon along the turnpike toward Hagerstown.[53]

Even after pulling back into northern Maryland, the Confederate troopers continued scouring the surrounding farms and villages for more livestock and runaway slaves. Storekeeper Hoke reported that they "sent out foraging parties in all directions in search of additional plunder." He insisted that "the whole southern portion of our county was plundered by those men." According to merchant Stouffer, Jenkins's men searched "the country in every direction about Waynesboro, Greencastle, Mercersburg [and] Finkstown for horses and cattle and Negroes."[54]

In the largest such incursion, a detachment under the command of Col. Milton J. Ferguson from the Sixteenth Virginia Cavalry rode northwest from Hagerstown into Pennsylvania. After passing through Mercersburg, the soldiers crossed the Cove and Tuscarora Mountains, reaching the town of McConnellsburg in the hours before dawn on June 19. "A force of about two hundred rebel cavalry made a dash into town, and surrounded it in a few seconds," the town's newspaper stated. "They then commenced their work of plunder, taking horses, negroes, and a large amount of store goods."[55]

The Confederate troopers rushed in so quickly that the townspeople had no opportunity to hide their valuables. An eyewitness reported that the cavalrymen "opened all the stores, helping themselves to boots, shoes, hats, provisions and everything else they could possibly carry away." He noted that the men from the raiding party "completely gutted the telegraph office, carrying away with them the instrument and all the messages." A woman from a nearby town, who had access to some of the first reports of the raid, informed one of her relatives that Ferguson's troopers "came in one door of the telegraph office there as the operator went out the other." Luckily the man "had a magnet concealed elsewhere and when they left he went back to his post & reported."[56]

Another squad entered the Fulton County jail, where they discovered two apparent Southern sympathizers being held under guard. "During their stay in town they went to the jail and released a rebel prisoner that was arrested near Greencastle, and also John Forney, who was in prison for the murder of Lieut. E. N. Ford," the local newspaper explained. Officials had apprehended the first man a few days earlier as a suspected spy. Forney faced charges for killing Lieutenant Ford as the officer attempted to arrest him as a draft dodger. The newspaper indicated that the "rebels took both of them away" when they departed from town.[57]

The searches eventually reached every major business in McConnellsburg. Merchant W. S. Fletcher complained that the troopers made him open his dry-goods store and "took by force goods of different kinds," noting that they seized $610 worth of boots, hats, shoes, and other valuable items. J. W. Greathead, who owned a general-merchandise business, estimated that his losses totaled nearly $2,000. Another resident admitted that "large numbers" of fine horses "fell into the hands of the rebels" during their stay. The cavalrymen also scoured the area around the town, seizing a "drove of fat cattle, valued at about six thousand dollars."[58]

The extent of the losses shocked nearly everyone involved. Farmer Adam Cook griped to his son that the raiders "carried off thirty thousand dollars worth of property" from McConnellsburg. He claimed that a "wicked boy" who used to live in the town accompanied the cavalrymen and "no doubt was of great service to them in plundering." Despite the losses, Cook managed to escape the worst of the damages from the raid. The wily landowner boasted, "we were a little too quick for them, and sav'd all our horses," adding that "our only loss is a few head of cattle."[59]

Prior to departing, Ferguson surprisingly offered the residents of McConnellsburg a chance to reclaim some of their looted goods. "After they had collected all their plunder and were ready to evacuate the place, the colonel commanding the rebels made known to the citizens that he was ready to listen to any claims for the recovery of horses, cattle, provisions, &c.," one newspaper account reported. "Many applied for the return of property, but for the most part were unsuccessful till a number of ladies came forward and interceded with the rebels, when a portion of the lost property was restored."[60]

The search parties that swarmed through the surrounding countryside were much less lenient. They proved so relentless that John B. Patterson went into hiding rather than hand over his livestock during a raid on his property, located about three miles south of town. His son, T. Elliott Patterson, acknowledged that the farmer came "very near losing every horse he had, as the rebels tracked us up on the hill to the woods leading to Mr. Jacob Pittman's." Young Patterson noted, however, that the intruders soon "got off our trail and rode down to his farm while we passed safely to the woods, not losing a horse." As a result, the troopers only confiscated the single mount that the family kept pastured in a nearby meadow.[61]

Another detachment rode farther south to Webster's Mill, where they seized nearly five hundred dollars' worth of footwear and clothing from the store owned by William M. Patterson. While searching the area for runaway slaves, the troopers stopped at the merchant's house. His daughter informed her brother that the commander was "mounted on a beautiful horse with one little darky in front of him and two at the back." The other men drove "a brand new two-horse carriage filled with darkies." As she watched in disbelief, they forced her mother to point out which of the captives were free and which were runaways.[62]

By late in the afternoon, Ferguson's main body had crossed back over the mountains to Mercersburg. Prof. Philip Schaff from the theological seminary of the German Reformed Church watched as the soldiers "rode up the Main street with drawn pistols and swords." Leading the way was Capt. James A. Crawford from the Seventeenth Virginia Cavalry, who threatened to retaliate at the first signs of resistance. Schaff described the cavalrymen as "a miscellaneous looking set of all sorts of dresses and countenances." Despite the initial show of force, their stay passed without any major problems. "They remained about two hours in town, without disturbing the citizens, who turned out in considerable numbers to witness the sight," he recalled.[63]

People in the town were stunned by the huge amount of plunder that Jenkins's men had seized from the neighboring valley. According to Professor Schaff, the loot included "a drove of about two hundred head of cattle captured at McConnelsburg, and valued at $11,000 and about one hundred and twenty stolen horses of the best kind and two or three negro boys." Rev. Thomas Creigh, the minister of the local Presbyterian church, caught a close-up view as the rebel cavalrymen trotted past his house "with many horses taken from the neighborhood and from the Cove, with immense numbers of cattle (a whole drove taken from Mr. Taylor of Chambersburg, 170) and negroes."[64]

By most accounts, Jenkins's forays through the lower part of Pennsylvania produced impressive results. One Maryland resident looked on in disbelief as "the rebels that went into Pennsylvania" passed by his residence "with a large number of horses, and a few mules." The haul also included "a large number of negroes who they alleged had run away from their masters in Virginia and Washington county Maryland." In typical Southern style the soldiers dutifully turned the "contrabands" over to their supposed masters. The eyewitness claimed that "those belonging about Hagerstown, were being returned to their rebel owners, and those said to be from Virginia were sent back under guard."[65]

Despite his apparent success, Jenkins discovered on his return that Rodes was seething over the conduct of the raid. The major general complained that the hurried withdrawal from Chambersburg directly contradicted his orders, which called for the cavalry to remain there until the main part of the division arrived in the area. "The result was that most of the property in that place which would have been of service to the troops, such as boots, hats, leather, &c., was removed or concealed before it was reoccupied," he fumed in his official report. Rodes deemed the cavalry leader's performance so unreliable that he ordered him to operate under Ewell's direct supervision during the rest of the campaign.[66]

All those problems had no effect on Rodes's preparations for resuming the advance to the north. The first move to consolidate his division came on June 17, when the men from Daniel's Brigade finally splashed over the Potomac River at Light's Ford, just downstream from the aqueduct near the major ferry crossing. After reaching the north bank, Daniel's men paraded through Williamsport to martial music. Lieutenant Green griped that the people they encountered along the way "seamed to Receive us with in difference." Lt. William Beavans, the acting ordnance officer on the general's staff, noted in his diary that the troops eventually settled into place just "out of town down the river."[67]

The following morning Daniel's Tar Heels swarmed into town for a long-awaited shopping spree. Capt. Charles F. Bahnson, the assistant quartermaster of the Second North Carolina Battalion, bragged to his father that they obtained "a large number of Boots & Shoes at this place, paying Government price, & I am now up to my knees in leather, for the sum of only $12.00." Lt. Pinckney Hatrick from the Fifty-Third North Carolina told his family that he also remained in "fine spirits" after purchasing some real coffee in one of the stores at the price of only forty cents per pound.[68]

During that time, Ewell met with Rodes at Williamsport to work out the final arrangements for the next phase of the summer campaign. In that session the two generals agreed on a plan that called for Rodes's troops to "move slowly toward Chambersburg until the division of General Johnson had crossed the Potomac." During the initial stage of the advance, Rodes would proceed to nearby Hagerstown, briefly halting there to await further instructions before crossing the border into Pennsylvania and pushing on toward Chambersburg.[69]

Rodes completed his preparations during the early hours on June 19, when the Alabama troops from O'Neal's Brigade waded over the main ford directly opposite Williamsport. For many of the soldiers, the trip across the Potomac River became the cause for open celebration. "In the morning we crossed the river, the men singing merrily, & all in high glee," Major Blackford from that brigade recalled. "The water here is from 3 to four feet deep, so the order came to strip, and a funny sight it was to see them all with nothing but their jackets."[70]

The buoyant mood stood in stark contrast to the unfriendly welcome the men received on their arrival north of the Potomac. Although the soldiers remained well

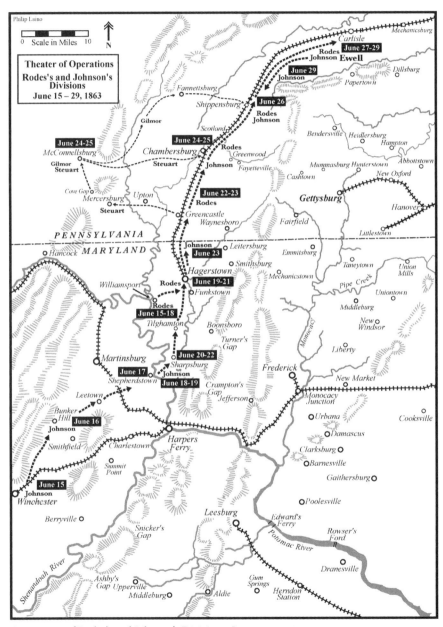

Operations of Rodes's and Johnson's Divisions, June 15–29, 1863

aware from their previous campaign that most of western Maryland was solidly pro-Union, the reaction of the citizens still proved disappointing. "No enthusiastic crowd thronged the bank to welcome us to the good old state of the Howards, the Carlisles, Carrolls and other great and good Southern spirits," one soldier from the Third Alabama grumbled to his hometown newspaper. "Cold indeed was our reception—rendered more so by wading that clear cold river so early in the morning." At the same time, he remained undeterred by their frigid greeting. "Our course lay through that abolitionized portion of the state," he proudly declared. "And through it we were bound to go."[71]

6

"Wherever Ewell Leads, We Can Follow"

With all five brigades safely in Maryland, Major General Rodes was ready to make his next move. Following a short halt, the newly arrived troops from O'Neal's Brigade headed straight through Williamsport and joined the rest of the division on the road to Hagerstown, already secured by Jenkins's troopers. After tramping six miles north on the turnpike, they reached the town during midmorning on June 19. With O'Neal's men in the lead, the soldiers swung directly onto Potomac Street. Major Blackford recalled that, "as we entered this town, each regiment broke into column of companies, and marched at the right shoulder shift, making a fine appearance."[1]

Hagerstown served as a busy manufacturing hub for the fertile valley that ran through central Maryland, renowned for its agricultural abundance. The area formed part of the much larger Cumberland Valley, which extends all the way from the Potomac River in Maryland on the south to the Susquehanna River in Pennsylvania on the north. This sprawling region is bounded on the east by the South Mountain range and on the northwest by North Mountain in the Allegheny range. The section in Maryland is sometimes referred to as the Hagerstown Valley.

The troops from Rodes's Division were overjoyed by what they found on their arrival in Hagerstown. Sgt. Maj. Preston H. Turner from the Fourth North Carolina in Ramseur's Brigade described it to his family as "an extensive and beautiful town." Most important, the Confederates had arrived there with hardly a hint of opposition from the enemy. "Our passage through Maryland was as peaceable and as quiet as a Quaker could desire," Capt. John Gorman from the same brigade quipped in a letter to a major newspaper in Raleigh. He noted with pride that "not a gun has been fired at us."[2]

Although loyalties among the town's residents remained about equally split between the Union and the Confederacy, crowds of well-wishers poured into the streets to welcome the Southerners. "As we entered Hagerstown the men cheered, the ladies

Entrance into Hagerstown, Maryland, on Potomac Street. Courtesy Washington County Historical Society.

waved handkerchiefs, and showered boquets upon our men," Surgeon John Shaffner from Ramseur's Brigade reported. Pvt. Samuel Pickens from O'Neal's Brigade pointed out in his diary that the troops "seemed to have a great many friends there, as the ladies all along the streets waved handkerchiefs & some Confederate flags." Lt. William Ardrey from Ramseur's Brigade spotted "white handkerchief[s] floating from every window."[3]

The wild celebrations that their arrival touched off shocked nearly everyone in the division. "Here we received such a welcome as we did not expect," Capt. James Beck from Doles's Brigade admitted in a letter to his hometown newspaper. "The streets were crowded with ladies, who, with bright smiles and waving handkerchiefs, cheered us on." Long gone were the stony grimaces and harsh stares that had greeted them along the river at Williamsport. Major Blackford made no secret of his feelings about the startling contrast between the two places, reporting to his father that the rebels were "met with a most enthusiastic welcome, very different from that tendered us at Wms.Port, which is a miserable little town."[4]

Their reception also differed considerably from what they experienced there during the earlier Maryland Campaign. Lt. Col. Charles Forsyth from the Third Alabama in O'Neal's Brigade noted that the greeting "was cordial beyond expectation, and showed plainly that a decided and marked change in favor of the South had taken place in the minds of the people since the Confederate army had entered the state nearly a year previous." Another soldier from the same brigade acknowledged that "last year everything was cold and timid, but this time there was a very gratifying demonstration." His best explanation for the turnaround was that "the Yankee soldiers have treated them so badly that they are desperate, and can suffer no more than they have already done."[5]

Surgeon Shaffner found the reasons behind the shift in public opinion much less perplexing. He insisted that all the changes there could be "accounted for easily" by major political events in the North during the previous year. "The abolition proclamation effected something—but the Yankee Conscription Bill much more," the Tar Heel opined in a letter to one of his friends. "These together have made many secesh sympathizers." Just as likely was that the Confederates' successes in the opening phase of the campaign had emboldened their supporters to turn out, while their opponents deemed it prudent to stay mostly out of view.[6]

Even the most hardened veterans from the Maryland Campaign quickly succumbed to the outpouring of apparent support they received from Hagerstown residents. "We expected to meet nothing but cold looks and averted eyes, so judge of our surprise and delight on finding the streets thronged with men, women & children of all ages & classes cheering and waving their handkerchiefs in unfeigned joy," Lt. William Calder told his mother. He noted that "bright eyes showered kind looks upon us from all sides and for the first time in my life I felt like fighting for Maryland." What remained open to question was what the attitudes in this area of mixed loyalties would be like if the Southerners' fortunes in the current campaign took a major turn for the worse.[7]

Amid these cheering crowds, Rodes's troops finally halted along Potomac Street in the middle of town. Ramseur's men set up camp on "a hill" near the Hagerstown Female Seminary, the general establishing his headquarters in the main building on campus. The troops from the Fourth North Carolina took on provost duties and soon moved into place at several key locations around the town. One soldier from that regiment reported that the men immediately "cut the Union flag down." He watched in amazement as "many of the citizens split the flag pole into pieces for souvenirs."[8]

Rather than remaining in town, the rest of the troops from the division eventually trudged south toward Boonsboro as a feint meant to hold in place the substantial Federal force at nearby Harpers Ferry. With that deception accomplished, the men at the head of the column finally halted alongside the road about two miles south of Hagerstown near the village of Funkstown. Major Blackford immediately took control as provost marshal, dealing mostly with an unending stream of bitter protests from the local German farmers about the conduct of some Confederates in confiscating their goods. "These people were all dutch and spoke such a jargon that I could scarcely understand them," the major complained.[9]

The bulk of the troops established camp directly opposite Funkstown on the banks of Antietam Creek. Nearly everyone in the division was already familiar with the surrounding area from their ill-fated campaign of the previous September, which had culminated along another section of the same stream. "This creek upon which we are encamped is the celebrated Antietam on which the great battle of Sharpsburg was fought," Private Pickens penned in his diary. He pointed out that "the battle ground is about 3 or 4 miles from here."[10]

Despite their proximity to the former killing fields, most of Rodes's soldiers were awestruck by the scenery surrounding them when they halted for the day. Asst. Surgeon William Marston from Iverson's Brigade described the location of their campsite as "a beautiful grove" alongside the main road. "This is the most romantic spot for an encampment I ever saw," he declared in his diary. "It is situated immediately on Antietam River—the site thickly set with majestic oaks, its ground is undulating & thickly interspersed by the most huge rocks imaginable." The only damper on their enthusiasm came from a series of torrential downpours that hit the area during the middle of the afternoon.[11]

Not even the terrible weather could keep the soldiers from making frequent trips into Hagerstown, where nearly everyone they met greeted them warmly. Captain Beck noted that the Confederates "had many private conversations with ladies and gentlemen, and we are satisfied that the intelligent and wealthy Marylanders are for the most part with us." While still skeptical about the allegiance of most people in the state, another soldier from the Forty-Third North Carolina in Daniel's Brigade acknowledged in a letter to his hometown newspaper that "even in this 'dark corner,' we met numbers of as loyal and devoted Southern men and women as can be found on Southern soil."[12]

To their delight the men soon discovered that most of the young women they encountered there were ardent Southern supporters. One soldier who set many female hearts aflutter was General Ramseur, one of the celebrated heroes of Chancellorsville. "In Hagerstown, Md, we met some fair and beautiful sympathizers of the South," he admitted to his fiancée. "I said some sweet things to some of them and kissed a few rosy ruby lips." The Carolinian joked that he took "some credit to myself for converting a Wisconsin girl, very pretty, pert and plump, from the error of her northern notions to be a proud and zealous sympathizer in our cause."[13]

Although Hagerstown remained about equally divided between "secesh" and Union supporters, a soldier from the Third Alabama found nothing to fault about the reception the troops received from the women during his stay in town. "I made the acquaintance of a number of ladies of both sides," he commented in a letter home. "It is amusing to see the 'Union girls' being escorted about by rebel officers and men." He pointed out that "our men tease them a great deal about whipping their friends, and, strange to say, they don't know how to deny it."[14]

Men throughout the division appeared completely smitten by their many young female admirers. Pvt. Louis Leon from Daniel's Brigade found that the "men greeted us very shabby, but the ladies quite the reverse." Sgt. John T. Nichols from the Thirtieth North Carolina in Ramseur's Brigade noted that the "ladies of town paid us a visit and said we Rebels looked fine." Major Blackford informed his father that "the ladies call us 'the dear rebels' in Hagerstown, and make great toasts of us you may be sure." Lieutenant Ardrey happily proclaimed in his diary that "Hagerstown is noted for the pretty ladies."[15]

Blackford even attended a party hosted by a local secessionist and his two daughters. "I was invited there to a dance last night wh[ich] I enjoyed very much as you can imagine, managing my new top boots and spurs very successfully," he reported to his father. Lt. Robert E. Park from the Twelfth Alabama took in a musical recital at the home of another prominent Confederate supporter. "With Captain Hewlett and Lieutenant Oscar Smith, of [the] Third Alabama, called on Misses Mary Jane and Lizzie Kellar, young ladies just from a Pennsylvania female college, and heard them play and sing Southern songs," he recorded in his journal.[16]

For many others, their safe arrival at Hagerstown called most of all for thanks to God. The best opportunity for taking worship came on the morning of June 21. One soldier from the Third Alabama noted in a letter home that "many of the men, accompanied by their company officers, were permitted to visit Hagerstown, to attend Divine services." A steady influx of officers and enlisted men crowded into the local Catholic, Lutheran, Methodist Episcopal, and Presbyterian churches, joined by a substantial number of residents.[17]

One of the biggest services that Sunday took place at St. Mary's Catholic Church near the corner of Walnut and Washington Streets. "Hundreds of soldiers went to Church in Hagerstown to-day," Private Pickens wrote in his diary. "Those from our Co. went to the Catholic where Gens. Ewell & Rodes were. Heard a very good sermon on the importance of prayer—St. Matt. 15th Chap. 21 to 29th verse. After service a good many ladies & men went to the carriage & shook hands & conversed with the Gens." The Alabamian noted with pride that "most of the Catholics are secessionists."[18]

The presence of General Ewell, who was in town for an important strategy meeting with Rodes, also attracted a good deal of attention from the crowd of people waiting outside the same church on a nearby street corner. Even a fleeting look at the lieutenant general as he hobbled out of the Catholic church and climbed into his carriage made Southern sympathizer Mary Louisa "Lutie" Kealhofer gush with excitement. "Gen. Ewell has just passed from the R. C. Church in a carriage," she exclaimed in her diary. "But has driven so rapidly that we had only a glimpse of him."[19]

The religious services that day were not limited only to the churches. Rev. J. A. Stradley, who was serving as a missionary with Ramseur's Brigade, pointed out that "a vast crowd was in attendance" during a series of baptisms that took place in the brigade camps along the banks of Antietam Creek. Lt. Thomas Land from Daniel's Brigade reported seeing thirteen soldiers "baptized in the Antietam river" that evening. Stradley found that location to be an especially ironic choice for such a sacred ceremony. "Over this Creek about a year ago the battle of Sharpsburg was fought," the minister declared in a letter to a statewide religious newspaper in North Carolina. "How different the scene!"[20]

Despite the religious fervor among the troops, at least some of the men still longed to take revenge against the many "southern traitors" whom they had encountered in the western part of Maryland. Even the rousing welcome at Hagerstown failed to assuage their doubts about the people's true loyalties. "We have been entirely too kind to these rascals, & have often been insulted by these animals & their relations of the female sex," Asst. Quartermaster Charles F. Bahnson from Daniel's Brigade complained to his father. The young supply officer knew exactly what he would do if anyone said anything disparaging in his presence. "I have not as yet been insulted by any of them, & hope they will not attempt it, for I do not want to kick up a fuss, & a fuss will be kicked certain if they attempt it," he pledged.[21]

Although the troops were in close proximity to Baltimore, much of the speculation in the division had focused by then on Pennsylvania as the most likely objective for their advance. "From what I can find out we are bound for Harrisburg, the capitol of Pennsylvania—but what the result will be, God only knows," Capt. David Ballenger from the Twenty-Sixth Alabama in O'Neal's Brigade told his wife. "If we do not have some hard fighting to do I shall be deceived." He described the campaign as "among the boldest movements that has been made during the war, and I think it will either shorten or protract the war."[22]

Another Alabamian became indignant at reports that the people in Pennsylvania were already "in a perfect state of fear and consternation" over their fate if the army crossed the Mason-Dixon Line. "They think we are going to destroy and burn everything to pay for all they have destroyed in our country," he wrote in a letter home. "I hope it will be the policy, but fear it will not. The devils have laid waste our most beautiful country, and they never will be ready for peace until we make them feel what war is." The soldier argued that the enemy had "inaugurated the policy, and I think self-defense requires that we should 'fight the devils with fire.'"[23]

As they awaited orders for an advance into the Northern states, the men took full advantage of the plentiful supplies on hand in Hagerstown. "We are living sumptuously now," Lieutenant Calder from Ramseur's Brigade told his mother. "We get rations of bacon, beef, flour, butter, & New Orleans syrrup, besides what we buy from the citizens." Lieutenant Ardrey noted in his diary that he was having "a gay old time, plenty to eat and to drink." According to Private Pickens, there also "was a great deal of whiskey in circulation" during their stay. "I saw and heard of a good many drunken men," he acknowledged in his diary.[24]

Aside from alcohol, the most sought-after items were new clothes to replace the old garments that many soldiers still wore. For some of them, their clothes were so threadbare that finding replacements became almost a necessity. "I now wear a Yankee overcoat, boots, shirt, socks, & hat; & if I dont capture a new pair of pants, I will have to go to bed whenever company comes to see me; for they need reseating powerfully bad; & my short jacket does not hide the deficiency," Assistant Quarter-master Bahnson playfully jested in a letter to his father.[25]

While Rodes's men enjoyed their visits into Hagerstown, the troopers from Jen-kins's Brigade continued their raids through the nearby Pennsylvania countryside. On June 20 a large detachment rode north through the mountains to search for live-stock. They soon reached Waynesboro, which stood just north of the border along the western slope of South Mountain. Pvt. Isaac Reynolds from the Sixteenth Virginia Cavalry reported to his wife that the men immediately began to "plunder through town." Local teenager Mary Clara Forney protested in her diary that the cavalrymen "came tearing into town, pressing horses and taking clothing from the stores."[26]

Over a few hours the rebel horsemen seized a huge amount of spoils in the town. "In this place large supplies of commissary stores, drugs, transports, etc., have been procured," one of the troopers declared in a letter to a Virginia newspaper. Despite all the looting, their stay did not last long. Young Lida Jane Welsh, who was the daughter of the town's burgess, described the raid as "a hasty visit." She noted that the rugged cavalrymen immediately "scurried back across the border" on "hearing of Federal troops on the mountain a few miles east of town."[27]

A smaller force from the Fourteenth Virginia Cavalry moved farther east from there along Emmitsburg Turnpike and then swung north to the tiny village of Fair-field. Jacob Hoke reported that "about 120 of them entered Fairfield, and returned again by the Furnace Road, taking with them all the good horses they could find." Ac-cording to Lt. Hermann Schuricht, they "succeeded in capturing a number of horses and some cattle." Their looting came to an abrupt end when a Federal force that in-cluded the Adams County Cavalry, under Capt. Robert Bell, and some horsemen from the Philadelphia City Cavalry under Sgt. M. E. Rogers arrived in the area from Gettysburg.[28]

After forming about a mile away along Mud Run, the Federal cavalrymen charged "into and through town." From there they chased the rebels south "to the mouth of the gap, between Kepner's Knob and Jack's Mountain." The main part of the Union force returned to Fairfield "after detaching a small squad to skirt the western slope of the hills and cut off any stragglers who might be found." Jenkins's troopers fled south past Monterey Gap with their spoils in hand. The Confederates continued to elude their pursuers until making it to safety just across the Maryland border at Leitersburg.[29]

Another detachment of Jenkins' horsemen dashed into Greencastle on June 21 and began looting the local shops. "In some of the stores, a great quantity of goods were destroyed," the local newspaper claimed. Just outside one of the businesses, an officer assigned to the detail ordered his men to "dismount and ransack the store." The newspaper noted that the owner "had, a day or two previously, suffered heavily by these men." The troopers eventually "took possession of the warehouses, and loaded the Confederate States wagons with flour, grain &c." The hunt for useable goods continued until the early evening, when the entire force departed.[30]

A much more troubling incident occurred on the previous day about four miles north of Greencastle near the village of Marion. After stealing some whiskey, three drunken stragglers from Jenkins's Brigade murdered forty-three-year-old farmer Isaac Strite and buried his body in a dung heap. "They . . . wanted his money," one of his neighbors reported. "He gave them part of it. They then wanted to burn his barn; he begged them not to do it. They thereupon shot him." The rogues also wounded Strite's wife when she refused to reveal where the family's money was hidden. In a desperate attempt to save her mother's life, a daughter provided the robbers with the location of the valuables, which amounted to only about forty-five dollars in cash. The offenders were never identified or punished for their crime.[31]

Throughout that time, General Ewell focused on the planning for the future course of the campaign. On June 19 he traveled to Leetown, Virginia, for a conference with James Longstreet, whose First Corps had moved into place along the major gaps through the Blue Ridge Mountains. By then the men from A. P. Hill's Third Corps had already left the vicinity of Fredericksburg for the lush Shenandoah Valley and were closing fast on the rest of the army. Ewell also made frequent visits to the headquarters of his three divisions, which remained widely scattered across a large swath of northern Virginia and southern Maryland.[32]

Despite all that activity, the Confederate advance remained on hold until all of Ewell's men crossed the river into Maryland. The first move to consolidate his forces came in the afternoon on June 16, when the troops from Johnson's Division shifted north from Stephenson's Depot to Smithfield. The Second Maryland Infantry Battalion, which had served in the mountains of western Virginia prior to participating in the attack on Winchester, joined them there and was assigned to Steuart's Brigade. During the stay in the lower Valley, Johnson temporarily detached Jones's Brigade for a brief raid "to destroy a number of canal-boats and a quantity of grain and flour stored at different points" along the Potomac River.

The main part of the division pushed forward the next day to within a couple of miles of Shepherdstown. This stronghold of Southern sympathy stood on the south side of the Potomac about ten miles downriver from Williamsport. Many of the town's Confederate supporters willingly welcomed the troops into their homes. "The house is full of soldiers of all ranks and grades—from the rank of general to the most humble private," one local woman wrote to her daughter. Despite severe shortages of food and other supplies, she had no hesitation in providing for the needs of the fighting men. "I greet all as brother, and am willing to share every mouthful with them," she declared.[33]

View into Shepherdstown, Virginia, from Ferry Hill. Courtesy Library of Congress.

Maj. Henry Kyd Douglas, who served as assistant adjutant general on Johnson's staff, took time that evening to visit his family's home, Ferry Hill Place, perched atop the heights directly across the river from Shepherdstown. The extent of the damage to the residence from repeated Federal occupations came as a severe shock. "My beautiful home was a barren waste," he complained. The veteran staff officer noted that "blackened walls of the burnt barn stood against the sky as a monument of useless and barbarous destruction." The sight left Douglas seething with anger toward the North. "I felt that it would be hard for me, going into Pennsylvania, to put aside all ideas of retaliation," he acknowledged.[34]

On the following morning the troops paraded through Shepherdstown to nearby Boteler's Ford. A soldier from the Twenty-Seventh Virginia in the Stonewall Brigade reported that they "passed through that staid old-time burg with colors flying and the blast of bugle and drum beat." Pvt. John B. Sheets from the Thirty-Third Virginia in the brigade spotted many "nice looking ladies" among the throngs who greeted them. Lt. Randolph McKim, who served as Steuart's aide-de-camp, pointed out that "the general and all his staff" even had "bouquets presented them."[35]

Amid cheering crowds, the troops soon splashed into the fast-flowing water at the crossing. The stirring music from one of the regimental bands added to the festive mood. "Before reaching the river the excellent band of this regiment had gone forward and taken position in the middle of the stream, a little above the broad and shallow ford," Capt. James H. Wood from the Thirty-Seventh Virginia in the Stonewall Brigade recalled. He noted that "as the head of the column entered the ford the melodious strains of 'Maryland, My Maryland' floated out from the band with such forceful expression as to stir to the depths the emotions of those war worn veterans of so many fields."[36]

A gunner from one of the Maryland batteries in the division reported that "hearty cheers burst from the throats of her patriotic sons" as they waded across the Potomac. The only problems came from a sudden downpour that hit the area. The torrential rain failed to deter General Steuart from expressing his overwhelming joy at making it onto the northern shore of the Potomac. Lieutenant McKim from his staff recalled that "our horses' feet touched the sacred soil of our native state at the same moment, but before I could guess his intentions the general sprang from his horse and dropping on his hands and knees kissed the ground."[37]

The ranks of the First Maryland Battalion immediately erupted with wild rejoicing at this gesture. Lt. Thomas Tolson noted in his diary that the troops "gave vent to their feelings in vociferous cheers." Pvt. John C. Henry reported that the long-anticipated arrival in their home state became "the occasion of speechmaking by [Lt.] Col. [J. R.] Herbert, Lt. James Franklin and others." Maj. William W. Goldsborough claimed that many of the soldiers "were moved to tears." According to another Maryland officer, the celebrations along the riverbank grew so frantic that the men "seemed to be demented."[38]

All that posturing did not go down well with everyone in the division. Surgeon Casper Henkel from the Thirty-Seventh Virginia in Steuart's Brigade was disgusted by their behavior. The doctor confided to his cousin that he had "no liking" for the Maryland troops, who had only recently joined the brigade, and "shall avoid having much to do with them." Most disturbing for him was their overwrought reaction on reaching their home state. "They made a great fuss, & many ludicrous demonstrations when they landed on Md. soil," he fumed. "Some of them went so far as to kiss the ground."[39]

Once the celebrations settled down, the men went into camp at the top of a hill near the Douglas home. From there a soldier from Jones's Brigade "could plainly see the 'Stars & Stripes' floating over the enemy's works in Maryland Heights some ten miles distant." Their proximity to a large force of Federal troops caused some concerns among the men. "We are in sight of the yankee camps," Col. John Q. A. Nadenbousch from the Second Virginia in the Stonewall Brigade wrote to his wife. "There is some 10,000 there." To his relief, the enemy soldiers seemed unwilling to provoke a confrontation. "There is no indications of a fight here," the regimental commander happily reported.[40]

The division's huge ordnance and supply train followed closely behind the main column of troops, utilizing the ferry at Shepherdstown, which operated directly alongside the remnants of a bridge that had been destroyed earlier in the war. Maj. Campbell Brown from Ewell's staff looked on as "the single flat-bottomed ferry" remained busy throughout the day, transporting the long line of wagons and horses over the Potomac. Old Allegheny Johnson established his headquarters at nearby Ferry Hill Place. Ewell arrived soon afterward and took up quarters in the same building.[41]

During this stay, the corps commander provided the men with a share of the spoils from their recent victory. "Gen. Ewel had all the eatibles captured at Winchester divided amongst the men such as candies, segars &c. which gave great satisfaction," Surgeon Abram Schultz Miller from the Twenty-Fifth Virginia in Jones's Brigade explained in a letter to his wife. "They are all very much pleased with it." He noted that the men "did not get very much a piece but they like the principle, and I think he [Ewell] will make himself as popular as Gen Jackson." Capt. Edward H. Armstrong from the Third North Carolina in Steuart's Brigade informed his father that the items they received included "candy, Segars, tobacco, cakes, &c. &c."[42]

Some of the soldiers took the opportunity to assess all that they had accomplished up to that point in the advance. Almost to a man they had nothing but praise for their new corps commander. Surgeon Miller insisted to his aunt that Ewell was "the right man to fill Gen Jackson's place." He pointed out that the "general is a splendid fighter, and was very popular with his old division." The doctor was most impressed by the skillful way he had "managed the affairs about Winchester." Pvt. Ted Barclay from the Stonewall Brigade echoed that positive assessment. "I think we have a very good successor to Gen Jackson," he proudly proclaimed in a letter home that day.[43]

But many of the men gave their division commander's performance more mixed reviews. For some of them, the fact that Stonewall Jackson had recommended Johnson for promotion after serving alongside him in western Virginia was enough to overcome the many doubts they had about his character. Others openly blamed Johnson for failing to finish off the enemy at Winchester. Surgeon Miller was among his harshest critics. "I don't think much of old Johnson," he complained in a letter home. "I think him a second or third grade man." Miller argued that "it was his fault that old Milroy got away." The veteran surgeon insisted that Johnson "is no comparison to old Gen Early."[44]

The troops remained in place opposite Shepherdstown until June 20, when they pushed on a few more miles north. Their route took them to the village of Sharpsburg and the battlefield of the previous September. Sgt. Watkins Kearns from the Twenty-Seventh Virginia described the town in his diary as "a very ordinary looking place of some 300 or 400 inhabitants." Like most of western Maryland, Sharpsburg remained a hotbed of pro-Union sentiment. A soldier from the Fifth Virginia in the Stonewall Brigade informed a friend, "we find very few that will speak to a rebble." Lt. Samuel Thomas McCullough from the Maryland battalion insisted that the town was "as thoroughly *Union* as Abe could desire."[45]

Lt. George Buswell from the Thirty-Third Virginia was especially struck by the shows of contempt from the women in the town. "The girls of Sharpsburg are as sour as vinegar & as ugly as any set of girls I ever saw," he grumbled to his brother. Another soldier from the Forty-Eighth Virginia in Jones's Brigade found the greeting

Turnpike at Sharpsburg, Maryland. Courtesy Library of Congress.

in Sharpsburg just as frigid. "The people look very sour on us and are mostly union," he wrote in disgust to his wife. "The ladies in Virginia cheered us on our way but I am induced to believe that white handkerchiefs in Maryland are rare."[46]

The troops eventually set up camp close by the battlefield in some woods just outside of town. Pvt. Gabriel Shank from the Tenth Virginia in Steuart's Brigade pointed out in his diary that "the signs of battle" were still "visible on the trees." Capt. Oscar Hinrichs from the division's staff claimed that "pieces of exploded shells, round shot, broken swords, and muskets, ever and anon mixed up with human skulls and bones of both man and beast, broken artillery wheels, in fact, everything which could bear witness of a terrible conflict were strewn around." All those signs of devastation had a profound effect on the troops. The German-born mapmaker acknowledged that "sitting around their camp fires at night there were no sounds of revelry and joy."[47]

Another soldier from Steuart's Brigade found the exposed corpses that littered part of the former killing grounds more upsetting than anything he had ever encountered in his life. "I saw dead Yankeys in any number just lying on the top of the ground with little dirt throwed over them and hogs rooting them out of the ground and eating them," Pvt. George Harlow from the Twenty-Third Virginia wrote in a letter to his father. He observed many bodies "lying on the top of ground with the flesh picked off and their bones bleaching." Even two years of hard fighting had not prepared him for such a scene. "What a horrible sight for a human being to look upon in a civilized country," he declared.[48]

The following morning the chaplains held a solemn Sabbath ceremony to commemorate their fallen comrades. An officer from the Third North Carolina recalled that the troops "assembled and with arms reversed and to the roll of the muffled drum marched to the battle field, where the Rev. George Patterson, chaplain of the Third, read the burial services." Lieutenant McKim from Steuart's staff noted that the beloved clergyman also "preached and administered the communion" for the many soldiers in attendance.[49]

Some of the men attempted to offset their somber mood by going shopping in town that afternoon. "The stores have been opened & the prices have been to us 'Dixie Boys' remarkably moderate," Sergeant Kearns happily penned in his diary. Cpl. William H. Proffit from the First North Carolina in Steuart's Brigade effused in a letter home that the goods were "much cheaper than I expected to find them." Sgt. Ferdinand J. Dunlap from the Thirty-Third Virginia remained less pleased with the results. The young soldier griped to his sister that he had "been trying to get some Cotton and Calico or something to send to you all but everything can not be got."[50]

While that was going on, Jubal Early's troops and the two battalions from the Second Corps Artillery Reserve rested outside of Winchester before going into camp just south of Shepherdstown on June 18. Pvt. Thomas Benton Reed from Hays's Brigade grumbled in his diary that "a very heavy rain fell this evening." Ignoring the inclement conditions, the soldiers pushed on through town to the Potomac River early on the following day. Colonel Evans from Gordon's Brigade noted that the men "were received with many demonstrations of joy by the citizens" as they paraded through the streets. After a short march, the rain-soaked troops reached Boteler's Ford in preparation for their crossing.[51]

On their arrival at the river, the troops went into camp alongside the ford, a decision that proved to be a major miscalculation. While the soldiers rested, massive storms raged throughout the night without pause. Lt. J. Warren Jackson from Hays's Brigade complained to his brother that the river rose so high that by the following morning "we could not cross." With the water nearly at flood stage, the Early's men were unable to make it over the Potomac into Maryland until early in the morning on June 22, their first opportunity to cross in safety.[52]

Throughout that time, Ewell remained in regular contact with the army's commanding general on what his orders would be for the next phase of the advance. "If you are ready to move, you can do so," General Lee finally informed him on the afternoon of June 21. "I am much gratified at the success which has attended your movements, and feel assured if they are conducted with the same energy and circumspection, it will continue." He explained that Ewell's "progress and direction will, of course, depend upon the development of circumstances." Most emphatic of all were Lee's directions that "if Harrisburg comes within your means, capture it."

Spurred on by Ewell's stunning achievements in the campaign, Lee had no hesitations about finally taking his army deep into Northern territory for the first time in the war. His plan called for Rodes's Division to lead the way along the main turnpike through the center of Pennsylvania's Cumberland Valley toward the state capital; he instructed Johnson's Division to follow closely behind. Lee ordered Early's men to move forward on the right into place a few miles outside Chambersburg and await further instructions. Jenkins's cavalrymen would again screen the front of the advance and capture supplies from the surrounding countryside.[53]

As part of the arrangements, Ewell temporarily assigned the Seventeenth Virginia Cavalry for duty with Early's Division. The arrival of the Baltimore Light Artillery, under Capt. Wiley Hunter Griffin, somewhat offset that reduction in Jenkins's main force. That battery had served in the mountains of western Virginia prior to the current campaign. As Ewell moved in for the attack on Winchester, he temporarily assigned it to support Early's Division. Following that battle, the Ordnance Department allowed the unit to replace its worn-out guns with four captured ten-pounder Parrotts. Despite that honor, Ewell soon ordered the battery into the artillery reserve for the corps.

This proposed transfer stirred up a huge wave of discontent among the Marylanders. "The order occasioned the greatest surprise and indignation throughout the command, for always before they had led the advance and covered the retreat," one of the artillerists grumbled. "Such an indignity as they considered it, could not be tamely submitted to." He noted that "a protest was immediately drawn up and forwarded to Genl Ewell." The men complained so vehemently against the transfer that the general allowed them to join up with Jenkins's Brigade at Hagerstown.[54]

With all his forces in place, Ewell finally issued the command for Rodes to resume the advance on the morning of June 22. At the appointed time, the Virginian led his division back through Hagerstown toward Pennsylvania. "Got orders early this morning," Quartermaster Sgt. John Tucker, who served in O'Neal's Brigade, recorded in his diary. "Struck tents and left for Pa. Went through Hagerstown & large crowds of people turned out to see us and many little sisish flags were displayed." From there the men tramped straight north to the village of Middleburg, which straddled the border between Maryland and Pennsylvania.[55]

About 10:00 A.M., Rodes's troops made their triumphant entrance into the Keystone State. Unlike the recent crossing of the Potomac, the honor of being the first infantry from the Army of Northern Virginia to cross into Pennsylvania did not go to the men from Ramseur's Brigade. With the Twentieth North Carolina in the lead, the soldiers from Iverson's Brigade instead took the position at the front the column. "Our Brigade led the division this morning & was first of rebel infantry that ever entered the state of Penn.," Assistant Surgeon Marston proudly boasted in his diary.[56]

The move immediately sparked open celebrations throughout the division. Major Blackford informed his father that one of the regimental bands "struck up the 'bonnie blue flag' most cheerily" just as O'Neal's Brigade reached the border. Few of the men doubted that their bold advance into the North would result in anything other than a final victory against their hated foe. One soldier from the Third Alabama noted in a letter home that "when the fact became known that Pennsylvania was our destination, a shout of joy ran along the lines." He added that "when our troops crossed the line it was with a proud and defiant step, conscious that wherever Ewell leads, we can follow."[57]

7

"No Signs of Sympathy with the Rebels"

After crossing into Pennsylvania late in the morning on June 22, the men from Rodes's Division proceeded north along a secondary road before finally linking up with Valley Turnpike at Greencastle. About noon a small detachment from the Fourteenth Virginia Cavalry stumbled into some Federal cavalrymen patrolling just north of the town. The enemy force consisted of about forty troopers from Capt. William H. Boyd's First New York Cavalry detachment who had escaped from Berryville and Martinsburg.[1]

Rodes responded to such signs of Federal troops to his front by hurriedly deploying the entire division in battle formation along the turnpike about a mile beyond Greencastle. "Fences were torn down to the right and left of the road," Charles Hartman, who served as a town councilman, recorded in his diary. As he watched, the "infantry took position on the high ground of Mr. John Kissecker's farm." Rodes's overly cautious reaction resulted from a false report that some 40,000 Federal soldiers under Maj. Gen. George B. McClellan had already arrived in the vicinity from the state capital at Harrisburg.

The division commander took the further precaution of sending part of Jenkins's Brigade a short distance ahead to guard against a surprise attack. Hartman reported that "Jenkins threw his cavalry forward, and formed a skirmish line upon the land of Mr. William Fleming, about a quarter of a mile in advance of the infantry." Pvt. George W. Wilson from the Fourteenth Virginia Cavalry noted that the men from his company soon set out in search of the Federal troopers operating along their front. "After going three or four miles, we went up a hill, and just as we got to the top we ran in a company hunting for us," he recalled.

Under Jenkins's orders, the Confederates began to draw the enemy cavalrymen back toward the Fleming House. "Just as we neared the camp the captain ordered us to dismount and get over the fence and let our horses run into camp," Wilson explained. Another rebel trooper reported that the men from the detachment galloped "back at full speed to a short turn in the road in full view, when they dismounted." As the Federals continued chasing the horses into the vicinity of the camp, Jenkins's men "took cover under a fence" and suddenly "poured a terrible volley into the column of pursuing cavalry."[2]

The civilians huddled inside the nearby house looked on in terror as a fierce firefight erupted right on their doorstep. "The noise and clatter were quite lively," Councilman Hartman wrote in his diary. "A sister of Mr. Blair Fleming going to the window to look out, barely escaped a ball which came crashing in through the glass in front of her head." During the ensuing exchange of volleys, the Federal cavalrymen suffered two casualties. Sgt. Milton S. Cafferty sustained a painful wound in his leg, while Cpl. William H. Rihl was killed by a bullet that tore through his upper lip.[3]

With that sudden burst of gunfire, the young trooper became the first combat fatality in Pennsylvania during the Confederate advance. "While huddled in a mass, directly in front of the house, which was on the right side of the road, Rhial [sic] was shot, falling on the left-hand side, where his body was left lying," an officer in Boyd's detachment recalled. Councilman Hartman noted that the fatal shot passed "through his head, his blood bespattering the paling fence in front of Mr. Flemings' dwelling." After some more sporadic firing, the Federal detachment galloped off toward Chambersburg, with Jenkins's horsemen in full pursuit.[4]

Once their path was cleared of enemy troops, Rodes's men settled into camp about a mile north of Greencastle. That prosperous market town, which had a population of about 1,400, was located in the southern section of Pennsylvania's rich

Entrance into Greencastle, Pennsylvania, on Carlisle Street. Courtesy Allison-Antrim Museum.

Cumberland Valley. Scotch-Irish immigrants first settled the area in the mid-1700s. The town's name reportedly traced back to a village in County Donegal, Ireland. It's lone brush with fame to this point came when Charles Mason and Jeremiah Dixon used it as the base for their border survey in the 1760s. Then with the completion of the vital Cumberland Valley Railroad in the early 1840s, Greencastle enjoyed a major economic surge.[5]

While Jenkins's horsemen set up their pickets on the edge of town, Rodes traveled back south to nearby Boonsboro for a conference with Ewell. The plan they worked out during the meeting called for Rodes to pause at Greencastle and await the arrival of Johnson's Division before pushing farther north. The corps commander also ordered him to seize an extensive list of supplies from the local residents and merchants. Ewell joined the division in Greencastle the following afternoon after riding in his carriage from Boonsboro. Capt. Frank A. Bond's Company A of the First Maryland Cavalry Battalion, which was attached directly to corps headquarters, escorted the general on the trip.[6]

From the moment of their arrival, Rodes's troops experienced a frigid welcome from the citizens at Greencastle. Lt. Col. Wharton Green from Daniel's staff complained that, when they first reached there, "it seemed that all of the Pennsylvania Dutch for a hundred miles around about had come to look glum at our audacity in venturing so far in their midst." Pvt. Louis Leon, another of Daniel's men, noted that the people "showed their hatred to us by their glum looks and silence, and I am willing to swear that no prayers will be offered in this town for us poor, ragged rebels." Pvt. Edwin R. Sharpe from the Fourth Georgia in Doles's Brigade admitted in his diary that "there was no signs of sympathy with the rebels shown after we crossed the Maryland line."[7]

As more and more Confederate troops poured into town, the mood among the residents quickly turned into open disdain for the invading soldiers. According to Pvt. Henry Wood in O'Neal's Brigade, "the cold shoulder is pointed at us hear as shure as we live." Pvt. Lucius Lovelace from Doles's Brigade found the reaction from the inhabitants so extreme that it appeared "as if they had been taking something very bitter." Lt. John Gay from the same brigade insisted to his wife that the citizens of Greencastle "hate us as bitterly as it is possible for mankind to hate."[8]

Rodes's men responded to their chilly reception with some harsh comments of their own about the people who lived in the staunchly pro-Union town. Asst. Surgeon William Marston of Iverson's Brigade left no doubt about his feelings when he wrote in his diary, "the sorriest set of Yankees you ever saw inhabit this place and the largest collection of ugly dirty looking women I ever saw." Major Blacknall from the same brigade described the residents as "trembling culprits." He pointed out that they "are all hostile to us, but we are quite docile as they are frightened out of their lives, & offer us everything we wish to save them from utter destruction."[9]

While both sides sized each other up over the course of the day, Col. Edward Willis from the Twelfth Georgia, one of Doles's regiments, took control of Greencastle as provost marshal. Under his directions, supply officers from the division confiscated needed goods from all over town. Willis ordered civilian officials to hand over large quantities of leather, tin, lead, and food of all kinds. The call for supplies soon extended to items of almost every description, even including two hundred curry combs and brushes and one hundred saddles and bridles. Willis allowed no excuses for failing to comply.[10]

The list of goods that they were required to turn over shocked the elected officials in the town. "These demands were so heavy that the Council felt it impossible to fill them," the local newspaper declared. Rodes's men guaranteed the cooperation of the council members in carrying out the seizures by detaining them under an armed guard. "Heavy demands made upon us for salt, meat, onions, and such," Councilman Hartman lamented in his diary. "Also bridles and saddles, harness. The town council was held till their demands were complied with." He described it as "the hardest day in all my life."

Quartermaster and commissary search details eventually uncovered an array of useful items that merchants had hidden away. "The Rebels got a few saddles and bridles, and some vegetables about town," the editor of the local newspaper reported. He complained that Rodes's men also "seized and carried away about $2000 worth of leather from Mr. Stiffel." Local officials further directed residents to turn over a huge quantity of onions to the commissary details at the central square. One resident quipped that "the Town Council owing to orders it had given was jocular[l]y named Onion Council, much to the disgust of several of the councilmen."

While Rodes's infantrymen gathered up their loot, Jenkins's troopers embarked on a major hunt for runaway slaves in the surrounding area. Hartman was horrified by what he witnessed as the riders relentlessly pursued the hapless black residents. "One of the exciting features of the day was the scouring of the fields about town and searching houses for negroes," he recorded in his diary. "Those poor creatures, those of them who had not fled upon the approach of the foe, [were] concealed in wheat fields about town." The councilman looked on helplessly as the "cavalrymen rode in search of them and many of them were caught after a desperate chase and being fired at."[11]

Some of the men from Doles's Brigade, and probably others throughout the division, joined in rounding up "contrabands" whenever the opportunity presented itself. Private Lovelace informed his father that "some of our Brigade have brought in several runaway negroes since I have been writing, they belong to a man near Guineas Station, the boys played off on them and caught the bucks." Lt. Thomas Hightower from the Twenty-First Georgia bragged that they had "recaptured some of the negroes that were taken in Virginia." Another Georgian estimated that they had seized "over a hundred negroes" by then.[12]

A newspaper correspondent attached to the army noted that groups of slave owners from Virginia followed closely behind the Confederate advance "in search of their stolen negroes and horses." During a brief stop at Hagerstown, he "met several gangs of negroes going to the rear who had been captured in the mountains in Maryland and Pennsylvania." Along the way the fugitive hunters gathered up whatever additional plunder they could locate. "Many of the owners of these slaves had procured wagons and other conveyances this side of the Potomac, which they filled with goods and groceries at the market price in Confederate money or gold, and were carrying into Dixie," the correspondent explained.[13]

One of those slave catchers made his way onto the campus of the College of St. James, just southwest of Hagerstown, on the same day that Rodes's troops arrived in Greencastle. "Near Tea time a person named Sever came from Winchester in search of the slaves of his father," an instructor at the school wrote in his diary. What followed proved shocking for the staunch Union supporter, who watched in utter disbelief as the man "carried off our cook and her two children." The distraught educator openly lamented that this unwarranted seizure "was a sad sight."[14]

Although Jenkins's cavalrymen carried out most of the slave hunting during the invasion, they were not part of some rogue unit conducting operations in secret. The seizures took place with the full knowledge of the top commanders in Ewell's corps, who kept a close eye on nearly everything the men did and clearly sanctioned their conduct. The infantrymen from the three divisions also joined in rounding up any blacks whom they encountered without any interference from their superiors. None of them made any real effort to distinguish between runaway slaves and those who had been born free. Every African American who came within reach of the Confederates was fair game for capture and a trip south into bondage.[15]

The kidnapping of blacks was so commonplace that most of Rodes's men paid little attention to the brutal acts going on around them during their occupation of Greencastle. They instead relished all that they had accomplished in making it nearly unopposed into Pennsylvania. Capt. John Gorman from Ramseur's Brigade bragged in a letter home that the troops were "as confident as when old Jackson infused us with his own ardor" in the months before his untimely death. "Trusting in the justice of our cause, in the wisdom of our leaders, and the help of the Omnipotent arm of Jehovah, we calmly await the issue," he declared. The Tar Heel insisted that "whatever fate befalls us individually, we have an abiding faith that victory and triumph awaits us in the end."[16]

By the morning of June 23, Johnson's men and the two battalions from the corps artillery reserve, which had linked up with the division on the previous day, were also on the move along the turnpike toward Greencastle. Their route took them through Tilghmanton, Maryland, which one Southerner described as "a small log village." The men could not resist taking out their frustrations over the chilly greeting from residents in that part of the state with some sharp-tongued comments about the local women. One soldier from the Tenth Virginia in Steuart's Brigade joked that the town was "renowned for its ugly wimmen." According to Chaplain William Robert Gwaltney from the First North Carolina in the same brigade, he actually spotted "some of the ugliest women in the world" as they passed through there.[17]

Their march came to a sudden halt when the gatekeeper on the turnpike outside Tilghmanton demanded payment of the toll before allowing the troops to proceed. "The toll-gatherer, stepped out of his toll house, let down his gate, and stood by it to bar our passage," Maj. Henry Kyd Douglas of Johnson's staff recalled. The man then "accosted" the general and his staff officers, demanding that they immediately hand over the money. The brazen gatekeeper finally relented when Old Allegheny informed him that he would only receive payment if he sent his bill directly to Jefferson Davis in Richmond.[18]

Despite the delay, Johnson's troops easily reached Hagerstown by midmorning. Lt. Samuel Thomas McCullough from Steuart's Brigade reported that they marched into that town "with fixed bayonets, flying colors, bands playing, &c." With the arrival of the troops, many pro-Southern citizens again felt free to show their support. Lt. George Buswell from the Stonewall Brigade admitted in a letter home that he "was much surprised to find a strong secession sentiment" in the town. Quartermaster Sgt. Albion Martin from the Thirty-Third Virginia in the same brigade insisted that they "never received such demonstration of welcome in any Va. town."

The only serious threat came from the many bushwhackers of mixed Union and Confederate sympathizes in this fractured region. That problem proved deadly for Capt. Johnson Orrick from the Thirty-Third Virginia, a former Confederate congressman and member of the Virginia Secession Convention with numerous political enemies in the area. "He was on his way home in Morgan Co. and riding along the tow path of the Canal and when near Clear Spring, Md. was shot," Sergeant Martin explained to his wife. He declared, "we all tried to persuade him against going at all and especially on this side of the River as there are many bad men in his region and he knew they were his personal and deadly enemies."[19]

Ignoring the danger, the soldiers resumed the advance during the late afternoon. After a short march, they halted for the night "about 100 yards" south of the Pennsylvania border near Middleburg. Pvt. John William Ford Hatton from one of the division's batteries described it in his journal as "a small and unattractive village." Although the town was far from appealing, the nearby area overflowed with all kinds of useful supplies. Lt. Henry H. Harris from the division's engineering staff effused in his diary that "foraging is profitable as every thing in plenty, and one need give only as much money as he chooses."[20]

The forces available to Ewell also included the First Maryland Cavalry Battalion, headed by Maj. Harry Gilmor. The renowned cavalry leader had only recently assumed command of the unit as the temporary replacement for Maj. Ridgeley Brown, who had suffered a leg wound at Greenland Gap, Virginia, during late April. After a stint in western Virginia, the battalion participated in the fighting around Winchester as part of the Maryland Line. Following that battle, the horsemen crossed the Potomac into their home state at Williamsport. Gilmor noted that Ewell immediately ordered him "to go forward to Boonesboro, feel my way down to Frederick, and, if possible, destroy the Monocacy Bridge."[21]

Maj. Harry Gilmor. Courtesy Library of
Congress.

From his camp outside Boonsboro, Gilmor dispatched about ten men to scout the nearby town of Frederick. The group arrived there in the afternoon on June 20. As the horsemen charged into the streets, they encountered a small force from Maj. Henry Cole's First Potomac Home Brigade Cavalry. "Our quiet town was startled by a dash of cavalry from the west end through Patrick Street," the town's newspaper stated. Local resident Jacob Engelbrecht reported that the rebels rushed in "at full speed firing as fast as they could." Catherine Markell, who also lived in Frederick, noted in her diary that the "Confederate pickets drove Cole's cavalry scouts through town capturing thirteen of them."[22]

After receiving some reinforcements, the invaders soon had the streets under tight control. They quickly rounded up some sick and wounded soldiers at the U.S. Army hospital on South Market Street. A story in the Northern press indicated that Gilmor's men also "captured nine of our men who were on duty at the Signal Station" and paroled "the invalid prisoners, numbering about sixty in the hospital." By nightfall, the Southern troopers were so relaxed that they began making the social rounds. According to the local newspaper, some of them, "having been formerly residents of Frederick," spent that time "visiting their friends."[23]

Events took a sudden turn in the early afternoon on June 21. Major Gilmor noted that his men "were getting on quite smoothly, when a small force of cavalry dashed in and drove them out, wounding one of them severely, who was left behind in the hospital." The Federal contingent consisted of about twenty-five troopers from

Major Cole's command under Capt. George W. F. Vernon, who chased the startled Southerners to the west end of Frederick. "The body of the Confederate cavalry resting near town retreated rapidly until they reached a point about a mile out of town," one of the local newspapers stated.[24]

Vernon's men soon ran into the main body of Gilmor's battalion, which had just arrived. The Confederate leader noted that "the head of their column came to the edge of the town, and opened on us with carbines." He responded with a forceful counterattack. "I dismounted twenty of our sharpshooters with long-range rifles to engage them," Gilmor recalled. "After deploying these on both sides of the road, I advanced boldly, as though we had plenty of support." His men quickly brought the Federal advance to a halt. "In a short time, the enemy retreated, and, when our skirmishers had gained the edge of town, I dashed in with the rest of my command," Gilmor remarked. The beleaguered Federal troopers were soon in full flight on the road to Harpers Ferry.

Although the citizens in Frederick remained decidedly mixed in their loyalties, a significant number of Southern supporters lived there. To Gilmor's relief, many of the residents gave his men a friendly reception. "The people of Frederick turned out *en masse,* and never did I see so much enthusiasm," he remarked. "The ladies particularly crowded around us, and it was with difficulty we could move along." Gilmor further noted that the jubilant townspeople "gave the men all they wanted, invited us into their houses for refreshment, and manifested unmistakably their sympathy with the South."[25]

The raiders quickly turned their attention to seizing additional plunder from the neighboring farms. The troopers remained busy confiscating necessary supplies until they finally pulled out of Frederick the following day. While the results were far from overwhelming, the Confederates still uncovered a substantial amount of livestock that could be added to the larder of the invading army. Union supporter Jacob Engelbrecht complained in his diary that "about 40 head of cattle were taken by the Rebels yesterday." He pointed out that "they were principally taken from Joseph Waltman & driven around towards Possomtown."[26]

With those duties out of the way, Gilmor "had the bugle sounded and went on to the Monocacy to try the bridge." That structure occupied a strategic position over a significant tributary of the Potomac River. The major quickly determined that the span was too stoutly defended for his men to carry out a successful attack, "there being a strong stockade at each end." Gilmor thus had little choice other than to call off the attempt. "I gave it up and returned through Frederick to the top of South Mountain, near Boonsboro," he explained.[27]

While Gilmor was busy at Frederick, a large detachment from Jenkins's Brigade carried out a major raid of their own into the nearby Pennsylvania countryside to search for some 2,000 horses that farmers there had reportedly hidden away. Maj. James C. Bryan, the quartermaster for O'Neal's Brigade, supervised this operation.

After departing from northern Maryland in the afternoon of June 22, the Confederate troopers reached Mont Alto Furnace, about six miles northeast of Waynesboro, just before midnight. After seizing several horses and some provisions from the owner, the cavalrymen settled into camp for the night.

Early the next day they headed north along an "unfrequented mountain road" to the Caledonia Iron Works, which stood west of Cashtown Gap along the turnpike running between Chambersburg and Gettysburg, arriving at the site just before dawn. The sprawling industrial complex consisted of several furnaces and rolling mills, a company store, and homes for its two hundred workers. The capture of the ironworks carried strong symbolic value to the troopers because it was owned by Thaddeus Stevens, a leader of the Radical Republicans in the U.S. Congress.[28]

Jenkins's men immediately ordered the resident manager to surrender all the saddle horses on the site. "Mr. Sweeney, who has charge of the works, agreed to deliver up the riding horses if the property should be protected," one area newspaper reported. "This they agreed to, but on going for the riding horses they met the teamsters and compelled them to produce all the horses and mules nearly forty in all, with gears, harness, &c." During the early afternoon, the Confederates finally set off after the "Yankee guard" and the other horses that had eluded them on their arrival.[29]

The cavalrymen initially galloped east along the road leading to Gettysburg. "About two miles beyond Caledonia Iron Works we discovered the road to be blockaded, just where it entered into dense woods," Lt. Hermann Schuricht from the Fourteenth Virginia Cavalry reported in his diary. A squad of nine men immediately moved forward to clear away the barricades. At that point the rebels encountered about twenty-five militiamen from the Adams County Cavalry, under Capt. Elias Spangler and Lt. Hiram Lady, who were hiding in the woods along the road. After taking a couple of the enemy pickets as prisoners, the butternut-clad troopers chased the militiamen toward the Cashtown Gap.

As they approached an old limekiln just west of Cashtown near Gallagher's Knob, Jenkins's distracted riders passed by four civilians lying in ambush. Using the underbrush along the road as a cover, Henry Hahn of nearby Hilltown suddenly fired a shotgun blast at the advancing troopers. The single shot mortally wounded Pvt. Eli Amick. Lt. John A. Hawver, who was riding alongside Amick, reported to the trooper's family that the unlucky cavalrymen slumped over in his saddle before his horse could be brought to a halt. The spread of shotgun pellets left the private with three gaping wounds in his abdomen. Hawver quickly confirmed that Amick was mortally wounded and nothing could be done to save him. As the bushwhackers made their escape, the cavalrymen determined that the area was too dangerous for further pursuit and hurried back past the ironworks to the village of Greenwood, where the Southerners' rear guard held the captured horses. After forcing some residents to feed the "men and animals," the raiders headed south and eventually linked up with the rest of the brigade the following day.[30]

The main part of Rodes's Division, meanwhile, resumed the advance north from Greencastle along Valley Turnpike early on June 24. Johnson's men trailed a short distance behind from their camp near Middleburg. After crossing the border that morning, Johnson's troops quickly pushed on to Greencastle. Pvt. Samuel Angus Firebaugh from Steuart's Brigade described the town in his diary as "a pretty hard looking place." A veteran from the Twenty-Fifth Virginia in Jones's Brigade spied "a pretty young girl" holding "a small United States flag in her hands" as they passed through the streets. To his surprise, the feisty youngster repeatedly "taunted" the soldiers with the banner. the Virginian sheepishly admitted that some of the troops "were not courteous to her."[31]

While his men took a brief rest, Johnson detached Steuart's Brigade and Capt. John C. Carpenter's four-gun Alleghany Artillery for a quick strike over the Cove and Tuscarora Mountains into Fulton County. Ewell's orders called for this force of about 2,250 men to proceed as far west as McConnellsburg, where they would "collect horses, cattle, and other supplies which the army needed." The general also expected that this move would protect his left flank from the Federal militia and the remnants of Milroy's command that had moved into place near the town. Meanwhile, the rest of Johnson's Division would continue north to Chambersburg and then move on through Shippensburg to Carlisle.[32]

After departing from Greencastle, Steuart's column headed northwest on the arduous march through the mountains past Upton and on toward Mercersburg, at the western edge of the Cumberland Valley. The brigade commander quickly moved to resolve his major problem: the lack of any cavalry to screen his advance through enemy territory. "When we were already eleven miles on our march, the general sent me back to Hagerstown after the Maryland cavalry, which had not yet reported to him as ordered," staff officer Lt. Randolph McKim recalled. He eventually located Major Gilmor and five companies of the First Maryland Cavalry Battalion resting in Hagerstown and ordered them to move forward as fast as possible.[33]

The cavalrymen had just arrived there after a brief stop at Boonsboro following their aborted raid on the Monocacy Bridge. After meeting up with Lieutenant McKim, they proceeded west along the turnpike leading to Mercersburg. During midmorning on June 24, Gilmor's troopers finally joined Steuart's Brigade "at the top of the mountain and immediately took the advance." With horsemen now at the front, the column pushed on for a few more miles to within sight of Mercersburg. About noon the major assembled his three hundred fearsome-looking troopers for a sudden dash into the unsuspecting town.[34]

Mercersburg, which had a population of about nine hundred, was best known as the home for the theological seminary of the German Reformed Church. Prof. Philip Schaff watched in despair from his house as "the advance pickets" charged down the main street and "dismounted before the gate of the seminary." The rest of Steuart's command followed closely behind the cavalry. Schaff noted in his diary that the soldiers "made a most motley appearance, roughly dressed, yet better than during their Maryland campaign last fall, all provided with shoes, and to a great extent with fresh and splendid horses."

Steuart immediately placed Maj. William W. Goldsborough from the Second Maryland Infantry Battalion in charge as provost marshal. While the guards moved into position, the general called together some of the "leading citizens" of Mercersburg for a brief meeting. According to Schaff, the brigade commander read Lee's proclamation "to the effect that the advancing army should take supplies and pay in Confederate money, or give a receipt, but not violate private property." Steuart followed up with a demand "that all the stores be opened." The frightened officials reluctantly complied with the orders.

Quartermaster and commissary details were soon busy searching local businesses for any usable supplies. The items that the troops found in the stores were all that they could have desired. "Some of them were almost stripped of the remaining goods, for which payment was made in Confederate money," Schaff grumbled in his diary. "They emptied Mr. Fitzgerald's cellar of sugar, molasses, hams, etc., and enjoyed the candies, nuts, cigars, etc., at Mr. Shannon's." Major Goldsborough reported that the details also obtained "a goodly quantity of shoes" for the men.[35]

The soldiers in the ranks were just as pleased with all the goods available. Lieutenant McCollough from the Maryland infantry battalion noted that they "bought bacon, coffee, Sugar, &c. paying in Confederate money at Baltimore prices." A man from the Tenth Virginia wrote in his diary that he "got plenty of apple butter and Butter to eat." Not surprisingly, they received a hostile reception from the citizens in this staunchly pro-Union town. Capt. Edward H. Armstrong from the Third North Carolina grumbled to his father that here too the people "look very sour at us." Chaplain Gwaltney from the First North Carolina complained that he encountered "some strong abolitionists" during his stay.[36]

While the bulk of the troops departed from town in the early afternoon, Armstrong's company remained behind as provost guards. Their presence caused a major stir among the citizens. "Some thought that I had been left behind to burn the town, and children came to me and asked if such was the case," the captain explained in a letter home. "I assured them it was not." The worst problems occurred when he prevented several local women from passing through the lines. Armstrong noted that "they became very much enraged said some pretty hard things but it did no good." He understandably complained that "the ladies in this state are decidedly the hardest looking people I have ever seen."[37]

From Mercersburg the rest of Steuart's force proceeded west through the tiny village of Cove Gap and over Tuscarora Mountain toward McConnellsburg. That town of about six hundred inhabitants was nestled in a bountiful valley just west of the junction of the main roads from Chambersburg and Greencastle. The settlement sprang up in the late 1700s along an old trader's trail that ran west from Philadelphia to the Ohio River. That path was later upgraded into a macadamized turnpike. The resulting influx of commercial traffic quickly transformed the town into a major transportation hub for the region, which had already made it the target for a raid on June 19 by Col. Milton Ferguson's cavalrymen.[38]

As Steuart's men continued their ascent of the mountain, a force of militiamen and a few survivors from Milroy's command took up position along the turnpike in an effort to block their further advance. The largest contingent consisted of 120 troops from the Forty-Sixth Pennsylvania Volunteer Militia under Lt. Col. Jacob Szink, who set up on both sides of the road at the top of the mountain. About a dozen troopers from the Twelfth Pennsylvania Cavalry under Lt. Col. Joseph L. Moss, who had escaped from the disastrous fighting at Winchester, assembled just to the west near the junction of the Chambersburg and Mercersburg Turnpikes. A single company of Huntingdon County militia under Capt. William W. Wallace remained farther in the rear at McConnellsburg.

During midafternoon, Szink spotted the Confederate troops moving rapidly on the road toward his position. He immediately fired a signal gun to notify Moss's cavalrymen that the enemy was fast approaching and sent a courier into McConnellsburg calling for Wallace to send his unit forward to reinforce the defenses. The company by that point numbered fewer than thirty militiamen, but despite the small size, Wallace hastened his troops out of town toward Szink's position. Along the way they linked up with Moss's handful of horsemen.[39]

To their surprise, the militiamen soon encountered Szink's entire command in full flight from the oncoming enemy. "Just as we reached the foot of the mountain we met Zinn's [sic] regiment on the retreat," Pvt. Samuel A. Steele from Wallace's command recalled. "Our company halted them and Wallace begged them to stay with us but they had business far in the rear and away they went with coat tails fluttering in the breeze." Steele pointed out that their panicked withdrawal also "stampeded the 12th cavalry who went to the rear as fast as their horses would take them."[40]

The exceptions to this general flight were a lieutenant and four troopers who bravely offered to stay behind as scouts for Wallace's intrepid band. The militia captain readily accepted their help. Despite Szink's shameful retreat, Wallace proceeded with his plans to ambush the Confederate column, instructing the cavalrymen to "ride on ahead as far as you can with safety and return with timely information of the approach of the enemy before they see us." With two of Moss's horsemen in the lead, the militiamen were soon on the march up the mountain toward the enemy.

During a brief halt along the way, the captain issued his final instructions for the proposed ambush. His plan called for the men to remain well hidden among the rocks and underbrush along the twisting mountain road. "Throwing the brave little band into single file, I cautioned them to follow me in silence and keep their eyes upon me, in readiness on a wave of my hand to leave the road, clamber up the bank, which no cavalry could have mounted, and each one to conceal himself securely in the thick brushwood that skirted the road," Wallace explained years later.[41]

While that was going on, Steuart's men pushed on toward McConnellsburg. The first hint the rebels had of an enemy presence along their front occurred when they came upon a barrier blocking their route. That obstacle caused only a momentary delay. "At the top of Tuscarora Mountain we encountered a barricade of stone across the road, guarded by but one person, who fled on our approach," Lt. Thomas Tolson from the Maryland infantry battalion explained in his diary. "Removing the obstruction we passed on, moving slowly and feeling our way."[42]

The sudden appearance of Confederate infantry sent the Federal scouts scurrying for safety in the rear. Private Steele noted that, "when about half way up" the mountain, they "heard the rebels coming driving our two scouts ahead of them." Captain Wallace immediately "divided his company into five squads placing them about sixty feet above the road and about the same distance apart." As the scouts pulled back, Steuart's men suddenly opened fire on them, which forced them into a hasty retreat. In the hustle to get away, one of the horsemen suffered a slight wound.[43]

The militiamen waited patiently until the advancing column moved closer before unleashing a barrage of their own. Lt. James Pott from Wallace's company admitted that they opened fire much sooner than planned when one "impetuous" young militiaman "prematurely discharged his musket." Steuart's troops reacted to the sounds of gunshots along their front by immediately deploying a line of skirmishers. Pott noted that "the Johnnies threw out flankers which came very near trapping us all, but we all escaped and not one of us was hurt, although volley after volley was rained in among us, but mostly over our heads."[44]

After a brief exchange of gunfire, Steuart halted the shooting and demanded the immediate surrender of Wallace's command. Although they were hopelessly outnumbered, the tiny band of Federals remained defiant. "We did not heed this request but kept up a continuous fire, the rebels all the while concentrating their fire upon us," Private Steele recalled. The relentless shooting sent the men scrambling for any shelter they could find along the slopes of the hillside, though even that cover provided little real protection from the steady barrage of musket fire. Steele complained that the incoming bullets were "striking the bushes and rocks like hail."[45]

Despite the close range, the return fire from Wallace's small force proved little more than an annoyance for the Confederates. Major Gilmor boasted that "a few shots were fired at us; but it did not amount to much." Within a few moments the men from Carpenter's battery unlimbered their guns and opened fire on the Pennsylvanians. "Finally they threw several shells into our midst and by this time had almost completely surrounded us," Steele recalled. "It was then surrender or run." He continued, "the result was that we all escaped in squads of two or three without losing a man." Although the action was lively for a time, Wallace's company sustained only two casualties during the encounter.[46]

The situation proved just as bleak for the small detachment from the Twelfth Pennsylvania Cavalry. Sgt. John H. Black reported in a letter home that their tiny group of horsemen soon became embroiled in "a pretty brisk skirmish" along the mountain road. Within minutes the advancing Confederates forced the troopers into a retreat from the rugged heights. "Finding they were too many for us we fell back slowly firing all the while," the sergeant explained. "Sorry to say we had three men wounded in the affray, among which was my highly esteemed friend Sergeant Stiffler."[47]

Even then the dangers for the handful of Federals were not over. Private Steele acknowledged that the defenders were quickly "scattered in all directions." A few of them had such a narrow escape that their clothing was "cut by balls." With enemy patrols scouring the countryside all around them, many of the men found it impossible to make it back to their own lines. In some instances they took shelter deep in the woods or at the home of a sympathetic farmer. Steele pointed out that some of the militiamen remained in such peril that they were trapped "between the rebel lines for several days."[48]

Although nightfall was fast approaching, the Confederates pushed on from the top of the mountain toward McConnellsburg. Surgeon Thomas Fanning Wood from the Third North Carolina was awestruck by his first view of the town spread out on the floor of the fertile valley in the distance. He noted that it "looked like a miniature village, as though you could throw your hat over it and cover it." The doctor found other sights just as impressive. "The road was beautiful and at the top was a fine spring from which the water was carried in wooden troughs to the village at the foot of the mountains," he recalled.[49]

As the troops reached the bottom of the hill, Major Gilmor readied his cavalrymen for an immediate attack. "When within a half mile of the town, we heard that a force of infantry and cavalry were there, and I was ordered to charge in," he recounted. "It was so dark we could see nothing in our front. I rode along the flank of the column, made the men dress up their sections, and then started down the turnpike at a trot." The horsemen quickly thundered into town. "Charging through the main street, I threw out detachments to right and left in each cross street, but no Federals could be discovered," Gilmor explained. The major immediately "returned to the centre of the town, sounded the 'assembly,' and formed in line."[50]

Residents looked on in terror as the riders sped past their homes. "The cavalry dashed into town on a charge, expecting, as they alleged, to find Milroy's forces here," the local newspaper reported. "In this they were disappointed, the small force which was here during the day having moved westward about dark, after having a slight skirmish with the rebel advance on the top of the mountain." The newspaper noted that "the invaders placed the town under guard, ordered the citizens to

Water Street at McConnellsburg, Pennsylvania. Courtesy Fulton County Historical Society.

remain in their homes, and took up and placed under guard for the night several citizens who were found on the streets."[51]

The infantry battalion followed just behind the horsemen into the center of town. The extent of the fear among the citizens came as a shock for the troops. Lieutenant Tolson reported in his diary that the Marylanders "moved forward rapidly, and occupied the place, finding the people scared to death." Lt. Whitfield Kisling from the Tenth Virginia insisted that the residents "were *literally* quaking in their boots" when the rest of the brigade entered the town soon afterward. Many of the people were so frightened that they fled into the surrounding countryside.[52]

One of the first tasks for Steuart's men was to restore some relative calm among the terrified populace. "We assured those remaining that they need expect no injury and soon brought them to feel comparatively at their ease," Tolson reported. Pvt. John C. Henry from the Maryland infantry battalion observed a similar turnaround in the attitude of the residents. "We found the people of McConnellsburg much frightened at our first appearance, but afterward very clever and hospitable," he commented in his diary the following day.[53]

Other troops moved into place as sentries on nearly every street corner. Major Gilmor quickly posted his cavalry pickets "on all the roads." He also sent a courier with reports to General Steuart, who set up his camp about a mile outside of town. While Maryland infantrymen secured the streets, the cavalrymen fed their horses "upon the oats and corn" they seized there. Gilmor insisted that his troopers enforced such strict order that "not a house was allowed to be entered until the next day, when the commissary and quartermaster came and took possession." Even the local newspaper acknowledged that "nothing was disturbed during the night."

Early the following morning, General Steuart established his headquarters in town at the historic Fulton House Inn, which had opened in 1793. From there he dispatched several squads to search local businesses for supplies. According to the town's newspaper, the soldiers assigned to those details "entered the stores and took such things as they wanted, in most instances, we believe, offering to pay in Confederate money." The results certainly proved better than Steuart's men could have expected. The newspaper reported, in fact, that "all our stores and shop keepers lost heavily by them."[54]

Among the biggest losers were Thomas and John Greathead, who had more than $300 in groceries, teas and spices, salt, tobacco, and dry goods taken from their mercantile business. The troops also confiscated about $190 worth of dry goods, shoes, threads, laces, and sewing silk from W. S. Fletcher's store. Local physician and druggist S. E. Duffield suffered the loss of fifty pounds of candy and a case of surgical instruments. Henry M. Hoke, who owned the Fulton House, fared no better. Before departing, Steuart's men seized nearly $500 worth of goods, including eighty gallons of rye whiskey. They even carried off Hoke's linen tablecloths, knives and forks, and all kinds of food.[55]

The soldiers gathered up huge quantities of provisions as they foraged through the town and the neighboring farms. Lieutenant Kisling wrote home that "pots of apple butter, milk, bread, &c. were forthcoming" from the residents. He watched in disbelief as some men returned from one foray "with a spring wagon loaded with onions, buttermilk, apple butter, hams, &c and the boys are now enjoying themselves over it highly." Lieutenant Tolson noted that the people remained so frightened that they "gave our boys plenty of bread and butter and would take no pay." Another soldier wrote in his diary that the citizens would provide the men with "the last thing they have if we only spare their lives."[56]

Lieutenant Kisling sat down that night to a sumptuous feast that proved far better than what he had any reason to expect. "We are now laying by today and I have just finished one of the best of dinners," the young Virginian effused in a letter to his cousin the day after their arrival at McConnellsburg. Kisling happily reported that he "had sliced onions with vinegar peppers etc, nice fired stake, boiled eggs, hot rolls, butter, apple butter, fruit, coffee with sugar, stewed peaches, milk, peach preserves and 'lastly' as our little chaplain says—some of the nicest kind of courant wine."

Kisling (and other Confederates) also went shopping in town for scarce goods to send home to his relatives. "I have bought a dress for you and some calico for Fannie," Kisling informed his cousin. "I don't know if you fancy the dress much but I think it will look pretty well." Surgeon Casper Henkel from the Thirty-Seventh Virginia had much less success in making such purchases. "I have found it a very difficult matter to procure anything in the way of goods that is desirable," he complained to a relative. "Persons owning them are very loath to sell." The need to obtain a written pass before entering town further added to the doctor's problems in obtaining clothing or household goods for his family.[57]

The situation proved more positive for Gilmor's cavalrymen, who remained busy sweeping through the nearby farms for all kinds of livestock. The major boasted that his troopers "brought in a number of horses and cattle." The losses to the landowners in the area, however, were not limited only to their animals. One farmer complained in a postwar claim for damages that "a squad of rebel cavalry" camped on his property for three days, destroying his "entire crop" of forage grass. John B. Patterson, who lived just south of town, reported in his claim that the raiders seized forty bushels of corn, a wagon, all his riding gear, nine barrels of flour, and six head of cattle from his farm.[58]

The men from Steuart's Brigade were overwhelmed by all the loot that fell into their hands during the raids around McConnellsburg. Pvt. John Futch from the Third North Carolina boasted to his wife that "we have prest a grate menny horses & bear of[f] evry thing we want." They were particularly impressed by the huge variety of goods among the plunder. "I will tell you what we seize as we go along," Pvt. Gabriel Shank from the Tenth Virginia gloated in a letter to his sister. "Anything we want for use of the army such as horses, cattle, molasses, bread, flour, coffee, shoes, hats, &c." The only downside to their experience at McConnellsburg was a massive rainstorm that engulfed the area later that night.[59]

Not surprisingly, the townspeople displayed open hatred toward the occupying troops. Pvt. Hiram Kibler from the Tenth Virginia noted in a letter home that the women "seem to look on a reble with contempt." Surgeon Henkel griped to his cousin that "sour looks would meet our eyes, & cutting speeches would greet our ears on all occasions." The doctor was so put off by the cold reception they received there that he dismissed the residents as unworthy of any sympathy. He insisted that they "are all uncouth in their manner" and was especially struck by their lack of education. "They are mostly of little intelligence about on a par with the most common peasantry of our own country," Henkel declared.[60]

Kisling was just as disgusted by the townspeople he encountered during his stay. Like so many others, the lieutenant took out his worst frustrations on the females who lived there. "As a general thing the people are a narrow minded, ignorant, selfish German population with the *ugliest* girls I ever saw," he vented in a letter to his cousin the day after their arrival. The Virginian unconvincingly argued that his harsh comments were not a matter of mere prejudice on his part, describing them as, in fact, "the most uncouth, ungainly females I ever saw."[61]

Even the people's compliant responses to the demands to turn over their goods left some of the soldiers fuming about them. Lieutenant Tolson proudly pointed out that such conduct stood in stark contrast with that of civilians in the Confederate states. The fawning behavior of the citizens in that part of Pennsylvania symbolized for him the clear superiority of the Southern culture he was fighting so hard to preserve in this brutal war. "Their servile and politic course toward us, so different from the independent and uncompromising manner of non-combatant Southerners hits off to a nicety the different natures of the two peoples," the Maryland officer declared in his diary.[62]

McConnellsburg's ordeal finally came to an end early on June 26, when the troops departed along the turnpike to the east. While Steuart's men proceeded past Fort Loudon and St. Thomas to Chambersburg in a driving rainstorm, Gilmor's cavalrymen swarmed through the surrounding valley as far north as Burnt Cabins. According to one account, "every nook and cranny from Mercersburg to Newburg was searched, and many valuable animals were captured and taken away." In one foray around St. Thomas alone, they reportedly gathered up forty horses, sixty head of cattle, and "a few mules." The raids continued during the next couple of days as the horsemen pushed on through Fannettsburg along the main road heading east.[63]

The first hint of opposition occurred when a group of citizens threw together some makeshift barriers a couple of miles southeast of Burnt Cabins at the entrance to the upper Horse Valley. Township supervisor Stephen Keefer noted that several hundred horses "belonging to residents of the valley, as well as those taken there from other parts," were hidden there. "On the top of the mountain covering the approach to Strasburg road, breastworks of logs and bushes were erected, and about thirty of the hardy mountaineers with tried rifles stood guard there for several days," the supervisor reported.

By chance, "a detachment of about one hundred cavalry" from Gilmor's force arrived while the defenders were temporarily absent. The horsemen entered through the undefended gap and penetrated a couple of miles into the valley. Luckily for the farmers, the troopers failed to locate the main group of horses. "They then turned about and retraced their steps by the same route, taking with them but six horses from the valley," Keefer recounted. He acknowledged that "had they gone on up the valley some eight miles, two or three hundred valuable horses might have been taken."

The cavalrymen moved on from there past nearby Keefer Gap, where another group had stashed more than a hundred horses. "The farmers in the neighborhood of this gap to the number of twenty or twenty-five formed a camp at this place, erecting several tents, and laying in a stock of food and provisions for their horses," Jacob Hoke reported. Fifteen to twenty people remained on guard at all times. "This deterred the enemy from approaching the place," Hoke claimed. After skirting around that gap, Gilmor's troopers continued through the mountains into the central Cumberland Valley.[64]

On June 27 a group of horsemen from the Maryland battalion galloped into Newville, located about twenty-five miles northeast of Keefer Gap. Teenager William McCandlish wrote in his diary that "some fifty rebel cavalry entered town to-day."

Zenas J. Gray, who was nine years old at the time, described them as "a squad of tough looking rebels." One local girl complained that the intruders seized "anything a soldier could make use of, especially horses." The cavalrymen seemed largely unconcerned about any interference from the Federal militia operating in the vicinity. According to McCandlish, the Confederate commander remained so relaxed that he "stood on one of our street corners talking politics with one of our citizens until nearly midnight." Young Gray watched with relief as the loaded-down cavalrymen finally "folded their tents" and galloped out of town early the following morning on "the road leading to Carlisle," where they would link up with the main part of Ewell's corps. McCandlish noted that their haul of loot included "some 350 head of cattle" and a large number of horses. Despite their exit, the teen remained on high alert. He still observed "a few straggling Rebels scouting through town" on the morning of June 29. Another frightened resident also spotted "a few rebels prowling round" the area later that afternoon.[65]

Although the expedition to McConnellsburg took Steuart's troops outside the confines of the Cumberland Valley, the results provided some valuable lessons for the rest of the men from Ewell's corps. They would repeat the same pattern of forced confiscations from local businesses and surrounding farms time after time during their own advance to the north. The skirmish with local defense forces also confirmed that the Federal militia they might face along the way would provide little or no real opposition. These lessons removed any remaining doubts in their minds that Lee's army could successfully live off the land in enemy territory. The excursion also served as an early warning of exactly what would be in store for the frightened citizens along the Confederate route through the central valley and the counties just to the east.[66]

8

"Going Back into the Union"

As the other two divisions in Ewell's corps moved north through Maryland into southern Pennsylvania, Jubal Early's division and the two reserve artillery battalions remained stuck just outside Shepherdstown on the Virginia side of the rain-swollen Potomac River. The waters finally dropped enough for them to make it across Boteler's Ford early in the morning on June 22. According to Sgt. Francis L. Hudgins from the Thirty-Eighth Georgia in Gordon's Brigade, the troops proudly marched to the crossing "with flags fluttering and bands playing 'Maryland, My Maryland.'"[1]

To their delight, crowds of townspeople, including numerous attractive women, turned out at the ford to greet them. "The road is enlivened by many secession ladies and demonstrations," Lt. William James Kincheloe from "Extra Billy" Smith's brigade effused in his diary. He pointed out that "nearly every home had a Confederate flag waving by the hand of some lady." Sgt. William S. White from the reserve artillery noted that many of the town's "fair daughters cheered us with gladsome smiles, waving their handkerchiefs, and bidding us remember them in the coming struggle."[2]

As they stepped into the river, the men quickly discovered that the crossing was fraught with dangers. "At sunrise we waded the Potomac," Col. Clement Evans from Gordon's Brigade informed his wife. "The water was deep coming up to the waists & breasts of the men." Even the surging waters failed to slow down their mad rush to splash across the Potomac. "The [river] was very high and it was amusing to see the long lines of naked men fording it—their clothes and accountrements slung to their guns and carried above their heads to keep them dry," Capt. William J. Seymour from General Hays's staff penned in his journal. "The water was very cold and the men as they entered it would scream and shout most boisterously."[3]

After arriving safely on the Maryland shore, the soldiers immediately ascended the nearby heights and crossed through the Sharpsburg battlefield. Their proximity to the former killing grounds stirred some deep emotions among the many veterans in the long line of troops. Pvt. George F. Agee from the Twenty-Sixth Georgia in Gordon's Brigade admitted that "we were forced by our inclinations to look out on all sides and to note some of the marks left at this place by war's relentless hand." The men from the reserve artillery here split off from the column and went into camp at the town of Sharpsburg. They later would move out to join with Johnson's Division.[4]

Ewell's instructions called for Early's Division to bypass the Federal garrison around nearby Harpers Ferry rather than carry out a direct attack. "I was ordered to proceed along the western base of the South Mountain," General Early explained. "Maryland Heights and Harper's Ferry were both strongly fortified, and were occupied by a heavy force of the enemy, which we left behind us, without making any effort to dislodge it, as it would have been attended with a loss disproportionate to any good to be obtained." He pointed out that "our movements through and from Sharpsburg were in full view of the enemy from the heights."[5]

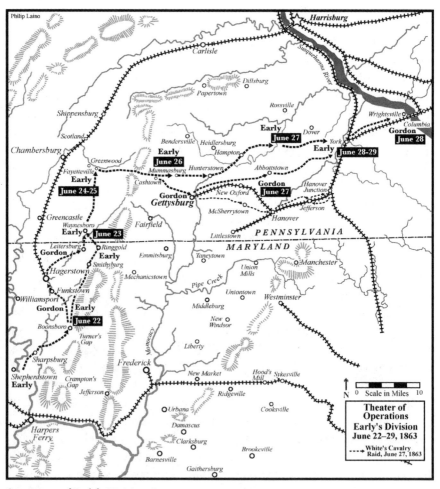

Operations of Early's Division, June 22–29, 1863

The Confederate column quickly pushed north from Sharpsburg on the macad-amized Hagerstown Turnpike. Along the way Col. William H. French's Seventeenth Virginia Cavalry, which had been detached from Jenkins's Brigade, linked up with the division. Those troopers, most of whom came from the mountains of western Virginia, had experienced their first real combat during the recent skirmishes at Bunker Hill and Martinsburg while attached to Rodes's Division. Early soon discov-ered to his dismay that this regiment remained in such a "state of inefficiency" that its usefulness remained in serious doubt.[6]

The fifty-one-year-old French was a former sheriff and state legislator from Mer-cer County, Virginia, with no military background prior to the war. Most of his men had little positive to say about the colonel's capabilities. "While his courage is undis-puted he was too kind hearted and easy going to discipline or keep order amongst his troops either in field or camp," Sgt. James Hodam admitted. He further declared that "the commonest soldier knew and showed more knowledge of military tactics than the colonel ever did." Even so, the affable leader had no problems delegating au-thority. "Luckily he knew his failings and left the command of his regiment entirely to his Lt. Colonel and other officers," Hodam explained.[7]

With French's horsemen at the front, Early's troops passed through the tiny settlement of Keedysville, the site of a large mill powered by the waters of Antietam Creek. The men finally halted for the day soon afterward about three miles north of Boonsboro, Maryland. That town, first settled by two of Daniel Boone's cousins, nestled on the western flank of rugged South Mountain astride the old National Road. By the time of the division's arrival, many of the men were almost broken down from their exhausting trek. Lt. J. Warren Jackson from Hays's Brigade com-plained that he "came near 'playing out' that day." The Louisianan admitted, "my feet were very sore and I straggled a little."[8]

As many of the troops expected, much of the area along their route was filled with Union supporters. "This section of Maryland is thoroughly Yankeeized, the women all wear the red, white and blue ribbons and look upon the rebels with con-tempt," Cpl. William Britton Bailey from the Louisiana Guard Artillery grumbled in his diary. The artilleryman had much less to say about the few military-aged men they encountered on the way, noting simply, "the male population kept in the background and make themselves scarce generally." Sgt. Osborne Wilson from the Thirty-First Virginia in Smith's Brigade complained in his diary that the people at both Sharpsburg and Keedysville "look very sour at us."[9]

Colonel Evans from Gordon's Brigade found the reception on their journey just as frigid. "The citizens of this county (Washington) are thoroughly Union & we met with not a single sign of encouragement until we reached Boonsboro," the Georgian griped in his diary. To his relief, at least some of the nine hundred residents in that town displayed clear signs of support for the Southern cause. The colonel noted that "here the feeling is better and many expressed their hearty wishes for our success against the tyranny of the Yankees." Lieutenant Kincheloe from Smith's Brigade was equally pleased to find "a good deal of demonstration in our favor" at Boonsboro. Topographer Jed Hotchkiss happily penned in his diary that he "made some purchase there at reasonable prices."[10]

The soldiers finally went into camp north of the town "in the woods" alongside the chapel for the United Brethren church at the tiny hamlet of Benevola. Prior to settling in for the night, the troops received the first official word of the commanding general's strict policy regarding their conduct while they remained in enemy territory. "Before we broke ranks General Lee's order was read forbidding us to trespass on private property under the pain of death," one of Gordon's men recalled. Despite those orders, he acknowledged that at least some of his comrades still thought "we ought to pay" the Northern citizens "back in kind" for the damages that their soldiers had inflicted in the South.[11]

Although the trip that day had been relatively easy, Cpl. Joseph H. Truitt from the Thirty-First Georgia in Gordon's Brigade could only speculate about what their next move might be. "I reckon I dont know where we are a going to or how long we will stay in these diggings," he admitted in a letter to his parents. "I think we will go to Pensilvaney before [we] stop if the yankees don't stop us and I don't think there is many of them clost to us at this time." Truitt gloated that General Lee "had got old Hookers army" so tied up that he could not intercept them. The corporal added that they also had "whipt old Milroy" and his men so badly that he did not think they "will attack us any more."[12]

Early's veterans resumed their advance north from Boonsboro just before dawn on June 23. The division commander immediately split his force into two columns. Gordon's men on the left trudged forward through a light rain along the turnpike to Hagerstown. From there they swung northeast through Leitersburg and on toward the Pennsylvania border. The main part of the right-hand column hugged the base of rugged South Mountain along a series of secondary roads that took them through the tiny villages of Beaver Creek, Cavetown, and Smithburg.

Most of the inhabitants the easternmost column encountered along the way remained staunchly pro-Union. "The nearer we get to the border the more grim the countenances of the people," Lieutenant Kincheloe from Smith's Brigade commented in his diary. Not surprisingly, many of the citizens appeared frightened for their lives at the sight of the invading army. According to the young Virginian, "the pall of death had stricken all these people and though bad enough looking by nature, fear had tortured them into the ugliest of creatures." The principal exceptions were the residents of Smithburg, where Pvt. Bartlett Yancey Malone from the Sixth North Carolina in Avery's brigade encountered "a good meney Secesh."[13]

Best of all was the sight of the tidy farms and lush field that dotted the landscape. "That part of Md through which we traveled is a very fine country for wheat, corn, clover, grass and cattle," Pvt. Samuel W. Eaton from the Fifty-Seventh North Carolina in Avery's brigade wrote in his diary. He was especially surprised that the area was so "thickly settled." The Tar Heel pointed out that "most all" of the farmers "live in neat, comfortable houses, built of brick and stone." He added that they "have beautiful farms and cultivate them well."[14]

The men from the main column reached Ringgold during late morning. Private Malone noted in his diary that this tiny cluster of houses stood "wright war the line run[s] between M.D. & Pa." Later that day the troops made their joyful entrance into Pennsylvania. "We shook the Md dust off our feet and marched into the Union to the tune of 'Dixie,'" Lieutenant Jackson from Hays's Brigade effused in a letter to this brother. "The men were quite lively & joked the cit[i]z[ens] by telling them that we had eat up the last mule and we had come over to get some beef & bacon." Some others taunted the onlookers by shouting at them that "we were going back into the union at last."[15]

Early's troops quickly diverged on nearby Waynesboro, Pennsylvania. That prosperous settlement of nearly 1,300 people stood about two miles north of the Mason-Dixon Line along the turnpike running west from Emmitsburg, Maryland, through the mountains at Monterey Gap. In 1797, John Wallace, a veteran of the Revolutionary War, laid out the town, calling it Waynesburg after Brig. Gen. "Mad" Anthony Wayne, who had been his commander during the war. The early settlers consisted mostly of Scotch-Irish and German immigrants. To avoid confusion with some other locations in Pennsylvania with that same name, in 1831 officials rechristened the town Waynesboro.[16]

The first reports of a large force of Confederates approaching sent many of the citizens from this solidly pro-Union community into a panic. John Philips, who was the cashier at the First National Bank, was among those who fled before the enemy troops arrived. The frantic bank employee hastily filled a small carriage with bags of money and other valuables stored at the bank and hurried east from Waynesboro on the turnpike, turning due north at Monterey Pass and reaching the nearby village of Fairfield. On his arrival Philips fully briefed Maj. Granville Haller and other military officials in Adams County on the harrowing developments.[17]

Soon after the cashier's departure, Colonel French's troopers rode into Waynesboro at the head of the advancing column. The bulk of Early's infantry followed closely behind them, while Gordon's Brigade trailed slightly farther back and would not arrive until later in the day. Most of the soldiers expressed outright enthusiasm at what they observed as they threaded their way through the streets. Cpl. William Henry Mayo from Hays's Louisiana brigade described Waynesboro in his diary as "a very pretty, neat and tolerably large town." Private Agee in Gordon's Brigade similarly described it as "a pretty little town," noting that so many people filled the streets that "the doors, piazzas and windows were crowded plumb full."[18]

The citizens who jammed the byways watched with mounting apprehension as the long line of Southern troops tramped into town. "On June 23, 1863, just before

Brig. Gen. John B. Gordon. Courtesy Library of Congress.

noon, we found our streets swarming with grayclad men," recalled Lida Jane Welsh, who was sixteen years old at the time. "That which we had so long anticipated with dread had happened, and the enemy was at our gates—indeed, he was within them." The immense size of the arriving column proved far beyond anything that the teenager could comprehend. "Never having seen a large body of troops, we were sure the whole invading army was passing our door, and we were surprised to learn that the larger portion had gone by way of Greencastle and Chambersburg," she admitted.[19]

The utter despair on the faces of the town's residents proved impossible to miss. Colonel Evans wrote in his diary that he found "the citizens uneasy at our approach, looking as if they scarcely knew how to conduct themselves." Lieutenant Kincheloe was even more startled by what he witnessed there. The Virginian reported that the streets were "lined with curious and frightened gazers, some crying, some shouting that they were good Democrats, some good secessionists." He insisted that the "people seemed perfectly crazy with fear."[20]

Some of the women in Waynesboro displayed such extreme terror that the soldiers took pity on them. "It was right touching to see how frightened the women were—some could be seen crying and wringing their hands," Lt. J. Arthur Taylor from the Eighth Louisiana in Hays's Brigade admitted in a letter to his father. He pointed out that "others could be seen at a distance standing in crowds looking at us, with every appearance of fear, very much in the same manner as the wild beeves of Louisiana gather round a person creeping through the grass in hunting ducks."[21]

Despite concerns about her own safety, young Lida Welsh could not help being impressed by the army's soul-stirring entrance. She noted that the soldiers "filled the town with their gay music, prancing horses, glittering musical instruments, bayonets and other bright equipment, and their banners—such beautiful banners—made by mothers, wives, sisters, and sweethearts in the South." Welsh openly pondered all "the tears and sighs, hopes and fears, stitched into their silken folds." She further noted that most of the troops in the column displayed courtesy toward the civilian population. The young woman acknowledged, in fact, that "the men all seemed cheerful."

The Southerners' friendly behavior toward the crowds of youngsters who lined the streets upon their arrival proved particularly reassuring. "They spoke kindly to the children on the porches; no doubt many of them were fathers of little ones," Welsh recalled. She was especially touched by an incident that occurred as the soldiers paraded through the town. The teenager watched with fright as "a two-year-old boy, left alone for a short time, stood on a rocking-chair and rocked with all his tiny strength until the chair moved along to the very edge of the porch." The response from the troops in the column was instantaneous. According to Welsh, "a dozen men" immediately "broke ranks and rushed to save the little fellow."[22]

Most of the other onlookers also found little to fault about the demeanor of the troops as they strutted into town. "The soldiers were well-armed, in perfect discipline and moved as one vast machine," as one resident described their entrance. "Not many stragglers were to be seen." This same witness recalled that "these southern boys" were mostly "polite and courteous." He acknowledged that "it was difficult for the citizens along the way to realize that these friendly and courteous men were their enemies." Yet the man remained much less impressed with the condition of the soldiers' uniforms, which "consisted of every imaginable color and style."[23]

Although the Confederates appeared less threatening than they had expected, many of the townspeople remained deeply concerned about what awaited them. The expressions on the citizens' faces made it abundantly clear to the arriving troops that they were far from pleased with having the enemy's army in their midst. "In Waynesboro the people are strongly 'Union' in their proclivities, and their countenances and actions did not indicate much joy at our arrival," Captain Seymour commented in his journal. Sergeant Mayo, a fellow Louisianan, insisted that the "people are all Union and seem very much dissatisfied at seeing so many rebels."[24]

At least some of the residents' worries about how they would be treated proved justified. As citizens watched in despair, a squad of soldiers secured the town hall for use as their headquarters during the occupation. Their commander quickly placed the first symbol of the invaders' authority over the town where every resident could see it with ease. As the people looked on, his soldiers pulled down a large Union flag from the front of the building and "tucked" it away; in its place a Confederate flag soon "proudly floated in the breeze."[25]

While the bulk of Early's troops went into camp a short distance from town "on a high hill, in a nice piece of woods," provost guards moved into position all over Waynesboro. "At once the town was placed under martial law," Lida Welsh recalled. She griped that "a requisition for provisions was made, and some of our returned soldiers and stay-at-homes were ordered to canvas for bread and meat, which in most cases were given very unwillingly." Additional orders called for town officials "to have all intoxicating liquors put out of reach."

The occupation proved especially trying for the young lady's father, Jacob R. Welsh, who served as the town's chief burgess. He "was promptly deposed," Lida explained, and "was told by the Provost Marshall the troops were under complete control and the residents need fear no depredations, as orders had been given that no person or private property should be molested and no houses entered." The officer further informed him, however, that the situation could change suddenly if his men came under a determined attack by Federal troops. "We may be repulsed, and if we have to retreat we may not have complete control," he cautioned. "Tell your people, in that case, for your own safety, not to taunt or offer our troops any insult."[26]

With that out of the way, Early's commissary and quartermaster details began rounding up needed supplies from local businesses and homes. The search parties largely focused on hunting for any hidden caches of footwear. "In Waynesboro we made the people hand over what boots and shoes they had," Lt. William D. Lyon, who served as the acting ordnance officer in Gordon's Brigade, reported in a letter home. The efforts to secure baldy needed shoes did not always go as well as they expected. Lyon openly complained to his brother, "we got few of them."[27]

The soldiers had much better luck gathering up a long list of other useful goods. Corporal Bailey from the Louisiana Guard Artillery reported that the search parties seized "a large quantity of Government stores." A soldier from Gordon's Brigade noted that they confiscated many "other articles that [wer]e needed for the comfort of the soldiers." One store owner reportedly lost merchandise valued at more than $3,000. Teenager Mary Clara Forney vented her frustrations by castigating the soldiers with the wild story that they "took all the clothes out of people's houses [so that] they had not a change for their children." She further noted that the rebels "took all the provisions they could gather."[28]

One squad forced its way into the building that housed the weekly *Village Record*, the town's only newspaper. In an act of apparent retaliation against the hated Northern press, the soldiers "went into the printing office, upset the type, broke up the forms and scattered things around generally." The men took special pains to pry up the type, which made "it impossible to issue the newspaper for some time afterward." The damage proved so severe that "it took two weeks to get the office and type in order." An outbreak of smallpox among the staff further pushed back publication of the next issue until July 31.[29]

While that was going on, the commissary details ordered citizens to turn over 2,000 loaves of freshly baked bread. "All over the town the women spent the day and much of the night baking bread, which was to be delivered to the Town Hall, where they made their headquarters," one resident recounted as the story she had heard. The woman noted that "the next day a huge pile of bread could be seen for a little while on the pavement, but it was soon stored in knapsacks and supply wagons and carried on by the moving soldiers." According to another account, most of the hungry soldiers did not "take the time" to cut the loaves into slices, but instead "just ate it in chunks."[30]

The provost marshal attempted to control the troops' access to alcohol by posting sentries around all the stills and warehouses in Waynesboro. "A few of the distilleries promptly complied with the instructions and stove in the barrel heads, letting the liquor run out on the grounds," one report stated. Even so, several owners attempted to salvage at least some of the alcohol for later sales. They reportedly "hid their barrels in out-of-[the-]way places and dug pits in the ground and covered them over with earth and were thus successful in saving some of it." Despite their efforts, "much of the whiskey was sought out and destroyed" by vigilant officers from the provost guards.[31]

Early also placed the local bars under tight supervision. Sergeant Hodam from French's cavalry regiment quipped that "all saloons and liquor shops were closely guarded, and the law of total abstinence was enforced in a way so complete that a modern prohibitionist might have been proud of it." Even those strict measures often failed to keep the intoxicating beverages out of the hands of the soldiers, especially the dreaded "Louisiana Tigers" of Hays's Brigade. Although drinking was strictly banned, Captain Seymour admitted that some of the Louisiana troops "got quantities of liquor here and I had great trouble keeping them in ranks."[32]

The quartermaster and commissary details conducting the seizures under the authority of General Lee's recent orders by most accounts acted "very carefully to give receipts for all horses, cattle and other property confiscated." They further informed the people that "if they won the war, their government would pay the bills and redeem the currency in gold, but if they lost the war the Federal government would be obliged to make settlement." But that mattered little to the rightful owners who lost their valuable goods without any immediate compensation. As most of them expected, the promises of future settlements would never come true.[33]

Despite the strict regulations, most of the men spent their time foraging through nearby homes and farms for additional food. "We camped near the town, and some of the boys were soon in the country in search of something to eat, in which they were very successful," Lieutenant Taylor from Hays's Brigade remarked in a letter home. He noted that "the people were so frightened they told the boys they might have everything they had, if they would only not destroy their property." Taylor attributed their fears to rumors spread by Northern officials. "It seems they were told by the authorities of the state that if we ever came over there that we would burn everything we could lay our hands on," he explained. In reality, the civilians' fright was the natural reaction to being confronted in their homes by armed enemy soldiers.[34]

Many senior officers went shopping for scarce goods to send home to their wives and families. "I have bought you twenty-four yards of red-check Gingham at 25cts. per yard," Colonel Evans reported to his wife. "If I could have been allowed to leave my regiment I would have been able to supply you with all you needed for yourself & children." General Gordon had less luck obtaining items for his loved ones. "I have made every effort to get you some goods," he informed his wife on the day of his brigade's arrival. "Intended to send back a box of articles for you but could get nothing you need." In the end he only provided his wife with one pair of shoes, which he feared were "too large" for her.[35]

For most of the men, the bounty available at Waynesboro proved to be all that they could have desired. "Some of the company went out foraging and got apple butter, lightbread, chickens, milk &c, &c," Lieutenant Jackson from Hays's Brigade effused in a letter to his brother. "The people were afraid of us and gave the men everything they asked for." Corporal Truitt from Gordon's Brigade reported home that the soldiers confiscated "all the sugar, coffee, and whiskey and shoes that was in the towns" along their route. The foragers also grabbed up any farm animals that came within their reach. According to one frustrated resident, the Confederates proved so thorough in seizing livestock that "a chicken or a pig running at large was not safe during this invasion."[36]

Some of the Southerners' favorite targets were the many hens and roosters that roamed freely through parts of town. Lida Welsh noted that one "long-necked Shanghai rooster that almost lived on the street fearlessly threaded his way through their feet, and occasionally a man would take him and carry him a few yards until a watchful officer ordered his release." The officers in charge remained so vigilant that the lucky bird survived every attempt to take him away. Welsh noted that "the rooster paraded long after the last gun of the Confederacy was silenced."[37]

The presence of Hays's Louisianans, who were renowned for their rowdy behavior, caused the biggest stir among the town's inhabitants. Most of the men from that brigade found the people's reactions so extreme as to be ludicrous. "One of the 7th La (a nice young man, not a raw) went into a house near camp and asked the lady of the house for some milk and bread," Lieutenant Jackson recounted in a letter home. "She told him to take a seat & she would go get the articles." The woman offhandedly inquired about which regiment the man served in. When the soldier replied that he came from the Seventh Louisiana, she fainted on the spot. The startled visitor quickly "went to work trying to revive the lady." At that moment her husband rushed into the room and inquired as to what had occurred. The soldier informed him that she had collapsed "very unexpectedly," and he had no idea why it had happened. Her husband immediately demanded to know what the soldier had said to her. The "Tiger" blurted out that he only told her that he belonged to the Seventh Louisiana, to which the homeowner replied that that fully "explained the matter." The man "then told him that the cavalry, when they passed thro, told everybody that the La. Tigers would kill, burn & destroy everything & everybody in the country and it was some time before Mr. 7th could convince the lady that he was not a cut throat &c."[38]

A much more disturbing incident occurred on the front steps of the National Hotel in the middle of town soon after the Southerners' arrival. As the troops passed nearby, several officers accosted prominent farmer Josiah S. Kurtz and demanded that he provide them with the names and addresses of the town's most well-heeled citizens. The man steadfastly refused to comply. One of his interrogators became so enraged that he pulled out his saber and continued to question him under the threat of bodily harm. The officer finally snapped and slashed the unarmed man across the hand, leaving a deep gash. Kurtz was so shaken by the attack that he fled Waynesboro and hid with some of his relatives until the occupiers departed.

The problems were not limited to this single violation of Lee's orders. Several soldiers reportedly waylaid two unsuspecting citizens along the street and shoved them into a nearby alleyway. The offenders immediately robbed the terrified men of their belongings and then "stripped them of all their clothes," picking through the pile of garments and shoes and taking whatever pleased them. After leaving behind "a few lousy rags" for the victims to "cover their nakedness," the perpetrators ran off as quickly as they had appeared. The townspeople reportedly only submitted "to these incivilities because the soldiers carried guns which were instruments of great persuasion."[39]

In another instance some drunken soldiers attempted to break into the back door at one of the homes in town. A group of women trapped inside became so terrified by the ordeal that they could do little more than cower behind the partially closed shutters and call out in desperation for help. To their surprise, one of the few Southern sympathizers in Waynesboro came to their assistance. Their rescuer, a prominent local doctor, immediately summoned a Confederate officer to the scene of the disturbance and urged him to place a sentry around the residence. The officer ordered a guard to take up position and assured the ladies that they would not be disturbed again.[40]

One man from Gordon's Brigade nevertheless insisted that misconduct by the troops remained far from common. "So far our men have behaved themselves, taking nothing without paying for it," the soldier remarked in a letter to his hometown newspaper during this time. He acknowledged that one exception occurred when "some men broke into a woman's cellar and took some of her provisions." In that case punishment from the top commanders in the division proved remarkably swift. The Georgian pointed out that a complaint "was made," and the men were "promptly put under arrest."[41]

Despite such breaches of the peace, some local women showed little hesitation about meeting the invaders in person. "In the evening crowds of ladies visited our camp to see the rebels," Corporal Bailey noted with astonishment. The soldiers responded by providing them with a friendly welcome. "They were treated with the greatest respect and had all the attention possible paid to them," the artilleryman penned in his diary. "I learned from them that they had never seen a cannon, and it was the first time that they had ever seen a large body of troops." It turned out to be a pleasant experience for everyone involved. Bailey insisted that the ladies "were pleased with the attention paid them by the rebs."[42]

The stay proved much less enjoyable for a Quaker conscript from the Twenty-First North Carolina in Avery's brigade, who was forced to serve in the army despite being a conscientious objector. "This evening I was before Colonel Kirkland," he recounted during his time at Waynesboro. "He asked me what I wanted. I told him that I desired a discharge or release from the army that I might go home." The colonel brusquely informed him that the soldier "might take a gun and go into the ranks, or he would order me shot that evening or the next morning, and I might take my choice." Even under that threat the man refused to give in. This long-running dispute remained unresolved when the brigade marched out of town the following day.[43]

While that was going on, most of the Southerners settled in for a much-need rest. Some of the troops took the time to celebrate their success thus far by attending religious services at one of their camps on South Church Street in "the yard of the Union Church." Their fervent thanks for all they had accomplished in the campaign soon became audible to nearly everyone in town. "The first night after the invasion of our town a large number encamped in a field at the end of our street," Lida Welsh recalled. The youngster noted that "we heard hundreds of men's voices join in singing familiar old hymns, and persons living nearer the camp told of hearing the chaplains' voices in prayer."[44]

As they waited for the order to resume the advance, speculation spread among the troops about what their next move might be. "I do not know where we are going," Colonel Evans admitted in a letter to his wife on the day of their arrival. "Ewell's corps can sweep like a hurricane over Pennsylvania, if he will just say the word. I hope we will go to Harrisburg, the capital." Like so many others in the army, the Georgian expected little or no serious opposition from the enemy if they made such a move. He strongly argued that the city could "be taken easily, for there is but little defence except Militia & very few volunteer regiments." Only upcoming developments would determine whether the top generals in the Army of Northern Virginia shared that assessment.[45]

9

"These People Certainly Must Have Lived like Lords"

While Early's men occupied Waynesboro, Rodes's well-rested troops continued north from Greencastle deeper into Pennsylvania. The main part of Johnson's Division followed closely behind the column through the heart of the renowned Cumberland Valley, which had long served as the major breadbasket for Pennsylvania. After more than two years of increasingly bitter fighting, this vast stretch of lush farmlands and thriving villages still remained largely untouched by the ravages of war. With Ewell's troops now on the move at the front of Lee's invading army, all that was suddenly about to change.

Most of the soldiers in Rodes's Division came away stunned by the prosperity of the countryside along their route. "Since we entered the valley of the Shenandoah in Va. up to the present time, we have passed through the most magnificent country I have ever seen," Col. Francis Parker from Ramseur's Brigade told his wife. "It is all a lime stone soil; such fields of wheat and clover, I have never looked at, and such cattle too." He insisted that "these people certainly must have lived like lords, before the war." According to Lt. Col. David R. E. Winn from the Fourth Georgia in Doles's Brigade, the citizens were "supplied with every comfort & convenience of life."[1]

The men from the Deep South soon discovered that this part of Pennsylvania was unlike anything they were used to seeing back home, which only reinforced their certainty that the North was truly foreign territory. "This country is very different from Ga both in climate and customs of the people," Pvt. Lucius Lovelace from Doles's Brigade commented in a letter to his father. "This is only suited for grain and pasturing while our state produces cotton, rice and various other commodities that will not grow here." The young soldier noted that most of the people in Pennsylvania had only "a small tract of land, while in Ga the farmers own their hundreds and thousands of acres."[2]

The troops in Johnson's Division were just as impressed by what they found in the valley. Everywhere he looked, Lt. Henry H. Harris from the division's engineering unit spotted "fine crops of wheat, rye, and barley and of clover and timothy hay." Capt. Henry H. Roach from the Twenty-First Virginia in Jones's Brigade described it as "the most beautiful and productive country I ever saw." Lt. William A. Smith from the Fiftieth Virginia in the same brigade told his fiancée that "the people have everything that heart can wish." According to Sgt. John Garibaldi from the Stonewall Brigade, the inhabitants in the Cumberland Valley were "living like princes almost."[3]

General Lee had anticipated the high potential for plundering in such a land of plenty and crafted explicit orders governing the conduct of his soldiers while they remained in enemy territory. The directives allowed little room for interpretation. "No private property shall be injured or destroyed by any person belonging to or connected with the army, or taken, excepting by the officers hereinafter designated," the orders stated. He further emphasized in his General Orders No. 72 that all the rules were to be "strictly observed, and any violations of them promptly and vigorously punished."[4]

Those regulations played an essential part in supporting Lee's aims for the invasion. They provided the army commander with the opportunity to take the moral high ground by highlighting the reasonable conduct of his men with what many regarded as the unconscionable behavior of Union commanders such as Robert Milroy and Benjamin Butler toward the helpless civilians in the Southern states. Such directives also allowed his army to gather huge quantities of badly needed supplies while providing political cover for the peace faction in the North. With those orders in place, Lee could reasonably argue that the invasion was not about retribution for the supposed excesses of the Federal troops in the South but instead represented a justifiable military attempt by the Confederacy to gain its independence.

Although Lee's morality and Christian beliefs certainly played a role in shaping his policy, his instructions had just as much to do with maintaining order in the ranks. The general certainly wanted no repeat of the widespread straggling and desertions that had crippled his army during the earlier Maryland Campaign. To achieve his goals, Lee needed a disciplined and well-fed fighting force at the maximum possible strength. None of that mattered to the civilians in the path of his army, however, who endured repeated seizures of their property with nothing to show for it other than worthless Confederate money or scrip.[5]

Ewell immediately had the regulations read to his troops and promised swift retribution against anyone who violated them. "General Lee has issued orders prohibiting all misconduct or lawlessness, and urging the utmost forbearance and kindness to all," Lt. Robert Park from O'Neal's Brigade commented in his journal. "His address and admonition is in contrast with the conduct of the Northern Generals, who have invaded the South with their soldiers. But it is in accord with true civilization." He argued that the South "cannot afford to make war upon women and children and defenseless men."[6]

The reality was often much different than what the commanding general had intended. Although foraging was strictly banned under the orders, soldiers throughout Rodes's and Johnson's Divisions were soon busy prowling the farms and homes near their campsites for any usable supplies. Cpl. John A. Stikeleather from the Fourth North Carolina in Ramseur's Brigade admitted that "light bread, apple-butter, buttermilk, and such like, were under heavy contribution by the boys in gray." Pvt. Jeremiah Tate, who served in O'Neal's Brigade, informed his mother that it was impossible to keep the troops "from getting what ever they want, especially when every thing is so plentiful as it is hear."[7]

At the same time, the troops generally stayed within the spirit, if not the letter, of Lee's order. Maj. Eugene Blackford informed his mother that, except for the theft of a few chickens, the men "behaved with much more propriety than I have ever observed in Virginia." Capt. John Gorman insisted that "nothing is wantonly destroyed, no private seizures are allowed, and nothing taken without due orders and authority." What none of them thought of mentioning was that the moral principles embodied in those rules clearly did not extend to the African Americans who were brutally rounded up and sent into bondage in the South.[8]

Other soldiers proved much more forthcoming about how the men in the field actually interpreted the rules regarding civilians. Pvt. Sidney Richardson from Doles's Brigade told his parents that "if they refuse to take our money we generally press things such as we need." Lt. Thomas Hightower from the same brigade conceded in a letter to his wife that "some give us what we want, while we take from others what we want." In Iverson's Brigade Capt. Oliver Mercer from the Twentieth North Carolina admitted to his brother that "some take our money very readily while others are forced to do it."[9]

Johnson's men displayed a similar disregard for the finer points of the regulations. Lt. Fleming Saunders, who served as the assistant quartermaster with the Forty-Second Virginia in Jones's Brigade, complained to his mother that the people "will not take our money for any thing, and our men are very much disposed to take whatever they want." Sgt. Daniel Sheetz from the Second Virginia in the Stonewall Brigade acknowledged that the soldiers often "took more than they ought to have any use for." Another officer from the same brigade summed up the prevailing attitude among the troops: "whilst you need not fear that I will be guilty of such conduct as the Yanks were whilst in Va, I do not think I will be as particular as I was in Va."[10]

The scattered groups of stragglers and deserters who followed in the wake the main columns were responsible for many of the worst violations. "I knew that the order was not respected by a good many of unworthy, straggling, thieving soldiers," Lt. John L. Hubbard from the Second Maryland Infantry Battalion in Steuart's Brigade fumed in a letter to his uncle. "But it was not the wish of our officers for citizens to be treated this way." He admitted that "it is hard for [us] to watch such men or to catch them as they are always away from their companies." The Marylander expressed hope that "the citizens will not be down on the whole southern army because of a few thieving soldiers."[11]

Despite those problems, only a few cases of outright violence against citizens and their property occurred during their stay in Pennsylvania. Other than the murder of one farmer by several drunken stragglers from Jenkins's Brigade, the exceptions to Lee's policies usually involved some extenuating circumstances. "Not a house was burned and I knew of but two that were plundered, one of these by orders on account of the owner's firing upon our men," Lt. Joseph B. Oliver from the Twentieth North Carolina recalled. He noted that "the other [dwelling] was deserted and plundered by stragglers, who were caught and severely punished."[12]

While Ewell's soldiers generally showed restraint, a recent incident in Georgia had left many of them seething with anger over the conduct of Federal troops in the South. On June 10, Federal gunboats and steamers landed a force of several hundred troops along the coast south of Savannah. The following day a group of about three hundred freed slaves under the command of Col. James Montgomery, a prominent abolitionist from Kansas, indiscriminately burned the town of Darien and plundered the property of the civilian population. Despite protests from their commander, Montgomery also forced regular black troops from the Fifty-Fourth Massachusetts to participate in the looting.[13]

Resentment over this outrage ran so deep that many soldiers reacted to General Lee's ban on retaliation in the North with mixed emotions. "When I see how frightened & polite the citizens are, I almost think we ought not to pester anything they have," Capt. Asbury Hull Jackson, who served as the assistant commissary for the Forty-Fourth Georgia in Doles's Brigade, declared in a letter home. He admitted, however, that "when I think of them giving so much aid & support & sending troops on our soil to invade us, committing all kind of depredations & fighting & killing our best men for our subjugation, I feel like killing everyone of them (the men)."[14]

Lt. Col. Thomas H. Carter, who commanded the artillery battalion assigned to Rodes's Division, found Lee's orders just as difficult to accept. "I know this humane & magnanimous course is right & that we shall be rewarded in some way but it is hard to practice when one recollects the barren & devastated waste between the Potomac & the Rappahannock & all the privations our grand old state has undergone," the Virginian explained to his wife. Carter was especially upset that the people in Pennsylvania showed no signs of suffering from the conflict. "They know nothing of war," he declared. "I never saw greater evidence of thrift & prosperity—everything from a house to a hogpen untouched & looking like the smiling day of peace."[15]

Lt. James Garland Pollard from the Ordnance Department in Rodes's Division had a much different reaction to Lee's directives banning retribution against the civilian population. The young officer admitted to his brother that he was initially "glad to make them feel some of the evils which they endeavor to impose on us." His attitude quickly softened when he "heard the orders of Genl. Lee read to the troops calling upon them to desist from any acts of retaliation on their property." What struck the deepest chord with him was the commander's appeal to his sense of honor, which was so much a part of the Southern mindset. Pollard reported, in fact, that he "was proud and at the same time thankful that we had such a general."[16]

The need to maintain discipline in the army remained the overriding issue for many of the officers in the two divisions. "I am happy to say that our men neither desire or are permitted to make robbers & outlaws of themselves," Lieutenant Colonel Winn commented to his wife. "They neither burn, pillage, or in any way injure property or persons. Such conduct permitted to [an] army of men burning to revenge most cruel & brutal wrongs would utterly demoralize & make it unmanageable." Despite those worries, he held out hope "that the people will yet be made to feel some of the horrors of war such as our people have been subjected to."[17]

Surgeon Abram Schultz Miller from Jones's Brigade expressed similar concerns in a letter to his wife. "If our orders were not so strict the whole country would be plundered and ransacked," he argued. "Our men would not have any mercy on them. But for [the] good of our army it is best to keep them in place. It does an army a great deal of injury to let them get to plundering." The doctor asserted, "it demoralizes them more than a defeat." He ascribed most of the problems in the Union army on their officers' failure to control the troops. "They let their men plunder our country and when they came on the field of battle they could not stand our men who had not been in the habit of plundering," Miller argued.[18]

Others insisted that an aggressive campaign of retaliation represented the only chance for decisively changing the attitudes of the citizens in the North and bringing about an end to the conflict. "They seem to be very unconcerned about the war, very seldom they see a soldier, and they hardly know what war is," Sergeant Garibaldi griped in a letter to his wife. He declared "that if the war was to be carried on there as long as it was carried on in Virginia they would learn the effects of it, and perhaps would soon be willing to make peace like we are."[19]

One soldier from the Corps Artillery Reserve was pleased with the chance to inflict at least some hardships on the citizens in the North. "While individual marauding and plundering are prohibited by the severest penalties and the strictest orders, you see that in a systematic and orderly fashion we are making the enemies support our army," Sgt. William Beverly Pettit from the Fluvanna Artillery wrote to his wife. "They are now feeling some burdens and pains and penalties of the war, which they have been so long inflicting on us." He hoped that "it may help restore them to a proper sense of their duties toward us."[20]

While generally holding to Lee's directives, a soldier from the Stonewall Brigade made no secret of his frustrations with the rules against forced seizures. "Our government is pursuing a very lady like policy here," Sgt. Watkins Kearns protested in his diary. He boldly complained that the commanders "are strenuous about the preservation of property &c just as though those scoundrels had not been the aider & abettor of all the pillage and rapine that has made Virginia a desert wherever they have been & rendered homeless thousands of helpless women and children."[21]

At the same time, even those men who disagreed with the policy seemed mostly willing to follow the rules set out by General Lee. "I feel sometimes, when I think how our country has been desolated, that the '*lex talionis*' should be applied," Captain Gorman explained in a letter to a Raleigh newspaper. "But in the language of our soldiery, 'Our Generals know best.'" The Tar Heel captain admitted in another letter home that he "was unchristian enough to think we treated these people too tamely while their sons were burning and despoiling the fairest portion of our own loved State."[22]

Major Blackford, who originally came from Virginia, told his mother that he also had "seen too much misery entailed upon my own dear old state by these miscreants, not to wish for a more vigourous policy." He conceded, however, that "outwardly I am forced to appear to acquiesce." Maj. Campbell Brown, Ewell's stepson and assistant adjutant general on the general's staff, found the strict rules just as troubling. He argued most of all that the restriction against forcing Confederate money on private residents was "a leniency which I think utterly thrown away upon people who behave as these have done, or at least as their troops have done."[23]

Although forced confiscations became commonplace, the top commanders consistently minimized the extent of the problem. General Rodes boasted that "the conduct of the troops of this division was entirely in accordance with those orders and challenged the admiration of their commanding officers, while it astonished the people along the line of march." He insisted that only "a few instances of forced purchases were reported but never established." On the surface at least, Ewell remained equally pleased with the actions of the men from Rodes's and Johnson's Divisions. He reported to his niece that "it is wonderful how well our hungry, foot sore, ragged men behave in this land of plenty, better than at home."[24]

Chaplain James Sheeran from Williams's brigade also found little to fault with their behavior during the advance. The Roman Catholic priest was especially heartened that the men refrained from any outright plundering or violence toward civilians. He dismissed any other violations as nothing more than minor slipups. "It was remarkable to see how orderly our men conducted themselves on this march," Sheeran wrote in his journal. "It is true many of them helped themselves to poultry, vegetable, milk, etc, but I saw no wanton destruction of private property." Most gratifying was how much their conduct contrasted with that of Federal troops in the South. "This I think rebounds more to the honor of our army than a dozen victories on the battlefield," he proclaimed.[25]

Maj. Sandie Pendleton from Ewell's staff insisted that the soldiers' strict adherence to Lee's policy resulted directly from "Southern chivalry" and the effects of rigid discipline in the army. "They move with thorough decorum through a country they would so gladly ravage," he wrote to his fiancée. "I came today 18 miles along the road traveled yesterday by Rodes' Divn. and the only sign of the passage of an army was that on one cherry tree the limbs were broken. This is literally true! And I am thankful for it." In another letter to his mother, the veteran staffer acknowledged that it was "rather a pleasant feeling to know that you have a country at your mercy & are magnanimous."[26]

While forced seizures were banned, Lee's orders allowed supply officers to procure necessary goods from local governments, businesses, and even individuals. At every town along the way, they requisitioned essential items ranging from hats and shoes to grain and flour. In many cases they also demanded luxury goods such as vinegar, coffee, dried fruit, and sugar. The supplies taken under this authority would be paid for at "the market price." Officers furnished receipts for all transactions and forwarded duplicates to the army department carrying out the requisition. Any person found "removing or concealing property" was liable to have all his good seized.[27]

Unlike the infantry, many of Jenkins's cavalrymen openly flaunted the regulations set forth in Lee's orders. Sgt. William S. White from the artillery reserve described the rough-hewn mountaineers in his diary as "a set of free-booting, hard-riding, hard-fighting fellows." At one point their violations of the rules became so flagrant that General Walker, commander of the Stonewall Brigade, finally took some decisive action. Sergeant Kearns noted that the general "arrested some cavalry who were engaged in plundering & behaving very badly & we have them now with the Brigade under guard."[28]

But such efforts did little to keep the ill-disciplined horsemen from relentlessly searching the countryside in every direction for all kinds of livestock. The troopers proved so adept at what amounted to outright thievery that many in the army were left shaking their heads in utter disbelief. Major Blackford from O'Neal's Brigade gloated to his mother that "thousands of horses & cattle, sheep, hogs, &c have been driven towards Va. besides the immense number needed to supply our own Army." Private Tate, another of O'Neal's men, insisted in a letter home that "the horses and beef cattle that we have captured since we have bin hear is beyond numbering."[29]

The quartermaster and commissary details secured most of the supplies by paying frightened merchants and farmers with nearly valueless Confederate money and scrip. "During our march through Maryland and Pennsylvania, a regular system of impressment at market prices was organized and executed by authorized agents only," a Tar Heel soldier explained in a letter to his hometown newspaper. "Wagons, horses, hats, shoes, clothing, saltpetre, stationery, &c, were thus seized and sent to the rear, except such as were needed for our immediate use." He pointed out that "subsistence was secured in the same way."[30]

Those in the path of the invasion who lost property with no meaningful compensation took little comfort from the legal niceties in the regulations. For them Ewell's soldiers were like a plague of hungry locusts that they had no way to stop. The seizures pushed some of the hardest-hit businessmen to the brink of financial ruin.

The situation proved just as dire for those farmers who had their draft horses taken away. With the animals gone, they faced the devastating prospect of having no way to bring in their crops during the upcoming harvest season. Although many of them responded to the danger by sending their horses to safety in the surrounding mountains, there remained little they could do protect their stores of grain and valuable farm equipment.

Most of the people also feared for their personal safety. After nearly two years of brutal warfare, they viewed the enemy troops with a mixture of hatred and dread. The drumbeat of anti-Southern stories in some of the more partisan Northern newspapers further fueled their worries. Such concerns ran so deep that terrified citizens often handed over their goods without asking for any kind of payment. Not even Lee's orders could convince them that the soldiers intended to do anything other than indiscriminately plunder the countryside. They instead counted it lucky if they came out the encounters without having all their property stolen and their homes and businesses burned.[31]

Although some farmers went to amazing lengths to keep their most prized possessions from falling into Confederate hands, soldiers assigned to securing the goods proved remarkably adept at ferreting out their hiding places. Many of those so detailed were farm boys themselves and knew full well the best places to secret livestock. One of the men from the Forty-Third North Carolina in Daniel's Brigade noted that they even discovered "a beautiful bay pony in the parlor, enjoying himself among the mirrors, cushioned chairs, sofas and near an elegant piano, while he tramped the fine brussels carpet with conscious pride of his exalted position."[32]

The quantity of supplies confiscated under this system far exceeded even the most optimistic expectations. Capt. James Beck, who served in Doles's Brigade, reported home that the army obtained "a large number of horses, cows, sheep, wagons, harness, saddles, bridles, boots, shoes, hats, &c., &c.; and when I say a 'large number' I mean it." Rodes noted that "some 2,000 or 3,000 head of cattle were taken, and either appropriated for the command or sent to the rear for other divisions." Ewell counted more than 5,000 barrels of flour that his troops secured during the advance. As part of his overall plan, Lee intended to transfer much of that hoard back to Virginia as a stockpile to sustain the army on its return.[33]

An officer on Johnson's staff placed the amount of spoils much higher. "The Quartermasters were occupied daily in gathering supplies and sending them to the rear, likewise with the medical and commissary departments," Capt. Oscar Hinrichs wrote in his journal. "I estimate the whole number of horses and cattle sent to Virginia and appropriated to our use while in the state at 4,000 and 20,000 respectively." He pointed out that "coffee, sugar, tea and other things of the kind" were also "gathered up and either disposed of on the spot or sent to the rear, most of which reached its destination safely."[34]

The men remained well aware of the devastating consequences that all of those seizures had on the populace and were mostly pleased by it. "We have given the people of Pennsylvania to understand that war is in the land, by capturing thousands of their cattle and horses," Lt. Medicus M. Ward from the Twelfth North Carolina in Iverson's Brigade boasted to his parents. Those sentiments were even stronger among Jenkins's cavalrymen. One of them openly bragged to his wife that "the dutch never knew any-thing of the war until we invaded them and fought all round them and stoled their horses and cattle."[35]

The only major disappointment was the poor quality of the horses they confiscated from local farmers. An officer from the Sixteenth Virginia Cavalry in Jenkins's Brigade complained that those animals of the Norman-Percheron breed were "almost useless for cavalry purposes." They proved no better for hauling artillery or the heavily laden wagons from the corps supply and ordnance trains. Pvt. W. P. Snakenberg, who served with the Fourteenth Louisiana in Williams's brigade, admitted that "what animals we bought and used in our wagon train soon gave out and soon got to be no account for wagon use." Musician "Nat" Raymer from Ramseur's Brigade insisted that the beasts were "too fat and clumsy for any use, but are peculiarly adapted to the farm."[36]

That problem mattered little to most of the troops. Almost to a man they described the rich bounty offered up from the rolling farms and prosperous hamlets of lower Pennsylvania as nearly beyond belief. "Never did men fare more sumptuously," an officer from the Second Louisiana in Williams's brigade remarked in a letter home. "The people of Penn—gave apple butter, rich yellow butter, chickens, ducks, and vegetables in abundance." Another soldier effused that "for a little Confederate note, and often for nothing, a soldier could get quantities of onions, apple butter, *cow* butter, ham, good Dutch loaves, cheese, and every delightful thing in the grand category of the production of the Great Cumberland Valley."[37]

For many in the two divisions, the best part of their stay was the ready availability of whiskey and other types of alcohol. Despite the best efforts of their commanders, drinking among the troops remained a nagging problem throughout the advance. "I've never seen so much liquor in a country as we struck there in Pennsylvania," one of Ramseur's men admitted. He found it just as easy to obtain all the ingredients needed to make whatever mixed drinks they wanted, including one particular Southern favorite. "There was more mint than I ever saw anywhere in my life; sugar, too, by the barrel, and ice packed away in the ice houses," the soldier effused. "Mint-juleps in tin cans were plentiful."[38]

At one point a group of soldiers from their brigade stumbled onto several barrels of whiskey hidden in some woods alongside the road. One of them remembered that the discovery of this cache came on the same night that their chaplain had scheduled a prayer service. What happened next was a scene that few in attendance would ever forget. "Apparently some men are more susceptible to good influences when under the influence of 'John and his corn,' as they had to crawl to the prayer service," he quipped years later. "It was ludicrous and to some, an amusing sight, to see with what eagerness they sought places in the congregation, crawling one over the other!"[39]

In addition to all kinds of food and drink, the solders secured a vast array of other goods for themselves and their families at home. Major Brown from Ewell's staff noted that "all these little Dutch Yankee towns are full of things we require, and we have clothing, shoes, provisions, letter paper even, in great quantities—less clothing and shoes in proportion, however, than anything else." Sgt. Joseph J. Felder of the Fourth Georgia insisted to his father that "there is but one thing liking, and that is tobacco, which is impossible to get in this state or Maraland."[40]

Capt. Seaton Gales, who served as assistant adjutant general on Ramseur's staff, found the shopping in Pennsylvania much less satisfying. Despite his best efforts, he only managed to send home three pairs of children's shoes and two pairs for his wife. The staffer placed most of the blame for his lack of success in procuring goods for the family on the strict orders issued by the commanding general. He especially complained to his wife that "Gen. Lee is so fastidious about the rights of the people, that it is next to impossible to get anything."[41]

Still, those restrictions did little to prevent the men from individually gathering up goods of all kinds from the surrounding countryside. "Of course we have had a splendid time, living on the fat of the land, having all the excitement, and all the fun, very much to the discomfiture of other Rebels behind, who follow on, only to find that we have stripped all the hen roosts and eaten all the butter for miles around," Major Blackford declared in a letter to his father. He noted that "it is all paid for however, the orders being very strict against taking anything against the will of the owners."[42]

The enthusiasm of the soldiers at the front of the advance stood in marked contrast with the increasingly gloomy mood among the area's residents as Ewell's command pushed deeper into Pennsylvania. "The people up here to hear them talk are all apprehensive," Sgt. George Wills from Daniel's Brigade informed his sister. "They are afraid we will imitate their soldiers and destroy all their property and for that many are profusely submissive." Lt. John F. Christian from the Fifth Alabama in O'Neal's Brigade described them in a letter home as "the worst scared people" he ever saw.[43]

At some locations the residents even lined the roadways handing out refreshments to the Southern troops. "The citizens here are so badly frightened that they stand at their gates, as we pass along the road, with large pails & tubs of water—men & women—and give to the soldiers as they pass along," as Lt. John Gay from Doles's Brigade described the scene. "They even excell our own Southern ladies in waiting upon the soldiers. Anything they have, if you ask for it, you can get. Confederate money is perfectly good with many of them." He admitted that "all this though is done to obtain favor and prevent us from destroying their property."[44]

Concerns about their own safety reached such an extent that many residents refused to answer the door when soldiers approached their houses. All that failed to deter the Southerners from their constant foraging. "Tom Tiotter and myself went out to buy something to eat, but when we came to a house, they would close their doors in our faces, or let us knock and not open," Pvt. Louis Leon from Daniel's

Brigade wrote in his diary. "We got the ear of one or two ladies, and after proving to them that we were not wild animals or thieves, they gave us what we wanted, but would not take pay for anything."[45]

Major Blackford found the response of local women to his simple requests for food so extreme as to be laughable. "In many places where we would go up to a house asking civily for butter, eggs, &c, the woman of the house would rush out screaming, begging us to take every thing but not to murder the children," the major joked in a letter to his mother. "Think of a great Dutch woman, large enough to whip me in a moment, begging your son not to murder the child she has at her breast and actually in her gratitude refusing to take any compensation for butter and eggs."[46]

Despite the signs of prosperity all around them, most of the invading Southerners had nothing positive to say about the people living there. Asst. Surgeon Abner E. McGarity from the Forty-Fourth Georgia certainly held little back in his outlandish description of the women he spotted along their route through the Cumberland Valley. "They are not only ignorant, but the ugliest people I ever saw," the doctor ranted in a letter to his wife. "I can safely say that I did not see a real pretty woman in Pa." A horseman from Jenkins's Brigade put it more colorfully when he reported to his sister that the girls he met were "as ugly as a stone fence."[47]

The Southerners were especially offended by the crude language that some of the careworn wives and daughters of the mostly German farmers used in confronting the troops. Sergeant White from the artillery reserve insisted that "most of the women we have met are about on a par with our mulatto house servants in the South, and are certainly less choice in their language." According to Lieutenant Hightower, the females were in "no way backward in saying curse words to our boys when they go to their houses." Another officer from Doles's Brigade claimed in a letter home that "swearing among the ladies was a very common practice in that country."[48]

The men attributed such behavior to a lifestyle in the North that emphasized wealth over education and social refinement. "Though I might say volumes in praise of the country, I have no word of commendation for those who inhabit it," Lt. Col. William Gaston Lewis from Daniel's Brigade told his fiancée. "They are a coarse, uncultivated set, & bent entirely on making money." Private Pickens wrote in his diary that he had "not seen any nice, refined people since we have been in the State." According to Lt. William Calder, a single overnight stay in the home of a typical "Dutch" family left him "more than ever devoted to our own Southern institutions & customs."[49]

Some of the Confederates' harshest words referred to the German populace in the rural areas along their route. With more than 10 percent of the Union army made up of German immigrants, the Southerners harbored deep contempt for their civilian fellow countrymen. Typical of their outbursts were those from Assistant Surgeon McGarity. "The people are all Dutch and they are certainly the most ignorant people I ever saw," the doctor vented in a letter home. "They know nothing but how to build fine barns. They know but little about the war or anything else." He argued that "our negroes, take them in mass, are far their superiors, in point of general information."[50]

The comments from Lieutenant Colonel Carter, who was General Lee's cousin, were no better. "The people are a miserable, unintellectual unrefined set & I have not seen a single gen[tle]man or lady since our army crossed the border," the artilleryman ranted in a letter to his wife. "With all their material prosperity they are poor indeed compared with our people on the barren soil of many parts of Virginia." Like so many others, Carter was struck by what he regarded as the utter lack of refinement among the women who lived in the valley. He insisted that "the finest houses are inhabited by [j]abbering, slovenly Dutch women (in nine cases [ou]t of ten in the family-way)."[51]

Even the citizens' submissive behavior offended the sensibilities of some Southern soldiers. To their disgust, nearly all the people whom they encountered displayed none of the manliness and proud defiance that they valued so highly. "It was really painful to witness the servile complacency rendered to all our acts, and the obedient manner in which they welcome one of our army into their houses," Lt. Leonidas L. Polk from the Forty-Third North Carolina wrote to his hometown newspaper. "They were completely subjugated, and certainly know something of the terrors if not the horrors of war." In another letter home he told his wife that their conduct was actually "painful to a bold Southerner to behold."[52]

Although Ewell's troops had penetrated deep into Union territory with no significant opposition, one big concern still lingered. Despite the ease of their advance, most of the men remained convinced that their bold incursion into the North would not end without a major battle against the Army of the Potomac, which by then was finally on the move somewhere to the east of South Mountain. "I expect we have stirred up the quiet denizens of Eastern Lincolndom immeasurably by our occupation of their sacred domain," Captain Gorman admitted in a letter to a Raleigh newspaper. "That we cannot remain long without fighting is evident."[53]

Unknown to the soldiers, a climactic battle north of the Potomac was exactly what General Lee had wanted since the beginning of the campaign. Ewell's brilliant handling of his troops during the advance had confounded Milroy and Hooker so completely that Lee was now ready to take on the Union army in a final engagement that he expected would earn the Confederacy its hard-fought independence. "We have out maneuvered the enemy and are in the heart of Penn.," Lee summed up the situation to one of his generals. With that accomplished, he could easily concentrate his forces "on any point east of South Mountain in forty eight hours or less." What remained to be decided was precisely where and when the anticipated showdown with the enemy would take place.[54]

⚛ 10 ⚛

"No Army Ever Fared Better"

Jenkins's troopers again led the way as Rodes's and Johnson's men pushed north from Greencastle toward Harrisburg, the state capital. By the morning of June 23, the first horsemen had once again reached Chambersburg. "They rode in as leisurely as you please, each one having his hand on the trigger though, to fire any minute," local resident Rachel Cormany remarked in her diary. "Now I judge we are shut out again for awhile—I just wonder what they want this time." She immediately realized that the riders were "part of those that were here last week." Merchant William Heyser watched with apprehension as the fearsome-looking horsemen proceeded into the center of town and "placed pickets at all points to prevent surprise."[1]

Those precautions proved necessary because of the recent presence of Federal troops in the town. On June 21 a small brigade commanded by Brig. Gen. Joseph F. Knipe marched into Chambersburg from outside of Harrisburg. This mixed force of infantry and artillery included the Eighth and Seventy-First New York State National Guard and a four-gun Pennsylvania battery. Plans called for the militiamen to maintain contact with the advancing Confederate forces while avoiding a direct engagement. Based on those orders, Knipe lingered at Chambersburg for nearly two full days before hastily pulling out his entire brigade just prior to the arrival of Jenkins's main force.[2]

Jacob Hoke, the thriving grocery-store owner, found that the arrival of Jenkins and his men this time differed considerably from what he had witnessed only a week earlier. The cavalrymen now showed no signs of nervousness as they pushed forward toward the central square. "On Tuesday morning, at about nine or ten o'clock, Gen. Jenkins again entered our town," the businessman recalled. "Unlike his former entrance, which was in the night and under evident alarm, and were made with a wild rush down our streets, he this time came in slowly and confidently."[3]

While the pickets remained on high alert, other Confederates severed Chambersburg's links with the outside world. Some of them immediately cut the telegraph lines and sawed down the poles in the town. A detachment also set to work disabling the tracks of the Cumberland Valley Railroad running straight through the town's center. According to one local newspaper, this contingent "went down the rail road, tearing up the rails, placing the cross-ties in heaps and burning them, and throwing the rails into the fire, for the purpose of warping them."

Another squad attempted to burn down the vital railroad bridge that spanned Conococheague Creek a few miles northeast near Scotland. Although the structure had suffered considerable damage during the previous raid, workmen had already completed major repairs by the time of Jenkins's return. The troopers assigned to this new detail now found it impossible to set the bridge on fire. "The timbers being wet, they failed in their attempt, and then proceeded to destroy it, as far as they were able, by cutting and sawing the timbers," a reporter explained.

While that was going on, Jenkins ordered local officials to turn over enough rations to feed his entire brigade, backing up his demand with open threats on the town. "There was no alternative but to furnish [t]hem," the newspaper reported. "At least there was only one alternative, and that was to have the provisions taken from their houses by force." People soon lined up on the main street, clutching all kinds of food. "A stranger, visiting town about this time, would have thought we were preparing for some grand picnic," the writer quipped. He noted that "old and young might be seen trudging along with their baskets or bundles of provisions."[4]

The commissary detail at the town square quickly secured a huge supply of useful goods. "A large four-horse wagon, loaded of bread, cold meats and etc. was gathered and loaded up at the courthouse steps," Rev. Henry Reeves from the Rosedale Female Seminary noted. To the preacher's surprise, Capt. Nicholas Fitzhugh, the assistant adjutant general on Jenkins's staff, personally supervised every detail of the operation. "For this liberal offering Captain Fitzhugh, the rebel in charge of the matter, returned his hearty thanks to the people of Chambersburg," Reeves remarked.[5]

Merchant Hoke watched in stunned silence from the crowd as the rebels gathered in their spoils. He noted that slabs of bacon made up the largest portion of the food residents provided. "And as flitch after flitch, and jowl after jowl, with a sprinkling of bread, cakes, and pies, were deposited upon the pile, in front of the court-house, the name of the unwilling contributor to the stomach of the Southern Confederacy was taken down, by which his residence would be exempted from search in case enough was not voluntarily brought in," the storeowner recalled.[6]

Despite the contributions from the inhabitants, Jenkins's men impressed huge quantities of other goods from businesses all over Chambersburg. These searches reached nearly every store and warehouse of any consequence. Rachel Cormany complained that several officers "took possession of the warehouses & were dealing out flour by the barrel & mollasses by the bucketful—they made people take them bread—meat—&c to eat." The most distressing moments came when "some dumb fools carried them jellies & the like." Their compliant behavior left her seething with anger. "Not a thing went from this place," she insisted.[7]

William Heyser also reacted with dismay as the commissary details gathered up the loot. "This afternoon they opened the warehouse of J. Allison Eyster, and made off with $4,000.00 worth of bacon, salt, beans, coffee, crackers, etc.," he recorded in his diary. "They also opened the warehouse of Oaks & Linn, and took almost 300 barrels of flour belonging to Jacob Stouffer." Even so, the rebels generally carried out their searches with real restraint. Heyser acknowledged that the troopers "behave very well," noting that there was "not a citizen molested or a house visited."

The citizens were especially pleased with the forceful steps that the officers in charge took to keep the town's stock of alcohol out of the hands of the troops. In many cases soldiers destroyed confiscated supplies of liquor right on the spot. "They broke in the heads of 20 barrels of whiskey, which they poured out," Heyser explained. "At Miller's Drug Store, they poured a barrel of brandy into the gutter. Capt. Fitzhugh gave orders that if any of his men were caught molesting a citizen, they would be severely punished." Heyser readily admitted that "they were a thoroughly disciplined lot of men."[8]

The main part of Rodes's Division arrived the following morning after an easy eleven-mile tramp from Greencastle. "On the 24th, starting early, we passed through Chambersburg, with bands at the head regiment playing dixie and other Southern airs, arms at the right-shoulder-shift, the boys stepping out lively to the music, laughing and shouting to the gloomy faced citizens, 'Here's your played-out rebellion,'" a solider from Doles's Brigade gloated. One of the local newspapers noted that the tunes blaring from the front of the column included the "Bonnie Blue Flag," "Dixie," and "the Marselaise."[9]

Rodes's troops had penetrated more than fifteen miles into the heart of Pennsylvania's Cumberland Valley with their arrival in Chambersburg. The town was named for Col. Benjamin Chambers, who purchased some land along Conococheague Creek in 1730, soon establishing a fort there for protection from Indian raids. Chambersburg was formally laid out in 1764 and became the seat of government for Franklin County about twenty years later. The completion of the railroad in 1837 transformed it into one of the most important agricultural and commercial centers in the middle portion of the fertile valley.[10]

The Georgia troops from Doles's Brigade led the way into town. According to Sgt. "Tim" Furlow from the brigade staff, they made their entrance "with colors flying and bands playing, horses prancing, everything looking as gay as it could." Capt. James Beck insisted that none of this exuberance distracted in any way from the display of rigid discipline among the troops. "We marched through in perfect order; not a man allowed to leave his place in ranks; our colors flying and our bands playing Southern airs," he described in a letter to his hometown newspaper.[11]

Central Square at Chambersburg, Pennsylvania. Courtesy Franklin County Historical Society
—Kittochtinny.

Reverend Reeves was struck by the constant music that the regimental bands performed as they paraded through the streets. Their repertoire included several easily
recognizable melodies. The minister informed his sister that the musicians "played
'The Bonnie Blue Flag,' a secesh air, sometimes they played 'Dixie' and once or twice
'My Maryland.'" One particular Southern favorite proved impossible for anyone in
town to ignore. Reeves joked that the bands struck up "The Bonnie Blue Flag" so
often that many of residents soon began involuntarily humming the tune.[12]

The majority of the citizens initially stayed out of view as the troops made
their entrance. "The doors are closed and the windows shut," Hospital Steward John
S. Apperson from the Second Corps Medical Department wrote in his diary. He
soon noticed that some of the local women were gazing at the men through partially closed shutters. "From the windows above, often peering through the blinds,
we see pretty faces staring at the rebels," he explained. Although he could catch only
a glimpse of them, their expressions made it clear that they viewed the Confederates with terror. "I wonder if they have seen any horned ones," the young Virginian
commented facetiously.[13]

A soldier serving with one of the batteries in Rodes's Division watched as many
of the inhabitants eventually emerged from their homes to catch a better look at the
passing invaders. He was shocked to find that the ladies in the crowd were the most
vehement Union supporters, some openly berating the men along their line of march.
"Many of the women boldly displayed U.S. flags, and though the latter frequently
taunted the Southerners almost to the extent of insulting rudeness, the Confederates
did not permit themselves to make return in kind," the artilleryman recalled.[14]

As the streets filled with onlookers, their hatred for the Southern troops soon became apparent on nearly every face. Pvt. Louis Leon from Daniel's Brigade acknowledged that "nary a smile greeted us as we marched through town." Sergeant Furlow wrote in his journal that "the men, women and children, as a general thing, looked sullen and dejected." Capt. John Gorman from Ramseur's Brigade was especially struck by the harsh glares that the ladies directed at the soldiers. "You ought to see the women look sour," he grumbled to his mother. The Tar Heel veteran complained that he had "not seen a pleasant face since we crossed the Pennsylvania line." At one point he even spotted "one little spiteful miss with broom in hand sweeping petulantly the rebel dust that soiled her door sill."[15]

Despite their unfriendly greeting, Captain Beck found that Chambersburg was "a beautiful place of some four thousand inhabitants." Sergeant Furlow pointed out that the town "had some very fine residences." Hospital Steward Apperson also reported that it was "a fine town," noting that "the streets are too narrow, but the houses well built and mostly of brick." He was especially struck by the many public buildings around the central square, recording in his diary that the courthouse was "a very fine building—erected in 1802 at cost $44,543." Apperson added that the town hall was "a large building too."[16]

The townspeople watched with trepidation as a seemingly endless column of rebels made its way into town. "About 9 o'clock Ewell's corps passed through, probably some 10,000 men with an immense train of artillery and army wagons," merchant Heyser wrote in his diary. "Among them many farm wagons and teams they acquired along the way." Most notable of all was the lack of regular uniforms among the men in the ranks. "No two hats alike, and their shoes could hardly be called that," Heyser remarked. "It was hard to distinguish the officers from the men, except those of high rank."[17]

Although most of Rodes's troops were well outfitted by that point in the campaign, many citizens could not see beyond the common stereotypes about the soldiers. "They came with banners and music, but generally were a sorry-looking set," Reverend Reeves pointedly commented to his sister. "They are fierce and independent enough, but their personal appearance and dress, especially, was bad." Storeowner Hoke insisted with little basis in fact that "many were ragged, dirty and shoeless, affording unmistakable evidence that they sadly stood in need of having their wardrobes replenished."[18]

Some others in the town were more forthcoming about what they witnessed. Jenny Love, a young student at Rosedale Female Seminary, came away with a largely positive opinion of the troops that she encountered that day. The schoolgirl had long anticipated that the soldiers would display their contempt for the North with open rudeness and arrogant taunts. Despite her concerns, she soon discovered that the men in the long column handled themselves very well in dealing with the people along the streets. "It is but just to say that our fears of insults had been groundless," Love acknowledged. "I never heard one insulting word from any of the soldiers."[19]

A correspondent from one of the local newspapers also found the men from Rodes's Division better equipped and more disciplined than he had expected. "Their clothes were much worn, faded and scuffed, but there were comparitively few whom you could positively call 'ragged,' and we did not see a hundred men in their bare feet," he admitted. The writer noted that "their general demeanor was civil and quiet, though several citizens were deprived of hats, coats, and shoes, which some of the dilapidated chivalry immediately appropriated to their own use, and one or two lost their watches and pocket books."[20]

Just after 10:00 A.M., Ewell finally arrived at the town square with an escort of several horsemen. The general's small carriage eventually pulled up in front of the Franklin Hotel. "When he emerged from the carriage, which he did only by the assistance of others, it was discovered that he had an artificial limb, and used a crutch," Hoke recalled. "After making his way into the hotel, he at once took possession of a large front parlor, and, surrounded by six or eight gentlemenly-looking men, he was prepared for business." The merchant noted that "a flag was run out of a window, and head-quarters was established."[21]

Rodes's men set up camp a couple of miles beyond town around some high ground known as Shirk's Hill. Farmer Jacob Shirk loudly complained about the damages that he and neighbor Abraham Bittinger suffered from the constant foraging by the occupying troops. "They burnt about forty panels of fence for me and five times that much for Bittinger," Shirk protested in a letter to his cousin in early July. He griped that "they went on to the Cherry trees, broke down limbs, took them on their sholders and carried them to their encampment." Shirk pointed out that the troops also "broke of[f] garden pailings, went and stole all Abrahams onions and radishes and broke the pailings at the yard fence."[22]

The bulk of Johnson's troops reached the area soon afterward and halted about a mile south of Chambersburg. Like the men in Rodes's Division, they encountered a cold reception from the citizens. While conceding that the town was "a handsome & business like place," Sgt. Watkins Kearns from the Stonewall Brigade grumbled in his diary that the "people scowl—ladies frown—boys are impudent." He insisted that "every body is Union to the back bone." Cpl. James Peter Williams from the Chesapeake Artillery described the residents to his father as "the meanest looking white people I ever saw."[23]

Lt. Robert W. Hunter, who served as the adjutant for the Second Virginia in the Stonewall Brigade, reported to his sister on the day of their arrival that he "rode this evening through Chambersburg and saw more ugly women than I ever encountered in my life." He remained less certain about exactly why that was so. "Whether they were ugly by nature or looked sour because the rebels were looking at them I could not say," the adjutant jested. Pvt. John Henry Vest from the artillery reserve wrote in his diary simply that the "girls look severe." As usual, such comments had much more to do with resentment over the hostile welcome they received in town than the actual physical appearance of the women.[24]

While his troops settled into place, Ewell made arrangements within town for their comfort. One of his "first acts" was to secure a large schoolhouse on King Street next door to the city jail for use as a temporary hospital for the sick and broken-down soldiers in his two divisions. "This was followed by a requisition upon some of the hotels for a number of beds, which were taken to this building and the sick of his corps were placed thereon," Hoke explained. Additional demands called for town officials to turn over medical supplies that could be used to treat the Confederates.

The corps commander assigned the Third Alabama in O'Neal's Brigade as provost guards for the town. Col. Cullen Battle, who headed the regiment, had rejoined his command only two days earlier after recovering from an accidental injury that he sustained just prior to Chancellorsville. To mark the site of their headquarters, the Alabama troops defiantly hoisted a large Confederate flag atop the county courthouse. Hoke noted that "this was the only hated symbol of the Confederacy which was put up anywhere in the town."[25]

General Ewell took immediate steps to prevent any alcohol from falling into the hands of his troops. One of the local newspapers reported that "as soon as the enemy entered town, guards were placed over all the liquor that was reported to the commanding general, [and] the soldiers were refused admittance into any of the bar rooms or saloons." Those efforts proved quite effective in preventing the worst abuses. The reporter readily admitted that he "only saw one or two cases of drunkenness" among the troops from Rodes's Division during their stay.[26]

Other soldiers confiscated a huge supply of alcohol stored at a nearby warehouse. Lt. William Calder from Ramseur's Brigade reported that he was assigned to guard "a distillery with about one hundred barrels of whiskey from which it is desired to keep the men." Major Brown from Ewell's staff recalled that the building was stacked high with barrels of fine whiskey, many of which were "several years old." He noted that Rodes "put a guard over them & had all knocked in the head, but what the surgeons took in the wagons for medical purposes—some six or eight barrels only."[27]

Once the provost guards were in place, Ewell shifted his headquarters to a Mennonite church just outside of town near an old mill. From there he issued a demand for the storeowners to turn over a long list of requisitioned goods. The items that his chief quartermaster, Maj. John A. Harman, required included 5,000 suits of clothing as well as hats, boots, and shoes; 100 saddles and bridles; 3,000 bushels of corn and oats; 10,000 pounds of sole leather; and 10,000 pounds of horseshoes. Another request later in the day called for 6,000 pounds of lead and 10,000 pounds of harness leather.

Maj. Wells J. Hawks from the Commissary Department submitted a requisition that was just as extensive. His list of required foods included bread, salt, molasses, flour, vinegar, beans, dried fruit, sauerkraut, potatoes, coffee, sugar, and hard bread. Most stunning of all were the huge quantities of each item that the businesses had to provide. Typical of the numbers involved was the demand for 500 barrels of flour, 11,000 pounds of coffee, and 10,000 pounds of sugar. Orders called for the owners to surrender the goods without delay or face immediate seizures by force.[28]

During a hastily convened meeting, all but one of the town's merchants declined to comply with the demands. Ewell quickly made good on his threat. "After this refusal, guards were sent to all the stores, [where] the military authorities took pos[s]ession of such groceries, hardware, flour, drugs, soaps &c. as they wanted," one of the local newspapers said. "And then the merchants were directed to keep their stores open and sell to those who wish to buy for confederate scrip, on pain of having their doors burst open and their goods taken without any remuneration."[29]

Later that same day commissary and quartermaster details from the division started rounding up the required goods from the shops. "About two, the pillage of our stores began," Heyser complained in his diary. "Not a place escaped, never in the history of our boro was there such a scene. The merchants were compelled to pack up the wagons with their goods, which is [sic] being sent to Richmond." He noted that the streets were "crowded with Rebels who try to interrogate our lesser citizens as to where things are hidden or sent to, and also as to the movements of the Federal troops that had left."[30]

Hoke griped that the stores in town were soon "relieved of a considerable part of their contents." According to one newspaper, the troops forced businessman Samuel Shyrock to sell "books and stationary to the amount of $8000." The demands on the other stores were nearly as heavy. "The Messrs. Eyster sold dry goods and groceries to the amount of $5000, and a number of others to the amount of $2000 and $3000," the article declared. "There was not a store of any prominence that did not suffer heavily. Those who did not open at the first demand were compelled to see their doors broken in."[31]

Many of the merchants desperately attempted to make the best of a bad situation, which often required considerable Yankee ingenuity. "Among the first lot of goods bought by the rebels was Sam Shyrock's stocks of paper, envelopes, and stationery," Reverend Reeves commented to his sister. He noted that the wily businessman "charged them about four times the value of the goods, and as they promised to pay— of course in Confederate money—he kept at them until they paid the bill, amounting to some $8000." That hugely inflated price allowed him to sell off or trade some of the rebel money at a massive discount and still recoup at least part of his losses.[32]

As elsewhere, some senior officers also went shopping at the dry-goods stores for items to send home to their wives and daughters. Jed Hotchkiss reported to his wife that he found plenty of goods to purchase on the shelves when he visited one of the shops in town. "This land is full of every thing," he declared. "The stores were opened & they had to sell goods at their old prices for Confederate money."

Like most Southern gentlemen, Hotchkiss took his role as patriarch and provider for his family so seriously that he happily bought "about $100 worth of calico, wool delaine, bleached cotton, hoops, gloves, thread, gingham, pins &c &c which I hope to get home in due time if we stop short of N.Y."[33]

A squad also requisitioned the printing press of the *Reformed Messenger,* located in one of the town's churches. The owner recalled that "an officer with a detail accordingly called at my home on East Market street, and after reading the requisition for 'the use of a printing office and two printers,' politely suggested that the superintendent open the office and take charge of the work." The officer informed him that "a guard would be furnished to protect the property; otherwise, forcible possession would be taken, and no guarantee would be given as to the contents of the building." He admitted that "the propriety of a compliance was at once seen."[34]

Their visit came in response to the constant requirement in the invading army for official documents of all kinds. "The task required of them was the printing of a large number of General Orders issued by Generals Lee and Ewell, several thousand parole papers intended for the parolement of the prisoners they expected to take, and a large amount of other blank work for use of the army," Hoke explained. The merchant noted that "execution of this work took several days, and when it was completed, war prices were charged and the bill paid in Confederate scrip."[35]

While that was going on, supply officers stationed at the town square continued to gather up a long list of food and other supplies from residents. The goods that the citizens were required to surrender even included their personal riding tackle. The presence of armed soldiers in their midst proved so intimidating that a steady stream of people meekly lined up along the main street in the middle of town with the required items in hand. "It was one of the most amasing sights I ever saw to see the broadclothed gentry coming in & bringing saddles, bridles, &c & making a pile of them in the square for the use of the Rebels," Hotchkiss gloated to his wife.[36]

The soldiers were just as pleased as their officers with all the goods they secured. "At Chambersburg the Qr Masters emptied every store in the place and our men are living luxuriously," an artillerist in Johnson's Division effused in a letter home. "We bought everything we wanted at our own prices in the town, & the country is full of everything good to eat." Lt. Fleming Saunders from Jones's Brigade reported to his mother that "our Quartermasters and Commissaries have procured very many supplies in Chambersburg." He noted with enthusiasm that the real coffee they seized during their stay "adds very much to our bill of fare."[37]

A member of the Third Alabama serving as a provost guard insisted, however, that they "did not find a great amount of spoil" during their searches. "Most of the merchants had taken the alarm on the approach of our cavalry, and run their goods off by railroad, or secreted them," he speculated in a letter to his hometown newspaper. "Shoes, hats and clothing, things that a few of our men needed, were not to be found, except in small scattering lots." The soldier conceded that "flour, molasses, whiskey, medicines, stationery, and hardware were more abundant, and the 2nd mess availed themselves of the opportunity to fill and sent to the rear sundry wagon loads."[38]

Colonel Battle, who served as provost marshal, quickly earned the grudging respect of residents. "He established his headquarters in the Court-House, he was courteous and gentlemanly, and his guard, with scarcely an exception, behaved well," one local newspaper acknowledged. The colonel even placed a few businesses off limits from confiscation. "My neighbor, Widow Murphy, who kept a small store, dispensing Queens Ware and shoes, nothing of value to the Rebels, did succeed in having her place exempt from being robbed," Heyser recorded in his diary. He openly admitted that "some of the Rebel officers were very considerate."[39]

That strict adherence to the letter of General Lee's orders did not always extend to the soldiers in the lower ranks. Jacob Hoke noted that their behavior often stood in marked contrast to the courtesy displayed by their officers. In a few cases the enlisted men made unauthorized seizures from local merchants. "Some of the privates . . . when they had access to the stores were the reverse," he commented, "and unlike the officers, who invariably asked for what they desired to purchase, went searching through the store, opening the drawers and looking for concealed goods."[40]

The "rather peculiar conceptions" that some of the men from the Deep South had of Pennsylvanians further complicated relations between the Confederates and the citizens. "Quite a number were astonished to find our people speaking English, as they supposed that the prevalent language was the German," the editor for one of the town's newspapers explained. "At first when they attempted derisive remarks, they would imitate the broken English of the Germans." Their misconceptions even extended to what they regarded as the typical diet among the local populace. "Judging from Ewell's demand for 25 bbls. of sourkraut at a season when it is unknown in any country, even the commanding officers must have considered our people as profoundly Dutch," the newspaperman fumed.[41]

Early in the morning on June 25, the quartermaster and commissary details were once again out in force, gathering up additional provisions from businesses all over the town. "All quiet until about 9 o'clock when the locusts began to swarm again," William Heyser grumbled in his diary. "On each side of the street, they stop and make further requisitions. There isn't much left to take." Rachel Cormany complained that the soldiers "must surely expect to set up stores or fill their empty ones judging from the loads they have been hauling away & they take every thing a body can think of."[42]

One of the medical officers assigned to the effort reported that they actually found little of value remaining in the drugstores. "The stores taken was very small indeed," Hospital Steward Apperson admitted. "Not so much as a country practitioner would keep. Miller & Hinsby, JS Nixon, and Heyser were the Druggists from whom we took articles." He noted that the most valuable items were nowhere to be found. "Only 1½ oz. Quinine & 1 dram of Morphine were among the captures," Apperson said. "These stores are taken and duplicate Bills and made out with receipts attached and the cash paid for them."[43]

Although many goods had been hidden away (or already seized earlier), Jed Hotchkiss still expressed amazement at the huge quantity of supplies that the rebels confiscated around Chambersburg. "Our success is wonderful," he declared in a letter to his wife. "We shall get nearly a million dollars worth of horses, supplies of all kinds &c from this county, (Franklin) & we have invaded Fulton & Adams Cos.—also and shall levy on them in like manner—supporting our army entirely on the enemy— they say they never felt the war before but the first taste is enough for them." He added, "they do not care for more."[44]

The forced requisitions had a devastating effect on local merchants. Many of them barely hung on until the following year, when Confederate troops again raided the town and burned much of it to the ground. "This much can be said, that many persons who had toiled and economized for years and years together to gain an honorable support for themselves and families were ruined financially," Hoke explained. "Although the most of them started again in a smaller way, they never recovered from the losses of that day [in June 1863], and some of them after meeting other losses were finally burned out a year later, and died in poverty."[45]

Not surprisingly, the Confederates received a worse reception there than at Greencastle. "After leaving Hagerstown the most of the inhabitants seemed excited only by idle curiosity—but when we arrived at Chambersburg, Pa. men, women and children looked as sullen as an opossum and as sour as a crab apple," Capt. James Harris from Ramseur's Brigade commented in a letter to a friend. Describing the town as "strictly a Union hole," Lt. William Ardrey from the same brigade noted that "all the citizens looked upon us with scorn and contempt." Even General Ewell reported to his niece that "the people look as sour as vinegar & I have no doubt would send us all to kingdom come if they could."[46]

The people in the surrounding area also suffered severely from constant raids by Jenkins's cavalrymen. Mennonite farmer Henry B. Hege, who lived south of Chambersburg near the village of Marion, lamented to his cousin that the intruders "took all of our corn, about 20 barrels; all our oats, about 9 bushels; and nearly all our chickens." In addition, they seized the "mowing scythes and axes, and all the salt they could find." The outcome was even worse for his father, who endured about $2,000 in damages from the search parties. "They burned many of his fences, destroyed a great deal of his grain in the fields and took 100 bushels of wheat out of the barn," Hege reported in his letter.[47]

Events took a more frightening turn at the home of farmer Levi Horst, who had sent his horses away to safety in the nearby mountains. His daughter recalled that three or four cavalrymen stopped by their house just north of Chambersburg and demanded that her father tell them where his horses were hidden. "Then they said if he did not tell they would shoot him," she recounted. "We were out on the porch, mother and all of us children, and needless to say, were very much scared. Father stuck to his story and insisted that he could not tell them something that he did not know." She noted that the troopers "must have believed his story for they soon ceased their threatening, and rode away."[48]

The raids proved especially devastating for local landowner and prominent merchant Jacob Stouffer. He grumbled in a letter to his sister that Jenkins's cavalry stripped his property just outside Chambersburg of all its livestock and many other valuable goods. The merchant insisted that "these men wanted almost every-thing—bread—butter milk—cheese—vegables." The intimidating horsemen quickly grabbed up "flour—and every thing they needed—beef cattle, young cattle and milk cows." Stouffer further complained that "my loss in flour—corn—Oats—hay grass and fences is heavy."[49]

J. A. Rohrer, who lived north of Chambersburg near Pleasant Hall, first encountered the invaders on June 25, when a single horseman approached his house. The intruder immediately "came on the porch and asked for something to eat." The trooper soon placed his father under guard, while he searched the property. The farmer somehow got away and eventually hid most of his horses in nearby Amberson Valley. A larger detachment returned two days later, only this time the rebels seized an "old gray mare," two "good colts," eight head of cattle, seventy-five chickens, two hundred bushels of corn, two hundred bushels of oats, a new mowing scythe, and other valuable farm implements.[50]

Jenkins's men especially targeted the millers and distillers in the area surrounding Chambersburg. Greenwalt S. Barr, who operated a gristmill in Greene Township just northeast of town, estimated the damages to his property at more than $10,000. His losses included about 1,100 bushels of wheat, 100 bushels of corn, 100 bushels of oats, and nearly 400 barrels of flour. Jacob Hargbroad, who owned two mills and two warehouses in the same area, suffered about $5,000 in losses. According to his postwar claim for damages, the rebel cavalrymen "poured out" about 3,000 gallons of whiskey onto the ground during an incursion at a distillery attached to one of his mills.[51]

Other raiding parties focused on rounding up horses. Stouffer griped that "those in authority took from us all the horses they could find—many were not moved far away and fell into their hands." Christian Bitner, who lived about three miles south of Chambersburg, reported in his damage claim that Jenkins's men seized nineteen prized mounts from his property alone. According to Reverend Reeves, horses were soon in such short supply that they could hardly be obtained at any cost. The minister complained to his sister a few days after the Confederate retreat that none "are about except blind ones, and they are scarce and at a premium."[52]

The vast destruction from the constant forays left most of the landowners in such financial ruin that they did not fully recover until many years later. "All those farmers who did not send away their stock had them taken, some of whom cannot well afford the loss," a Chambersburg newspaper reported. "What the general loss in this county will be when booked up, we have yet no means of telling; but it is safe to say, that, leaving out of consideration the general damage to property and land, it will not fall under two hundred thousand dollars [a stunning amount equivalent to about $5.6 million in 2018]."[53]

With the infantry finally on hand, Jenkins's Brigade resumed the advance north along Valley Turnpike toward Shippensburg on the morning of June 24. Even the presence of Captain Boyd's small detachment from the First New York Cavalry failed to slow down Jenkins's progress. About 2:00 P.M. the Confederate troopers finally galloped into Shippensburg in hot pursuit of Boyd's beleaguered cavalrymen. Eunice Stewart, who was the wife of a prominent local doctor, reported to her parents that the rebels charged through the streets as "so many devils yelling like h—l-hounds."[54]

Jenkins soon established his headquarters in one of the hotels and, as usual, began requisitioning supplies. The general called for a meeting with the officials and businessmen of Shippensburg, during which he laid out his specific demands for goods of all kinds. "There he summoned the principal men and told them that he wanted rations for his men and the towns people must provide them," one eyewitness reported to a newspaper in Harrisburg. "If this was done plundering could be prevented." The correspondent noted that "the logic of this argument seemed so good to the citizens that they set about getting food and forage for their visitors with a will."[55]

Later in the day the commissary and quartermaster details from the brigade began seizing additional items from the stores around town. One major target for their searches was the drugstore owned by the prominent merchant John C. Altick. He recorded in his diary that "a Surgeon came in & took about 250 $ worth of drugs" on the evening of the Southerners' arrival. Altick complained most of all about the payment for his goods, which came in the form of Confederate scrip. At the same time, he acknowledged that the town remained "verry quiet all evening."[56]

The relative calm lasted until just after dark, when some of Jenkins's pickets confronted Boyd's troopers a few miles north of town on Walnut Bottom Road. A boy who lived on a nearby farm noted that the "shooting began, over our head, from the hills on both sides of us, by the retreating rear guard of the Union army and the advance guard of the Southern army." The incessant firing put the family in fear for their lives. "Just then my mother came running down toward me calling me," he recalled. "I hurried and saw that she was terribly frightened—the only time as far as I can remember, I ever saw fright on her face."[57]

The fighting along the roadway became so noisy that it attracted the attention of the troops in Shippensburg. According to a member of Capt. Wiley Hunter Griffin's battery, Jenkins's cavalrymen immediately "sprang to their horses, and artillerymen to their guns." Their frustrations turned into real concern when the "enemy could not be induced to come within range of Griffin's Parrotts." Although the encounter was brief, the skirmish left the general so alarmed that he immediately sent a panicked message to Ewell calling for him to send infantry reinforcements as soon as possible.[58]

Ewell assigned the duty of assisting Jenkins to Daniel's men, who had to be aroused from their sleep before heading north at top speed. The Tar Heel troops were hardly in the best of moods as they stumbled along in the darkness. "We were woke up in the middle of the night and marched off; waded a river which was so cold that it woke us up," Private Leon griped in his diary. General Daniel reported that his brigade "commenced the march about 1 o'clock, and arrived about there [Shippensburg] about 5 a.m." Lt. James Green complained that the men had "to march in quick time" for ten or twelve miles because Jenkins was in such a hurry for them to come to his assistance.[59]

The rest of the division arrived in town early in the afternoon on June 26 after slogging through a heavy rainstorm. Eunice Stewart watched with increasing despair as the long column of infantry proceeded through the streets. "This morning our eyes and hearts were pained again at the sight of some ten or twelve thousand of our assured foes pass[ing] through our streets accompanied by Gen. Ewell who was strapped on to his horse," she declared in a letter to her parents. Rodes's troops finally settled into place about a half mile southeast of town near Indian Spring. Johnson's men followed soon afterward and halted just west of there around some high ground known as Timber Hill.[60]

Shippensburg, Pennsylvania, from Timber Hill on the edge of town. Courtesy Shippensburg Historical Society.

Shippensburg, which directly straddled the turnpike, was the oldest settlement in the Cumberland Valley and the second oldest in Pennsylvania west of the Susquehanna River. The town took its name from Edward Shippen, who obtained the original land grant from the heirs of William Penn. Several Scotch-Irish families built the first cabins along Burd's Run in the 1730s. That tiny cluster of buildings eventually grew into a thriving community, with a population of about 1,800 by 1860. Pvt. Samuel Pickens from O'Neal's Brigade described the town in his diary as "a place of considerable length, being built along on each side of the road."[61]

Once the two infantry divisions arrived, Jenkins deployed his horsemen just north of town. During the late afternoon, his troopers surprised a squad of thirty-four men from Capt. Frank Murray's company of Pennsylvania militia cavalry along Walnut Bottom Road near historic Stone Tavern. According to Lt. William Fisher, who commanded the Federal detachment, his men came under attack as they approached within a hundred yards of the tavern. He noted that "about one hundred rebel cavalrymen swarmed from either side of the road, and succeeded in cutting off and taking in ten of our men prisoners." At least two other militiamen were wounded during the mad scramble to get away.[62]

While that was going on, provost details from Rodes's Division moved into place in Shippensburg. "Every Street and Alley in town is guarded and we are Prisoners in our own homes," Stewart griped to her parents. The situation proved most frightening for the town's African American residents, who sought safety anywhere that they could find. Stewart acknowledged that she had "four colored persons concealed in my house." To prevent them from being discovered, she kept "all the lower part" of the home locked while her family and the hideaways remained upstairs throughout the enemy occupation.[63]

Later in the day the division's commissary and quartermaster officers began gathering up loot from all over town. One of the merchants loudly complained in a letter to his son that the Confederate troops "plundered all the stores" in their search for useful goods and quickly cleaned out a large portion of his stock. At one point he had "5 different Sergeants" in his shop who confiscated "such drugs as would suit them." The shopkeeper noted that "as near as can be sumbd up about 20 or 25 thousand dollars worth" of medical supplies were seized by Rodes's soldiers during their stay.[64]

Altick, a druggist, found the situation just as trying. He grumbled in his diary that "three Rebel Surgeons" visited his store that day and "took some drugs." The merchant reported that some of the soldiers even "searched all the cellers for Liquers." Those efforts eventually uncovered numerous valuable items from various businesses in town. Among the biggest losers in Shippensburg was prominent merchant Thomas P. Blair, who had $30,000 worth of grain and flour seized from his large warehouse on the corner of Martin Avenue and North Earl Street.[65]

William McLean, who owned the local tannery, avoided a similar fate by hiding most of his finished leather goods inside false bottoms for the vats at his factory. John

John W. McPherson Hardware Store, Shippensburg, Pennsylvania. Courtesy Shippensburg Historical Society.

W. McPherson, the proprietor of a nearby hardware store, stashed the most valuable possessions in the fireplace at his home and covered the opening with wallpaper. The proprietor of the Union House hotel was so terrified that he hastily painted over the name on his building just prior to the arrival of Jenkins's horsemen. In lieu of handing over a large sum of cash, many of the town's women labored the entire night preparing bread, cakes, and pies for the occupying troops. They turned in the resulting array of freshly baked goods the following morning to a commissary detail on the central square.[66]

The occupation proved especially difficult for farmer Hugh Craig, who lived on the property adjacent to one of the main Confederate encampments. "Uncle Hugh lost one horse, a wagon and some feed," his nephew reported to another relative. "He had the horror besides of furnishing a camping ground for almost all of Ewell's rebel corps. His loss is probably $1000." One of his neighbors also "lost his sheep, cattle, and hams, but saved his horses." Another nearby landowner was much luckier in avoiding any major problems. "Watson strange to say, was not visited at all by the enemy, although he had taken his horses away as a precautionary measure," the letter explained.[67]

Craig bitterly resented his treatment, which proved much worse than what his nephew reported. He grumbled to his niece that "the rebels took six head of cattle from me and all my sheep and a lot of my meat." The farmer complained that they "even stooped so low as to take the card and curry combs." He had nothing but contempt for those who claimed that the enemy had acted well during their stay. "Some people may talk as they please about the gentlemanly conduct of the rebel army," Craig protested. "I from experience have come to the conclusion that—the cavalry at least—they are a wicked set of thieves and robbers."[68]

For their part, Ewell's men certainly found little that was appealing at Shippensburg. Capt. Joseph Reese, one of Doles's Georgians, reported to his hometown newspaper that the town was "not so beautiful, nor the buildings so magnificent as those at Chambersburg." According to Private Pickens from O'Neal's Brigade, it was "a common looking place & inhabited by common looking people." Asst. Surgeon William W. Marston from Iverson's Brigade described the residents in his diary as "a hard looking set I can tell you—mostly Dutch." Lt. Henry Harris, an engineer in Johnson's Division, especially complained that "good-looking ladies are very scarce."[69]

Just as at other stops in the Cumberland Valley, the inhabitants of this usually peaceful town reacted with open disgust at the arrival of the Confederate troops. Lieutenant Green acknowledged that most of the townspeople "looked mad at us as usual in this Country." Lieutenant Ardrey insisted that "there was nothing to attract our attention but the fear and stiffness of the citizens." Hospital Steward Apperson put it more bluntly when he wrote in his diary that Shippensburg was "another pretty place but O Lord they do dispise us so much."[70]

By that stage in the campaign, however, not even the frigid reception from local residents could dampen the spirits of the men from Ewell's two divisions. "You see we are well into the enemys country, weeding a wide row as we go," Capt. Oliver Mercer from Iverson's Brigade declared in a letter to his brother on the day of their arrival at Shippensburg. "This is the richest part of Pa. and it is the most beautiful country I ever saw." The Tar Heel captain pointed out that "we are faring sumptuously—no army ever fared better in the world than we do—plenty to eat, light marches and a squad of Pennsylvania Militia before us too badly frightened to make a stand."[71]

⪡ 11 ⪢

"Enough to Frighten Us All to Death"

Jubal Early's soldiers joined in the renewed advance on June 24, packing up their extensive gear and heading north from Waynesboro deeper into the Cumberland Valley. Their route took them along the western base of South Mountain through the rustic hamlets of Quincy and Altodale. The people in Waynesboro greeted their departure with open joy. Although other Confederate troops were still on the move in their direction, young Lida Welsh acknowledged that they were relieved "when the last straggling soldier and the last rumbling wagon had vanished over the hill north of town."[1]

The situation proved less pleasurable for the citizens living to the north. Cpl. William B. Bailey from the Louisiana Guard Artillery noted in his diary that the people "were badly scared and brought forward provisions of all kinds and distributed them among the soldiers." The extent of their fear was never more apparent than during a brief halt at one of the villages along the way. Bailey reported that "several ladies" approached the troops and demanded to know "if we intended to burn the town." While flabbergasted by the question, he assured "them that we did not enter Pennsylvania for the purpose of destroying private property or warring against women and children."[2]

Pvt. John J. English from the Sixth North Carolina in Avery's brigade found the terror among the residents just as palpable. He reported in a letter home that the women in that section of the state "seemed like they wer[e] scared to death." The Tar Heel admitted that "we dident have to pay for nothing much for they dident want our money." Cpl. Joseph H. Truitt from Gordon's Brigade informed his parents that "the Pennsylvania women would give us anything to eat that they had." To his delight, the troops easily obtained large quantities of "milk and butter and chicken and eggs." He insisted that they "lived on the best that there was in the state."[3]

Typical of their success in securing needed items was an occurrence at Quincy on the march north from Waynesboro. Col. Clement Evans, who also served in Gordon's Brigade, penned in his diary that the merchants in that town "were selling their goods to our soldiers, taking Confederate money freely." The only downside was the easy availability of all kinds of alcohol, which remained a constant concern among the commanders. "The citizens supply our troops *too* liberally with the article of *whisky,*" Evans grumbled. "Certainly they can ruin our army by a liberality of that sort unless the orders are enforced."[4]

Little in the way of food seemed to escape the attention of the hungry soldiers. "Our men are living finely, applejack, fresh butter and milk and most everything else," Lt. William James Kincheloe from Smith's Brigade effused in his diary. He admitted that the much-feared Louisiana Tigers "particularly pay no regard in foraging and supply themselves on all occasions." Pvt. G. W. Nichols from the Sixty-First Georgia in Gordon's Brigade pointed out that the quartermaster and commissary details also "took every cow, sheep, horse, mule and wagon that they could lay hands on."[5]

The men could not help being impressed by the clear signs of wealth that greeted them around every turn in the road. "I can inform you that Pennsylvania and Maryland is the best contry I ever saw," Pvt. Marcus Hefner from the Fifty-Seventh North Carolina in Avery's brigade remarked to his wife. "Thar barns is finer than any house in NC." He insisted that the inhabitants were the best provided people "in the world." Capt. Reuben Allen Pierson from Hays's Brigade was especially struck by the countless flourishing fields. "In Maryland & Penn. the crops were remarkably fine," he wrote in a letter home. "I have never seen such heavy grain crops anywhere as in those states."[6]

Many others in the advancing column found that the lush fields and tidy houses reminded them of what they were accustomed to seeing in the Shenandoah Valley prior to the war. The contrast left no doubts about how little the Cumberland Valley had suffered compared to its counterpart in Virginia. "On every side, as far as our alert vision could reach, all aspects and conditions conspired to make this fertile and carefully tilled region a panorama both interesting and enchanting," General Gordon remarked. "It was a type of the fair and fertile Valley of Virginia at its best, before it became the highway of armies and the ravages of war had left it wasted and bare." Pvt. Samuel Easton from Avery's brigade wrote in his diary simply that "the country is very fine indeed."[7]

Such stunning sights caused at least some of the men to question just how long the South could hold on without a decisive victory to undermine public support in the North. "They have not felt the effects of this war," Private Hefner reported to his wife after seeing firsthand the huge material bounty that the enemy could draw on. With the Southern economy frayed to the breaking point from the effects of the conflict, the Tar Heel veteran knew that the North's wealth would prove decisive in the long run. "The north can fite twenty years yet, that is my opinion," he admitted.[8]

After an exhausting trek through the verdant countryside, the troops finally halted about eight miles northeast of Chambersburg at the inconsequential village of Greenwood, which stood near the entrance to Black's Gap through South Mountain. Located near Thaddeus Stevens's huge ironworks along the turnpike from Chambersburg through Cashtown to Gettysburg, the settlement, as described by a soldier from Gordon's Brigade, was "a small place scarcely deserving the name of a village." Nevertheless, from Greenwood the division could easily push north through the center of the Cumberland Valley or swing east through the South Mountain gaps to Gettysburg and York in neighboring Adams and York Counties, depending on their final orders.[9]

Early was buoyed by the apparent willingness of his troops to comply with Lee's strict ban on retribution and plundering during their operations in Pennsylvania. "We were now in the enemy's country, and were getting our supplies entirely from the country people," he explained. "These supplies were taken from mills, storehouses, and the farmers, under a regular system ordered by General Lee, and with a due regard to the wants of the inhabitants themselves, certificates being given in all cases." The general proudly pointed out that "there was no marauding, or indiscriminate plundering, but all such acts were expressly forbidden and prohibited effectually."[10]

Despite those directives, many of the men were soon busy foraging through the countryside around Greenwood for additional provisions. "Our troops are faring finely," Colonel Evans reported to his wife that day. "Whatever is needed for the army is impressed & paid for just like we do in Virginia." Lee's lenient policy of paying for goods hardly went down well with the Georgia veteran. "This does not seem right after they have plundered Virginia so much," he grumbled. "But we can be gentlemen as well as soldiers, and that mixture seems to be an impossibility with the Yankees."

At the same time, the colonel showed little sympathy for the constant protests from residents about unfair treatment. "These people who have been unaccustomed to any army think that the loss of a beehive or a dozen poultry quite a hardship," Evans fumed. "But they ought to see the Virginia farms despoiled, houses burned, Negroes run off, women & children turned out of doors—then they would not complain." Capt. William Seymour from Hays's staff took special pleasure in seizing provisions from Stevens's nearby ironworks. He boasted in his journal that the men thoroughly enjoyed "luxuriating on old Thad's provider and good things generally."[11]

Like the men from the other two divisions in Ewell's corps, the troops serving with Early had no compunctions about seizing any "contrabands" who came within their reach. Sgt. Joseph C. Snider from the Thirty-First Virginia in Smith's Brigade gloated in his diary that the soldiers captured some "runaway Va. negroes" while on picket duty near Greenwood. With no hint of the obvious contradiction involved, he remained firmly committed to enforcing Lee's ban against plundering. Snider reported that he "went to a house" that evening "to guard it." To his delight, he "got dinner and also my supper" from the grateful homeowner.[12]

Lt. Col. Elijah V. White. Courtesy Thomas Balch Library.

While his soldiers rested in camp, Early traveled to Chambersburg on the morning of June 25 for a meeting with the corps commander to discuss plans for the next
phase of the campaign. The final arrangements called for his division to turn east
into the neighboring valley. "In accordance with instructions received from General Lee, General Ewell ordered me to move with my command across the South
Mountain, and through Gettysburg to York, for the purpose of cutting the Northern Central Railroad (running from Baltimore to Harrisburg), and destroying the
bridge across the Susquehanna at Wrightsville and Columbia on the branch railroad from York to Philadelphia," Early reported.[13]

As part of the plan, Ewell directed the Thirty-Fifth Virginia Cavalry Battalion,
headed by Lt. Col. Elijah V. "Lige" White, to accompany the division on the march.
During the early part of campaign, White's men were heavily engaged in the fierce
fighting at Brandy Station on June 9 and later carried out a stunning raid along the
Potomac at Point of Rocks, about a dozen miles downstream from Harpers Ferry.
On his arrival in Maryland, Ewell temporarily attached the six companies of the battalion to his headquarters. According to one of the cavalrymen, they mostly served
during that time "as provost guards & couriers." Their new assignment called for
them to conduct scouting operations and screen the division's movements through
Adams and York Counties.[14]

Early's troops finally pushed forward across South Mountain late in the morning on June 26. Col. William H. French's Seventeenth Virginia Cavalry Regiment and some of the troopers from White's battalion led the way at the front of the column, followed closely by the infantry brigades and a line of supply wagons. Before getting underway, Early carried out what some in the North regarded as an egregious violation of Lee's rules banning the destruction of private property. In an act of apparent retribution, the division commander ordered "the iron works of Mr. Thaddeus Stevens near Greenwood, consisting of a furnace, a forge, a rolling mill— with a saw mill and storehouse attached,—to be burnt by my pioneer party."[15]

On their arrival at the site, resident manager John Sweeney pleaded for the general to spare the complex because its destruction would plunge the workers into poverty. Early, overseeing the operation from his horse, steadfastly refused to back down. Sweeney recalled that the division commander then launched into a long rant about the owner's antagonism toward the Confederacy. "Mr. Stevens is an enemy of the South," he shouted at him. "He is in favor of confiscating their property and arming the negroes. His property must be destroyed." As Sweeney looked on in despair, Early immediately ordered French's cavalrymen "to apply the torch." The general felt fully justified in his actions because the furnace served as an important source of iron for the Northern war effort.[16]

Under Early's personal directions, the troopers quickly set the main part of the compound ablaze. "The work of destruction was well done, and soon all the works were in ashes," one of the local newspapers reported. "The houses occupied by families were not fired." The account noted that "some $3,000 worth of charcoal was destroyed, 7,000 lb. bacon stolen, leaving the families of the laborers without food, in spite of the earnest representations made by Mr. Sweeney as to their necessitous condition." The newspaper estimated the total losses at "not less than $50,000." Stevens placed the damages at nearly double that amount. "They could not have done the job much cleaner," the Radical Republican leader complained after visiting the site a few days later. "It is rather worse than I expected."[17]

Stevens, who lived in nearby Lancaster, had become a particular target for bitter hatred in the South due to his policies as a congressman. Southerners' assessment of the Pennsylvanian differed markedly from that of most Republicans, who revered him as a progressive thinker and a pillar of their party. That point of view mattered little to Captain Seymour, who branded him as "one of the vilest, most unprincipled & most fanatical of the Yankee Abolition Congressmen." Pvt. Gordon Bradwell from Gordon's Brigade insisted that Stevens was "one of the bitterest enemies of the south, and an advocate of every extreme measure enacted before, during, and after the war."[18]

Even in later years Early made no apologies for his torching the complex. "Finding in my way these works of Mr. Stevens, who—as a member of the Federal Congress—had been advocating the most vindictive measures of confiscation and devastation, I determined to destroy them," the Virginian admitted. He acknowledged that "the burning was simply in retaliation for the various deeds of barbarity perpetrated by Federal troops." Early went to great pains to take sole credit for the decision, thereby deflecting any criticism away from his superiors. "This I did on my own responsibility, as neither General Lee nor General Ewell knew I would encounter these works," he insisted.

Despite that postwar admission, Early claimed that he took great care to protect the workers from any direct harm. "A quantity of provisions found in store at the furnace was appropriated to the use of my command, but the houses and private property of the employees were not molested," he explained. Captain Seymour acknowledged, however, that the burning of the ironworks "was the only occasion during the Pennsylvania Campaign when private property was destroyed by our troops." Even so, most of the men in the ranks remained more than happy to see the hated politician suffer for his antagonism toward the South. Sgt. James Hodam from French's regiment joked, in fact, that they "were anxious to give Mr. Stevens a free ride to Richmond to offset his losses at Greenville."[19]

Following the destruction of the complex, Early's men tramped east on the turnpike through nearby Cashtown Gap. From there they moved on toward the crossroads town of Gettysburg. "On getting to the eastern slope of the South Mountain, where the road forks about one and a half miles from Cashtown, I heard that there was probably a force in Gettysburg," Early recalled. He quickly dispatched part of his force "along the pike, which was the direct road to Gettysburg, in order to skirmish with and amuse the enemy in front, while I moved with the rest on the road to the left, by the way of Hilltown and Mummasburg, so as to cut off the retreat of such force as might be at Gettysburg."[20]

The thriving community of Gettysburg had about 2,400 residents and served as the seat of government for Adams County. It was home to both a well-regarded college and a Lutheran seminary. The town also enjoyed a direct railroad connection to Hanover, Pennsylvania, where other branch lines linked the town to most of the major cities in the East. A series of steep ridges and several rugged hills dominated the surrounding countryside. Most important, Gettysburg stood at the intersection of ten major roads that radiated in all directions like spokes on a wheel.[21]

With "Lige" White's troopers at the front of its column, Gordon's Brigade pushed forward on the right through a light rain along Chambersburg Turnpike toward Gettysburg. By then about seventy-five horsemen from the Adams County Cavalry under Capt. Robert Bell had established a picket line some three miles west of town along the roadway. From there Bell deployed his scouts to detect as quickly as possible the fast-approaching Confederate troops. The first reports of sighting the enemy arrived soon afterward.

In addition to Bell's men, the force defending Gettysburg included some 750 troops from the Twenty-Sixth Pennsylvania Volunteer Militia under Col. William

View into Gettysburg, Pennsylvania, from the northwest on Chambersburg Pike. Courtesy Library of Congress.

Jennings, most of whom took up position just in the rear of Bell's pickets along the banks of Marsh Creek. This unit, which included one company made up largely of bookish students from what is today Gettysburg College, had only mustered for duty a few days earlier. Jennings protested that his militiamen were too inexperienced to take on a large body of regular troops, but Maj. Granville Haller, whom Federal officials had assigned as overall commander of Union forces defending York and Adams Counties, refused to reconsider.

Despite Jennings's concerns, a contingent of about twenty men from his regiment joined Bell's horsemen along the front line. Another detachment from the regiment and some other men from the First Troop of the Philadelphia City Cavalry under Capt. Samuel J. Randall remained behind on the east end of town to guard the supplies stored in the several railroad cars that had carried the militiamen to Gettysburg. The remainder of the colonel's troops set up camp in a swampy clover field west of town alongside Marsh Creek. From there the young soldiers watched with fear for any sign of the Confederate invaders.[22]

Bell's pickets soon spotted in the distance White's horsemen thundering toward their position along the turnpike. Capt. Frank Myers, who commanded a company in White's battalion, reported that the rebels charged forward "with barbarian yells and smoking pistols, in such a desperate dash, that the blue-coated troopers wheeled their horses, and departed towards Harrisburg without firing a shot." The onrushing Confederates gathered up a number of prisoners from the picket line right on the spot. "Of course, 'nobody was hurt,' if we except one fat militia Captain, who in his exertion to be the first to surrender, managed to get himself run over by one of Company E's horses and bruised somewhat," Myers joked.

As the enemy closed in on their position, the troops from Jennings's regiment in the rear hurriedly gathered up whatever equipment they could carry. One of them noted that the order soon "came to strike tents and fall into line as quickly as possible"; in a few moments they "marched away on quick time." Another militiaman claimed that he "never saw anything done so quickly in my life." Captain Myers bragged that those who could not get away fast enough immediately "threw down their bright, new muskets, and begged frantically for quarter." General Early described the young soldiers as so frightened that they were "rejoicing at this termination of their campaign."[23]

White's men largely ignored the remainder of Jennings's troops as they fled north on Belmont Schoolhouse Road to Goldenville Road, where they turned east. The Confederate cavalrymen instead continued to pursue Bell's retreating horsemen straight into the center of town. The sight of White's fearsome-looking riders charging through the streets of the normally peaceful community reminded Rev. Abraham Essick from St. James Lutheran Church of a vision straight from the depths of hell. The clergyman declared in his diary that the men "rode at the top of their speed and yelled like demons, their faces black with dirt, and their hair streaming in the wind."[24]

Schoolgirl Matilda "Tillie" Pierce also watched in terror as the riders charged by her home on Baltimore Street. "What a horrible sight!" she remarked. "There they were, human beings! clad almost in rags, covered with dust, riding wildly, pell-mell down the hill toward our home!" She noted that the men were "shouting, yelling most unearthly, cursing, brandishing their revolvers, and firing right and left." Prof. Michael Jacobs from the local college found the scene just as frightening. He reported that the troopers were "yelling and shooting like so many savages from the wilds of the Rocky Mountains, firing their pistols not caring whether they kill or maimed man, woman, or child."[25]

Sarah "Sallie" Broadhead, who lived in the west end of town on Chambersburg Street, could hardly believe the soul-piercing sounds emanating from the ferocious-looking horsemen. She claimed that they let loose "with such horrid yells that it was enough to frighten us all to death." Some of the children in Gettysburg had a much different reaction to what they witnessed that day. Nine-year-old Gates Fahnestock caught a close-up view with some of his friends as the riders charged past his home on the corner of Middle and Baltimore Streets. "The boys looking through the slatted shutters on the second floor saw it and enjoyed it as much as they would a Wild West show," he recalled years later.[26]

The Confederates' arrival also attracted the attention of John Charles Wills, whose father operated the Globe Inn. The young man looked on as White's cavalrymen charged along Chambersburg Street "at full speed with carbines up, as if ready to shoot." The troopers soon halted and deployed around the central square. Willis noted that the commander immediately "divided them into three squads; the first went out Carlisle Street, the second out York Street, and the third out Baltimore Street." The horsemen then "gave chase, out each street" after the fleeing militiamen.[27]

Most of the men from Bell's Adams County Cavalry scrambled for safety along Hanover Road. Some of White's pursuing cavalrymen soon encountered Pvts. William Lightner and George Washington Sandoe along Baltimore Turnpike about a quarter mile north of Rock Creek. Lightner quickly rode off unharmed at the first sight of their pursuers. After firing his pistol, Sandoe attempted to escape by having his horse leap over a nearby fence. When his mount stumbled, one of White's troopers shot him dead on the spot, inflicting wounds to his head and left breast.[28]

While that was going on, another group of rebel cavalrymen rode south on Baltimore Street to Evergreen Cemetery. Elizabeth Thorn, the acting caretaker while her husband served in the Union army, watched in fear as six troopers approached the grounds. "Before they came into the Cemetery they fired off their revolvers to scare the people," she recounted. "They chased the people out and the men ran and jumped over fences." Their sudden presence left her frightened nearly out of her mind. "When they rode into the Cemetery I was scared, as I was afraid they had fired after my mother," the woman recalled. "I fainted from fright, but finally reached the house."

The troopers assured her that she "should not be afraid of them, they were not going to hurt us like the yankeys did their ladies." The men instead seemed most interested in obtaining something to eat. Thorn noted that "they rode around the house on the pavement to the window, and asked for bread and butter and butter-milk." While her mother gathered up some food, another cavalryman arrived on the grounds with a riderless horse in tow, one of those who had ambushed Sandoe. The man informed his friends that the militiaman "shot at me, but he did not hit me, and I shot at him and blowed him down like nothing, and here I got his horse and he lays down the pike."[29]

Besides killing Private Sandoe, White's troopers took many of Bell's men pris-oner as they attempted to get away. They also captured all twenty of the pickets from Jennings's regiment in the initial attack along Marsh Creek. The cavalrymen later rounded up about thirty-five additional militiamen, who had remained in town to guard the train cars. Some others from that contingent eventually escaped east to Wrightsville, along the Susquehanna River. The men from the Philadelphia City Cav-alry fled for safety along York Street. From there they galloped north to Hunterstown Road and, after a brief exchange of gunfire, made their way to Hanover with no loss.[30]

With the troopers from French's Seventeenth Virginia Cavalry at the front, the rest of Early's Division pushed east through the rain along Hilltown Road in an at-tempt to cut off any enemy forces fleeing north from Gettysburg. The commander placed two regiments from Hays's Brigade in support of the cavalrymen, while the other three regiments, along with the men from Smith's and Avery's brigades, trailed behind in the rear. The advancing column soon reached Mummasburg, where Early received information that "there was but a small force at Gettysburg." He halted there "to wait for the infantry whose march was impeded by the mud, sending out one of French's companies toward the latter place to reconnoiter."

As they scoured through the area, French's scouts gathered up a handful of pris-oners "from whom it was ascertained that the advance of Gordon's force . . . had encountered a regiment of militia, which fled at the first approach." The informa-tion further indicated that the retreating unit was "only four miles away." Based on those reports, Early "immediately sent forward Colonel French with his cavalry to pursue the militia force." While the horsemen hustled off to the east, the general dispatched the two lead regiments in Hays's Brigade to aid in chasing down the retreating Federal troops.[31]

After an "exhausting chase of several miles," the cavalrymen spotted about six hundred militiamen resting at Henry Witmer's farm on Goldenville Road, about three miles northeast of Gettysburg. The troopers immediately set up on some high ground known as Bayly's Hill for an attack. Sergeant Hodam bragged that French's troopers charged into the ranks of the militiamen "as if they were so many sheep." According to him, the Southerners punctuated their devastating attack with an

ear-piercing yell that "would have done credit to a band of Comanche Indians."
Jennings's men got off only three or four shots apiece, which unseated a couple of
cavalrymen, before finally giving way in terror.

The onrushing Confederates quickly rounded up the panicked militiamen by
the dozens. "Those on the right side of our approach were captured before they had
a chance to run," Hodam recalled. "Those on the farther side including most of the
officers fled as fast as their legs could carry them, leaving everything behind except
their arms and knapsacks." Soon the ground was "strewn with guns, knapsacks,
musical instruments, blankets and clothing." The rest of the Pennsylvanians scrambled for cover in any hiding place they could find. "The main body of the fleeing
enemy kept together in the highway, but many, as they became exhausted, sought
refuge in the fields, orchards, and farm buildings by the way," Hodam explained.

The cavalryman claimed that "many laughable incidents" occurred as they gathered up the terrified youngsters from the surrounding area. They found six of them
clinging to "the branches of a large apple-tree." Eight more militiamen cowered
"under a corncrib." Lt. Col. William C. Taverner from French's regiment ordered
some of his men to dismount and join in the search on foot. The detail soon spotted
a regimental officer "hid in a bake oven" inside one of the nearby dwellings. Hodam
reported that the disheveled gentleman "made a fit subject of the boys fun with his
fine uniform all covered with soot and ash."[32]

Captain Seymour openly mocked the enemy's cowardly behavior. "The militia,
who no doubt had previously resolved to die if need be in defense of their homes and
friends, changed their mind when they caught a glimpse of our two little regiments
in the distance and most precipitately and ingloriously fled the field," the Louisiana
staff officer remarked in his journal. The comments from Sue King Black, who lived
near Bayly's Hill, were hardly better. She reported to a friend that "one of the boys hid
under a bed where a reb found him and asked if his mother knew he was out."[33]

In all, French's troopers captured about 120 of Jennings's troops around the Witmer Farm. Most of the frightened militiamen surrendered without the least sign of
resistance. The mere sight of the pursuing cavalrymen most often proved sufficient
to end their flight. "On every side the blue coated fellows could be seen waving
their handkerchiefs in token of surrender," Sergeant Hodam remembered. All that
was required to finish the job was "to make them break their guns over a stump or
fence and send them to the rear as prisoners."

The only casualty came when a militiaman was "struck in the face by a ball, which
glanced from a rail" on a nearby fence. The injury proved so minor that the youngster
did not require the attention of a surgeon. The cavalrymen mostly failed to pursue
the defenders who had evaded the initial charge on their lines. Hodam complained
that the enemy troops interfered with their effort to track them down by tearing up "a
bridge delaying us a short time." Adding to the problems was "a hard rain" that soon

began. Most of the remaining militiamen fled northeast along the backroads toward Dillsburg. After a harrowing retreat, they eventually reached safety at Harrisburg.[34]

Both Smith's and Avery's brigades remained in place near Mummasburg throughout the attack. The three reserve regiments from Hays's Brigade established camp just south of there around some high ground known as Oak Hill. This area, located about a mile and a half north of Gettysburg, would become the site for some of the hardest fighting in the war less than a week letter. The troops from the other two regiments in the brigade, who had played only a minor role in gathering up the prisoners, rejoined their comrades soon afterward. "Darkness coming on, our men returned to camp weary from their long and useless march in the rain and mud," Captain Seymour grumbled in his journal.[35]

While French's cavalrymen rounded up Jennings's men, Gordon's troops paraded into the center of town. Private Bradwell noted that they entered Gettysburg from the west and then "turned down the main street to the south and halted while our military band took position on the principal corner and played 'Dixie' and many other selections." Those martial flourishes failed to impress sixteen-year-old Margaretta Kendlehart, who dismissed the passing soldiers as "the filthiest looking pack of men we had ever seen." Fannie Buehler, wife of the town's postmaster, watched from her porch as the troops continued down Baltimore Street and eventually stopped "in front of the courthouse almost opposite to our house."[36]

A crowd soon gathered to observe the invaders close up. Private Bradwell was shocked that most of the children had only one pressing concern on their minds. "They were anxious to know when we were going to burn the town," the Georgian remembered. "Crowds of these youngsters hung to us everywhere we went, asking the same question." Their unexpected pleas for mercy left him almost at a loss for words. Even Lee's recent orders banning all types of retribution while the Confederates remained in enemy country mattered little to the terrified townspeople. Bradwell admitted that "our only answer was that Southern soldiers didn't burn towns."[37]

Although plundering was strictly off limits, General Early made it clear to the citizens that they would not escape without making a substantial contribution to the army's larder. The division commander initially inquired for the chief burgess. On learning that the man had fled town, Early tracked down merchant David Kendlehart, who served as president of the town council, and immediately presented a demand for him to turn over items from a long list of supplies, including sixty barrels of flour, 7,000 pounds of pork or bacon, 1,200 pounds of sugar, 600 pounds of coffee, 1,000 pounds of salt, forty bushels of onions, 1,000 pairs of shoes, and 500 hats—or $5,000 in cash.

After briefly conferring with the other council members, Kendlehart submitted a formal written reply. "The requisition asked for can not be given, because it is utterly impossible to comply," he declared. "The quantities required are far beyond that in our possession." Instead, the council president defiantly agreed only to a compromise solution. "In compliance, however, to the demand, we will request the stores to be opened and the citizens to furnish whatever they can of such provisions, etc., as may be asked," Kendlehart offered. He added that "further we can not promise."[38]

While far from pleased, Early decided not to carry out any major retribution on Gettysburg, later explaining that "it was then late and I had to move early in the morning towards York." Teenager Albertus McCreary noted that the council president, "after much parley, convinced the officer that it would be impossible to agree to their demands, since, having been warned of their coming, the citizens had removed their money and goods to places of safety." Catherine Mary White Foster, who lived nearby, noted that the rebels "boldly raised their flag over our town and played Dixie tunes in the court house but they did not succeed in gathering any booty in the place."[39]

Fannie Buehler was just as satisfied with the results of the negotiations. "After matters had been satisfactorily arranged between our Burgess and the Rebel officers, the men settled down and the citizens soon learned that no demands would be made upon them by the Rebel soldiery, and that all property would be protected, and it was," she remarked. Buehler acknowledged that "some horses were stolen, some cellars were broken into and robbed, but so far as could be done, the officers controlled their men, and all those in and around the streets behaved well." She was especially relieved that the much-feared "'Louisiana Tigers' were left and kept outside of town."[40]

Unknown to her, the rowdy Louisianans failed to keep completely out of trouble during their stay. A group of them sneaked into town sometime after dark and gained access to a large stock of whiskey. "The whole brigade got drunk," Lt. J. Warren Jackson griped in a letter home. "I never saw such a set in my life." Private Bradwell, who was serving with the provost guards from the Thirty-First Georgia, explained that "some of the Irish soldiers" in the brigade "found some people of the same nationality in the southern suburbs who sold liquor, and a fight began which resulted in our men beating up the old citizens." He admitted that "the whole thing was over when we arrived on the scene to put a stop to the riot, and we made no arrests."[41]

Rather than rounding up the unruly soldiers, the provost guards spent most of their time assisting the commissary and quartermaster details as they scoured through Gettysburg for additional supplies. "Soon the town was filled with infantry, and then the searching and ransacking began in earnest," young Tillie Pierce complained. "They wanted horses, clothing, anything and almost everything they could conveniently carry away. Nor were they particular about asking." She griped that "whatever suited them they took." Reverend Essick grumbled in his diary that the soldiers "took a great many things from the stores, for which they paid Confederate scrip or left a receipt and order upon their government."[42]

Although the supply details secured a few scattered items, their efforts to gather up any significant plunder proved disappointing. "As the store-keepers had previ-

ously removed nearly all their goods, there was little left for the rebels," a local newspaper explained. Colonel Evans, who commanded the provost guards, especially
complained that they uncovered "very few boots, shoes, or hats for the men." Despite
their lack of success, the troops carried out the searches without any major trouble.
Their conduct stood in stark contrast to what the townspeople had anticipated. "The
citizens expected us to revel & riot all night, burning & destroying property," Evans
remarked in a letter home "They were therefore very much surprised by the quiet of
the town."[43]

Most inhabitants found the constant unauthorized foraging for additional food
more intrusive than the organized searches. Gettysburg resident Kate Bushman
watched with disgust as a group of soldiers pillaged a grocery store near her home.
To her consternation, some of the men soon arrived at her front door. "What was
our feelings you can imagine when I turned around to see three of them standing in
our dining room," she declared. "However I tried to look as fearless as possible and
bid them the Time when they asked me for some Dinner which I gave them." Luckily the unwanted visitors turned out to be well behaved. "They were gentlemanly
and polite," the young woman recalled. "Especially one of them."[44]

Elizabeth Thorn spent nearly all day providing provisions for the hungry troops
who swarmed over the grounds of Evergreen Cemetery. "We were trying to feed
them all we could," she explained. "I had baked in the morning and had the bread
in the oven." The terrified woman "stood before the oven and cut this hot bread for
them" as fast as she could. Many other men stopped by to get a quick drink. "We
had all the glasses and tins and cups and tubs and everything outside filled with
water," Thorn remarked. "All the time our little boys were pumping and carrying
water to fill the tubs." She noted that the youngsters "handed water to the soldiers
and worked and helped this way until their poor little hands were blistered."[45]

Schoolteacher Salome "Sallie" Myers was relieved that the invaders seemed more
interested in simply conversing rather than in plundering. "Two of them were at our
door about two hours talking to father about the war and their southern rights etc.,"
she penned in her diary. "We talked to them as we would to anyone else." Mrs. Buehler
also had a relatively carefree encounter with a small group of soldiers who stopped on
her porch that evening. "They were not as ragged and dirty as some of the men I had
seen earlier in the afternoon and were very civil and well behaved," the woman admitted. "We had a long pleasant talk, no bitterness expressed by them or me."[46]

The presence of the Confederate troops proved much scarier for the few African
American residents who had not fled town prior to their arrival. "My mother had two
Negro servants," Jacob Taughenbaugh, who was a teenager at the time, recounted.
"We were sure if the Confederates found them they would be taken away." His family
quickly provided them with a secure hiding place. He recalled that "our front porch
was a few feet above ground, and at one end there was an excavation below ground
where you could get to the cellar from the outside." Taughenbaugh noted that his

mother "took away the stones enough to let the servants crawl through, then put them back carefully just as they had been."

The deception required constant vigilance to keep the fugitives out of the hands of the patrols, which repeatedly stopped by their home about five miles outside of town. "Someone had to keep a sharp lookout all the time, and as soon as a soldier was seen coming Mother would take the servants down and stow them away," he remembered. The Confederates often lingered long enough to threaten exposure of the hiding place. "Sometimes there would be men hanging around the house all day long almost," Taughenbaugh remarked. "The best she could do then was to take down some food and slip it to them through the space of one stone when some of the men were near about."[47]

The outcome was somewhat better for black minister Abraham Cole and his wife and daughter. "The daughter's husband was in the Union army," recalled Mary Warren, who lived near the family on West Middle Street. "They were alone and did not know what to do." Offering them a place of refuge, her "mother told them to come to our house." The woman informed her guests that "she would hide them in the loft, take away the ladder, and they would be safe." By the following day "no Confederates were about and they felt safe to go home again."[48]

While the troops rounded up whatever loot they could find, Early remained busy dealing with his haul of captured soldiers, the bulk of whom remained under guard north of town around the Witmer farm. He placed those who had been seized around Marsh Creek and inside Gettysburg into temporary custody at the Christ Lutheran church on Chambersburg Street, soon ordering them transferred under armed escort to the courthouse. That sight left Sallie Broadhead in total despair. "I cannot tell how bad I felt to hear them, and to see the traitor's flag floating overhead," she declared. "My humiliation was complete when I saw our men marching behind them surrounded by a guard."[49]

Early displayed utter contempt for the hapless militiamen, who had surrendered in droves without a fight of any consequence. "This was a part of Governor Curtin's contingent for the defence of the State, and seemed to belong to that class of men who regard 'discretion as the better part of valor,'" the Virginian later declared. "It was well that the regiment took to its heels so quickly, or some of its members might have been hurt, and all would have been captured." According to one account, Early directly lectured the Pennsylvanians from the front steps of the courthouse with the derisive comment, "you boys ought not to be out here in the field where it is dangerous and you might get hurt."[50]

Other details fanned out across the town searching for any militiamen who might be might be hiding. Lydia Catherine Ziegler, who was thirteen years old, watched from the steps of the Lutheran seminary in the northwestern section of town as a detachment arrived. "A squad from the main body was sent over to the Seminary to find out whether any Yankee soldiers were concealed there," she re-

called. "After the investigators were informed that the building was a theological
school edifice," the horsemen called off the hunt. Instead, "a guard, was placed
around it, and we felt perfectly safe," Ziegler admitted.[51]

A different squad stopped at the local bank to locate any hidden stashes of cash.
Unknown to them, the clerk had already transferred the bank's funds to safety in a
nearby town. "When I returned I found the Rebels in possession of the town," the
diligent employee recounted. "They took me to the bank and made me show 'em
that we hadn't any money there." He claimed that one of them even "threatened to
send me and the treasurer to Richmond." To their disgust, the Southerners quickly
determined that the clerk's protestations were correct. The youngster gloated that
"they didn't get the money or much else in the town."[52]

Another detachment secured about a dozen railroad cars that had remained
parked on the southeastern edge of town. John Wills protested that one of them
contained private property destined for delivery to his family's hotel. "We had in
that car, for the Globe Hotel, six barrels of whiskey, forty bushels of potatoes, three
barrels of sugar, one barrel of syrup, and one tierce of hams and shoulders of cured
meat," he explained. "We called on General Early and asked him to give us a guard
while we were getting these goods out of the car and removing them to the cellar."
The rebel commander surprisingly complied with his request.[53]

With that out of the way, the men assigned to the railroad detail confiscated
"about 2,000 rations" from the other packed carriages. They immediately turned
over the food to the provost guards from Gordon's Brigade. After cleaning out most
of the other contents, the soldiers destroyed the boxcars by setting them ablaze.
They also torched the railroad bridge spanning nearby Rock Creek, sparking a huge
inferno that quickly consumed most of the structure. "The cars, numbering 10 or
12 were burned, as was also a small railroad bridge," General Early boasted in his
official report.[54]

According to one newspaper account, the fire grew so intense that "the centre
span of the bridge was burnt and fell in," while the other two sections remained
"standing, but badly damaged." Aaron Sheely watched the roaring blaze from his
home around Red Hill, just north of the bridge. "A dozen or more cars, some filled
with merchandise and others empty were set on fire and started down the track,
probably for the bridge," he remarked. Rather than crashing into the burning span,
the railroad carriages wildly skidded well past their intended target and "were consumed a short distance beyond."[55]

The massive fire sent a wave of terror rippling through town. Elizabeth Thorn
could clearly "see the cars drop down" in flames from as far away as Cemetery Hill.
Henry Eyster Jacobs, who lived on the corner of Washington and Middle Streets,
noted that the sky during the evening turned "red with the reflections of the fire."
Fannie Buehler speculated that the inferno marked the beginning of the widespread
destruction and plundering she had feared so much before eventually concluding

that "the town was not burned down." She was especially pleased that "the court-house remained uninjured as far as I could see."[56]

While Gordon's men patrolled the streets, the other troops remained in camp just north of town. White's cavalrymen eventually took up position about two miles east of Gettysburg along York Road. Sarah Barrett King caught sight of them as they rode past her house on the edge of town with a huge haul of plunder in hand. "Some of them had a pile of hats on their heads looking comical, strings of muslin, and other goods trailing on the ground, quilts and shawls were piled up on their horses, shoes tied to the stirrups, altogether forming a laughable picture," she recounted.[57]

The majority of the townspeople eventually settled in for a largely sleepless night. Sallie Broadhead remained especially apprehensive about the presence of so many armed on the streets. "I was left entirely alone, surrounded by thousands of ugly, rude, hostile soldiers, from whom violence might be expected," she fumed. "Even if my neighbors were at hand, it was not pleasant, and I feared my husband would be taken prisoner before he could return or whilst trying to reach me." Albertus Mc-Creary was most upset by the sounds of revelry that punctuated the evening calm. He admitted that it was "very exasperating" to hear "their band through the night playing 'Dixie' and other Confederate airs."[58]

"Our Army Left a Mark Everywhere It Went"

After paroling the prisoners from Jennings's regiment, Jubal Early's men headed east from Gettysburg toward York early in the morning on June 27. The only troops not ready for the trip were some of Hays's Louisianans, who had been issued a ration of whiskey. Capt. William Seymour griped that many of them became drunk and "caused me much trouble to make them keep up with the column." The brigade staffer forced some of the worst offenders to ride in "the cook utensils wagon" amid "the sharp sides and projecting legs of the pots & kettles." He joked that the hungover "Tigers" endured a very "rough and disagreeable ride," which "sobered them speedily."[1]

Early divided his advancing column into three parts. The brigades of Smith, Avery, and Hays, on the left, followed a route from Mummasburg that took them through the small settlements of Hunterstown, New Chester, and Hampton. The bulk of William French's Seventeenth Virginia Cavalry and three of the division's batteries accompanied them on the march. Much of the journey took place in a driving rainstorm that swept through the area. Lt. J. Warren Jackson from Hays's Brigade complained that the mud soon became "nearly Knee deep." The footing proved so treacherous that the troops began "straggling by the hundreds."[2]

Gordon's Brigade, on the main body's immediate right, traveled east from Gettysburg along York Turnpike toward New Oxford. The column also included a single company from French's regiment and Capt. William A. Tanner's Courtney (Virginia) Artillery. Because the turnpike was macadamized, the Georgians encountered fewer problems due to muddy conditions than the rest of the division. The crushed-rock surface of the turnpike resisted the rain so much better than the dirt road to the north that the troops made good time as they pushed though the eastern part of Adams County. On the far right, Lieutenant Colonel White's horsemen split off on a major raid southeast to Hanover in order to gather supplies and disrupt traffic on the railroad running to Gettysburg.[3]

The men in both columns soon discovered that this section of the state was just as lush as the neighboring Cumberland Valley. One soldier from Gordon's Brigade effused in a letter home that it was "the most beautiful and highly cultivated country I ever beheld." He proclaimed that "every thing was in the most perfect order and every thing that man or beast could want abounded in great plenty." Capt. Reuben Allen Pierson from Hays's Brigade was astonished to find that the farmers "sow their grain with patented machines covering it at the same time." He noted that "they reap, pile in bundles, thrash and fan the grain all with different machines."[4]

Lt. William Lyon, who served as the ordnance officer in Gordon's Brigade, was stunned by the huge quantities of food available from the people along the way. "They brought out in the greatest abundance everything they had to eat and drink, and would not be prevailed upon to take pay for it," he remarked in a letter to his brother. "I don't think any men of the brigade lived so well before." According to another officer from the Thirty-Eighth Georgia in the same brigade, the Southerners were determined to take full advantage of whatever else they found in the region. To his delight, they "gobbled up all the horses, wagons, cattle and sheep for miles on either side of the line of march."[5]

Early's soldiers focused much of their attention on confiscating horses. Like the men from the other two divisions, they remained disappointed with the poor quality of the animals that they seized along the way. "After all, we gained very little by our horse stealing," Lt. Robert Stiles from the Charlottesville (Virginia) Artillery conceded. He noted that "the impressed animals were, for the most part, great, clumsy, flabby Percherons or Conestogas, which required more than twice the feed our compact, hard-muscled little Virginia horses required, and yet could not do half work they did, nor stand half the hardships and exposure."[6]

The items procured along their march often included more than just food and livestock of all kinds. An officer from the Sixth North Carolina informed Colonel Avery's family about a month later that the brigade commander had purchased a large supply of "ladies goods" for them during the advance through Pennsylvania. Following Avery's death during the fighting at Gettysburg on July 2, this man faced the problem of how to ship the items to the colonel's relatives. "If I had any way in the world to send them home to you I would do so," he explained to the fallen commander's father. His biggest worry was that the massive bundle would "be lost or stolen" in transit.[7]

The huge amount of goods that they confiscated from the Pennsylvanians proved particularly satisfying for those soldiers seeking revenge for what they regarded as the despicable conduct of Federal troops in the South. Lt. Joseph Hilton from the Twenty-Sixth Georgia in Gordon's Brigade gloated to his cousin that the Southerners "have inflicted serious injury upon the corpulent Dutch farmers of that loyal state, in the destruction of Bee Gums, Fowls, Eggs, Butter, Cherries, Green Apples, Cider, and Apple Butter." He estimated that "it will take at least three seasons to replenish the stock, besides playing havoc with their horses and cattle."[8]

Rather than admitting the obvious benefits of the North's free-labor economic system for the average farmer, many of the men chose instead to demean the looks and character of the people they encountered. "From the imperfect view which I had of the country and its inhabitants in thus passing through it, I know of nothing which I could name for which it is more noted than its fine grain, nice large cherries, Dutch farmers and ugly females," a soldier from Gordon's Brigade jabbed in a letter to his hometown newspaper. "If the other portions of the state are to be judged by this, I should express it as my conviction that handsome females are much more scarce than Copperheads."[9]

Even when the soldiers encountered some undeniably attractive females, they openly questioned their morals. "I never saw the whole time while I was in Pennsylvania, a single woman who appeared delicate and refined," another Georgian remarked in a letter home. "I saw a great many well-dressed ones in the cities and towns, through which I passed, but they all showed unmistakable signs of lowness and vulgarity." His comments about the male inhabitants were no better. "The men whom we met, who were almost all Dutch, were certainly the most cowardly wretches I ever saw," he ranted. The soldier complained that they "would tell any tale and act any part" to keep their valued property from being confiscated.[10]

Many of the people along their route attempted to mollify the troops by declaring that they were Peace Democrats or Copperheads, which is hardly surprising in a section of the state where the majority of voters failed to support Lincoln in the 1860 election. Pvt. John Hundley from the Twenty-First North Carolina in Avery's brigade pointed out to his wife that "a great many claimed to be Southern people and were bitterly opposed to the war." The Tar Heel acknowledged, however, that they "found some few who were in favor of prosecuting war and thought they would eventually conquer us." Pvt. John Cleek from the Fifty-Second Virginia in Smith's Brigade remained convinced that whatever Southern sympathy the people showed "was more through fear than anything else."[11]

The men were especially perplexed by the strange hand signals that many of the citizens flashed at them. "Much to our surprise, hundreds of people in the towns through which we passed greeted us with those signs and we joyfully accepted them as proofs of the anti-war feeling that pervaded the country," Captain Seymour remarked in his journal. Only later did he and others learn that the inexplicable gestures were the result of an elaborate hoax perpetrated by some conmen. "When we reached York we found that those professions and demonstration[s] were hollow and hypocritical," Seymour acknowledged.

The Louisianan could hardly believe the extent of the fraud. He noted that "two Yankees from one of the New England States traveled through the country professing to be high officials of a New York lodge of the 'Knights of the Golden Circle' and that they were empowered to receive any number of persons as members of the Order, on the payment of the small fee of five dollars per capita." The hucksters insisted that the soldiers would respect the signs and exempt them from retaliation. To Seymour's surprise, "thousands of people were induced to pay their money for the privilege of being accounted as friends of the South, hence our apparently cordial greeting along the line of march."[12]

Some of the more sophisticated citizens in the larger towns were stunned by the apparent gullibility of the farmers in the rural areas of the state. One York resident complained to a relative that "now, those poor ignorant people come into town to some smart people here, bringing their tickets of the Knights of the Golden Circle and saying: 'Here we want our dollar back, we showed the ticket, and made the signs, but it did no good.'" The woman claimed that most of the soldiers treated those farmers much worse than their neighbors. "In many cases, when they were told that the horses had been sent away, they made them pay as much as the horses were valued at," she remarked.[13]

Even the most impassioned protestations of ardent Southern support usually failed to prevent soldiers from carrying out forced seizures. "It is related that a prominent peace democrat of York county, Pa., when he discovered a party of cavalrymen leading five or six horses and some cattle from his barnyard, endeavored to persuade them to take them back, assuring them that he was deeply sympathetic with the cause of the South, and was opposed to the war and the administration, and had done all in his power to aid them," one newspaper recounted. The commanding officer reportedly "thanked him heartily for his sympathy, but told him he would take the horses and cattle as a contribution from a friend of the Confederate government."[14]

Those distractions did little to slow down Early's advance. During the late morning, the long column of troops from Gordon's Brigade, accompanied by some of French's troopers, arrived in New Oxford, home to about five hundred people. Local resident Charles Himes observed "a citizen on a horse watching their entree, until a cavalry man got a square from him, when there was a race." As the onlooker sped away, the trooper immediately "threw his reins over his arms, drew two pistols & rode as hard as horse flesh could carry him crying halt." He soon began interrogating the man about the presence of any Federal troops. Himes noted that the cavalryman "asked many questions using threats, honeyed words, or anything that promised to get at the truth."

The other rebel horsemen spread out all over the town, "with pistols in hand prying into every corner." Their behavior quickly changed once they determined that New Oxford remained undefended. Himes admitted that the invaders soon "became social and amiable, even friendly." The men "placed guards at stores & taverns," Himes observed, "told the storekeepers not to open except under orders from an officer," and "paid for all they got in Confed. scrip." He pointed out that the troopers "looked every inch fighting men." At the same time, they remained "very orderly, only calling out 'we're back in the union again, ain't we glad.'"

During the transit of Gordon's column, Himes engaged in "conversations with a number of officers & privates of the cavalry advance guards & infantry officers." Rather than halting, most of the infantrymen "passed through on a rapid march near four miles an hour paying their respects as they passed to a warehouse, carrying off sugar etc. & filling their canteens with molasses." Some of them assured Himes, however, that "they only wanted to let us know the meaning of the word war that they had felt it but that they would not imitate the conduct of our soldiers, who wasted every section they passed through."

As the last of the troops paraded out of town, Himes spotted a huge cloud of dark smoke rising from a warehouse "a few miles" from there at Goulden's Station, which the soldiers had torched and reportedly contained 1,000 bushels of grain. He noted that they set it on fire only after the owner's wife refused to hand over the keys. "On learning that it was private property they said they were very sorry," Himes remarked. The young man admitted that the troops "destroyed nothing" in the village itself, though, "not even a large quantity of hay ready for packing because it endangered the town."[15]

From New Oxford, Gordon's men continued east along the turnpike leading to York. The troops took another break soon afterward at Abbottstown. Numerous soldiers crowded around a water pump on the town square to quench their growing thirst. Others questioned the citizens about the location of any Federal troops. Some of the pickets soon caught sight of a lone driver approaching in a carriage. This turned out to be York businessman Arthur B. Farquhar, who arrived there in hopes of meeting with the Confederate general. After conferring with a committee of top officials in York that morning, he had volunteered as an emissary to work out terms for a peaceful occupation of the town in order to prevent its destruction.

As he was being taken into custody, Farquhar, who had extensive family and business connections in the South, spotted an old acquaintance among his captors. The startled officer immediately escorted the businessman to Gordon's headquarters for an impromptu meeting. "The General was exceedingly courteous," Farquhar recalled. "I did not know General Gordon personally but I knew him well through mutual friends." When the brigade commander inquired what was on his mind, the wealthy entrepreneur explained that his sole aim was to protect York from danger. "General Gordon, unless you have entirely changed from the character you used to have, you are neither a horse thief nor a bank robber, and fighting is more in your line than sacking a city," he declared.

When the general pressed him for more details, Farquhar calmly spelled out his plan. "You and your men enter York quietly and then you sit down and make requisitions for whatever you reasonably want and our committee will see that they are honoured," he answered. Gordon replied that he was more than happy to make any arrangements that would spare York from "the horrors of war." Even so, he initially balked when Farquhar asked him to sign a formal agreement. "When I explained that it was not because I doubted his word but only to satisfy the Committee, especially the women of the town, who were very uneasy, he at once signed what I had written," the businessman stated.[16]

Following the envoy's departure, Gordon's men proceeded east from Abbottstown and went into camp a couple of miles across the York County line alongside a cluster of about twenty buildings known simply as Farmers Post Office. Colonel Evans from the Thirty-First Georgia described it in his diary as "a little town of two stores." The general made his headquarters at a large farmhouse owned by Jacob S. Altland, which stood nearby on the south side of the turnpike. While his troops settled into place, Gordon had the gunners from Tanner's battery dig some artillery emplacements in case they came under attack.[17]

Later that evening a larger delegation from York, which included Farquhar, Chief Burgess David Small, and three members of the town's Committee of Public Safety, arrived at Gordon's camp under a flag of truce for another meeting with the general. After conferring with Farquhar on his return earlier that day, the officials had reluctantly agreed to the basic arrangement worked out with Gordon. In a single act of defiance, the men decided that they would leave a huge Union flag flying from its 110-foot pole in the central square at York as an indication that the town had not formally surrendered.

After being escorted to Gordon's headquarters, the officials pleaded with him to protect the people in the town from harm and ensure the safety of their property. The general assured them that the Confederates "didn't intend pursuing the same system of warfare" that Union troops had carried out in the South and that "they respected private property." He acknowledged, however, that his soldiers would destroy any supplies intended for use by the Federal government. Gordon also informed the delegation that "the particulars would be arranged by General Early the next morning when he entered the town." The Georgian initially declined to allow the visitors to leave, but after he finally relented, they hurried back to York to await the arrival of the invaders.[18]

Early's two brigades on the left of the advance followed a different route to York that took them northeast through the tiny village of Hampton before turning east on an unpaved road. Following an exhausting march, the troops halted for the day about a mile beyond New Berlin. Pvt. Charles Moore Jr. from the Fifth Louisiana in Hays's Brigade described this community of about five hundred residents as "a beautiful place." Early established his headquarters a short distance away at the home of a frightened German widow. The general took over most of the building for his own use, while his staff officers slept that night on the large front porch.[19]

The men from the Forty-Ninth Virginia in Smith's Brigade served as provost guards during their stay. Lt. William James Kincheloe borrowed a horse and joined some other troops on a foraging expedition into the surrounding countryside. The Virginian noted that he met "with good success in bread, applebutter, butter, etc."

Just as at their other stops during the advance, the citizens most often handed over their goods without demanding payment of any kind. "The people are scared into fits and break their necks nearly to wait on me," Kincheloe remarked in his diary.[20]

Soon after their arrival at New Berlin, Early rode to Gordon's camp, located about four miles south of there on the turnpike, "to arrange with him the means" of seizing York the next day. During their meeting, the Georgian informed him that the latest reports from his scouts indicated that there were "no troops" in the town. He also briefed the general about his session with the municipal delegation. If York proved to be undefended, Early directed him to continue east to Wrightsville, on the west bank of the Susquehanna River opposite Columbia, and "get possession" of the nearby bridge "at both ends," holding it until the rest of the division joined them there.[21]

While all that was going on, the 250 horsemen from "Lige" White's battalion set off early on June 27 to the southeast toward Hanover, which stood at the junction of the two railroad branches connecting York to Gettysburg. Their first halt came about 10:00 A.M. at McSherrystown, near the boundary of Adams and York Counties. "During the forenoon, we heard that a squadron of confederate cavalry was approaching McSherrystown from Gettysburg," recalled Lewis J. Conrad from nearby Hanover, who was in town supervising some construction. "I had a good horse and I decided it was best not to let the enemy have him." The contractor quickly gathered up his tools and galloped off at top speed.[22]

As they entered the town, White's troopers spread out through the streets in search of all kinds of plunder. A quartermaster detail immediately forced its way into Isaac Reily and Vincent Sneeringer's dry-goods store. The owners looked on helplessly as the Southerners rummaged through the contents of the business. The cavalrymen eventually departed with a small haul of loot that included sixty hats, ten caps, twenty pairs of shoes, and a quantity of socks, pen knives, and handkerchiefs. Their stay proved much more trying for a terrified resident forced to serve as their guide as the band of horsemen continued east.[23]

The column of riders soon reached Hanover, which had a population of about 1,600. Jesse Kohler and his brother-in-law Eli Kindig were among the many frightened citizens who fled as the Confederates approached the town. "They had started when they were commanded to halt, by a cavalryman, who came dashing on behind them," one newspaper account stated. "Not obeying they were fired on, and heard the bullet whistle in rather dangerous proximity." As they came to a stop, Kohler somehow managed to slip away, while "Kindig was captured and ordered to stand by the sidewalk and await orders." Despite his predicament, he escaped soon afterward with his horse and buggy.[24]

By the time White's cavalrymen occupied the town, officials had already transferred most of the locomotives and railroad cars normally kept there to safety on the far side of the Susquehanna River at Columbia. The local newspaper reported that the townspeople "were soon greeted with the sight of one, and then another horseman, with cocked pistols in their hands, moving slowly and steadily up the avenue and commanding all who attempted to flee to halt." According to another account, the main part of the column proceeded "slowly up Carlisle Street, nearly every man with his finger on the trigger, ready for any emergency."

After posting pickets on the main streets, the rest of the troopers halted in front of the Central Hotel on the town square. From a perch atop his fine horse, Lieutenant Colonel White addressed a large crowd of citizens who had gathered to gawk at the invaders. He immediately assured them that they had no cause to fear for their safety and that his men would fully abide by the strict rules issued by General Lee. The cavalry leader declared to the assembled throng that "although his soldiers wore faded suits of gray, they were gentlemen fighting for a cause they thought to be right, but would harm no one."[25]

Following White's impromptu oration, most of the cavalrymen on the square dismounted and entered the nearby stores in search of shoes and any clothing that they might uncover. Daniel Skelly, who had recently escaped to Hanover from Gettysburg, looked on in disgust as a detail burst into the local express office. The youngster, who worked as a clerk for the prominent Fahnestock Brothers store in Gettysburg, noted that one of the packages they seized "was for my firm and which I saw them open." The items inside the container proved to be a shipment of gloves, which the intruders immediately appropriated.[26]

Another group entered a large shoe store on Baltimore Street that belonged to Joseph C. Holland. Even when the soldiers began waving their guns at him, the

Central Square at Hanover, Pennsylvania. Courtesy York County History Center.

feisty merchant at first refused their orders to unlock the door. "I don't like that, and you are cowards if you continue it," he defiantly shouted back at them. Holland eventually gave in to their demand with the comment, "if want to go in my store, I will open it." To their consternation, the men in the search party discovered that the shop was nearly empty of merchandise and left with only a handful of shoes.[27]

Other soldiers pillaged through nearby Heiman's Clothing Store, where they uncovered a number of useful items. Other searches extended to Wintrobe's Hotel, which the men ransacked by shuffling through the cabinets and busting open a safe. Several brazen troopers also forced their way into A. G. Schmidt's drugstore and immediately demanded that he serve them some whiskey. Although he had none on hand, the terrified owner actually crossed the street to a hotel, where he purchased a supply of alcohol for them to drink. Some others arrived soon afterward and forced him to sell much of his extensive merchandise. Schmidt remained so frightened that he politely declined to take any payment for most of the goods.[28]

The bulk of the troopers focused on damaging the equipment in the railyard. They pried up some of the rails, disabled several of the switches, and also cut down most of the telegraph wires that connected the town to the outside world. Some others forced their way into the telegraph station at the yard, where they smashed a pair of old transmitters as they rummaged through the office. The men from the detail eventually left after turning the room into a shambles. Unknown to them, the operator had stashed a fully functional set of equipment in the building's loft.[29]

Despite the Confederates' zeal, the results of the searches proved a major disappointment. By most accounts, the efforts hardly appeared worth their trouble. "Some of the stores were robbed of a few articles but the soldiers did not obtain much clothing, because all wearing apparel and valuables had been concealed or taken away," one report stated. In all, the men spent only about an hour in their largely futile effort to gather up any useful goods. The townspeople watched with relief as their unwanted visitors quietly dashed out of town soon afterward along York Street.[30]

About a mile outside of Hanover, White's horsemen overtook local jeweler William Boadenhamer, who was fleeing in his carriage with a large box of merchandise from his shop on Broadway Street. They immediately seized his entire load of goods and rode off to the east. The troopers halted soon afterward at a nearby mill owned by Samuel Mumma and began shuffling through the container. Following a thorough search, they discovered a stash of about one hundred watches and pieces of jewelry, which the owner later valued at about $200. Lieutenant Colonel White noted that "after supplying ourselves, we buried the balance."[31]

The Confederates pushed on from there through the eastern part of Adams County toward Jefferson, which stood at the junction of two major roads. Along the way squads of cavalrymen plundered through neighboring farms. "We gave the old dutch in Penn. fits," one of the horsemen bragged in a letter home a few days later. "Our Army left a mark everywhere it went. Horses, cattle, sheep hogs, chickens,

Railroad yards at Hanover, Pennsylvania. Courtesy Library of Congress.

spring Houses suffered alike." He gloated that the farmers in that section of the state "cried peace most beautifully." The men also torched several wooden railroad bridges spanning Codorus Creek and cut down the telegraph lines along their route.[32]

After skirting just south of Jefferson, White's troopers arrived outside of Hanover Junction, located about eleven miles south of York, at about 2:00 P.M. As the site of a huge railroad complex, the hamlet served as a major transportation hub for the region. Main lines for the Northern Central Railway extended south to Baltimore and north to Elmira, New York. The Hanover Branch Railroad ran west through Jefferson and on to Hanover, where it connected with the lines running to Gettysburg and to Littlestown. The train yards included a maze of tracks and switches as well as a large wooden depot.

By then, three companies from the Twentieth Pennsylvania Volunteer Militia, totaling about two hundred men, under Lt. Col. William H. Sickles had moved into place in front of the depot near a bridge over Codorus Creek, where they attempted to hold off the advancing cavalrymen. The line of defenders soon faced a ferocious attack, punctuated with wild yells, from White's onrushing riders. Harry I. Gladfelter, who was twelve years old at the time, watched as the troopers charged into town. "Looking toward Seven Valleys and Hanover Junction from our home, we could see men galloping along the highway over the creek and Rail Road," he recalled.

The rampaging horsemen pushed on toward the enemy's position, their pistols blazing and their sabers flashing in the sunlight. As the Confederates closed in on the bridge, Sickles's line began to falter. After firing a few shots, the militiamen quickly lost their will to fight and withdrew in a panic about a mile to the rear. Not a single defender remained in place as the troopers finally swarmed over the bridge. One of White's officers noted that the cavalry commander did not "deem it prudent" to press the attack and allowed Sickles's militiamen to escape unharmed.[33]

A northbound train from the Northern Central Railway was passing through town just as the troopers entered the railroad yards. One railroad employee noted that the engineer "was on his way toward York when in the vicinity of Hanover Junction, he discerned a small troop of rebel cavalrymen galloping along the road-bed of the intersecting railway." A swarm of Confederate troopers soon nearly surrounded the train. The defiant conductor immediately instructed the engineer to "hurry away" as fast as possible. "We need no more pressing orders to leave than the approach of the enemy," the conductor yelled at him. "They shall not have this train if we can help it."

According to the employee, the engineer "opened the throttle to the limit and, calling to the fireman to follow, left the unprotected cab for the sheltering side of the locomotive tender, which in those days carried wood instead of coal." The railroad men hunkered down well out of view as the train accelerated off amid a hail of gun-fire from the pursuing troopers. "Hurriedly dismounting, the cavalrymen fired shot after shot at the fleeing train, but not a bullet struck the engine or tender," the man recalled. Despite that close call, the engineer and his companion eluded capture and made it safely to York by midafternoon.

Another locomotive with a tender and a single coach pulled out of the yards at Hanover Junction at about the same time. The telegraph operator at the main depot quickly jumped aboard as the terrified driver sped off to the south. "Just then, the Confederates caught sight of the train and they galloped ahead with all possible speed, expecting to catch it before it rounded the curve below the junction, but they did not succeed," one of the railroad men recalled. After navigating that stretch of track, the train sped off amid sporadic gunfire from a group of pursuing riders.[34]

Once they ended the chase, White's horsemen began destroying as much rail-road property as they could. One squad burned down the wooden bridge spanning Codorus Creek; they reportedly "performed this work by pouring coal oil on the wooden beams and setting fire to them." Another detachment smashed the railroad turntable and knocked the switches in the main yard out of commission. Other soldiers slashed the telegraph wires and ransacked the stationmaster's office. The worst damage occurred when they torched four railcars parked along the tracks, including two boxcars that the owner had sent there to protect them from destruc-tion during the recent raid on Gettysburg.[35]

Several raiding parties thereafter scoured the neighboring towns in search of plunder. "A company of more than fifty Rebel cavalry" reportedly gained entry to the general-merchandise store owned by Henry Bott and Ephraim D. Hartman in the tiny village of Seven Valleys. The men seized whatever clothing and other goods they could uncover, including calico, muslin, gingham, dress goods, hats, shoes, and boots. They also attempted to force their way into a large safe on the premises. Bott complained that they "took an axe and damaged the fire-proof safe in their efforts to open it."

When the businessman protested about this outrage, one trooper handed Bott's wife a one-dollar Confederate note as payment for a small item he had confiscated. She immediately complained that the money was worthless to her. "It will soon be worth more than your Yankee greenbacks," the cavalryman sternly replied. "We are going on to York and will soon cross the Susquehanna and move toward Philadelphia. The war is nearly over, and the South will win." The owners later filed two separate damage claims totaling nearly $650 in lost merchandise.[36]

Another group of "about 300 Rebels" stopped at the nearby property of Henry Fishel. The distraught farmer looked on in terror as the men "broke open [the] locked door of the distillery room" in one of his outbuildings. The raiders consumed a large quantity of rye whiskey right on the spot "before an officer intervened" and halted the drunken spree. The chastised troopers then destroyed forty-six barrels of whiskey "by smashing in the barrelheads." Fishel reported in his postwar claim for damages that the Confederates poured more than $1,200 worth of alcohol "onto the floor."[37]

After seizing numerous horses and goods from several other farms and villages, the raiding parties rejoined the main part of the battalion at Hanover Junction. The Virginians then retraced their route back to Jefferson. One trooper traded a brooch from the recent jewelry seizure for a glass of water from a young girl on the town square as he passed through the streets. Several others approached one home and demanded that the residents use some cornmeal and flour that they had obtained to bake them a supply of bread. The woman of the house took pity on them and reluctantly complied. She was shocked to find that the visitors looked like "typical farm boys."[38]

Before leaving town, White's cavalrymen stopped at the railroad depot, where they "knocked in the head[s]" of two barrels of fine whiskey belonging to Jacob Rebert, who owned a general-merchandise store. The horsemen also set fire to several railroad cars full of tanning bark that belonged to Henry Rebert. White's men eventually turned north through Spring Forge, the site of a large paper mill, before riding a couple of miles farther to the village of Nashville, halting there for the night on the John Weist farm, not far from Gordon's location.[39]

13

"I Want My Requisitions
Filled at Once"

Before dawn on June 28, General Early's soldiers were once more on move eastward. With a screen of cavalrymen along their front, the men from Gordon's Brigade and Captain Tanner's Courtney Artillery led the way toward the borough of York on the macadamized turnpike. The brigades of Smith, Avery, and Hays, along with the division's other three batteries, followed just behind on the unpaved Canal Road, leading to the village of Dover. "Just as the sun was rising in the east, the bugle was sounded and we took up the march toward York, passing a short distance south of Davidsburg over a wide road to Weigelstown, leaving Dover to my left," Early reported.[1]

Early assigned White's cavalrymen to scout through the surrounding farms and villages. The general noted that they "scoured the country, and gathered in many horses needed for our cavalry and our officers, for our own horses were tired and many of them nearly worn out." At Weigelstown he dispatched another detachment of troopers from Colonel French's regiment to ride north of York through Manchester to the Susquehanna River at the mouth of Conewago Creek near York Haven. "We didn't know they were coming until we saw them coming across the road toward Manchester from Weigelstown," area resident Michael Gross recalled. "There were about 200 of them all on horseback, cavalrymen, I believe."

To his surprise, the invaders trotted through town without halting. From there the column continued north to the nearby village of Mount Wolf. This time the horsemen lingered just long enough to pillage one of the local businesses. "They rode on through Manchester without disturbing any property, but stopped at Mt. Wolf, where they took a lot of shoes and other goods out of George Wolf's store," Gross recounted. "They didn't take anything in our township but horses, but they got a lot of them from some of our farmers and rode away with them."[2]

As they approached the river, the troopers spotted about four hundred men from the Twentieth Pennsylvania Volunteer Militia under Col. William B. Thomas in battle formation along the main crossing. The defenders fled in a panic over the Susquehanna to Bainbridge at the first sight of the Confederate horsemen. George W. Finlaw, who lived in that town, noted that French's troopers immediately "dashed down" to the riverbank and "commenced to ford the river." The cavalrymen also shot off a few rounds from the shoreline at some civilians who were trying to escape the scene of the fighting. "They opened fire on a flat loaded with men, women and children that was fleeing from them," Finlaw protested. "But strange to say, no one was hurt though they were in easy range and it was crowded with men, women and children."

The Federal troops quickly assembled a new defensive line on the opposite shore in a desperate attempt to keep the enemy from following them. "Soon as they showed a disposition to cross, the Soldiers were filed down from the town on the front and formed in line of battle," Finlaw explained. He noted that "this side of the river" was soon "dotted with boats filled with sharp shooters pulling out to an island to meet them." From there they unleashed a fierce fire on the invaders. "For a few minutes the popping of their rifles was quite brisk on both sides, but the rebs saw we were likely to give them the worst of it and returned," the man remarked. At least one Confederate was shot off his horse while crossing the Susquehanna.

After calling off the pursuit, French's men used coal oil to torch the railroad bridges that spanned the two nearby branches of Conewago Creek. One of the militiamen described the huge plume of smoke billowing from the structures as a "sorrowful and humiliating spectacle." With that task completed, the troopers galloped off to the south. Finlaw reported that the invaders "were soon out of sight and nothing but an occasional picket has been seen since." Later that day some of French's horsemen moved on to Hanover Junction, where they destroyed some of the bridges and railroad infrastructure that White's troopers had missed during their earlier raid on the town.[3]

While that was going on, the main part of Gordon's column pushed on toward York. That commercial and political hub, which had a population of about 8,600, ranked as the largest prize yet during the invasion. Settlers from eastern Pennsylvania established the town in the early 1740s. When the British occupied Philadelphia in 1777, the Continental Congress took refuge there, making York the temporary capital of the fledgling nation. During the following years, the town became home to a fast-growing number of mostly Scotch-Irish and German immigrants. It also emerged as a hotbed of support for the Democratic Party. In 1862 the U.S. Army opened a large military hospital there.[4]

After conferring with the chief burgess on the outskirts of town, Gordon split his force into three columns. The general accompanied the men from the Thirty-First Georgia into the city on Market Street, while the rest of his troops followed behind on two parallel streets. Colonel Evans, commander of the Thirty-First Georgia, described the parade to his wife as "a triumphal entry." Capt. William H. "Tip" Harrison from the same regiment noted that "a small squad of cavalry, followed by one of infantry of perhaps sixty," entered town at the front of the main column. As they marched along, the Confederates secured York by "stationing a sentinel at each cross street in the town."[5]

Gordon's troops arrived just as many of the townspeople were gathering for Sunday religious services. "The church bells were ringing, and the streets were filled with well-dressed people," the general recalled. "The appearance of these church-going men, women, and children, in their Sunday attire, strangely contrasted with that of my marching soldiers." Not surprisingly, nearly all of the citizens displayed unmistakable signs of outright fear. "Begrimed as we were from head to foot," the Georgian found it "no wonder that many of York's inhabitants were terror-stricken as they looked upon us."[6]

One woman was busy taking in an inspiring sermon when she suddenly heard the distinct sounds of a band playing "Dixie" from outside the sanctuary. Just then, someone rushed into the church to announce that the Confederates had arrived. The distraught pastor immediately dropped his notes and, after dismissing the congregation, suddenly broke into tears. The startled parishioners filed out of the building onto the front steps. A few of them stood gawking at the sights, while the majority headed off to the central square to catch a close-up view of the occupying troops.[7]

Many other townspeople spilled onto the main thoroughfare to witness the rebels' arrival. Lt. George Agee from the Twenty-Sixth Georgia noted that "the streets were lined from end to end with citizens, both men and women, as though there was no war going on." Colonel Evans reported to his wife that their entire path was filled with people "dressed in the best, all full of curiosity to see the rebels." The throng of onlookers soon crowded in on them from all sides. Pvt. Gordon Bradwell pointed out that "so great was the pressure that our officers marched us through the town in single column of twos," rather than their normal four-abreast formation.[8]

Cassandra Small, the thirty-four-year-old daughter of a prominent local businessman, looked on with growing concern as the Confederates paraded through the streets. "They came with loud music, flags flying," she reported in a letter to a relative. The officers took immediate steps to secure the town from any disruptions. "First we saw a picket in front of our door," the young woman remarked. "Where he came from or how he got there, no one knew, he came so suddenly and quietly." When Small gathered enough nerve to speak to him, the guard informed her that he was there "only to keep the men in line."[9]

Troops from the Thirty-First Georgia continued along Market Street into the center of town. Martin L. Van Baman, who was a teenager at the time, recalled that "it took but a short time for them to arrive in the square, with General Gordon at their head." Here stood the York County courthouse and several other major government buildings. The square was also the site of the town's market house, which consisted of "two market sheds, extending east and west." Van Baman noted that "a large flag staff upon which floated the Stars and Stripes" towered high over the center of this impressive public space.[10]

Market Sheds at Centre Square in York, Pennsylvania. Courtesy York County History Center.

From the front of the column, Colonel Evans soon caught sight of the Union banner waving in the light breeze atop the flagpole. The Georgian became so perturbed by this open sign of defiance that he determined to remove the offending Union symbol from its lofty perch. "I found the Yankee flag flying over the city," he informed his wife, "and as our troops had to pass directly under it, I hauled it down and sent it to the general." The colonel was stunned by its massive size, which he described as "being nearly thirty feet in length."[11]

Gordon immediately took the colors into his possession. Businessman Arthur Farquhar happened on the scene at about that time and begged the general not to replace the Stars and Stripes with the hated Confederate flag. This request touched off a heated exchange between the two leaders. After much deliberation, Gordon eventually gave in to Farquhar's impassioned pleas. Soon afterward some other troops spotted a smaller Union flag fluttering from the front of Pearce's Bookstore just east of the square. A squad quickly rushed forward and pulled this second banner down.[12]

Although most citizens greeted the soldiers with disdain, York remained a Democratic Party stronghold, home to many people who opposed Lincoln's war policies, including the Emancipation Proclamation. A few Southern sympathizers made their presence known as the troops threaded through the crowds. Cassandra Small fumed in a letter to a relative that "some ladies received them with waving handkerchiefs and red streamers." She claimed that others stopped the men on the street and begged for their uniform buttons as souvenirs. Such actions struck particularly close to home for this staunch Union supporter: one of her cousins served

with the Second Maryland Infantry Battalion in Johnson's Division and was reportedly in town on detached duty as a guide for Early's troops.[13]

Some ardent Copperheads took more overt steps to aid the occupiers. Lawyer
James W. Latimer griped in a letter a few days after the troops arrived in York that
the traitors "gave them all the aid and comfort in their power." One Southern supporter even stepped forward from the crowd and helped the soldiers pull down the
flag from the front of the bookstore. The attorney learned further details of their
treachery after questioning several of the Confederate guards assigned to protect
the town. "Reb officers said they had many sympathizers here; that they could get
any information they wanted," he complained. "One Copperhead, hearing a Union
man asked by an officer for a map of York Co. which of course was refused, volunteered to take him to his house and give him a map."[14]

Even that was not the most troubling instance of disloyalty among the residents.
As he moved farther into town, Gordon was shocked by the sight of "a little girl,
probably twelve years of age," who ran up to his horse and handed him "a large bou-
quet of flowers, in the centre of which was a note, in delicate handwriting, purport-
ing to give the numbers and describe the position of the Union forces of Wrightsville, toward which I was advancing." He noted that the message "bore no signature,
and contained no assurance of sympathy for the Southern cause, but it was so terse
and explicit in its terms as to compel my confidence."

Despite such displays of Southern support, most citizens exhibited so much
trepidation that Gordon felt compelled to assuage their fears. The general immediately halted along the street "in order to speak to the people" from his horse. He
pledged to the terrified onlookers that "the Confederate soldiers have entered your
state in no spirit of retaliation" and insisted that "we are here simply to fight the
armies that are invading our soil and destroying our homes." Gordon took great
pains to let them know that they had no cause for concern. "I beg to assure you that
no private property will be disturbed, and if one woman in this city is insulted, I
promise you the head of such a man," he declared.[15]

The brigade commander soon pulled up in front of Small's home, where several
of her friends had gathered to watch the arriving troops. "General Gordon stopped
his horse at our door, came up to [the] pavement and said, 'Ladies, I have a word
to say,'" the woman reported to a relative. His sudden appearance caught her completely off guard. To her surprise, he informed them that "you need not have any
fear of us, whilst we are in your midst." The rebel commander insisted that "you are
as safe as though we were a thousand miles away." With that comment, he abruptly
"bowed and turning his horse rode off."[16]

The general's efforts to calm the situation seemed to have the desired effect. An
officer from the Fifty-Seventh North Carolina in Avery's brigade recalled that most
of the people "gazed at the troops as they passed with something like stupefaction,
but there was no sign of alarm, even among the ladies." He pointed out that most of

the women soon "went to their homes and during our stay there they were rarely ever seen on the streets." The Tar Heel noted that "the men, however, mingled freely with the Confederate officers, and there was little or no sign of bitterness apparent."[17]

As Gordon's men secured the town, General Early arrived from the north on Harrisburg Turnpike with the rest of the division. "I moved into York at the head of Avery's brigade of North Carolina troops, and with them took possession of the Public Common, where the hospital buildings were stationed and the Fair Grounds, southeast of town," the division commander recalled. The Tar Heels immediately took over provost duties from the Georgians. That arrangement allowed Gordon's men, along with Tanner's battery, to head off about ten miles east in an attempt to seize the bridge over the Susquehanna River at Wrightsville.

The troops from Hays's and Smith's Brigades trailed slightly behind Avery and went into camp a short distance away along Codorus Creek. Early noted that "they pitched their tents" about two miles northeast of York around two large flour mills. The nearby waterway provided the motive power for the mills, which housed about 2,000 barrels of flour in adjacent warehouses. The men from the Louisiana Guard Artillery quickly fortified the area against an enemy attack. Early reported that the gunners "planted their cannon east of the mills, along the hill sides, overlooking the town, and threw up some earth works."[18]

The division commander proceeded on to Centre Square, where he established his headquarters at the courthouse. One of the town's newspapers noted that the general occupied the sheriff's office, while Maj. Samuel Hale from his staff, who served as provost marshal, set up shop in the adjacent register's office. Early soon sounded a bell at the building to summon Chief Burgess David Small and a delegation of leading citizens for a meeting. He immediately informed the assembled group that he "had taken possession of your town, by authority of the Confederate government." Early then issued a demand for them to hand over a long list of supplies for his troops.

The huge quantity of goods that they were required to surrender caused a major stir among the town's leaders. Capt. William Thornton, who served as the division's commissary officer, issued a requisition for 165 barrels of flour, 3,000 pounds of sugar, 1,650 pounds of coffee, 300 gallons of molasses, and 32,000 pounds of fresh meat or 21,000 pounds of bacon. The list that the division's quartermaster, Maj. Charles E. Snodgrass, submitted proved just as burdensome. He ordered the townspeople to provide 2,000 pairs of shoes and boots, 1,000 pairs of socks, and 1,000 felt hats. The most humiliating moment came when Early directed the civilian leaders to hand over $100,000 in cash (equivalent to about $2.8 million in 2018).

Early again showed that he would be much harsher toward civilians than either Generals Ewell or Rodes. Although the officials had allowed his troops to enter town with no signs of resistance, the general was not inclined toward any leniency. "You are living in a land of plenty and have not suffered from the results of war, like my own countrymen down in Virginia," he brusquely declared. "I want my requisitions filled at once." Early made it clear what would happen should they not produce the required items in a timely fashion. "If you do not comply with my demands, I will take the goods and provisions from your stores, or permit my soldiers to enter your houses and demand such things as they need for assistance," he threatened.[19]

The terrified officials set about gathering up the goods with a will. Attorney Latimer noted that the local "Ward Committees were appointed to collect money." Several of the town's merchants "furnished the groceries and flour, and the hatters & Shoemakers were called on for the shoes & hats, with understanding that the Boro' would assume the debt & repay the money & pay for the supplies." Lt. William Kincheloe from Smith's Brigade quipped in his diary that York's frightened burghers "could not have evinced more industry and zeal if they had been selling at large profit." In the end the townspeople obtained the majority of the goods Early demanded. The major exception was the cash, where their best efforts fell well short of the required amount.[20]

While the civilians scrambled to meet the imposing levy, Early completed his defensive preparations by placing the Staunton (Virginia) Artillery in position on the south end of town along Webb's Hill to protect against any enemy attempt to reclaim York; the Charlottesville Artillery remained in reserve at the nearby fairgrounds. Generals Smith and Hays posted sentries around their camps on the outskirts of town, while Avery's Tar Heels moved into place on the municipal streets as provost guards. White's cavalrymen spread out through the surrounding countryside to gather up additional plunder.[21]

The men from the provost details mostly carried out their duties with courtesy and restraint. "Guards were placed at hotels, stores, etc., and the town was kept comparatively quiet, the soldiers being under very strict discipline," a local newspaper stated. "Places of business were generally closed, though in many cases were on request opened and articles were purchased, the soldiers and officers paying for them in confederate money." While far from pleased about being under rebel occupation, the citizens had no cause for direct complaints. "So far as we are informed, their promise to respect the rights of persons and property was kept," the correspondent acknowledged.[22]

With the situation at York well in hand, during the early afternoon of June 28, Gordon's men and Tanner's battery headed east on the turnpike toward Wrightsville, on the western bank of the Susquehanna. Plans called for them to seize the 5,630-foot bridge that connected that town to Columbia on the opposite side of the river. This massive covered structure was wide enough to accommodate a carriage path, a pedestrian walkway, railroad tracks, and a canal towpath. Its capture intact would open the way for Early's Division to cross the Susquehanna and advance from there on Harrisburg, the state capital, from the east.

Along with Gordon's troops and artillery, the column included White's cavalry battalion and a single company from French's regiment. The soldiers took their first break early in the afternoon about three miles east of York near a former wayside tavern. There Gordon divided White's command into two parts: one company would accompany the advancing column, while the rest of the battalion spread over the surrounding countryside to cut telegraph lines and destroy railroad bridges. Other squads would hunt through the area for horses and additional plunder of all kinds.

Following this brief stop, the main column pushed east through the village of Hallam. The company from the Seventeenth Virginia Cavalry screened the infantry as they moved toward the Susquehanna. About 5:00 P.M., Gordon's soldiers finally halted just outside of Wrightsville. Some of French's horsemen reported seeing enemy cavalry moving off in the distance. As they approached within about one mile of town, the scouts discovered a large body of Federal troops spread out around its perimeter. By all indications, Gordon's men would encounter some considerable opposition as they attempted to seize the bridge.[23]

The force defending Wrightsville totaled about 1,400 troops commanded by Maj. Granville Haller and Col. Jacob G. Frick. The largest contingent was Frick's Twenty-Seventh Pennsylvania Volunteer Militia, which had about 900 men in the ranks. Three companies from the Twentieth Pennsylvania Militia under Lt. Col. William Sickles, which had fled from the earlier attack at Hanover Junction, were also on hand. The First Troop of the Philadelphia City Cavalry served as provost guards. In addition, four local militia companies, a detachment from the Twenty-Sixth Militia, and some patients who had been evacuated from the military hospital in York were available to protect the town. One of the local militia companies included fifty-three African Americans, who had helped construct the defenses around Wrightsville.[24]

From a steep ridge in front of the town, Gordon got his first look at what he faced, soon determining that the enemy's positions corresponded almost exactly to the information in the anonymous note he had received at York. "There, in full view before us, was the town, just as described, nestling on the banks of the Susquehanna," he explained. "There was the blue line of soldiers guarding the approach, drawn up, as indicated, along an intervening ridge and across the pike." The general could clearly see "the long bridge spanning the Susquehanna and connecting the town with Columbia on the other bank." He added, "not an inaccurate detail in that note could be discovered."

Gordon quickly maneuvered his troops into place for an attack. The key terrain feature along their front was a "deep gorge or ravine running off to the right and extending around the left flank of the Federal line and to the river below the bridge." The general decided to send his troops through that gorge into "the flank, or possibly in the rear, of the Union troops and force them to a rapid retreat or surrender." In preparation for the assault, Gordon ordered the four guns of the Courtney Artillery to set up around some high ground known as Strickler's Hill.[25]

Private Bradwell from the Thirty-First Georgia watched as the men from the lead regiment moved forward "across a field of rye now headed out and up to their shoulders." He and the rest of the troops followed just behind in battle formation with a screen of skirmishers at the front. "Soon the entire brigade was in line, and Capt. Warren D. Wood, of our regiment, was ordered to deploy his own company (F) and two other companies and develop the position of the enemy," the Georgian explained. Bradwell pointed out that there was "low ground for some distance" in front of them and "on the rising ground on the other side could be seen a line of excellent earthworks."[26]

Although the defenders had posted pickets to detect the enemy's approach, Gordon's men easily outmaneuvered them. One of the militiamen reported to a local newspaper that the enemy's line of skirmishers eluded their sentries "on the right by passing to the west and east." The bulk of the attackers then moved "through a ravine, and those flanking parties approached within a short distance of the left centre of our rifle pits, where the firing suddenly commenced about six o'clock." He noted that "a brisk skirmish ensued on our left and front, during which time the Rebels could be seen moving up the hills to the left through the woods and wheat fields."[27]

Despite facing some initial resistance, the advancing troops made good progress. "Captain Wood and his men moved forward in skirmish formation about one hundred and fifty yards when the fun—the old-time familiar crack of rifles—began," Private Bradwell recalled. "This was immediately responded to by the popping of muskets and whizz of balls over our heads." Just then, two of Tanner's guns opened fire on the Federal positions. The artillery barrage immediately sent the enemy into a panicked retreat. "In a moment we were ordered to advance to the enemy's works, which we found abandoned, and from there to the town the enemy had divested themselves of their equipment in their hasty flight," the Georgian boasted.[28]

Sgt. James Hodam from French's regiment looked on from the outskirts of town as Gordon's infantry rushed forward "under brisk fire" and drove the militiamen from their breastworks. He bragged that "our men entered the entrenchments on the double quick," capturing some of the defenders. The Federal losses totaled one man killed, nine wounded, and about twenty taken prisoner, including Lieutenant Colonel Sickles. Hodam noted that the only Confederate casualty in the attack "was one man wounded" from the Sixtieth Georgia. Lt. William Lyon from Gordon's staff commented simply that "after a brisk battle of a half an hour, we routed them."[29]

The remaining militiamen were soon in full flight over the bridge to Columbia. Colonel Evans informed his wife that "the timid Militia, who equaled us in numbers fled at the bursting of the first shell." The veteran hardly found that outcome surprising, considering the defenders' lack of any meaningful combat experience. "They had not been in action before, and believed that the shelling was terrible, although only two pieces were fired," the colonel gloated. At the same time, he conceded that the terrified militiamen "fled so rapidly that we captured only about thirty."[30]

Unknown to Gordon's troops, the Federals had placed explosive charges on the bridge to prevent it from falling into Confederate hands intact. "We bored all the arches and charged them heavily with powder, attached fuses to the powder, and had them all ready for the matches," reported Robert Crane, one of the men assigned to that duty. "There were four men placed in charge of the matches and fuses on a given order." Others from the detail sawed away on the main supports to weaken the central span. One of the men noted that they also saturated the bridge "with oil and combustible matter."

Once the bulk of the militiamen had made it over the bridge, one of Major Haller's aides ordered Crane "to apply the matches to the fuses which was accordingly done." The attempt to blow up the span proved only partially successfully. "When the blast went off it was effective but not sufficient to throw a span of the Bridge," Crane admitted. That disappointing result left the Federals scrambling to come up with another method of knocking the structure out of commission. Colonel Frick eventually made the final decision. "There was no time to cut the spans down as the Rebel cavalry had entered the bridge from Wrightsville," Crane reported. "Col. Frick then gave orders to the men to set fire to the Bridge which was done as directed."[31]

A trooper from the Philadelphia City Cavalry watched as the fire rapidly engulfed the entire structure. "The Susquehanna is more than a mile wide at this point, and the old wooden bridge with timbers dried and seasoned by years, burned with a vigor and intensity I have never seen equaled," he recalled. "For more than two hours the flames shot heavenward, lighting the surrounding hills and valleys for miles in all directions." A member of the U.S. Sanitary Commission "could see the light distinctly" from the roof of his hotel more than thirty miles away in Harrisburg. A soldier from the Twenty-Seventh Pennsylvania Volunteer Militia watched in awe from the east shore of the river as the billowing smoke began "rolling up the firey clouds toward the heavens."[32]

Burning of the bridge at Wrightsville, Pennsylvania. From *Harper's Weekly*.

The massive blaze, fueled by the liberally applied oil, quickly spread into the nearby buildings. "We had just crossed their works, when we heard a great explosion, and, looking toward the town, we saw the timbers of the bridge rising high into the blue sky and almost immediately the black smoke rising from the burning bridge and buildings in the village," Private Bradwell recalled. He noted that the Confederates "hastened on unopposed and found the merchants in the business part of town near the bridge rolling their goods out into the street and the greedy flames eating their way from house to house up the street on the north side."[33]

As darkness fell, the inferno threatened to consume Wrightsville. Rather than let that happen, Gordon's men stepped forward to help. "With great energy my men labored to save the bridge," the general explained. He insisted that the soldiers "labored as earnestly and bravely to save the town as they did to save the bridge," quickly creating a makeshift bucket line. "In the absence of fire-engines or other appliances, the only chance to arrest the progress of the flames was to form my men around the burning district, with the flank resting on the river's edge, and pass rapidly from hand to hand the pails of water," Gordon recounted.[34]

The fire raged so fiercely that it seemed like none of those efforts would be enough to quell the blaze. "In spite of our labor the conflagration continued to make headway until our pioneers came with kegs of powder," Bradwell remarked. "These were placed under the building most exposed to the fire, and our officers ordered our men to put on their bayonets and force our soldiers back up the street out of danger of the explosion." The resulting blast knocked the affected building into pieces and cut off the spread of the flames. Those heroic measures eventually brought the blaze under control. In all, only about eight or nine structures burned to the ground.[35]

According to Lt. B. R. Doster from the Thirteenth Georgia, their brigade commander himself came up with the plan to use the gunpowder to prevent the flames from spreading. "General Gordon, on horseback, was passing around and about during this time, when I heard him ask three ladies who were on a front porch where he could get some powder," the Georgian remembered. "They told him, and he rode rapidly away, and in reasonable length of time afterwards, I heard the explosion." Doster pointed out that the men in the brigade took on the task of saving the town "with free hearty, good will, and soon accomplished this commendable objective."[36]

Colonel Evans remained just as proud of their willingness to prevent a total disaster. "Seeing that the town of Wrightsville on this side would be burned also our noble hearted men, who had marched twenty five miles that day & chased the Yankees a mile or more stacked their arms and worked until nearly midnight to arrest the fire," he told his wife. The colonel was especially pleased that their conduct contrasted so sharply with that of the Federal troops in pillaging Darien, Georgia. "It was a singular sight to see those marching Rebels work so eagerly to save a Yankee town which the scamps had themselves set on fire, and this too after reading in Northern papers of the entire destruction of Darien in our own state by some Massachusetts & two other Negro regiments on the 16th of this month," he declared.[37]

Despite their heroic actions, not everyone felt good about saving the Northern town. "Those efforts I joined in, but I must say I did not fully approve of our exerting ourselves to any considerable extent, for I could not help thinking that in a similar case in our country a Yankee army would not exert themselves much to save our towns from burning," Lieutenant Lyon confessed in a letter home. Lt. Joseph Hilton, whose hometown was located near Darien, lamented that they had allowed the chance to inflict some much-needed retribution on the North to slip away. "Next time I think we will be apt to apply the torch instead of putting out the fire," he groused darkly in a letter to his cousin following their return to Virginia.[38]

French's horsemen joined the rest of the Southerners in Wrightsville just as the firefighters gained the upper hand in putting out the flames. "We entered [the] town where all was confusion and dismay, many large buildings, mills and a lumber yard had taken fire from the bridge and a great conflagration was only prevented by timely exertions of the citizens and our soldiers," Sergeant Hodam remarked. Despite their attempts to douse the inferno, nothing could be done to save the bridge. Hodam noted that "the great bridge was one vast sheet of flame from end to end and in the coming darkness was a sight not soon forgotten by friend or foe."[39]

The only disorder occurred when some men broke into a couple of abandoned boxcars along the tracks on the west side of the river. "After the fire was under control, then it was that the soldiers came up from the river and broke open the cars," which contained whiskey, Lieutenant Doster admitted. "Then the picnic commenced; the boys 'held the fourth of July,' and some, I am sorry to say, drank too much." Gordon attempted to get the plundering under control by having the heads of the barrels knocked in and pouring out the spirits onto the ground. Soon afterward he ordered the bulk of the troops into camp about two miles outside of town on George W. Dellinger's farm.[40]

Later that night General Early arrived to check out the situation in person. "By the time I got outside of the town I saw the smoke arising from the burning bridge, and when I reached Wrightsville I found the bridge entirely destroyed," the Virginian recalled. Up to that point he had expected his troops to push through Lancaster on the east side of the river toward the state capital while Ewell advanced "against that city from the other side." To his disappointment, that plan was "thwarted by the destruction of the bridge, as there was no other means of crossing the river." Before departing, Early reluctantly directed Gordon to return to York the following day.[41]

After a much needed rest, the Confederates resumed their duties in Wrightsville early on June 29. Gordon immediately appointed Capt. George W. Lewis from the Thirty-First Georgia as provost marshal. Lewis quickly placed guards around "a large and well-selected stock of liquors" stored in the cellar of an abandoned hotel on the corner of Hellam and Front Streets. During that time, Sergeant Hodam got his first daylight look at the massive destruction caused by the fire. "On the river bank the remains of iron foundries and mills strew the ground while nothing of the bridge remained except some thirteen great stone pillars with here and there a piece of burned timber clinging to them," he remarked.[42]

The provost guards soon began gathering up supplies from the town's businesses. One detail entered the store owned by Jacob G. Leber, securing ten hats, thirteen caps, fifteen pairs of boots, and ten pairs of shoes. They further obtained a large quantity of food, including twenty gallons of molasses, one and a half barrels of sugar, spices, crackers, and various confections. The owner also lost all the pails and buckets in his shop, which were used for putting out the fire. In his postwar claim for damages, Leber placed his total losses at about $230.[43]

Most of the citizens' homes remained untouched during the Confederate occupation. "Very little pilfering was done, and aside from demands for food, private property was not molested to any great extent," one resident admitted. "The rebel officers stationed guards at most of the houses, and no one was permitted to enter without the consent of the citizens." But the situation proved much worse for many of those living in the surrounding area. "Some houses in the suburbs of Wrightsville, and some farm houses with[in] a radius of a mile or two of the town, were pretty thoroughly sacked," the same man fumed. "In some cases every portable article was either thrown about the premises or carried off."[44]

The townspeople experienced the worst problems from the invaders' constant foraging for food. "They behaved pretty civilly while passing here," local resident Rachel Bahn conceded in a letter to her nephew. "Hundreds of them came in, one wanted bread, another wanted butter, the next wanted apple butter, milk &c." The disabled woman especially complained that "they wanted to pay everything with their worthless money, but of course we did not take any." Bahn's hatred ran so deep that even the soldiers' mostly respectful demeanors could not keep her from unleashing a vicious rant. "A dirtier, more motley, obnoxious-looking set of fellows I never saw," she fumed.[45]

General Gordon, meanwhile, took in breakfast that morning at Mary Jane Rewalt's residence. The invitation to visit her home came the previous evening in response to his men's efforts to protect the town. "The lady who owned the house, late that night, sought out Gen. Gordon and when she was directed to his quarters told him that she had come to invite him and as many of his men who could get in her dining room for breakfast the next morning," Pvt. George W. O'Neal from the Thirty-First Georgia recalled. "She wanted to do something to show her appreciation for saving her residence from the fire."[46]

Even years later the brigade commander fondly remembered her kind gesture. "At a bountifully supplied table in the early morning sat this modest, cultured woman, surrounded by soldiers in their worn, gray uniforms," Gordon recalled. He noted that "the welcome she gave us was so gracious" that he inquired if she was a Southern supporter. Rewalt instantly replied, "I can candidly tell you that I am a Union woman." Not wanting to leave her motives in doubt, she added, "you and your soldiers last night saved my home from burning, and I was unwilling that you should go away without receiving some token of my appreciation."[47]

While Gordon's troops finished up their duties around Wrightsville in preparation for their departure later that morning, General Early remained busy gathering up supplies from York and the neighboring farms and businesses. Those efforts raised some major concerns among the citizens in that town. Samuel and Philip Small, who owned one of the mills along Codorus Creek, received several disturbing reports that some soldiers had ransacked their property and destroyed much of the equipment there. Lawyer James Latimer claimed that Philip Small became so distraught over the news that he "was quite demented for a while."[48]

Samuel Small Jr. eventually lodged a formal protest with Early over this apparent outrage. The general informed him that the reports could "not be correct," directing Small to ride there and confirm that no such damage took place. "My troops dare not waste and destroy the wheat and flour or tear down the buildings," Early thundered. "Go out yourself and tell General Hays, who commands the brigade, that his men must obey my orders." The Virginian further pledged that the offenders would be arrested or even put to death if the reports were true. Early then issued a pass for the owner's safe passage while making the trip. After a brief hesitation, Small finally agreed to the plan.

Accompanied by Early's chief quartermaster, Small soon set off to the site of the mills northeast of town. To his relief, he discovered that the stories about the plundering there were false and the milling equipment remained undamaged; a commissary detail had only confiscated some flour for preparing bread in a makeshift bakery at their campsite. General Hays had even placed sentries around mill site to prevent any soldiers in his brigade from breaking in and stealing the flour or other goods stored on the property.[49]

Later that day Chief Burgess Small appeared at Early's headquarters to update him on the efforts to fill the general's massive requisition for goods. Although the civil authorities had gathered up most of the items, the number of shoes and boots and the amount of cash fell short of Early's demands. "In compliance with my requisition some twelve or fifteen hundred pairs of shoes, all the hats, socks, and rations called for, and $28,600 in money were furnished by the town authorities," the Virginian reported. Small informed him that they made a good-faith attempt to round up all the cash. "The mayor assured me that the money paid over was all that could be raised, as the banks and moneyed men had run off their funds to Philadelphia," Early explained.

The division commander seemingly accepted the burgess's excuses at face value. "I believed that he had made an honest effort to raise the money, and I did not, therefore, take any stringent measures to enforce the demand, but left the town

indebted to me for the remainder," Early recalled. Rather than carrying out any retaliation, he only required the officials to post a bond against future payment of the
debt. Early immediately issued the shoes, hats, and socks "to the men, who stood
very much in need of them." The general later used some of the cash to purchase
additional cattle for feeding his troops. He eventually handed over the remainder
of the money to the Quartermaster Department.[50]

His measured reaction to the shortfall proved short lived. During midafternoon,
Early unexpectedly summoned Judge Robert Fisher to his office and ordered him to
hand over the keys to the other offices in the courthouse. When Fisher demanded to
know the reason for the request, the general replied that he intended to destroy all
the county records stored there in retaliation for a similar act perpetrated by some
Federal troops at the Fairfax County courthouse in Virginia. The judge appealed so
forcefully to his sense of honor toward a defenseless town that Early eventually gave
up his threat.

Even then the general was not done with his attempts to force full payment of
the levy on the town. He soon traveled to the main railroad yard with Chief Burgess
Small. Unknown to the official, the division commander wanted to see if the repair
shop and depot could be torched without putting the rest of the town in danger of
destruction, quickly deciding that his plan was impractical. "I determined not to
burn but thought I would make a further effort to get the balance of the $100,000,"
Early admitted. He informed Small that he would set the entire complex on fire
if all the cash was not turned over immediately. The burgess again protested that
there was not a single dollar left in town to meet the ransom. With his bluff called,
Early backed down and left the railroad yards largely untouched.

The general later issued a formal proclamation to the citizens explaining his
decision not to burn the complex. It proved to be a prime example of Confederate
propaganda at its best. "Had I applied the torch without regard to consequences, I
would have pursued a course that would have been fully vindicated as an act of just
retaliation for many authorized acts of barbarity perpetrated by your own army on
our soil," Early declared. "But we do not war on women and children." He further
expressed his hope that "the treatment you have met from the hands of my soldiers
will open your eyes to the monstrous inequity of the war waged by your government upon the people of the Confederate States."[51]

To the surprise of many, Early took strong measures to protect the town from
looting during his stay, having assigned Colonel Avery's soldiers as provost guards
to secure the streets and keep the men away from the local saloons and liquor stores.
Their duties allowed the North Carolinians to get a close-up view of the town. Pvt.
Samuel Eaton described it as "a beautiful place" and was especially pleased that "the
ladies appear to be very kind & have a great curiosity to talk with the rebels." Pvt.
Marcus Hefner was so impressed by the sights that he joked to his wife that "the
worse York town is the best town that I ever saw."[52]

Although orders strictly limited access, Captain Seymour from Hays's staff used his friendship with Major Hale, who served as the provost marshal, to obtain an official pass into York. With the required papers in hand, the staffer "got into the back door of a large very fancy store," where he "purchased a bottle of old Cognac brandy and a few other articles." Even that was not the end of his good luck. The female shopkeeper surprisingly informed him that she was willing "to accept Confederate money in exchange for anything in her store."[53]

Many other soldiers visited York without permission from their superiors. Lt. J. Warren Jackson from the same brigade informed his brother that he "took French leave and went into town" during their stay. He noted that he and some of his friends "had lots of fun, saw some pretty girls—and amused ourselves extensively until 10 P. M." In a few cases, such as Seymour's, Confederates gained entry into the local shops. Although the stores were "closed to everyone expect the authorized officials," Lieutenant Kincheloe from Smith's Brigade admitted that he "succeeded in getting some shirts, etc." during one of his unauthorized trips.[54]

Local businesses suffered the worst damages, however, from the commissary and quartermaster details that were assigned to gather up the requisitioned goods. Nathan Lehmayer and Brothers general-merchandise store sustained about $1,300 in such losses. The confiscated items included 100 hats, 125 coats, more than 200 shirts, fifty pocket handkerchiefs, and fifty pairs of socks. Other details targeted Jacob A. Sechrist's grocery store, which lost three pounds of cheese, five pounds of tea, thirty pounds of sugar, and eight pounds of coffee. Search parties also visited Charles Spangler's dry-goods shop, where they secured a long list of goods, including notions, gingham, calicoes, gloves, vests, and stationery.[55]

While that was going on, other Confederates scoured the countryside outside of town for additional loot. Zachariah Loucks, who owned a mill near Hays's camp, placed his losses at more than $1,100. He complained that details seized sixty bushels of corn, fifty bushels of oats, and twenty-five tons of hay from his storehouses. The businessman further reported that some foraging soldiers "filled their haversacks with flour, amounting to 25 barrels." Josiah E. Myers, who operated a gristmill a couple of miles away along Codorus Creek in Manchester Township, also lost eight barrels of flour and fifteen bushels of corn.[56]

Another detachment from Hays's Brigade raided a farm located just northeast of Emigsville in the same township. "When they heard that the southern soldiers were coming, they hid the horses in the river hills, a wooded area near the Susquehanna River," one of the owner's descendants recounted. Upon their arrival the unwelcome visitors asked the farmer's six-year-old son for some milk. The youngster immediately informed his father, who "sent them down in the cellar where ice from the river was stored to keep milk and food cold." The men soon uncovered something more appealing than a supply of cold milk. "Instead, the soldiers found the wine cellar and stayed a long time sampling the contents," the relative reported.

Unknown to the intruders, the family, who were fervent abolitionists, had an African American hidden in the barn on their property. The men remained so distracted by the stash of alcohol in the cellar that they failed to locate the fugitive. "If the rebels had found him they would have carried him back into slavery as they did with many blacks whom they captured during their stay in Pennsylvania," the family's descendant acknowledged. After consuming their fill of wine, the troopers headed off to a nearby farm, the site of a distillery. They soon emptied it of its entire contents and departed the area without further harm.[57]

Additional squads relentlessly tracked down any horses stashed away by their owners. Captain Seymour noted that the Southerners sometimes found the animals secreted "in bedrooms, parlors, lofts of barns and other out of the way places." During one search, the quartermaster from Hays's Brigade "called at a large, finely furnished house," whose owner reportedly possessed "a splendid" mount. "The proprietor stoutly denied that he had such an animal," Seymour remarked. The quartermaster eventually opened a nearby "door and there in an elegant parlour, comfortably stalled in close proximity to a costly rosewood piano, stood a noble looking horse," which he immediately confiscated.[58]

The men in the ranks mostly foraged for food and clothing of all kinds on the properties around their camps. Sgt. William Henry Mayo from Hays's Brigade bragged that "any one of the messes can go out in the country and get as much butter, apple butters, milk, pies, bread, &c, &c, as he can carry free of charge." In a few instances such forays took the soldiers into the central part of town. "Some of the boys made a raid on the merchants in York and got a lot of hats and shoes," fellow Louisianan Pvt. Thomas Benton Reed gloated in his diary. "I got a nice hat which I was very proud of."[59]

Those same "Tigers" were likely responsible for a more disturbing incident that occurred at a local clothing store. After being tipped off that a large quantity of new shirts was hidden there, some Louisianans arrived at the shop and demanded access to the goods. When the owner denied them entry, they forced their way into the building. The men then locked him out and began shuffling through his merchandise. Beside the shirts, they uncovered "a small supply of old whiskey and other choice liquors." Their spree soon attracted a large crowd of angry onlookers. The Louisianans eventually escaped with the shirts and the stock of intoxicating beverages in hand.[60]

The soldiers in Smith's Brigade proved just as adept at uncovering hidden caches of alcohol. Sgt. Joseph C. Snider admitted in his diary that "whiskey was plenty and we had a good many drunken men." Lieutenant Kincheloe acknowledged that "our whole camp" was soon "drunk on Dutch whiskey," which was "diffused profusely" to the troops. Capt. William French Harding from the Thirty-First Virginia in the same brigade claimed that some of "the boys aided by an auger and a hole in the bottom of a nearby freight car, extracted a supply of liquid refreshment from a barrel which they had in some way located in the car." He added that the drink was so potent that "the exuberance of the boys lasted until late on the evening of the next day."[61]

The worst abusers of alcohol came among Hays's rowdy Louisianans. "'Old Red Eye' took great effect on the boys today," Private Reed jotted down in his diary on the day after their arrival in York. "Company E of our regiment, who are all Irish, all got drunk." The result was an alcohol-fueled brawl among the troops. The Louisianan admitted that they "had a general family fight, and one of the lieutenants got pretty badly used up." Regimental officers immediately placed the main culprits under arrest in "the Bull Pen." Some of the most boisterous drunks threated to overpower the guards. According to Reed, the miscreants "finally went to sleep, and we had no more trouble with them."[62]

During the midafternoon, Gordon's troops arrived back in York from their expedition to Wrightsville. "Lige" White's horsemen, who trailed just behind the main column, spent much of the return journey raiding the lush Pennsylvania countryside, severing numerous telegraph lines and burning several railroad bridges. While Gordon was off at Wrightsville, the main part of French's regiment focused on rounding up supplies from Dover Township. At one stop alone they confiscated 247 bushels of corn, 68 bushels of oats, and twenty-two acres of hay. The horsemen then forced the landowner to provide them with 300 meals and six barrels of homemade whiskey.[63]

Gordon's men gathered up some additional plunder as they marched back to town. James Gall, who was visiting York as a relief agent for the U.S. Sanitary Commission, reported that the Georgians brought along "some horses and cattle which they picked up on the way." The arriving column also included eight loaded-down "supply and ammunition wagons." Those troops eventually settled into camp just west of town along the turnpike leading back toward Gettysburg. The men from the other brigades remained in place on the outskirts of York for the remainder of the day.[64]

Soon after their return, Gordon's troops received their share of the spoils from the levy on the town. Private Bradwell recalled that "it was surprising to see the amount and variety issued to us." According to Lieutenant Agee, the rations included "sugar, coffee, candy, raisins, and some good old rye whiskey, which was sure a rare treat for a Confederate soldier." The other troops in the division took that time to rest up while waiting for the command to resume the march. Lieutenant Kincheloe from Smith's Brigade noted in his diary that orders finally arrived late that evening "to have three-day's rations on hand cooked and be ready to move at daylight in the morning."[65]

For many of the men, the best part of their stay was the surprisingly pleasant reception that the numerous Peace Democrats in this Northern community gave them. Capt. James Carrington from the Charlottesville Artillery recalled that the Confederates "were treated with much kindness by many of its citizens, and there I met friends and acquaintances who were cordial and hospitable." Private Bradwell from Gordon's Brigade insisted that "the people of York were the most refined and intelligent folks we met in the state and reminded us of our friends at home, both in manners and personal appearance." Lieutenant Jackson also informed his brother that the people there "were very friendly." The Louisianan effused, "I shall ever remember York with pleasure."[66]

14

"We Did Not Come Here
for Nothing"

While Early's Division was on the move through Gettysburg to York, the cavalry-men from Jenkins's Brigade proceeded north from Shippensburg on the morning of June 27. After a hard ride of about twenty-five miles along Valley Turnpike, they arrived at Carlisle. General Jenkins moved cautiously because of widespread re-ports that the town was defended by a large militia force. He deployed most of his brigade just west of town in case an attack was necessary. Gunners from the Bal-timore Light Artillery under Capt. Wiley Hunter Griffin unlimbered two of their four ten-pounder Parrotts and placed them in "a position to rake the main street."[1]

By that point, however, the Federal troops in Carlisle had already withdrawn to the north. The force that had assembled there following the Confederate occupa-tion of Chambersburg consisted of General Knipe's small brigade and two com-panies of local militia; Capt. William H. Boyd's cavalry detachment guarded the main approaches to the town. Charles Himes, who was visiting Carlisle at the time, reported to a friend that the "negro population" was also "impressed to dig rifle pits & make barricades about a mile west of town." The makeshift barriers obstructed the entrances from both Valley Turnpike and Walnut Bottom Road.

The troops assigned to protect Carlisle further included a few raw recruits from the U.S. Army barracks there, known as the Third U.S. Cavalry Scouts under Lt. Frank Stanwood. Himes noted in his diary that "the cavalry belonging to the barracks were posted in the street and picketted out the streets." Knipe's brigade eventually pulled back from the defenses late in the evening on June 25, while Boyd's troopers galloped off only hours before the Southerners reached there. The cavalrymen from Stanwood's company lingered in town until just prior to Jenkins's arrival.[2]

As the Confederate horsemen finally approached the edge of town, a group of frightened officials, including the assistant burgess, emerged under a flag of truce to inform Jenkins that all the militiamen were gone. Based on their assurances, the cavalrymen proceeded into the west end of town along High Street without firing a shot. Lt. Hermann Schuricht from the Fourteenth Virginia Cavalry indicated in his diary that they quickly "passed the obstructions and fortifications, and occupied the city at 10 o'clock." From Carlisle it was only eighteen miles to the state capital at Harrisburg.[3]

The town Jenkins now occupied had a population of about 5,700 and served as the seat of government for Cumberland County. Several waves of Scotch-Irish immigrants arrived in the area during the 1700s. A later influx of thrifty farmers and merchants from Germany further shaped the character of the region. Carlisle had a long history of electoral support for the Democratic Party. Over the years it had also been the home for many Southerners who attended Dickinson College or served with the dragoons and cavalry at the army barracks on the outskirts of the community.[4]

The lead troopers from Jenkins's Brigade initially rode east through the center of Carlisle. According to one of the local newspapers, the force was "about four hundred in number, mounted infantry, and every man carried a gun in a position to use it on an instant with his hands on the hammer." James W. Sullivan, who was fifteen years old at the time, reported that they were "big men, wearing broad-brimmed hats, and mounted on good horses." He noted that they carried their carbines "butt resting at the knee and barrel pointed upright." Most impressive of all was "their picturesque air of confidence and readiness for action." Local teenager Mary Matilda Loudon described them in her diary as "a hard looking Set."[5]

The rebel column carefully continued along High Street all the way to the junction of Trindle Spring and Dillsburg Roads, where a squadron turned off to the north. Jenkins's orders called for that force to secure the barracks, located a short distance from there along the turnpike to Harrisburg. Another small detachment set up a picket line to the east just outside of town to protect against an enemy attack. The remainder of the men, according to a newspaper report, "dismounted for a few minutes, when they again took their saddles, returned to the town and stopped in the public square."[6]

Some of the cavalrymen threatened the people gathered in the square with forceful retaliation to any signs of resistance. One onlooker complained to a New York religious newspaper that "a major, sitting on his horse in the public square, with a large whiskey bottle protruding from his pocket, was very loud in his declarations of authority, saying among other things, that if his rear guard was fired upon he would burn the town and lay waste to the country for ten miles around." At the same time, the eyewitness admitted that most of the troopers "were very orderly, and under the most rigid discipline."[7]

Jenkins immediately called on the chief burgess to hand over enough food for all his men. "That request had to be complied with, and was done with alacrity as Jenkins had threatened that on failure to furnish [the goods] his men would be helping themselves," the local newspaper explained. "In less than an hour, the stalls of the market house were filled will all kinds of eatables, and considerable hungry secessionists were filling themselves with good food." Other troopers took up positions as guards at various locations. The newspaper acknowledged that the soldiers so assigned "conducted themselves generally speaking with decorum."[8]

The main part of Rodes's Division arrived at Carlisle soon afterward not on the macadamized Valley Turnpike, but on Walnut Bottom Road, a dirt track that ran directly alongside the turnpike. Heavy rains during the previous night added to the difficulty of the trip. Lt. William Calder from Ramseur's Brigade complained that "we were not on the pike and it was awfully muddy, and of course much more tiresome." Pvt. Samuel Pickens from O'Neal's Brigade estimated that they traveled more than twenty-three miles that day. "It was worse than 30 on a good dry road," he griped. "I was completely broken down & my feet hurt me very much."[9]

Despite their worn-out condition, the troops entered Carlisle with all the appropriate military flourishes. "At five o'clock in the afternoon, the sound of music announced the arrival of Ewell's corps," the local newspaper said. "It came by way of the Walnut Bottom Road down South Pitt to Main Street, thence to Bedford Street." One eyewitness informed the wife of the army barracks commander, who had recently fled town that the Confederate troops defiantly paraded through the streets "to martial music, banners flaunting and posted their guards at each corner."[10]

Another bystander reported to a friend that "the road was covered with cavalry and then infantry all the time." She was relieved that the troops remained "very orderly" as they passed by her home. Nearly all of them showed courtesy toward the people who lined roadway their route. "A great many officers stopped at the area and rested," the woman reported. She admitted that they proved "quite gentlemanly" and "talked very pleasantly." The only problem involved one of her neighbors. According to her account, the man had "considerable controversy with some of them."[11]

James Sullivan also got a close-up look as the Confederates marched into town. To his surprise, they appeared to be a superbly equipped and disciplined group. "Knapsacks and the whole personal kit was in order," the youngster admitted. "Arms were at every man's command. A significant touch to neatness was a toothbrush at hat band or buttonhole." Sullivan recalled that "further opportunity for inspection of the cavalry, infantry, artillery, and transportation service confirmed my first impression of a fit, well-fed, well-conditioned army." Local resident Hanna Culver could hardly believe the huge size of the occupying force. She was astonished that "their supply train" alone was more than "three miles long."[12]

Although Rodes's troops maintained strict discipline, many citizens along the street reacted with fear at the sight of their arrival. The signs of their despair soon became impossible for the arriving soldiers to miss. "The townspeople were terribly frightened and we saw many anxious faces peering behind closed shutters," one of the men from the Forty-Fourth Georgia in Doles's Brigade recalled. He soon spotted "a little girl huddled on the floor of a wagon." The soldier noted that "she was speechless, but as we passed by we assured her that there was nothing to fear."[13]

Old West at Dickinson College. Courtesy Cumberland County Historical Society.

O'Neal's Brigade, which led the way at the front of the column, proceeded east to the junction with the turnpike leading to Baltimore. Private Pickens noted that the troops finally halted just outside of town near "a large orchard." According to another Alabamian, they set up camp "on the roadside of the Baltimore Pike, about one mile from Carlisle, where we now are, doing picket-duty, and living on the fat of the land." The open countryside around their camp provided O'Neal's men with clear views of the eastern and southern approaches to the town, which they had been assigned to guard.[14]

Next in line came Doles's troops, who turned off on the west side of town into the "ample yard" of Dickinson College, which was founded in 1783. Lt. Thomas Hightower noted that it was "one of the oldest institutions in the once United States." The school was especially renowned because its first permanent building, known as Old West, had been designed by Benjamin Latrobe, the major architect for the Capitol in Washington, D.C. Another imposing structure named East College stood alongside Old West. Capt. James Beck described the two as "large stone edifices of huge proportion." A smaller stucco building known as South College was located on High Street, directly opposite the main grounds.[15]

As they entered the central campus, Doles's men quickly secured the major buildings. The Medical Department took over East College for use as a hospital. Some of the officers pitched their tents next to Pres. Herman Merrills Johnson's residence, also in East College. While Doles established his headquarters at Old West, the bulk of the men set up camp and began cooking some sides of beef that they had procured during the march to Carlisle. "One barbecue frame was made at a point in the front campus about where the NE corner of Bosler Hall is now," one the professor's sons remembered. "Another was directly north of the center of Old West about 1/2 way to Louther Street."[16]

According to President Johnson's son, his father's membership in the Masonic Order played a key role in ensuring the safety of the school. "Father went out to meet the commander, and gave him the Masonic sign, which was returned," he recalled. The younger Johnson noted that the colonel immediately deployed "a guard around our home and around all the college buildings, and although the rebel soldiers camped on the campus, not a thing of our's was destroyed, nor was the least bit of damage done to college property." He claimed that the troops remained so respectful of the campus that "the fires had to be built on the walks to protect the grass."[17]

Most of the youngsters in that part of town viewed all that military activity as more a cause for curiosity than real concern. "One can imagine how excited we were when Doles' Brigade took over the college campus," recalled Edward Beetem, who was a teenager at the time. He and his friends made repeated efforts to get a close-up view of the Georgia infantrymen. "The picture these troops presented on the campus with their tents, stacked rifles, and baggage was one which attracted us boys as much as the circus come to town, only it was so entirely different," Beetem admitted.[18]

While that was going on, Ramseur's, Daniel's, and Iverson's Brigades tramped northeast to the barracks on the outskirts of town. The column also included Capt. Frank Bond's company from the First Maryland Cavalry Battalion, which had been attached to Ewell's headquarters on "special" assignment during the advance into Pennsylvania. "It became my duty to place reliable guards over the stores that fell into our hands, particularly the stores of liquor," Bond explained. "When the commissaries and quartermasters came alone, we turned these things over to them, and advanced to the next town. In this way, we came to the city of Carlisle." According to one of the troopers, Ewell even authorized them "to make occasional scouts in the vicinity, to replenish our larder or pick up something good for the boys."[19]

The bulk of Johnson's Division, with three of its four batteries, and the two battalions of the Corps Reserve Artillery followed behind Rodes's men on Valley Turnpike. The column halted in a large grove about three miles west of Carlisle near Alexander Spring, with the exceptions of Steuart's Brigade and Carpenter's battery, which had not yet rejoined the division following their raid to McConnellsburg. The men from the other two corps in Lee's army stretched out in a long line extending south from Chambersburg to the Potomac River crossings.[20]

A scary accident occurred just as the Confederates reached camp that marred the arrival of the reserve artillery. Sgt. William S. White from the Third Company of the Richmond Howitzers noted that "a percussion shell in the 'limber chest' exploded and that communicating with the other charges (fifty in number, one pound each)

made a pretty big blow." Pvt. Henry R. Berkeley from the Amherst (Virginia) Artillery also witnessed the huge blast. "The top of the box was blown up almost out of
sight," he exclaimed in his diary. "Two men had just gotten off the box. The wheel
horses were badly burnt by the explosion." Luckily no one was hurt in this incident.[21]

Steuart's troops, meanwhile, continued their march from Chambersburg, where
they had halted the previous night at the local fairgrounds. The long trip proved
more difficult than expected. Lt. Thomas Tolson from the Second Maryland Infantry Battalion grumbled that the men were "very much fatigued, and there is some
straggling." Their route took them north through Shippensburg and Stoughstown
on to Springfield, where they went into camp alongside a "magnificent" spring. The
young Marylander pointed out that the fast-moving water from nearby Big Spring
Creek "furnishes motive power for two large mills."[22]

Many of the soldiers visited the town to buy scare provisions and other items to
send home. Their purchases sometimes extended far beyond just the usual food and
luxury goods. "At Springfield I bought seven copies of the New Testament for dis-
tribution among the men," recalled Lt. Randolph McKim, who served on Steuart's
staff. "The surprise of the storekeeper when an officer of the terrible Rebel Army
desired to purchase copies of the New Testament may be imagined." On the morning of June 28, the long column of troops turned southeast along the turnpike before
finally linking up with the rest of the division outside Carlisle later that day.[23]

While waiting for the last of his men to arrive, Ewell placed Maj. Rufus W.
Wharton from the First North Carolina Sharpshooter Battalion in charge as military governor of Carlisle. The two companies that made up his battalion had served
with Ewell's corps headquarters as provost guards since the beginning of the campaign. The troops assigned to secure the town also included the Fifty-Third North
Carolina of Daniel's Brigade. Ewell followed up that show of force by providing
his personal assurances to several prominent citizens that no one would be unduly
bothered during the Southerners' stay.[24]

The provost details quickly moved into place throughout Carlisle. One local
newspaper noted that "guards were placed on the corners of principal streets, and
during the evening excellent order prevailed." The correspondent pointed out that
those men "would not allow any soldier to pass unless he had a written pass." Rev.
Thomas Miller Griffith, who lived near the college, admitted that the troops protecting the campus were "exceedingly orderly." Despite some initial qualms about his
safety, he quickly determined that "there was no cause for fear" from the troops occupying that part of town.[25]

According to the newspaper, Ewell soon sent a staff officer into town "with a
demand on the authorities for supplies, medicines, amputation instruments, &c."
The quantity of goods included in this requisition proved so huge that it drew loud
protests from a group of town officials, who had arrived for a meeting with the
officer. Many "prominent citizens were present when the demand was made," the

report stated, "and informed the officer of the utter impossibility to comply with the requisition." The gathering finally broke up late in the evening with orders for residents to turn over all the required items or face a mandatory search of their businesses and homes by armed soldiers on the next day.[26]

When the merchants failed to open their stores on the morning of June 28, Ewell dispatched several quartermaster and commissary details to scour the town for food and military goods of every kind. Among the soldiers who "went in town with a party" to carry out the required seizures was Quartermaster Sgt. John S. Tucker from O'Neal's Brigade. He quickly realized that there were few items of real value left on the shelves of the businesses. "Opened nearly all the stores but found them empty," the Alabamian complained in his diary. "Everything having been hid or removed."[27]

Men from the Medical Department encountered similar problems in securing a long list of hospital supplies, including three hundred ounces of quinine, ninety pounds of chloroform, and fifty pounds of gum opium, from the town's druggists and physicians. "They responded that they had nothing to give," Hospital Steward John Apperson griped in his diary. His frustrations continued to mount as the soldiers' best efforts failed to turn up much in the way of useful drugs. The doctors in Carlisle especially resisted filling the requisition for four full cases of amputation implements. "Having to give up the med[ical] stores was a trial for them," the young Virginian finally admitted.[28]

Those assigned to the detail eventually instructed the doctors to surrender all their surgical equipment at the town square, orders that soon led to an open confrontation. According to a newspaper report, the physicians "felt it was a most unheard of demand, in violation of the rules of war, and at war with the rules of humanity." As a result, they immediately "protested in strong language against the outrage, but it was in vain." When one defiant doctor attempted to hand over a collection of obsolete instruments, the officer in charge of impressing the medical goods brusquely ordered him to take back his "antiques" and return immediately with "his regular kit."[29]

Despite such difficulties, Confederate commanders remained well pleased with the final results. Ewell reported that the details located "many valuable stores" once the shops in Carlisle were searched. Rodes pointed out in his official report that the troops uncovered "large supplies of cattle, horses and flour" throughout the town as well as "a large quantity of grain" in the barracks' stables. He added that "most of the Government property, excepting the grain, had been removed by the enemy, but musketoons, holsters, tents, and a small quantity of subsistence stores were found in the barracks."[30]

Ultimately the search parties from the division confiscated goods from almost every merchant in the town. Reverend Griffith noted that "those who had warehouses & groceries suffered most." According to another eyewitness, the soldiers even "went into [the] local Adams' Express office and took away all the boxes in it." Although the quantity of materials fell short of their initial demands, the men who gathered up the hospital supplies eventually secured "all the drugs and medicines they wanted, also medical instruments." Jed Hotchkiss from Ewell's staff estimated in a letter to his wife that they "obtained some $50000 of medicines & large supplies of provisions &c."[31]

Ewell also required many Carlisle business owners to provide a variety of services for the invading army. "I was detailed the last day of our stay to do some printing for the Quartermaster's Department," Capt. John Gorman from Ramseur's Brigade explained in a letter home. "With a guard, I visited all the printing offices, selected the best one out of the four, and done the work, and afterwards distributed the type." He took special pride in forcing this "rank Abolition office" to perform printing work for the Confederate army. "It would have afforded me much pleasure in turning it topsy-turvy," Gorman declared.[32]

Even so, the men from the quartermaster and commissary details generally carried out their duties at Carlisle with minimal disruptions. "Nothing was taken from dwellings except such articles as were evidently in storage," one of the local newspapers acknowledged. The writer noted that "the officers commanding the squads were gentlemanly and polite and performed their work in as mild a manner as possible." He admitted that Ewell's assurances about the town's safety "were fully realized and while his command were here the citizens felt satisfied that they would be protected."[33]

While the searches were underway, other soldiers, equipped with "axes, crowbars, and firebrands," began dismantling the railroad bridge that spanned LeTort Spring Run on the east side of town. "Track rails were ripped up and thrown down to the surface road," young James Sullivan remembered. "Next came ties, which were set on fire, and then all the 15 or 20 piers were stripped of their half-dozen upper courses of heavy stone." Captain Gorman reported that the division pioneers took great pains to tear up the railroad tracks for "a long distance" before finally setting fire to the ties. He complained that the men assigned to this detail were "berated strongly" throughout their work by a group of people on the street.[34]

Despite the flurry of activity around them, many soldiers still found time to tour Carlisle. After strolling through the streets, Pvt. Louis Leon, one of Daniel's men, declared that "this city is certainly a beautiful place." Hospital Steward Apperson insisted that it was "the prettiest inland town I have ever seen." Major Blacktord from O'Neal's Brigade spent nearly half a day taking in the local attractions. "'Tis a very handsome place, much more so than any town of like size in the South, and is handsomely laid off," he wrote in a letter to his father. "I rode through it this morning and visited the U.S. Cavalry barracks which are elegant and very extensive."[35]

The well-known barracks dated back to 1776, when the Continental Congress established the first permanent military post at Carlisle. During the following years, the facility served mainly as a recruiting depot. The U.S. Army finally converted the post into the School of Cavalry Practice in 1838. For most of the remaining nineteenth

Officer's quarters at
Carlisle Barracks,
Pennsylvania. Cour-
tesy Cumberland
County Historical
Society.

century, except for a brief period during the Mexican War (1846–48), Carlisle Barracks operated as the primary location for recruiting and training cavalrymen and
dragoons for duty on the frontier. Among those who served there prior to the war
were a number of high-ranking officers in the Army of Northern Virginia.[36]

Because of its huge size, this historic facility proved nearly ideal as a resting place
for the three Tar Heel brigades in Rodes's Division. "We are occupying the old U.S.
barracks, which in the days of yore were inhabited by the gay and happy young officers of Dragoons & cavalry," General Ramseur explained to his fiancée. Most of the
six officers and 268 enlisted men from the current garrison had pulled out nearly two
full days before Rodes's troops arrived. Ramseur noted that "so hurried was the flight
of the Yankees that many household ornaments & luxuries were left behind."[37]

Sgt. George Wills from Daniel's Brigade informed his sister that the barracks
were constructed "in splendid style and show a good deal of taste." He argued that
it would be "a pity to destroy such pretty property, but as it is government property, suppose it will be." Capt. Weldon Davis from the Thirtieth North Carolina in
Ramseur's Brigade reported that the complex consisted "of seven or eight buildings, each about one hundred yards long, and each containing about fifty or sixty
rooms, besides numerous smaller buildings." The Tar Heel declared with a note of
nostalgia that "the place reminds me very much of Chapel Hill."[38]

For General Iverson, the barracks must have stirred much more poignant memories than those of a beloved college campus. He was stationed at the post from 1857
to 1858 while serving as a lieutenant with the First U.S. Cavalry. Many of the citizens
still recognized him on the street from his happier days as a young officer. They

cheerily greeted him as "Mr. Iverson," the term "mister" being the common form of respect for officers serving at the barracks. More bittersweet was that Carlisle had been the place where he first lived with his now-deceased wife and they had conceived their oldest child.[39]

On the surface at least, Iverson appeared completely unfazed by his unexpected homecoming. "Gen. Iverson (on whose staff Don Halsey serves) is occupying the same quarters he did while stationed here as Lt. of Cavalry some years ago," Major Blackford, who came from the same hometown as Halsey, commented in a letter to his father. "I called upon him and found him about to go out on a visiting tour among his old friends. I am curious to know how he was received and shall inquire tomorrow on the march." He noted that Captain Halsey, who served as Iverson's assistant adjutant general, was "in high glee at the prospect of making the town with him."[40]

Ewell also served at Carlisle during his time in the U.S. Army. After graduating from West Point in 1840, he received his initial training at the barracks before joining the Second U.S. Dragoons. Ewell was again assigned there on recruiting duty in 1848, following his tour in Mexico. His latest return as a rebel commander proved more problematic. Although he still had many acquaintances in town, a severe headache prevented him from making the social rounds, having instead to rely on several of his staff officers to check on the welfare of old friends. Personal concerns about how he would be received likely played an even bigger role in his decision not to contact them himself.[41]

Although a few citizens gave the former army officers a warm reception, most of them responded to the occupiers with barely concealed contempt. "They were the sourest looking people when we marched through that I ever saw," Lieutenant Calder told his mother. "It almost put my teeth on edge to look at them. They haven't a bit of use for the rebels." Captain Gorman complained to his family that Carlisle "is a red-hot abolition hole, and the hostility they bore us was marked on every face, male and female." Quartermaster Sergeant Tucker described it in his diary as "a very nice Town but inhabited by very mean people."[42]

At the same time, Carlisle residents compared favorably with the mostly uneducated German farmers the men had encountered up to that point in their advance. Hotchkiss insisted to his wife that "the people here are not half as sullen as they are farther down the Valley." Based on some deep-seated prejudices, he ascribed the difference to "the German element not being as strong & the humanizing influences of the schools &c have made a better population." Major Blackford also reported to his father that the citizens there "seemed somewhat more refined than the almost God forsaken people we had encountered all thro' that beautiful valley."[43]

Many of the officers in Rodes's Division held out especially high expectations for the professors and students at Dickinson College. Over the years a large number of young men from the South had attended that school. "Many soldiers who were in our corps met with those with whom they had spent pleasant days while at this place,"

Captain Beck from Doles's Brigade explained in a letter to his hometown newspaper. "This is the *Alma Mater* of many a Southern gentlemen." He further pointed out that "many a noble Confederate soldier received his tuition at old Dickerson."[44]

Although only a handful of students from the Border States stayed on during the war, Sgt. R. W. Freeman from the Forty-Fourth Georgia noted that the remaining "college boys who were from Dixie were very kind to us, offering their rooms and beds to us for the night." Other men had connections to the college through their acquaintances and relatives who had studied there. Pvt. William J. Underwood from the Fourth Georgia was shocked to find himself camped at the same school where some of his friends had graduated. "Little did I think when I heard them talking of college that I would ever see it," he declared in a letter home. At least two soldiers from the occupying force were even Dickinson graduates.[45]

One of the school's most distinguished alumni was Rev. Charles Force Deems, whose son served with the Fifth North Carolina in Iverson's Brigade. Rumors long persisted among the professors that the famed minister and educator had played a key role in protecting the college from harm. While saying "Goodby and good luck" to a colonel from one of the Tar Heel brigades just prior to their departure for the North, he supposedly "told him to take good care of his old college home in Carlisle, if he ever got there." That colonel turned out to be one of the senior officers from the division who bivouacked in the town and supposedly went to great efforts to fulfill his promise.[46]

At least some of the men found the chance to visit the college quite enjoyable. Asst. Surgeon William Marston from Iverson's Brigade "was much pleased" with his reception there. "Professor Nelson was kind enough to show me around," he wrote in his diary. Lt. Clement Fishburne from the military court in Ewell's corps also had "a very agreeable interview" with some of the professors. Chaplain Alexander D. Betts from the Thirtieth North Carolina in Ramseur's Brigade, who had close ties to Reverend Deems, even arranged a brief conference with President Johnson. Betts later met with Johnson's daughter and participated in a lively debate with her about the merits of the war.[47]

Tensions ran much higher during another tour by several of Ewell's staff officers. Maj. Sandie Pendleton and Dr. Hunter H. McGuire, the medical director for the Second Corps, at first engaged some of the faculty in an amiable conversation. The mood quickly changed when Prof. Samuel D. Hillman openly defended the recent destruction of Darien, Georgia, and the burning of William and Mary College in Virginia during the previous year. The professor acknowledged that their discussion soon "rose to a strong gesticulatory heat." Pendleton became so outraged that he was ready to take vengeance on the man. "I'll pay him for that sentiment," he pledged to his fiancée. "McGuire & I are going this afternoon to confiscate his chemicals, etc. in reprisal for William & Mary College."[48]

Despite that threat, cooler heads prevailed, and the professor's science laboratory, located in the South College building, suffered no damage during the Southerners' stay. Yet it still remained a close call. Hospital Steward Apperson reported that he actually went to the campus on the following day "for the purpose of taking the Chemical Apparatus from the College, but for some reason it was forbidden."[49]

The mood was hardly better during a visit by Sgt. Maj. Elihu Wesley Watson from the Sixth Alabama in O'Neal's Brigade. Watson noted in a letter home that he held "a long conversation" with President Johnson while there. "I like the man well enough but his principles are as bad as Wm. H. Seward's," the Alabamian complained. "He is as rank as rankness itself. He is an unmitigated abolitionist and a bitter enemy to the South." Sgt. Tim Furlow from Doles's staff was equally blunt about his feelings toward the college. "For my part I wanted to see the buildings burned to the ground, for it is one of the most intense abolition literary institutions in the whole North," he raged in his journal. The commanding generals were not open to anything of that sort, however, and left the school untouched.[50]

The time in Carlisle proved just as frustrating for Ewell, who had to deal with the sudden appearance of Maj. Gen. Isaac R. Trimble on the morning of June 28. After a long absence from the Army of Northern Virginia while recovering from a wound, the sixty-one-year-old Trimble took over the Valley District in western Virginia following the victory at Winchester. He quickly moved on to Carlisle in the hope of obtaining a better assignment and soon began pestering Ewell with all kinds of unwanted advice about how to conduct the campaign. At one point Trimble called for a quick strike to seize Harrisburg. "Told General Ewell it could be easily taken, and I thought General Lee expected it," he pointedly recalled. "I volunteered to capture the place with one brigade."[51]

Despite those problems, most of the troops found that Carlisle was filled with nearly forgotten pleasures. "I have long hird of the land where Milk and honey flowed," Pvt. Jeremiah Tate from O'Neal's Brigade proclaimed to his mother. "I think this comes as near the place as any I have ever seen." Ramseur bragged to his fiancée that he "breakfasted on Salmon left in ice, &c, &c." Sgt. Thomas Cleveland from the Fluvanna Artillery in the Corps Reserve Artillery effused to his wife that "we are living in waste on flour, bacon, beef, mutton, maceral, molasses, milk, and butter." Lt. Samuel H. Pendleton from the headquarters staff for the Second Corps artillery even "had ice cream" during a visit into town.[52]

Delicacies of all kinds proved so abundant that sumptuous dining soon became almost commonplace. Private Pickens from O'Neal's Brigade noted that he "had an excellent dinner—Biscuits, butter, mutton, goose, molasses, apple-butter & milk— to which we did ample justice." Lt. Robert Park, a fellow Alabamian, also sat down to a veritable feast at the home of a sympathetic resident. "We were served with hot rolls and waffles, butter and honey," he recorded in his journal. "Fried chicken also graced the table, and, I need not say, everything was hugely enjoyed."[53]

The handful of other Southern supporters among the populace provided the soldiers with some of the most delicious items. Capt. John Key from Doles's Brigade watched in amazement from the street corner as some citizens passed out food to his men from the third story of a building. "I saw a basket being let down by a string and when the basket was let down in reach of the men, its contents consisting of pies, cakes and all sorts of good things to eat, were taken out and handed a round to the men," he remarked. Key acknowledged that the only thing the residents asked in return was for the soldiers to keep their generosity to them secret.[54]

The large number of attractive women in Carlisle compared to the rest of the state made their stay even better. Major Pendleton reported that "until yesterday when we reached this place, I have seen nothing approaching good looks in the women." Sergeant Wills from Daniel's Brigade told his sister that he had not "seen a pretty lady after Maryland until I arrived at this place where I saw some very pretty ones." Lt. John Gay from Doles's Brigade insisted to his wife that it was "the first place I have been to in the state where the women wear clean clothes & look really nice."[55]

Unlike the rural areas, at least some of the women in Carlisle were willing to spend time with the occupying soldiers, which may account for the favorable comments about their looks. Hospital Steward Apperson spotted several officers from Rodes's Division "walking with the ladies of this place." Lieutenant Pendleton from the headquarters staff for the Corps Artillery Reserve also met "some nice girls" during his stay. Private Leon from Daniel's Brigade pointed out in his diary that the troops were "treated very good by the ladies." He added that "they thought we would do as their soldiers do, burn every place we passed through, but when we told them the strict orders of General Lee they were rejoiced."[56]

Despite the lures of town, most of the Tar Heel troops remained content simply to enjoy their brief sojourn in the barracks. After settling in his room, Assistant Surgeon Marston effused in his diary that "everything is comfortable." Lt. Leonidas Polk from Daniel's Brigade reported to his wife that they "are splendid quarters and are comfortably furnished." An officer from Ramseur's Brigade declared in his regiment's record of events that "in ease and luxury we reveled in the United States barracks." The only complaint for Pvt. Joseph Cowand from the Thirty-Second North Carolina in Daniel's Brigade was that he remained "a long wais from home."[57]

The soldiers soon discovered that a building along nearby LeTort Spring Run contained a large quantity of ice, which had become nearly impossible to obtain in the South. "There was an ice house right across the road from our camp, and we made what use we could of the ice," Cpl. Thomas Catesby Jones from the King William Artillery recalled. "I do not expect there was much ice left, as it was being carried to the officers' quarters continually." Sgt. Alexander S. "Sandie" Murdock from the Second North Carolina in Ramseur's Brigade insisted in a letter home that they obtained "as much ice as we could use."[58]

The chance to sleep indoors came as another rare treat for the broken-down men from Rodes's Division. Sgt. B. Frank Hall from the Forty-Third North Carolina in Daniel's Brigade admitted that they "were not accustomed to being housed even in

winter, and much less in the last of June:—nor were we accustomed to unlimited supplies of sugar and lemons for lemonade." All that high living did not come without
some unintended consequences. "We staid there only two or three days, but those
extraordinary luxuries wrought havoc amongst us, in the form of 'summer complaints,'" Hall recalled.[59]

Those at the barracks who were so inclined also had ready access to the comforts
of religion. Rev. Beverly Tucker Lacy, who had been Stonewall Jackson's favorite
chaplain, conducted worship there on the day after their arrival. In addition, Chaplains Betts from Ramseur's Brigade and Henry E. Brooks from the Second North
Carolina Battalion in Daniel's Brigade were on hand to minister to the troops that
Sunday. "Bro. Lacy preaches to three North Carolina Brigades in the forenoon,"
Betts wrote in his diary. "I preach in the afternoon and baptize five by pouring."[60]

Other chaplains held a prayer meeting for Doles's men on the grounds of Dickinson College. "On Sunday, there was preaching in the campus by rebel chaplains,"
Reverend Griffith, who lived near the college, remarked. "From my window I could
hear an occasional word." He pointed out that "the forenoon service, lasted, I think
nearly two hours." Johnson's troops mostly took in services that morning at their
camps near Alexander Spring. Catholic chaplain James Sheeran from Williams's brigade noted that he arose before dawn and "offered up the Holy Sacrifice but owing
to the early hour we had but a small congregation."[61]

A few of the men even attended local churches. "The Gen. sent word to the
clergy to have their services as usual, as no one would disturb them," Jed Hotchkiss
explained in a letter to his wife. During a hastily called meeting, most of the town's
minsters declined to comply. Although the response from the clergymen proved
far from overwhelming, two churches in the town conducted normal services that
morning. Hotchkiss reported that "the preachers, though nervous, prayed for their
country in peril and their friends in danger—they also prayed for the strangers that
were among them; some of them prayed for peace."[62]

The Second Presbyterian Church, on the corner of Hanover and Pomfret Streets,
was one of the locations that remained open. When Major Pendleton and Lieutenant Fishburne arrived there, they discovered that Confederate soldiers made up
much of the congregation. The minster happily avoided all mention of the war
and focused instead on the need to pray for the "dear ones left at home." Fishburne
noted, in fact, that "there was nothing offensive in anything he said." On leaving the
church they learned that the young pastor, Rev. John Collins Bliss, had once lived
in Florence, Alabama, and personally knew several of the men at the service.[63]

Circumstances proved much different at nearby First Lutheran Church, where
more than half of the sixty people in attendance came from Rodes's Division. Rev.
Jacob Fry chose the text for his sermon from Psalms 139, which included the line
"depart from me, therefore ye bloody men." Fry remembered only after the reading
began that the psalm included those words and passed over them "as lightly as

Second Presbyterian Church, Carlisle, Pennsylvania. Courtesy Cumberland County Historical Society.

possible." Despite that slip up, there were no indications that anyone took offense. Hotchkiss insisted to his wife, in fact, that the minister there proved to be "very sensible."[64]

The rest of the clergymen steadfastly declined to open their doors that Sunday. Reverend Griffith resorted to the usual stereotypes about the soldiers to justify their refusal, insisting that the decision came "because we did not wish to appear like greeting the rebels & meeting them on friendly terms but rather to show our sense of the calamity by staying at home in silent grief & partly because the rebels were so exceedingly dirty that they were not fit to enter any decent church." He took such exaggerations even farther with the comment that "their smell was offensive, their clothes ragged & filthy & moreover we could see that they were lousy."[65]

Rather than searching for a church to attend, most of the soldiers assembled at the barracks that morning to hear Lacy deliver a stirring oration on the career of Stonewall Jackson and a fiery sermon from Paul's letter to the Galatians. "Be not deceived, God is not mocked," Assistant Surgeon Marston recorded as the primary text for the service that day. "Whatsoever a man soweth, that he shall reap. He that soweth of the flesh shall of the flesh reap corruption; he that soweth of the spirit shall of the spirit reap life everlasting." Lieutenant Pendleton described it in his diary as "an excellent sermon."[66]

Despite the acclaimed preacher's words of admonition, many of the men turned to alcohol rather than religion as their primary source of solace while at Carlisle. "There was the greatest quantity of lager beer here and almost everything else we wanted," Sergeant Furlow declared in his journal. Lt. William Beavans from Daniel's staff contentedly recorded in his diary that he was "sleeping in the Barracks drinking ice water and whiskey." Maj. William W. Sillers from the Thirtieth North Carolina in Ramseur's Brigade admitted to his sister that he consumed a whole bottle of "claret with plenty of ice in it" while quartered there.[67]

The hunt for alcohol soon became an obsession for many of the soldiers in the ranks. Some of the most successful foragers came from the Twenty-Third North Carolina in Iverson's Brigade. At one point a group of them accidently discovered a "great deal of brandy" hidden inside one of the rooms at the barracks. They quickly distributed their plunder to soldiers throughout the rest of the brigade. "Many men of the 23rd and I presume of other regiments drank pretty fully of the Yankee treat," one officer recalled as the final payoff from their startling find.[68]

An enterprising soldier from Ramseur's Brigade surprised nearly all his comrades with what he discovered while foraging near the barracks. "He came to an old haystack and kicked his foot amongst the straw and found a whole barrel of whiskey," one of his messmates recalled. The huge stock of whiskey that Major Blackford uncovered while on picket duty just outside of town topped even that find. "In knocking about our camp, I found 80 barrels of liquor concealed under the hay in a barn," he explained. Although he eventually turned most of the cache over to the division's quartermasters, the veteran officer retained several barrels for the benefit of his own men.[69]

With so much liquor available to the troops, the task of maintaining order in the town sometimes required extreme measures. One particularly troubling breach of discipline took place soon after their arrival. "Four of our men broke into and pillaged a house near the barracks," a soldier from the Forty-Third North Carolina reported to his hometown newspaper. He noted that "as soon as it was made known to Gen. Ewell, he adopted means for their detection—placarded them with the words 'Thief and Rogue' in large letters, and marched them through our division to the 'Rogue's March.'"[70]

Fifteen-year-old John Cabell Early, who had arrived at the town in the hope of joining the staff of his uncle, General Early, also witnessed that scene. "Orders were given that they should be preceded by the band, playing 'The Rogue's March,'" he remembered. The young Virginia Military Institute cadet reported that "a great many citizens, having assembled to witness this humiliation, the band became indignant at their evidences of delight, and after getting away from the officers in command, turned the tables on the crowd by substituting 'Yankee Doodle' for the 'Rogue's March,' whereupon they soon dispersed."[71]

Despite that public display of punishment, the men from the Twenty-First Georgia in Doles's Brigade, who had taken over as provost guards from the Fifty-Third North Carolina, continued to encounter problems with large groups of drunken soldiers. Some of the worst offenders came from the Twenty-Third North Carolina.

"Many of our jaded, weary boys, drank too much United States Government whiskey and a battle with a Georgia regiment, for the time likewise drowning their weariness, was narrowly averted," a North Carolinian admitted.[72]

The access to endless supplies of confiscated whiskey occasionally fueled something more than a brawl. A musician from the Fourteenth North Carolina in Ramseur's Brigade described in graphic detail what took place during one drunken celebration at Carlisle. "Some of the Pennsylvania women, hearing the noise of the revel and the music, dared to come near," he recounted years later. "Soon they had formed the center of attention and joined in the spirit of the doings." He noted with satisfaction that "after much whiskey and dancing, they shed most of their garments and offered us their bottoms."[73]

Many of the ranking officers also abused alcohol during their stay in town. While preparing for a Sunday ceremony at the barracks, someone from Rodes's staff found a large keg of lager beer. He soon passed the contents around to everyone in attendance. The division commander quickly became "somewhat affected" by the potent brew. "The beer was the strongest I ever saw, I must add by the way of excuse—probably mixed with whiskey," Maj. Campbell Brown from Ewell's staff remarked in his journal. Brown insisted that he "never saw Rodes intoxicated before or since—& it was an accident this time."

No one knows for sure if General Iverson took part in the drinking, although the events that day apparently sparked later rumors that he was drunk at Gettysburg. Several other officers definitely took the opportunity to drown their sorrows that afternoon. General Trimble, temporarily attached to Ewell's staff, soon became "quite jolly." Some of the heaviest drinking occurred among the officers from Rodes's staff. One of them became so "utterly incoherent" that another staffer had to grab his coattails to keep him from falling flat on the ground.[74]

The open drunkenness among the general officers drew especially harsh condemnation from Rev. J. A. Stradley, who was serving as a missionary in Ramseur's Brigade. "Many officers, some occupying important positions, have been drunk, and many others have been drinking freely, and at the same time punishing men for doing the same thing," he chastised in a letter to a statewide religious newspaper in North Carolina. The minister found such actions so intolerable that he called for alcohol to be banned for men of all ranks. "O that this fatal destroyer of all that is good were itself destroyed!" he proclaimed.[75]

The ostensible cause for all the revelry was the scheduled raising of the newly authorized Second National Confederate flag. Although the design was not yet in general use, the officers at Carlisle soon came up with a reasonable substitute by incorporating some white bunting with a battle flag from one of Daniel's regiments. "Finding a number of U.S. garrison flags at the barracks & the flag-staff standing, we concluded to raise a Confederate flag for the benefit of the ignorant citizens," Major Brown remarked. He noted that "the Battle flag of the [32nd] N.C. was made the ground-work, two or three tailors were procured, and in an hour or two we had a handsome flag ready for hoisting."

As the improvised banner fluttered over the parade ground that afternoon, some of the top officers stumbled onto the balcony of the commandant's quarters to give short speeches for the men assembled just below. "The troops were gathered round, the flag raised," Brown recalled. "A short, neat speech [was] made from the balcony of the house by Rodes, another by Junius Daniel, and then old Trimble made a few remarks, not so very neat." Ewell was suffering from a severe headache and managed to say only "a few words to the men at the first raising of the flag" before returning to his sickbed.[76]

The corps commander's sudden disappearance hardly put a damper on the huge ceremony. In place of a formal speech, a staff officer read a proclamation from Ewell praising the troops for all that they had accomplished thus far in the campaign. Sgt. Bolling H. Hall from the Sixth Alabama, who witnessed the event from the crowd, reported to his uncle that the message thanked "us for our noble deeds." Just as important, it called on the veterans from the division to prepare "to meet the enemy again whom we had beaten on so many battle fields."[77]

Despite those stirring words, at least one officer from Daniel's staff found the generals who spoke at the gathering far from inspiring. "It would seem that if there was ever opportunity to let fall a flow of eloquence, it was on that auspicious occasion," Lt. Col. Wharton Green explained. As each one made his appearance on the balcony, the men in the crowd eagerly awaited a fiery speech. To his surprise, Green heard "no adequate response from any of our distinguished leaders to calls made upon them, thus showing that heroism and oratory do not always go hand in hand."[78]

Although a few were disappointed with the speeches, most of the men in attendance greeted the ceremony with unbridled enthusiasm. Assistant Surgeon Marston recorded in his diary that they "raised our new flag today in the barracks—great cheering & speech making." Jed Hotchkiss described it in his journal as "quite an animating scene." Lt. William Ardrey from Ramseur's Brigade noted that "speeches were made by Generals Trumbell, Rhodes, and Daniels." He declared with pride that the generals "complimented the North Carolina troops that they had raised the Confederate flag in a greater latitude than any other Southern troops."[79]

The Fourth North Carolina's band also performed some rousing music, which provided one of the highlights of the event. "We hoisted the Confederate flag over this place to be attended or greeted by Dixie from one of our best bands," Sgt. Maj. Preston Turner from that regiment effused in a letter to his parents. Sergeant Wills from Daniel's Brigade was just as impressed by all the pageantry on display. He informed his sister that "the band played Dixie & Bonnie-blue-flag, and we heard little talks from Genl. Ewell, Trimble, Rodes, Daniel & felt like going on to N.Y."[80]

At least one soldier, and probably many others, left the parade grounds that day more inspired than ever to fight the enemy anywhere General Lee took them. "No one has the least idea what we are going to do," Lieutenant Calder admitted to his mother. "Some say we are to take Harrisburg, others say not, and so it goes." Despite his uncertainty about their destination, he remained supremely confident that their leaders had the situation well in hand. "This much is certain," Calder declared. "We are far advanced into Pennsylvania and we did not come here for nothing." He insisted that "Gen Lee knows what we are to do and it is our part to obey orders with out questioning."[81]

"The General Was Quite Testy"

By the time of the flag-raising ceremony at Carlisle, Richard Ewell had Harrisburg squarely in his sights. Orders already called for him to advance to the Pennsylvania capital on the afternoon of June 29. General Lee badly wanted to capture the city, which would place his troops in position to threaten the major population centers in the East. Seizing the bridges there would also severely disrupt the Union's crucial east–west supply lines. The potential political consequences of taking Harrisburg outweighed even its considerable strategic value. The fall of an important state capital seemed likely to spark widespread panic in the North and further undermine public support for continuing the long fight against the Confederacy.[1]

As early as 1861, Federal engineers had identified several locations as the most likely points of entry into the city. They expected that the 4,300-foot wagon-and-pedestrian bridge spanning the Susquehanna River near the town of Wormleysburg would be the primary target for an enemy attack. The railroad bridge that stood alongside it to the south also served as a potential objective for invading forces. Another area of concern was a large ford across the river, located only a short distance downstream from the railroad bridge. A survey conducted at the beginning of the war found that the water level there was surprisingly shallow.

Two major fortifications directly opposite the city provided the primary defenses for the capital. Workers completed construction on Fort Washington, which stood closest to the river in the area known as Bridgeport, in early June 1863. The compound consisted of several earthen embankments that covered more than sixty acres on Hummel's Heights. A smaller set of entrenchments occupied slightly higher ground about seven hundred yards to the west. This fort was named for Maj. Gen. Darius N. Couch, who commanded the newly created Department of the Susquehanna.[2]

The Federal forces stationed around Harrisburg totaled nearly 12,000 inexperienced troops, most of whom came from New York and Pennsylvania militia units.

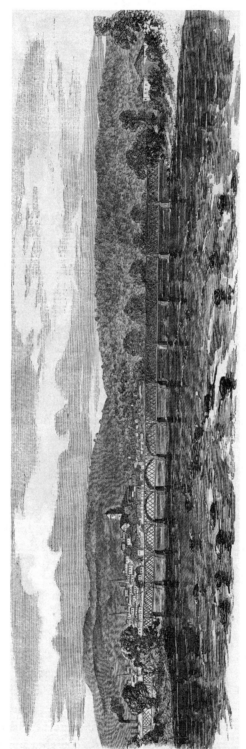

Railroad bridge over the Susquehanna River at Harrisburg, Pennsylvania. From *Harper's Weekly*.

About one-third of the men served on the west bank of the Susquehanna. Beside General Knipe's small brigade, several other regiments under the command of Brig. Gen. William Hall manned the two forts defending the western approaches to the capital. Another force of two regiments under Brig. Gen. John Ewen occupied a camp about three-quarters of a mile downstream from Bridgeport. On June 26 Brig. Gen. William F. "Baldy" Smith assumed overall command of the troops defending Harrisburg.[3]

The first probing operations by the Confederates began late in the afternoon on June 27, when Jenkins pushed east with his troopers along Trindle Spring Road. The horsemen eventually halted about five miles from Carlisle near the small village of Hickorytown. After a short ride the following morning, Jenkins split his force into two parts. The portion of the brigade that remained under his direct command included the Fourteenth and Sixteenth Virginia Cavalry, the Thirty-Sixth Virginia Cavalry Battalion, and the four-gun Baltimore Light Artillery under Capt. Wiley Hunter Griffin. His plan called for that force to secure a supply base at nearby Mechanicsburg before moving on toward Harrisburg.[4]

Mechanicsburg was a fast-growing community of about 2,000 residents. During the late 1830s, the town emerged as an important watering station on a main branch of the Cumberland Valley Railroad from Carlisle to Harrisburg. Several large grain and feed companies, a major lumber yard, and numerous factories soon sprang up along both sides of the tracks that ran through the center of town. Mechanicsburg also served as the home for two schools of higher education, the Irving Female College and the Cumberland Valley Institute.[5]

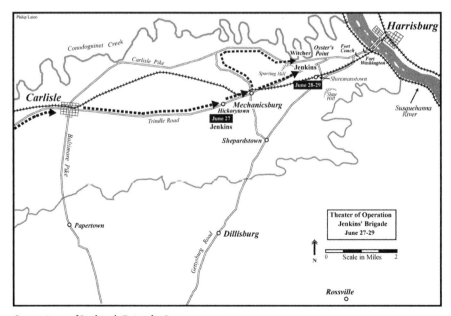

Operations of Jenkins's Brigade, June 27–29, 1863

As his troopers approached the outskirts of town during the early morning on June 28, Jenkins halted the column near the point where the road forked off onto Main and Simpson Streets. Their appearance prompted the hasty withdrawal of Capt. Frank Murray's company of Pennsylvania militia cavalry, which was one of the few Federal units operating along that part of Jenkins's front. According to the local newspaper, Murray and his men "dashed into town" about 8:30 A.M. After sending a hurried telegram to Harrisburg, the Federal troopers galloped off along the main road to the east.

From his vantage point along Trindle Spring Road, Jenkins spotted a large Union flag flying over Mechanicsburg. The general decided to scout the area carefully before moving forward. After firing a single artillery shell as a warning, he dispatched a small detachment under a white flag to find out if the town was being defended. "At nine o'clock two butternuts, bearing a flag of truce, dashed into town, and halting at the square inquired for the civil authorities and the flag which had been kept floating until a short time before their entrance," the newspaper reported.

After questioning several residents, the cavalrymen eventually tracked down the town's mayor. Following a short ride down East Main Street, the troopers pulled up in front of Burgess George Hummel's home. "They halted at Mr. Hummel's residence, and demanded of him the flag and that the town would be shelled on the refusal of this demand," the newspaper explained. The burgess immediately informed them that there were no longer any Federal troops in town. After a brief hesitation, the frightened official reluctantly handed over the flag that he was holding for safekeeping.

With that report (and the flag) in hand, Jenkins and his main column swarmed into Mechanicsburg during the late morning. The rebels' harsh expressions and intimidating stares left no doubts that the residents faced some hard times. One local woman described them to a friend as "the hardest looking pack" that "ever were created." The editor of the town's newspaper pointed out that "the men were, with a few exceptions, a stout looking set of fellows—picked men for hard service and would have done some good fighting had they been attacked." He further noted that their horses "were generally very good, having been stolen from farmers in the upper end of the valley."

As the long column of riders trotted through the streets, the townspeople got the chance for an even closer look at the soldiers from the invading army. "Some were clad in the butternut uniforms, while the majority had no uniform on at all, many indeed, having nothing but shirt, pants and hat," the town's newspaper reported. They brandished a surprising assortment of weapons, including pistols and sabers. The editor pointed out that "the majority had nothing but muskets, while a few had double barreled fowling pieces." Despite their fearsome looks, he admitted that Jenkins's men "were, as a body, pretty well behaved."

While the troopers set up their camp about a mile east of town, Jenkins and his staff established their headquarters at the Ashland House Tavern in the Railroad

Main Street at Mechanicsburg, Pennsylvania. Courtesy Mechanicsburg Museum Association.

Hotel, directly across the street from the railroad station. With those preliminaries out of the way, the general immediately demanded a meeting with the elected officials. "Jenkins sent for the Burgess, and issued his first proclamation, calling for fifteen hundred rations to be delivered at the Town Hall within an hour and a half, under pain of permitting his men to hunt provisions themselves," the newspaper explained. Jenkins reportedly backed up this ultimatum by placing some of his artillery "at the upper end of town" with orders to fire if the items were not turned over within the allotted time.[6]

Town officials quickly determined that they would face forcible seizures or worse retribution if they failed to comply with the demands. "As this was not the most agreeable alternative, our citizens at once set about furnishing the number of provisions required," the newspaper's editor declared. He noted that "it was rather a novel spectacle in town, to see a large number of citizens wending their way to the Town Hall, on a Sabbath day, carrying baskets of provisions for a band of rebel invaders." One woman reported that "the name of the donor was to be attached to each basket, so that, if there was not enough furnished, the men might have the privilege of helping themselves from those who had not contributed."[7]

The huge spread of food thus procured certainly proved much better than the Confederates had any reason to expect. "Upon requisition were treated by the citizens to a delicious dinner," Lt. Hermann Schuricht from the Fourteenth Virginia Cavalry commented in his diary. He admitted that "probably the frightened people gave up to us the meals prepared for their own table." Local grain merchant C. B. Niesley pointed out to his parents that the items the townspeople turned over included "baskets of ham, bread, butter and whatever else they choose to bring."[8]

The troopers hauled off the bulk of their loot to the brigade camp just outside of town. The editor of the local newspaper noted, however, that "a large number" of the men ate their share of the food at the town hall. Jenkins soon issued a further demand for the harried officials to turn over a huge supply of feed for his horses. "A quantity of corn and oats yet remaining in the warehouse of Brandt and Company and Johnson and Son, was drawn upon for this purpose," the newspaper stated. As at their previous stops, when the Southerners obtained the fodder from civilians, "payment was made in confederate scrip."

During the early afternoon, quartermaster and commissary details "visited some of the stores" in town. Most of the businesses had already shipped their goods away for safety just prior to the arrival of Jenkins's force. The newspaper's editor insisted that the horsemen's "purchases were not large from the fact that our merchants just then had a very small stock of goods on hand." According to another report, the exception was a local boot-and-shoe dealer who "was completely cleaned out of his entire stock, and all he had to show for it was $4,000 in worthless rebel currency."[9]

Some troopers turned to foraging for additional food at individual houses. One citizen reported to a friend that the hungry soldiers who showed up at his doorstep "only asked for bread, some for water, but dident disturb enything at this home." Other cavalrymen passed the time by "trading hats" with the people on the streets. "It did not usually take long to make a trade," the local newspaper explained. "The rebel riding up to a man whose hat pleased him would remove it from his head, hand him down his own in return, which he might wear or not, as he choose."[10]

The occupation proved especially dangerous for the handful of African Americans remaining in Mechanicsburg, who became targets for Jenkins's horsemen. The Southerners displayed so much brutality in gathering them up from their hiding places that it had a major effect on residents' attitudes. "I heard expressions of sympathy too for the poor slave from those who had been silent before," one woman reported to a friend a couple of weeks later. "It is said the Rebels captured six about town, among the number a woman with two babies a week old." She noted that the slave hunters seized them while they "were concealed in a cornfield."[11]

About 2:00 P.M., Jenkins finally settled his bill at the Ashland House and leisurely rode out of Mechanicsburg. He initially proceeded just east of town to his brigade's main camp. After briefly consulting with some of his scouts, the general then hurried off toward the north to check on the other part of his command. The rest of the men from the main body galloped out of camp soon afterward. That force, under the temporary command of Col. James Cochran from the Fourteenth Virginia Cavalry, headed straight east toward Harrisburg along Trindle Spring Road.[12]

The departure of Jenkins's cavalrymen left Mechanicsburg temporarily free from enemy troops. The residents were relieved that their town had suffered only minor damage during the Confederate occupation. Jenkins's men had limited their efforts to seizing provisions and disrupting the lines of communications. The local newspaper noted that the troopers "cut down several of the telegraph poles, and tore down the wire for a considerable distance." The only other loss of any consequence consisted of "a few rails" that they tore up on the railroad line running east toward Harrisburg.[13]

During that time, the other detachment from the brigade moved into place northeast of town. That force consisted of about three hundred troopers from Lt. Col. Vincent A. Witcher's Thirty-Fourth Virginia Cavalry Battalion. From the area of Trindle Spring, those seven companies first headed north along Hogestown Road. Jenkins's orders called for them to turn east from there onto the turnpike from Carlisle to Harrisburg. After traveling about a mile and a half along the toll road, the cavalrymen halted just past Silver Spring Creek near Salem Church.

At that point the Confederates suddenly confronted a large militia force under General Knipe. This mixed command of infantry and artillery consisted of two regiments from the New York National Guard and a battery commanded by Capt. Elihu Spencer Miller. After pushing forward from the fortifications outside Harrisburg, Knipe's troops took up a defensive position about a mile away from Witcher's location on some high ground known as Sporting Hill. The Virginians immediately formed a line of battle in preparation for an attack on the Federal force.

By then, part of Capt. William L. Jackson's Charlottesville Horse Artillery had arrived from Virginia. After linking up with the battalion's troopers, the gunners quickly unlimbered their three pieces and started firing toward the enemy lines. The volleys soon began to take a toll. The artillerymen eventually forced the militia forces to fall back to the east along Carlisle Pike. Witcher's cavalrymen then pursued the Northerners to the area where Orr's Bridge spanned Conodoguinet Creek.

General Jenkins, who had made his way safely from Mechanicsburg, soon joined Witcher near the bridge. From there the cavalrymen continued east to the farm occupied by Samuel Eppley and his family, located about halfway between Sporting Hill and the two major fortifications outside Harrisburg. Federal forces established a line of battle just west of Fort Couch near the junction of Carlisle Turnpike and Trindle Spring Road. A cluster of about twenty buildings, including Prof. David Denlinger's recently shuttered White Hall Academy, stood just to their rear. Because the Oyster family owned a large tavern there, locals referred to the area around the fork in the road as Oyster's Point.[14]

After determining that everything was in order along Witcher's front, Jenkins galloped off to the south. He eventually arrived at Peace Church, which stood at the intersection of St. John's Church Road and Trindle Spring Road. The structure dated back to 1798 and was used jointly by the local Reformed and German Lutheran congregations. Jenkins met up with Colonel Cochran, who had just arrived from Mechanicsburg with the rest of the brigade. The general immediately ordered Captain Griffin's Baltimore Light Artillery to deploy its four guns around the church and begin firing at a suspected enemy position along Oyster's Point.[15]

About the same time, the guns of Jackson's battery, positioned on some high ground just in front of the farmhouse, also unleashed a barrage of artillery rounds from the Eppley farm. Their target was the same enemy force at Oyster's Point that had attracted the attention of Griffin's guns. "About four miles from Harrisburg, the capital of Pennsylvania, we took position on a dominating hill," Lieutenant Schuricht from the Fourteenth Virginia Cavalry wrote in his diary. "Jackson's Battery, belonging to our brigade, came up, and the artillery fire with the enemy ensued, lasting until nightfall."[16]

Just after dusk, Jenkins withdrew his troops a short distance to the rear to a farm owned by John Neidig. Despite all the action in the area, the family members still remained on the property and were generally treated with courtesy by the soldiers. Neidig's wife acknowledged that the Confederates were "very well behaved and were strictly disciplined by their officers." Jenkins set up his headquarters nearby at the John Rupp house on Trindle Spring Road. Unlike the Neidig family, the residents of that home had fled to Lancaster for safety. Lieutenant Schuricht's company from the Fourteenth Virginia Cavalry took up position near Mechanicsburg in an effort to maintain the lines of communication with Carlisle.[17]

By then, about 250 troopers from the Sixteenth Virginia Cavalry had already set off on a major raid through northern York County to Dillsburg. Maj. James H. Nounnan, a hardened veteran of the brutal conflicts in the Kansas Territory, commanded the detachment. An officer from his regiment described the major as a man of stunning contrasts. "In the camp—he dressed like a servant—never washed, nor combed his hair nor put on clean garments, but presented at all these times the appearance of some day laborer, digging ditches in the swamps—dirty, haggard and worn," he recalled. Once he entered a battle, however, Nounnan suddenly transformed into one of the most magnificent leaders the officer had ever encountered.[18]

The cavalrymen arrived late in the afternoon on June 28 and set up camp just south of town. "They sent squads of their soldiers into Dillsburg for provisions, such as bread, meat, coffee and tobacco, &c, and offered to pay for it in Confederate scrip, but it was worthless to our people," local postmaster Augustus N. Eslinger complained. Many residents had prepared for the arrival of the invading cavalrymen by burying their most valuable goods or hiding them inside their barns. Most of the area farmers also sent their prized horses off for safety in the mountains.

Despite the efforts to conceal their property, several residents suffered severely during the incursion. James J. Moore's general-merchandise store lost thirty pairs of shoes and boots, several yards of cloth, twenty-five pounds of leaf tobacco, and one hundred fine cigars during this raid. Jenkins's cavalrymen also confiscated more than fifty pounds of finished leather from the local tannery and even ransacked the town's post office, where they grabbed up thirty dollars in cash, a pile of postage stamps, and the postmaster's overcoat. Eslinger noted that the troopers eventually "left camp on Monday morning the 29th, after taking all the good horses in the borough and from the farmers all around the country."[19]

Jenkins's men continued searching the surrounding area throughout most of that day for additional horses and supplies. These efforts took the rebels as far east as Rossville, where they ransacked the store owned by William R. Smith. The unlucky merchant suffered losses valued at $1,180, including large amounts of groceries, tobacco, clothing, calico, muslin, and various dry goods. The troopers also seized three full barrels of whiskey (126 gallons), 35 gallons of aged brandy, and 10 gallons of wine from the store. They next turned their attention to the adjacent property, confiscating several horses as well as 20 bushels of corn, 125 bushels of oats, and 3 bushels of other grains as feed for their mounts, before finally rejoining the rest of the brigade outside Harrisburg.[20]

While Nounnan's men were off on their raid, Capt. Frank Bond's troopers hunted around Carlisle for additional plunder. Hanna Culver reported to her brother that the horsemen "spread themselves over the country in quest of forage & horses." Although many items had been stashed away, the intruders seized huge quantities of goods. The woman admitted that many "barns were emptied of corn & oats and quite a number of cattle were driven off." She claimed that even "the mills in the country were in their posession [sic], grinding all the grain that could be obtained."[21]

Young Nettie Jane Blair watched in disbelief as six riders galloped up to her family's farm just outside of town and began hunting for any "contrabands" who might be hiding there. Her grandfather, a staunch abolitionist, had already escorted a number of African Americans to safety at Harrisburg the previous day. Although one terrified black girl remained hidden in an outbuilding, the searches came up empty. The Southerners next tried to force their way into the house. "They told Uncle Lank not to touch a thing that they would send out a detail to cut the wheat, and would then go through the house to see what they wanted," Blair recalled. Despite that threat, the men soon rode off without further incident.[22]

An African American laborer working on land owned by Josiah S. Carothers just west of Carlisle had much less luck evading capture. The farmer looked on in despair as the "body of rebels" turned their attention to a black workman who was present in the field as they rode up. The startled Pennsylvanian could do nothing to stop the horsemen as they "took with them" the African American whom he had hired to help with hauling away his crop of newly cut hay. In his postwar claim for damages, Carothers noted that the cavalrymen also confiscated five horses, one sheep, and two beehives from his property.[23]

The Givin Brothers' paper mill at Mount Holly Springs, Pennsylvania. Courtesy Cumberland County Historical Society.

Another citizen complained to a friend that a squad of seven horsemen stopped at her dwelling on the outskirts of town and demanded entry. The frightened homeowner found on opening the door that "all were armed with Carbines, Sabres &c." Once her neighbor arrived at the scene of the disturbance, the troopers "asked for several items," which they purchased with worthless scrip. The men then inquired if there were "any abolitionists about here." When the neighbor answered in the negative, they galloped off "in search of Horses." Some of them later returned to the woman's homestead and seized "a new farm wagon" and "young cattle in large numbers" from several of her neighbors.[24]

At one point Ewell ordered Bond to take four wagons and carry out a raid on a paper mill located a few miles away at Mount Holly Springs. The captain recalled that his command approached the village "very quietly, and were not noticed until well into it." As the horsemen entered the main street, the citizens shut themselves inside their houses. Bond and his troopers immediately "went to the mill," probably the extensive paper mill owned by Robert and Samuel Givin, "and got a load of paper, and started the wagon on its return." The remainder of the horsemen obtained dinner from some frightened residents before making their way back during the early evening.[25]

Another contingent of riders made a brief foray about six miles north of Carlisle to the resort town of Carlisle Springs. According to one account, about "20 Rebel cavalrymen" rode into the village on the morning of June 28. The men briefly interrogated businessman Nathan Woods, who managed the town's renowned spa hotel. Woods attempted to deceive the invaders with a false report that more than 50,000 troops had moved into place along the mountains a short distance away at Sterrett's Gap. Ignoring that warning, the cavalrymen eventually headed off to the north.

A group of children feasting on cherries along the road encountered the horsemen soon afterward, about a mile outside of town near the Joseph Miller farm at the foot of the gap. Several troopers "with pistols in hand" approached the youths. One cavalryman even engaged them in a brief conversation. At a frantic signal from his comrades, the man suddenly broke off the discussion. The group then turned their horses around and galloped back to the south. Whether those men were from Bond's company or Gilmor's battalion remains impossible to confirm.[26]

Unknown to the Confederates, the defenses at Sterrett's Gap consisted of little more than a series of hastily constructed barricades just over the border in Perry County around the Mountain Hotel. William McCandlish noted in his diary that "the Perry county people have the gaps in the mountains blockaded with felled trees and 'defended' by themselves, with shot guns old muskets, etc." The approximately three hundred defenders included a few women and clergymen as well as the editors and printers from some of the county's newspapers. Capt. Joel F. Frederick, who had previously served in the One Hundred Thirty-Third Pennsylvania, commanded the contingent.[27]

The former Union officer quickly organized his band of ragtag defenders into a reasonably credible force. "He soon had the road picketed and his skirmish lines properly advanced," one of the men recalled. "Fortifications were erected and the place made as nearly impregnable as possible." He noted that "the arms were of all descriptions, yet would have been effective, as nearly all were well supplied with buckshot." According to some unconfirmed accounts, the citizens around the gap actually fired on a force of Confederate cavalrymen probing the area along their front on the twenty-eighth.[28]

Less reliable are stories that a handful of troopers crossed the Susquehanna River about fifty miles farther north at Trevorton Junction, aiming to destroy some train cars from the Northern Central Railway parked upstream at Sunbury. According to one report, the town's telegraph operator sent a hurried warning to officials in Harrisburg after he spotted eight Confederate horsemen passing over the bridge. Another tale indicated that "a hired girl" working at a local inn deceived the troopers by changing the direction on a large weathervane, causing them to lose their way before reaching their objective.[29]

While all that was going on, the main part of Jenkins's Brigade resumed its operations outside of Harrisburg on the morning of June 29. After the cavalry pushed forward along two parallel roads, both supporting batteries were soon back in action from the same positions they had occupied the previous day. The Charlottesville Horse Artillery on the Eppley farm was bolstered by the sudden appearance of its three remaining artillery pieces. With their arrival, Captain Jackson's battery finally had its full complement of six guns, including four "Dahlgren Boat howitzers" and two three-inch rifles, on the field for the first time during the campaign.

The tardy guns and their crews had briefly halted at Mechanicsburg during the early morning before linking up with Witcher's men. "On Monday another party with three pieces of artillery passed through the upper part of the town," the local newspaper reported. "Like their predecessors they sent in a requisition for rations, but this time for only one hundred and fifty." Lt. Micajah Woods from the battery pointed out that the items they procured in town included "eggs, ham, beef, apple butter, pies, and vegetables of every description." The newspaper noted that only a few of the men "came down as far as the hall, and only tarried while they secured the rations."[30]

With their supplies in hand, the men moved north on Hogestown Road and then east on the turnpike, where they joined the rest of the battery on the Eppley farm. The newly arrived artillerymen soon unlimbered their guns and took direct aim at the enemy positions around Oyster's Point. "Without being halted one of Lt. Blain's Howitzers and my rifle 3-inch piece were ordered to front," Lieutenant Woods informed his mother. He explained that the two guns were located "about 400 yds. in front [of] the first line of works." The gunners immediately "opened fire with shell and succeeded in dislodging the enemy from his front in about a half an hour."

That portion of Jackson's battery performed well in what was its first taste of real combat since being reorganized. The only damage that the battery sustained that day came when the enemy's return fire disabled one horse. At the same time, their guns apparently inflicted some significant losses on the militiamen. Lieutenant Woods reported that "our dismounted cavalry entered the works afterward and reported several of the enemy killed and left." He declared with pride that the firing by their battery had "proved imminently successful & efficient."[31]

According to the plan that Jenkins and Witcher had worked out the previous night, the artillery barrage would provide needed cover for a major reconnaissance of the Harrisburg defenses. Jenkins's orders called for the cavalrymen "to simply demonstrate" while the general rode south to obtain a clear view of the city. Despite those arrangements, the lieutenant colonel was itching for any excuse to turn the demonstration into a full-blown attack. He quickly determined that the enemy "position could be carried" and decided to launch a "direct assault" around Oyster's Point.

About 11:00 A.M., two companies from Witcher's Thirty-Fourth Virginia Cavalry Battalion moved forward toward the enemy lines. Some troopers from the rest of the brigade soon joined in the advance as did a single gun from Jackson's battery, which followed closely behind the main body of horsemen. Opposing them were about 150 men from three different regiments under the temporary command of Lt. Col. John Elwell from the Twenty-Second New York State National Guard, who set up a defensive line behind some logs and fallen trees just east of Oyster's Point.

One of Jenkins's troopers noted in a letter to a Richmond newspaper that the attack quickly overran "the enemy's outpost." Despite that promising start, the horsemen soon faced a fierce volley of gunfire from the Federal troops behind the makeshift barricades. At least three Confederate troopers suffered wounds in the charge. Following a flurry of action, Witcher's men pulled back to their original position but, in the confusion of the fighting, left their lone artillery piece behind on the field. Jackson's artillerists were unable to retrieve their abandoned gun until late in the afternoon.[32]

While the remainder of the two batteries kept up a steady fire on the militia positions, Jenkins was busy meeting with Capt. Henry B. Richardson, who served as Ewell's chief engineer. Earlier in the day the corps commander had dispatched the captain and two other staff officers to carry out an extensive survey of the defenses around Harrisburg. After completing the mission, Richardson was expected to report back to the commanding general as soon as possible with detailed information on the likely prospects for an attack against the capital.[33]

Using the artillery barrage as a diversion, Jenkins and the group of officers proceeded south from Peace Church along St. John's Church Road. After a short ride they passed through the village of Shiremanstown and ascended nearby Slate Hill. That high ground provided a nearly unobstructed view of the Federal defenses around the state capital. Lieutenant Schuricht's company from the Fourteenth Virginia Cavalry escorted the officers. "We reconnoitered to the right of the Harrisburg turnpike, charged on the enemy's outposts, and viewed the city of Harrisburg and its defenses," Schuricht wrote in his diary.[34]

The action around Oyster's Point provided so much of a distraction that the militia failed to notice all the activity to their south. Although not a single soldier attempted to interfere with the rebel reconnaissance, several civilians reported seeing the enemy detachment in the area that day. One resident observed some Confederate cavalrymen "to the number of about sixty" moving along Lisburn Road during the late morning. Another clearly recalled seeing "a line" of Southern troops around Slate Hill soon afterward.[35]

Early that afternoon Captain Richardson made his way back to Carlisle with his report, which generally proved quite favorable. The reconnaissance showed no obvious signs that a large number of regular Federal troops had moved into place at Harrisburg. The fortifications around the city also appeared much less formidable than those at Winchester. Jenkins further reported that the river in the area was "apparently fordable." News that Gordon's Brigade had already reached the west bank of the Susquehanna to the southeast at Wrightsville further bolstered Richardson's positive assessment.[36]

With the city's defenses manned largely by state militia, Harrisburg seemed ready to fall at the first sight of the invading army. Capt. William C. Ousby from the Forty-Fifth North Carolina in Daniel's Brigade informed his family that he did not "think that the Yankees will give us much of a fight at Harrisburg as we learned that most of their forces at that place are militia." Lt. Thomas S. Taylor from the Sixth Alabama in O'Neal's Brigade boasted to his wife that "the Capital of this State is most certainly gone up the spout." Even so, Pvt. William A. Heirs from the Third Alabama in the same brigade admitted to his cousin that "it will be queer" if the enemy does "not make a stand and show fight at some point."[37]

Some of Doles's Georgians, who were seeking retaliation for the recent outrages committed by Federal troops in their state at Darien and at other locations in the South, found the prospect of seizing a Northern state capital especially attractive. "I sincerely hope we will capture it," Lt. John Gay explained in a letter home. "There we will probably be revenged for [the] burning of Jackson, Miss. & Darien, Geo." Capt. Shepherd Pryor told his wife that he also held out high hopes that they would "make the yanks feel the sting of this war, some of which they are now beginning to feel, I assure you."[38]

Sgt. William Beverley Pettit from the Fluvanna Artillery in the Corps Reserve Artillery remained undeterred by rampant rumors that more than 60,000 militiamen had assembled at Harrisburg. "The greater the body of militia brought in conflict with this army, the more complete and disastrous will be their route [sic]," he boasted to his wife a couple of days prior to reaching Carlisle. In fact, the Virginian eagerly awaited the chance to take on such troops. "I think we shall go there and, having taken the capital of the state, go on next to Philadelphia and take the great metropolis," Pettit declared.[39]

Many others were certain that they had entered the final phase of hostilities, no matter where their destination might be. "Our troops are in fine spirits," Sgt. Joseph Felder from Doles's Brigade told his father. "All seem to be perfectly confident of success, and [a] great many think they are now experiencing the closing seen [sic] of this war. God grant that it may be so." Pvt. James P. Garrison from the Twenty-Sixth Alabama in O'Neal's Brigade predicted to his wife that the upcoming move would bring the campaign "to a close before long." Lt. Leonidas Polk from Daniel's Brigade insisted that "this campaign is pregnant with great events & how or when or where it will end, is with Gen. Lee, & our God."[40]

But plans suddenly changed during the afternoon of June 29. Just as his troops were preparing to leave Carlisle, Ewell received a message from General Lee that canceled the movement toward Harrisburg and directed the entire Second Corps to concentrate in the vicinity of Chambersburg. Those new orders resulted from intelligence received from a scout on the previous day indicating that the Federal army under its new commander, Maj. Gen. George Gordon Meade, had already crossed the Potomac River and was fast approaching from the east side of South Mountain. That news left Lee with little choice other than to abandon seizing the state capital and to consolidate his troops for the long-awaited confrontation with the advancing Army of the Potomac.[41]

Instead of leading his men to Harrisburg, Ewell immediately dispatched Johnson's Division, which was camped about three miles outside of Carlisle, toward Chambersburg along Valley Turnpike on the western side of South Mountain. The two reserve artillery battalions and the corps's massive supply train accompanied the division on the march. This column also included the troops from Steuart's Brigade, which had finally rejoined the main part of the division the previous day. One of the men from the Maryland battalion in that brigade griped that they only "got one good night's rest and sleep at our encampment outside of Carlisle."[42]

The unexpected sight of Johnson's entire division moving south caught most of the people along its route by surprise. Their glee in seeing the invading troops pulling back soon became impossible for anyone in the long column of troops to overlook. Lt. Thomas Tolson from Steuart's Brigade noted that "the people along the road think we are retreating and seem pleased." Sgt. William S. White from the Corps Artillery Reserve also found that the citizens "look more cheerful and better pleased since we commenced to march backwards and say we are going to get a terribly bad whipping in the next few days."[43]

After a grueling march, the played-out troops went into camp just north of Shippensburg. Search parties were soon prowling the surrounding area for whatever supplies might remain. The wife of one nearby farmer protested to a colonel in the division when some of his men began rummaging through her barn with lighted torches. "The soldiers were looking for chickens for their suppers," her son recalled, taking "all except an old rooster." The youngster complained that the family also "suffered a considerable loss that night when the Confederates took a crib full of corn to feed their horses."[44]

As Rodes's Division prepared to depart Carlisle along the same route, a second courier arrived from Lee with updated instructions calling for them instead to move straight south through the mountains to Heidlersburg, located a few miles northeast of Gettysburg. From there Ewell could "either move directly on Gettysburg or turn down to Cashtown." The orders also directed the troops from Early's Division to proceed toward the same area from their main encampment near York. Jenkins's troopers would secure the rear as they pulled back from the outskirts of Harrisburg.[45]

Ewell assigned the duty of informing Early about the new arrangements to a detachment of scouts serving with Jenkins's Brigade. These instructions, however, would not reach him until late in the morning on the next day. "At Carlisle I was

Baltimore Turnpike looking north to South Hanover Street in Carlisle, Pennsylvania. Courtesy Cumberland County Historical Society.

detailed on a scouting party of thirty and traveling all night took a dispatch from Ewell to Early," an officer from the Fourteenth Virginia Cavalry recalled year later. "We, of course, didn't know the nature of our mission then, but it afterwards developed 'twas to recall Early from his advanced position back to Gettysburg."[46]

Rather than leave so late in the day, Ewell decided to hold Rodes's men in Carlisle until the following morning. The corps commander, who so recently had expected to take Harrisburg with little or no opposition, found the cancellation of the attack especially frustrating. "The General was quite testy and hard to please, because disappointed, and had every one flying around," Jed Hotchkiss remarked in his journal. Ewell's only satisfaction came when General Lee agreed that they would not need to burn Carlisle Barracks, where he had served during his earlier days as a young officer in the dragoons.[47]

Nevertheless, when Rodes's men finally marched out of town along South Hanover Street during the early morning on June 30, their destination was not one of the major cities in the East, such as Baltimore or New York, or even the Pennsylvania capital as most of them expected. Writing to his family a little more than two weeks afterward, Pvt. John F. Coghill from Iverson's Brigade reported that, following the last-minute change in orders, the soldiers "came back through Carlisle and took the road that went to Baltimore but instead of going to Baltimore wee went to the horrible place of Gettysburg."[48]

⚛16⚛

"We Had No Idea of Our Destination"

With the attack on Harrisburg cancelled, Robert Rodes's troops headed south from Carlisle along Baltimore Turnpike. As they passed by a tollhouse about a mile from town, some of the men forced the frightened gatekeeper to hand over food from his kitchen. In addition, the hungry soldiers soon emptied the home of all the bread, butter, and molasses they could find. This breach in discipline came to a sudden stop when General Rodes arrived on the scene. The gatekeeper's daughter noted that the division commander immediately ordered "his men to desist" from their foraging. She recalled that the admonition was "not a stern, harsh command" but rather a calm directive that prompted their "instant obedience."[1]

Their first halt came soon afterward at Papertown, home to the Kempton and Mullen Paper Company, one of largest manufacturers in the North. Maj. Eugene Blackford from O'Neal's Brigade noted that he "went in and saw more paper than I ever heard of before." The massive stock of high-quality goods proved too tempting for Ewell to pass up. Jed Hotchkiss indicated in his diary that the general and some of his staff officers "stopped awhile to examine the extensive paper mill there." The disgruntled proprietor eventually conducted a brief tour of the factory for them, during which Ewell selected more than $5,000 worth of supplies for seizure by the Quartermaster Department.[2]

After having the plunder loaded up, Rodes and Ewell led their men through the mountain gap at Mount Holly Springs. Along the way they passed by the Givin brothers' paper mill, which had been the target of an earlier raid by Bond's troopers. Despite intermittent rain, Hotchkiss described the day as "quite pleasant." Best of all was the spectacular mountain scenery along the route of march. Capt. John Gorman from Ramseur's Brigade insisted in a letter home that he had "never seen, in all my travels, a more lovely spot than Mt. Holly Gap." He further declared that "its picturesque beauty and grandeur must be seen to be realized."[3]

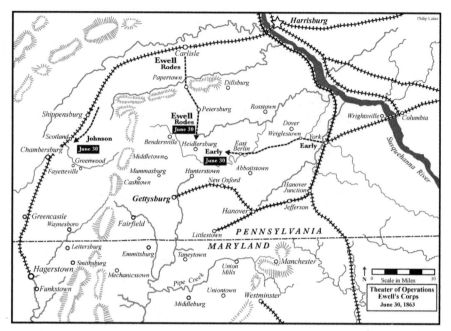

Operations of Ewell's Corps, June 30, 1863

Capt. James Harris, who served in the same brigade, was just as impressed by the sights that they encountered along the way. "I think that there are more rocks at this place than in all of No. Carolina," the Tar Heel veteran proclaimed in a letter to a friend. "The whole side of the mountain seems completely covered for 2 or 3 ft. deep altogether with small stones." Despite the rugged terrain, Harris found the trip through the gap to be relatively easy. He noted that the road they took that day "was as straight as you ever saw a stretch on a R.R., the ascents and descents being gradual."[4]

The men especially welcomed the chance to feast on the cherries that filled the trees along their route. A soldier from the Jeff Davis Artillery effused in a letter home that "they have the finest cherries in Pa I ever saw & more of them I never saw." The ripening fruit proved to be a special favorite for the corps commander. "As we rode along, we saw many fine wax cherries on the road," recalled John Cabell Early, who accompanied Ewell on the journey. "I enjoyed these hugely, and so did the General." Young Early spent most that day gathering up the heavily laden branches for Ewell to eat his fill and joked that he "brought him so many boughs of them for his consumption that I began to wonder, boy-like how so small a man could hold so many cherries."[5]

The only anxious moments came when it appeared that some bushwhackers had fired on the column as it "passed through the gap in the South Mountains." Ac-

Kempton and Mullen Paper Company at Papertown, Pennsylvania. Courtesy Library of Congress.

cording to a soldier in the Jeff Davis Artillery, the shots came "from an overhanging bluff covered by scrub undergrowth, forming a dense thicket." He claimed that "a volley of perhaps a dozen shots was fired." The commotion also caught the attention of General Early's nephew. The teenager recalled that "toward midday, upon approaching a rather high hill which the road crossed, there was an alarm of the enemy in front, and skirmishers deployed." He noted that the report of an attack "proved to be a mistake, however, and we resumed our march."[6]

Despite that scare, the troops pushed on a few miles without further incident to Petersburg, the site of the famed York Sulphur Springs resort. One resident noted that "our quiet town" was suddenly "thrown into a state of unusual excitement by the advance guard of Ewell's division dashing over the hill." Several search parties immediately moved into place and demanded "the stores to be opened." A local merchant complained that the troops entered his business "by force" and seized dry goods, hats, boots, and shoes. The loot even included "ginghams, calicoes, silks, hoop skirts, etc."[7]

Following a short break, Rodes's men were once more on the move along the turnpike toward Baltimore. Most of them still remained uncertain about exactly where they were headed. "We had no idea of our destination," Sgt. Charles D. Grace from the Fourth Georgia in Doles's Brigade acknowledged. "We knew we were going in a southeasterly direction and on a forced march, and that, too, on a most intensely hot day." To their surprise, they proceeded only about three-quarters of a mile before turning onto the main road running to the southwest. That highway served as the primary connection between the state capital of Harrisburg and the crossroads town of Gettysburg.[8]

By then, a light rain had begun to cause difficulties for some of the troops. Pvt. Louis Leon from Daniel's Brigade described June 30 as "a hard day for us, as we

Junction of Harrisburg and Gettysburg Roads at Petersburg, Pennsylvania. Courtesy Adams County Historical Society.

were the rear guard of the division." He complained that they had "a terrible job to keep the stragglers up." For many others the rainy conditions provided a welcome relief from the searing heat they had endured during much of their operations in the North. One soldier from the Third Alabama in O'Neal's Brigade admitted in a letter to his hometown newspaper that "our journey today was not so tedious as many previous ones, owing to the fact that the road was quite good, the sun hid by clouds, with an occasional light shower of rain."[9]

The only Confederate troops not on the march that morning were the two companies from the First North Carolina Sharpshooter Battalion under Maj. Rufus Wharton and the cavalry company under Capt. Frank Bond, which stayed behind in Carlisle to finish up provost duties. The men set out with a will readying the town for final evacuation. "My orders were to remain in Carlisle until two hours after the last of the troops had left, and then to release one thousand prisoners who were under guard in the market house, and to overtake the army and report," Bond explained.[10]

Those prisoners were mostly ill-trained militiamen who had been transferred there after being rounded up a few days earlier by Jubal Early's troops during their advance to York. As part of the final arrangements, Major Wharton worked out an agreement with Lt. Col. David M. Carter, who served with the military court in Ewell's corps, which would allow the men to be released on parole. "After some trouble we got them into a long line, single file, and requiring every man to hold up his right hand, administered to them, *en masse* an oath that they would not take up any arms against the Confederacy until they had been regularly exchanged," Wharton reported.

The major soon discovered that many of the young soldiers had no shoes. He insisted, though, that his men "had nothing to do with" confiscating the footwear from the captives. "The prisoners were just as we received them," he protested. Wharton speculated that the prisoners most likely had their footwear confiscated because Lee's soldiers had discovered few if any new shoes in that part of Pennsylvania. "Possibly their captors may have taken their shoes from them as a punishment for sending out of our reach all the shoes that should have been in the stores," he remarked.[11]

A clear example of this type of retaliation occurred the previous day. The incident took place just north of Shippensburg, where the retreating soldiers from Johnson's Division encountered about 150 paroled militiamen making their way home after being captured by Early's troops near Gettysburg. Pvt. John William Ford Hatton from one of the Maryland batteries in the division noted that "our boys considered the shoes and hats of the prisoners as public property, and did not hesitate to appropriate those articles to their own use as fast as an exchange could be made."[12]

Sgt. Watkins Kearns from the Stonewall Brigade reported that the rebels secured 126 pairs of shoes from the hapless youngsters on direct orders from General Johnson. Another soldier from his regiment claimed that the directive offended some of the troops so much that they "spurned the proffer, and the shoes had to be returned to their owners." Despite those protests, most of the men moved ahead with the seizures. The effect on the militiamen was devastating. "As we first saw them they were greatly crestfallen," a Virginian from the Corps Reserve Artillery explained. "But after losing their footgear all spirit seemed to have gone out of them."[13]

Despite their pitiful condition, the prisoners at the market house in Carlisle provided some tense moments for Captain Bond's company, which provided the guards for several hundred men. The impending release of the militiamen quickly attracted a throng of civilian spectators. The problems began when Bond allowed people in the crowd to pass bundles of food to the prisoners. He soon found that some of the baskets contained bottles of strong whiskey. "The soldiers began to get boisterous," the cavalryman recalled. "And, with a thousand men inside my thin line, and as many more close up outside, I considered the situation critical."[14]

Bond remained convinced that a major confrontation could erupt at any moment. "The situation became very interesting when they realized that there were but one hundred cavalrymen to hold them in check," he explained. The captain quickly responded with some forceful threats to head off the possibility of a mass escape. "For a time it seemed that a collision was inevitable, but I announced that if we were attacked I should retaliate to the utmost," he remarked. His firm stance quickly averted any trouble and restored relative calm in a few minutes.

The Maryland troopers eventually completed the paroles without any further problems from the huge group of prisoners. "Their old men counseled peace, and we departed in peace, although I am convinced that it was only the perfect coolness and discipline of the company which prevented a bloody fight," Bond declared. The provost guards then gathered up any remaining arms and usable supplies that they could locate around the town. After finishing up those duties, both Bond's and Wharton's commands prepared to leave Carlisle.[15]

With all the arrangements in place, the last of the occupying troops finally marched out of town late in the morning. Bond's cavalrymen led the way at the front of the column. The captain noted that his company "formed in the square, and paraded up one street, and down another with the proverbial chip on its shoulder." To Bond's relief, the frightened residents looked on in complete silence as the company of riders maneuvered its way south along Hanover Street. The cavalry leader recalled that "no demonstration was made, and we marched out with colors flying."[16]

Following their departure, Carlisle was empty of Confederate troops for the first time since early in the morning on June 27. The citizens soon found that Ewell's men had caused little harm to their community. Local resident Hanna Culver noted that "except the trouble they gave us in furnishing them rations we are none the worse for their being here." The townspeople were especially pleased that Ewell left the U.S. Army barracks largely untouched. "With exception of the considerable litter and filth which attended his occupation of the barracks, no other damage was done," one of the town's newspapers acknowledged.[17]

Another newspaper editor had a much harsher reaction to what residents had endured during the enemy occupation. Not even Lee's strict rules against plundering did anything to mute his outrage. "The rebels receive a good deal of credit in certain quarters, mostly copperhead, for the respect which they are said to have paid to private property, and the forbearance they manifested towards citizens whose persons and property were in their power," the editor bitterly commented. He insisted that this "'respect,' as we understand it, consisted in taking precisely what they wanted wherever they could find it, and paying for it sometimes, in worthless trash called 'Confederate notes.'"[18]

The town's relief came to an abrupt end about 2:00 P.M., when some four hundred fearsome-looking troopers from the Fourteenth Virginia Cavalry in Jenkins's Brigade galloped down the streets. The general had ordered these horsemen back to Carlisle from the vicinity of Harrisburg during the early hours that morning. Col. James Cochran immediately set up camp in the east end on the grounds of Dickinson College. A single company from the regiment remained behind at Mechanicsburg to secure their lines of communication with the rest of Jenkins's cavalry forces still just outside of Harrisburg.[19]

Without Jenkins around to restrain their conduct, the rugged backwoodsmen began to harass and intimidate citizens throughout Carlisle. "These men were under the command of Col. Cochran and it soon became evident that they were not under the same discipline which characterized those which had been here," the correspondent for one of the local newspapers explained. He pointed out that "they had not been in town half an hour until they were riding wildly through the streets." Young Edward Beetem noted that the troopers were "yelling like Texas cattle-men." Worst of all was the noise from their constant mock charges through the streets, which "made a great stir and racket."

Their ready access to large supplies of alcohol caused many of the Virginians to lose all control. "By some means and at some place, they procured liquor, and this ex-citing drink appeared to madden them," the newspaper reported. "They tore through the streets cursing and yelling and playing the demon, as only demons can play it." The writer acknowledged that "the feeling of safety which prevailed while Ewell's command was here vanished and the entire community felt the utmost alarm." He added that the "terror increased" even more as the first signs of darkness approached.

A group of prominent citizens eventually sought out Cochran at his regimental camp and pleaded with him to restrain his men. The colonel initially appeared to take their concerns seriously, assuring them that he fully intended to follow Ewell's orders and would immediately bring a halt to the problems in town. Yet the "disor-derly conduct did not entirely cease," noted a newspaper article. The only chance to fix the scary situation appeared to rest with the arrival of Jenkins and the remainder of his cavalrymen from outside the state capital.[20]

The bulk of the men from Jenkins's Brigade, in fact, had already begun pulling back though Mechanicsburg early that afternoon. By all signs, they carried out the retreat with great haste. Federal scouting reports indicated that the cavalrymen departed "with so much precipitancy that in some cases provisions had been left uncooked." The situation was much the same for the men from Griffin's Baltimore Light Artillery, who left the area about the same time. According to the same Fed-eral reports, the horses hauling the guns and caissons "had gone through Mechan-icsburg at a fast trot."[21]

Lt. Col. Vincent Witcher's cavalry battalion and Capt. William L. Jackson's horse artillery served as the rear guards during the retreat. The gunners set up just west of Silver Spring Creek on the south side of Carlisle Turnpike in front of Salem Church. Some skirmishers from the battalion deployed in a strip of woods and a nearby barn owned by Moses Eberly. From there the troopers confronted the men from the Twenty-Second and Thirty-Seventh New York State National Guard under General Ewen, who had moved into place about a mile to the east near Sporting Hill.

Ewen's troops initially departed from Fort Washington about 10:00 A.M. in re-sponse to reports that the Confederates had abandoned their positions in front of Oyster's Point. Major General Smith accompanied the men as they slowly pushed forward to Orr's Bridge. After confirming that the enemy was gone, the general ordered the militiamen back to the fort. While Smith rode off to his headquarters, Ewen's men followed him on the retreat back to the fort. Just as they reached Oyster's Point, Lt. Frank Stanwood's company from the Third U.S. Cavalry Scouts suddenly galloped up with news that they had spotted the enemy west of Sporting Hill near Salem Church.[22]

That report brought their withdrawal to a sudden halt. "After proceeding about a mile on my return, I was overtaken by a small company of dragoons, the commandant of which informed me that he had been driven by the enemy about three miles distant," General Ewen explained in his official report. He responded to the information by turning his small force around and hurrying off to the west. The general immediately "went in pursuit, employing the dragoons as an advance guard; despatching an aide to headquarters with intelligence of my information and movement."[23]

As they approached the vicinity of Sporting Hill, the militiamen came under fire from Witcher's troopers. "The enemy were concealed in a wood on the right of, and about a quarter of a mile distant from the road, and they promptly announced their presence by a volley as soon as the brigade reached the crest of a hill," a soldier from the Twenty-Second New York recalled. He pointed out that the Confederates "had also taken possession of one of the large brick barns for which this section of Pennsylvania is noted, and which they had loop-holed and filled with their skirmishers."

The two sides soon engaged in a lively exchange of volleys. Ewen admitted that the "severe fire" from the Confederate troopers in the barn wounded several of his men, including "Lieut. Colgate, who was shot in the neck, and a drummer boy, who was shot in the hip." Jackson's battery joined in the action by firing some shells at the New York troops posted around the hill. A newspaper correspondent traveling with the militia force reported that soon "came a shell directly over our skirmishers, and over the battalion, and exploded just beyond." He added that "things began to look serious, as the shell was followed quickly by two round shots."

Some of the Federal troops took cover in the nearby woods, while others moved into place in a wheat field on their left. "The enemy opened a smart artillery fire upon them and upon the companies in the wood," a young militiaman from the Twenty-Second New York recalled. "This was aimed too high, so that the shells, although making a great noise in the woods and showering down many leaves and branches from the trees, did no harm. In the field they burst and tore up the ground, but passed over the regiment." He acknowledged, however, that one of the enemy shells "burst in the Thirty-seventh, wounding a number."

Just then, a section of two guns from Capt. Henry D. Landis's First Philadelphia Battery arrived on the scene. Lt. Rufus King, who served as the chief of artillery for General Smith, quickly took command of the guns and opened a return fire. "The first shell burst in the barn with such effect that instantly its two great doors were swung open and a swarm of Confederates came rushing out and made for the woods, where the main body was posted," the militiaman explained. He pointed out that "the fire of the section was then directed at the Confederate battery with good effect."

According to Federal accounts, the shots from King's two guns soon caused the enemy fire to slacken and then cease. The Union gunners finally halted the barrage and took up a defensive position around the hill only after hearing the distinct sounds of artillery fire in the distance. "Artillery being then heard on the left, the Twenty-Second changed line from front to rear to be in readiness to repel an attack from this direction," the militiaman remarked. "But this force did not show itself, expect by a few cavalry." The disturbance turned out to be nothing more than the noise from a minor confrontation a short distance away on the outskirts of Mechanicsburg.[24]

Lt. Micajah Woods insisted that Jackson's battery actually gained the upper hand during this afternoon artillery exchange. He noted that the Confederates quickly forced the enemy "to limber up & disappear by a few well directed rounds from our guns." With five of the six guns from the battery opposing a single section of two guns from Landis's battery, the odds certainly seemed to be in the Southerners' favor. No matter who was right, the slackening artillery fire on both sides marked the end of the fighting on that part of the field. Federal losses amounted to two officers and seven enlisted men wounded. Exaggerated reports in the Northern press claimed that Jenkins's force suffered sixteen men killed and about twenty men wounded.[25]

During that time, Lt. Hermann Schuricht's company in the Fourteenth Virginia Cavalry remained in position just outside Mechanicsburg. They had served on detached duty there since earlier in the day, with orders to cover the rear as the rest of their regiment moved back to Carlisle. Schuricht recorded in his diary that Jenkins's instructions called for the troopers "to hold this town until ordered otherwise, and to destroy the railroad track as far as possible." After scaring off a small Federal force from Capt. Frank Murray's militia cavalry, Schuricht's company occupied Mechanicsburg during the late morning.

Within minutes his men started carrying out their assigned task. "I posted my command on an elevation east of the town, overlooking both the railroad and the turnpike, and ordered my men to demolish the railroad track," Schuricht explained. He noted that they "were repeatedly interrupted in this work by the reappearance of Yankees, and had to keep up a lively skirmish all day." At one point an artillery piece attached to his command from Jackson's battery fired some warning shots in the direction of the Federal troops. In the late afternoon the lieutenant finally received orders to withdraw toward the south.[26]

The last of the rebels to depart the area were the men from the Thirty-Fourth Virginia Cavalry Battalion under Lieutenant Colonel Witcher, who started pulling back from the vicinity of Sporting Hill in the hours just before dark. Their orders called for them to move slowly toward Carlisle while providing a protective screen for the rest of the retreating column. "I was in command of the rear guard, and directed to hold the enemy in check at all hazards until Gen. Jenkins could gather in his detachments on both sides of the road as we marched along," Witcher recalled.[27]

About 11:00 P.M., Jenkins and his remaining troopers made their way into Carlisle. "Their arrival was really hailed with joy," one of the town's newspapers declared. "The outrageous conduct of Cochran's men made the arrival of any other command desirable, and as Jenkins had acted well he was preferable to Cochran." The general's actions quickly confirmed that their expectations were largely justified. "As soon as he learned the conduct of the drunken demons he sent squads of men in search of them, and had them gathered up," the newspaper admitted. Jenkins immediately took full control of the town, even arresting some of the worst offenders from Cochran's regiment. "Quiet was again restored, and people retired not to sleep, yet in much more peacefulness than they would have done had they remained at the mercy of Cochran's men," the correspondent remarked. As most of the people there slumbered, Jenkins's entire cavalry force departed Carlisle by about 2:00 A.M. on July 1. The newspaper reported that residents "found the town deserted" when they woke up that morning.[28]

Unknown to the townspeople, their ordeal was far from over. This time Maj. Gen. J. E. B. Stuart's cavalrymen, rather than Ewell's troops, threatened Carlisle with destruction. On his arrival later on the first, Brig. Gen. Fitzhugh Lee demanded the surrender of the Federal militiamen who had taken up posts in town following the departure of Ewell's men. When the commander refused to comply, "Fitz" Lee unleashed a barrage of artillery that damaged numerous buildings in town and wounded several defenders. The horsemen also set fire to the army barracks and the town's gasworks, leaving them in ruins. With that accomplished, the Confederate troopers moved on to the south toward their own showdown with the enemy troops at Gettysburg.[29]

While all that was going on, Rodes's Division continued on the march until the late afternoon of June 30, when the men finally stopped about eight miles northeast of Gettysburg near the village of Heidlersburg. The town stood at the junction of two major roads and had a couple of hotels. Rodes's troops set up camp in an area of woods and meadows just north of town. From there they were in an excellent position to move forward the following day to either Cashtown or Gettysburg, depending on General Lee's final instructions.[30]

During that time, Early's troops were also on the move from their camps just outside York. The general got the first orders to pull back during the evening of June 29. Early stated in his official report that he "received through Capt. Elliott Johnston, aide to General Ewell, a copy of a note from General Lee, and also verbal instructions, which required me to move back, so as to rejoin the rest of the corps on the western side of the South Mountain." Because of the late hour, Early remained in place until the following day.

The main part of the division finally set off just "at daylight" on June 30 along a route taking them west through Weigelstown to East Berlin. Before their departure, Early dispatched Lt. Col. Elijah White's cavalry battalion "on the pike from York toward Gettysburg to ascertain if any force of the enemy was on that road." About noon, the long column halted a mile beyond Davidsburg. Early soon joined Brigadier Generals Hays and Smith and about twenty other officers for a conference at a roadside tavern. Just as the meeting broke up, they heard the clear sound of artillery firing in the distance, which turned out to be the noise from a skirmish involving Stuart's cavalrymen at nearby Hanover.[31]

Following a short halt, Early's entire force resumed the march toward South Mountain. The cavalry operating with the division once again led the advance. The only action occurred when White's horsemen encountered "a small squad of the enemy's cavalry" near East Berlin. After a brief skirmish, they chased the enemy off the field. With the area cleared of Federal forces, the cavalrymen pushed on to East Berlin, where they stopped for a break. The infantrymen trailed closely behind and finally joined them there at about 3:00 P.M.[32]

Col. William H. French's Seventeenth Virginia Cavalry, accompanying White's battalion during the trip, had the satisfaction of capturing one of the Federal cavalrymen during the encounter outside East Berlin. The Virginians immediately brought the prisoner to General Early at his temporary headquarters in town. Under interrogation, the man defiantly refused to provide any information on the location of Federal forces in the area. The division commander eventually gave up his efforts and turned the prisoner over to one of the Louisiana regiments in Hays's Brigade.[33]

As Early prepared to resume the advance from East Berlin, he received updated instructions from the corps commander that changed their destination. "A courier from General Ewell met me here with a dispatch, informing me of the fact that he was moving with Rodes' division by the way of Petersburg to Heidlersburg, and directing me to march in that direction," Early explained in his official report. The troops proceeded on a few more miles before halting in the late afternoon "about 3 miles" east of Heidlersburg along Plum Run. While his troops settled in for a much-needed rest, the division commander "rode off to see General Ewell."[34]

The soldiers from Johnson's Division, meanwhile, were camped more than twenty miles away on the western side of South Mountain. The trip on June 30 took them south through Shippensburg along Valley Turnpike before turning east at Green Village. A gunner from one of the division's batteries noted that it was "a cloudy day with frequent showers passing over." According to Lt. Thomas Tolson from Steuart's Brigade, the men "moved at a very slow rate, halting often." The troops finally stopped during the late afternoon just northeast of Chambersburg close to Scotland.[35]

This settlement of about two hundred residents consisted of a few houses, two churches, three stores, and a grist and saw mill. Sgt. William S. White from the Corps Artillery Reserve described it as "a dirty little village" situated "in a wildly beautiful country." He was especially struck by how much the surrounding area differed from the war-ravaged countryside in his home state of Virginia. "The high, rolling hills and beautiful valleys, some heavily covered with timber and others teeming with the fast-ripening grain, present a sad and marked contrast with the devastated fields of our once smilingly fair and happy Old Dominion," the artillery-man lamented in his journal.

Soon after their arrival, the division's pioneers began disabling the bridge over nearby Conococheague Creek. Lt. Henry H. Harris, one of the division's engineers, bragged that they quickly "completed the destruction of the rail road bridge." Other details swarmed into town to hunt for supplies. Sergeant White reported that the search parties "ferreted out a lot of hats and shoes which had been hidden." Chaplain James Sheeran from Colonel Williams's brigade noted that they secured "a considerable number of guns, shoes, and some other stores." With that duty out of the way, the soldiers finally went into camp for the night.[36]

After pulling back from outside Harrisburg, Jenkins's tired cavalrymen only made it as far as Petersburg before halting about noon on July 1. The brigade commander immediately ordered all the businesses to close and banned access to any alcohol. According to one resident, the general then called on "the citizens to prepare rations for his men, which was anything else than an agreeable task, but they had to make a virtue of necessity in this case." Several search parties set to work scouring the area for any usable plunder. The eyewitness reported that the troopers were soon "busily engaged in gathering up the horses, cows, and oats in the immediate neighborhood."[37]

Many of the horsemen resorted to foraging for additional food. A former resident who was visiting his father at the time recalled that "the soldiers came to the house, asking politely for something to eat, and the family began feeding them." He noted that "they continued to drop in till the porch and yard were full of them." While all that was going on, Jenkins enjoyed a hearty midday meal at the home of prominent businessman Ephraim Hiteshew. At the end of the dinner, the general finally received word from a courier that major fighting was underway in the vicinity of Gettysburg.[38]

The rest of Lee's army remained several miles west of Gettysburg on the night of June 30. Maj. Gens. Richard H. Anderson's and William Dorsey Pender's divisions from A. P. Hill's Third Corps and all three divisions from James Longstreet's First Corps were still on the opposite side of Cashtown Gap along the road between Chambersburg and Greenwood. Maj. Gen. Henry Heth's division from Hill's corps had moved into place near Cashtown. Earlier in the day a single brigade from that division carried out a brief reconnaissance toward the nearby town of Gettysburg. Plans already called for Heth's men to return there the following morning.[39]

As his troops settled into place outside Heidlersburg, General Ewell dispatched Captain Bond's cavalry company, which had finally rejoined the column, to scout around Gettysburg for any signs of the enemy. "We marched about eight miles, to within full sight of Gettysburg, without encountering opposition," Bond recalled. Although the exact time his command arrived remains difficult to pin down, the captain claimed that "there was nothing to be seen, but a quiet city with a heavy backing of mountains behind, and a large area of fertile fields in front and on the right." Before making his return, he posted some pickets under the command of Sgt. Hammond Dorsey about three miles north of town.

Bond's foresight paid off that night when the cavalry patrol captured three enlisted men from a Pennsylvania battery just outside Gettysburg. "It seems they found themselves within a few miles of home for the first time in a year or more, and asked for leave to see their folks," Bond explained. Although their commander refused permission, the men slipped out of camp under cover of darkness anyway and were soon picked up by Dorsey's cavalrymen. The troopers eventually escorted the prisoners to General Ewell. Under questioning they "furnished the first information of the whereabouts of Meade's Army."[40]

While Bond's troopers carried out their reconnaissance, Ewell held a strategy session with Generals Rodes and Early. The gathering also included General Trimble, who continued to pester Ewell for an active assignment since his arrival three days earlier. The major topic for the meeting was a discussion of the latest dispatches from Generals Lee and Hill. "At Heidlersburg, I received orders from the general commanding to proceed to Cashtown or Gettysburg, as circumstances might dictate, and a note from Gen. A. P. Hill, saying he was at Cashtown," Ewell explained in his official report.[41]

The only surviving account of the conference came from Trimble, who claimed that Ewell "read over the order of Gen'l Lee several times, commenting on its 'indefinite phraseology,' as he expressed it, in very severe terms, and asking each one what was meant by 'according to circumstances.'" While Rodes and Early had little to say, Trimble forcefully argued that Lee wanted them to advance directly to Gettysburg the following day. He noted that "this explanation did not satisfy Gen'l Ewell, who more than once impatiently remarked, 'Why can't a commanding General have some one of his staff who can write an intelligible order?'"[42]

Ewell eventually decided to push forward to Cashtown on the morning of July 1. His plan called for Rodes's men to proceed west from Heidlersburg through Middletown, just north of Gettysburg. From there they would move on to Cashtown, where General Hill had camped the night before with Heth's Division. Ewell ordered Early to follow closely behind along a route that would take him through Hunterstown to Cashtown. Once that decision was made, everything seemed to be in place for both divisions to finally link up with the main part of Lee's army the following day. With huge quantities of supplies already in hand, all that remained was to engage the Federal Army of the Potomac in the battle that Lee hoped would bring an end to the war.[43]

Epilogue

"The General Results . . . Are Not All Unsatisfactory"

Just before dawn on July 1, the men from Ewell's two divisions were aroused from their camps with orders to resume the advance. Rodes's troops were soon on the move to Cashtown along the road through Middletown, while Early's men headed south through Heidlersburg. Their destination suddenly changed with the arrival of a fresh dispatch from General Hill during midmorning. "Before reaching Middletown," Ewell wrote in his official report, "I received notice from General Hill that he was advancing upon Gettysburg, and turned the head of Rodes' column toward that place, by the Middletown Road, sending word to Early to advance directly on the Heidlersburg road."[1]

As soon as they turned off to the south, Rodes's men heard the sounds of artillery fire coming from the vicinity of Gettysburg. The action there had begun earlier in the morning when Heth's Division from Hill's corps encountered some enemy troops just northwest of town. Those men were first thought to be nothing more than a small militia force but proved instead to be veteran troopers from Brig. Gen. John Buford's division of the Army of the Potomac. Using delaying tactics, Buford's dismounted cavalrymen slowed Heth's advance long enough for the infantry from the Federal I Corps to arrive on the field. By late morning the men from both Heth's and Pender's Divisions were engaged in a fierce and growing battle along both sides of the Chambersburg Pike leading into Gettysburg.[2]

Spurred on the sounds of cannon fire in the distance, Rodes's men arrived within three miles of Gettysburg on the road from Middletown at about 10:00 A.M. The general quickly led his men to the right along the main ridgeline toward "a prominent hill" that overlooked the area just northwest of town. "On arriving on the field, I found that by keeping along the wooded ridge, on the left side of which the town of Gettysburg is situated, I could strike the force of the enemy with which Gen. Hill's troops were engaged upon the flank, and that, besides moving under cover, whenever we struck the enemy we could engage him with the advantage in ground," Rodes stated in his official report.[3]

The soldiers pushed on for almost a mile before halting about noon around Oak Hill. After conferring with Ewell, Rodes decided to launch an assault with O'Neal's, Iverson's, and Daniel's Brigades against the Federal troops posted along nearby Oak Ridge. Doles's Brigade would hold off another enemy force moving forward from town on his left until Early's Division could arrive on the field from Heidlersburg along Harrisburg Road. The men from Ramseur's Brigade would serve as the reserve force, to be called on to provide needed support for any of the other brigades if they ran into major trouble during the advance.[4]

The initial attack against the troops from the I Corps began to unravel almost as soon as it got underway. O'Neal's command quickly fell back in disarray after moving forward on the left of the line. Iverson's men blundered ahead on their right without a screen of skirmishers along their front into a deadly trap that resulted in one of the worse slaughters in the entire war. Daniel's men faced some stiff resistance before finally dislodging the enemy troops around an unfinished railroad cut north of Chambersburg Pike. The tide of battle only turned decisively when Ramseur's troops moved onto the field and pushed the enemy off Oak Ridge.

Progress proved much smoother on the other end of their line, where Doles's troops, together with those from Early's Division, overran the Federal XI Corps in the area north of Gettysburg. After arriving on the field late in the afternoon, Gordon's Brigade quickly dislodged the Federals around some high ground known as Blocher's Knoll. Hays's and Avery's men soon joined with Doles's troops in sweeping the rest of the enemy from the field. The soldiers from Heth's and Pender's Divisions enjoyed similar success during some fierce fighting with the I Corps on the far right of the Confederate line.

By late in the afternoon, the entire Federal force was on the run through the narrow streets of Gettysburg in a panicked flight toward Cemetery Hill on the south side of town. To the surprise of many in the ranks, Rodes suddenly ordered his men to stop in the middle of town. Early's troops also halted at about the same time. In one of the most controversial decisions in the battle, Ewell failed to resume the attack against Cemetery Hill. "Receiving no orders to advance, though my superiors were upon the ground, I concluded that the order not to bring on a general engagement was still in force, and hence placed my lines and skirmishers in a defensive attitude, and determined to await orders or further movements either on the part of Early or of the troops on my right," Rodes stated in his report.[5]

Whether justified or not, the decision to remain in town as Federal forces regrouped on the hill caused at least some of his men for the first time to question the abilities of their new corps commander, especially in comparison to the lamented Stonewall Jackson. The comments about the contrast between the two generals were often far from flattering for Ewell. Capt. John Gorman from Ramseur's

Brigade reported about a week after the battle that the Confederates had clearly "missed the genius of Jackson" that day. "The simplest soldier in the ranks felt it, and the results have proven it," he grumbled in a letter home. "But, timidity in the commander that stepped into the shoes of the fearless Jackson, prompted delay."[6]

Rodes also faced some criticism for his failures during the attack north of town on the first day of battle. Many questioned the Virginian's decision to allow his two worst brigade commanders to lead the initial assault on Oak Ridge. He also weakened O'Neal's forces by detaching one of that brigade's regiments prior to the initial attack. Rodes then compounded that error by allowing Iverson's Brigade to advance onto the field without a screen of skirmishers along its front, leading to an unprecedented disaster. Only the supreme gallantry of Ramseur and the intrepid leadership of Daniel and Doles allowed the new division commander to recover and eventually sweep the enemy from the field.[7]

While Rodes's exhausted soldiers rested in town, General Lee evaluated the stunning results on July 1. The three divisions of Hill's bloodied Third Corps occupied Seminary Ridge west of Gettysburg, while Ewell's Second Corps wrapped through town to the north, directly opposite Cemetery Hill and Culp's Hill. By the early afternoon on July 2, both John B. Hood's and Lafayette McLaws's divisions from Longstreet's First Corps had also moved into place on the south end of the Confederate line. The primary question Lee faced that day was whether to continue the battle or maneuver his army elsewhere in search of more favorable conditions.

The army commander eventually decided to resume the attack rather than reposition his forces. With two of the three divisions from Longstreet's First Corps now on the field, Lee planned to launch an assault against what he believed was the vulnerable left flank of the Federal line running south from Cemetery Hill along the main ridgeline. The attack would roll northward from there across Hill's front. Lee ordered Ewell to "make a simultaneous demonstration upon the enemy's right to be converted into a real attack should opportunity offer."

Ewell quickly moved ahead with the final arrangements for his divisions. He eventually ordered Johnson's Division, which had arrived on the field late on July 1, to launch an attack on Culp's Hill. Early's Division on Johnson's right would follow up with an assault on the eastern heights of Cemetery Hill. The corps commander directed Rodes to provide support by threatening the Federal positions on the western side of Cemetery Hill. His troops would join the fight on Early's right "as soon as any opportunity of doing so with good effect was offered."[8]

The effort began to fall apart when Longstreet's attack on the south end of the line failed to get underway until the late afternoon. Despite the tardy start, the Confederate troops enjoyed some initial successes. The assault quickly caved in the salient created by Maj. Gen. Dan Sickles's III Corps around the Peach Orchard and swept across the slopes of Little Round Top to the east. Once both of Longstreet's divisions were fully committed, several brigades from Hill's Third Corps joined in the action by advancing on Cemetery Ridge. The attack eventually broke down along that part of the front. As the fighting drew to a close, Lee's battered troops fell back to Seminary Ridge, leaving the final outcome to be decided the following day.

The outcome was little better on the northern end of the line. Although Johnson failed to make much headway in his attack against Culp's Hill, two of Early's brigades assaulted Cemetery Hill just before dark on July 2. Early noted that they "commenced ascending the steep side of the hill in gallant style, going over fences and encountering bodies of infantry posted in front of the main line on the slope of the hill behind stone fences which they dislodged." Following a flurry of fighting, the men from Hays's and Avery's brigades "succeeded in entering" the entrenchments and "compelling the enemy to abandon his batteries." When no support arrived, Early was eventually forced to withdraw.[9]

Rodes's efforts to assist Early's Division in the attack on Cemetery Hill ran into difficulties from the start. He fell so far behind schedule that the assault did not get underway until well after dark. Once his men approached within about two hundred yards of the enemy lines, Ramseur ordered a halt while he carried out a reconnaissance along their front. After concluding that the Federal positions were nearly impregnable, he hurried back to confer with Doles. About that time Ramseur also received word that Early's troops had already concluded their attack on the other part of Cemetery Hill. The final order to stop the advance came from Rodes, who was convinced by Ramseur and Doles that "it was a useless sacrifice of life" to continue in the darkness against such a strong position.[10]

Although Rodes had solid reasons for aborting the attack, his lack of action upset Early so much that he complained directly to Ewell. "General Early's indignation was great," Lt. Thomas Turner from Ewell's staff recalled. "He rode to Gen. Ewell's Headquarters bitterly commenting on Rodes' failure to fulfill his promise to support him." In later years the embittered division commander described Rodes's failure to carry through on the attack against Cemetery Hill as "the solitary instance of remissness on the part of any portion of the corps in the battle." At the same time, Early remained open to criticism for leaving Gordon's Brigade in reserve on the edge of town rather than committing it to the contest.[11]

The corps commander himself clearly blamed Rodes for this missed opportunity. Ewell pointedly remarked in his official report that he had "every reason to believe, from the eminent success attending the assault of Hays and Avery, that the enemy's lines would have been carried." According to Maj. Campbell Brown, Ewell was convinced that Early's attack on Cemetery Hill had been "admirably timed" and only "failed because of Rodes' failure to co-operate." In the general's view Rodes's lack of support directly caused the withdrawal of the attacking troops after they had penetrated the enemy's defenses at the top of the hill. Brown noted that Ewell held Rodes "fairly censurable" for allowing one of the best chances for turning the enemy's flank to slip away.[12]

Although he later distinguished himself as one of the top division commanders in the Army of Northern Virginia, Rodes suffered so much damage to his reputation at Gettysburg that he was never seriously considered as a potential corps commander. A possible explanation for this uncharacteristic performance was his apparent poor health. At least one eyewitness from Early's staff reported that Rodes appeared noticeably ill and flushed with fever during a meeting late in the afternoon the previous day. Early's nephew recalled that Rodes was "so sick that he was compelled to ride in an ambulance whenever practicable."[13]

At the same time, Early earned widespread praise for his determined attack on the heights on July 2. Johnson also came out of the battle with his reputation as a hard fighter largely intact. While unsuccessful, he fought with real grit and determination in attacking the nearly impregnable Federal positions along Culp's Hill on both July 2 and 3. Even so, his conduct at Gettysburg hardly went down well with Pvt. Ted Barclay from the Stonewall Brigade. "The division suffered proportionally through the folly of our *hard fighting* Johnson," the Virginian griped to his sister. "He has none of the qualities of a general but expects to do everything by fighting."[14]

The battle ended on the afternoon of July 3, when what came to be known as Pickett's Charge failed to penetrate the center of the Federal line along Cemetery Ridge. The army's defeat and subsequent withdrawal to Virginia left nearly all of Lee's military and political objectives unfilled. The one bright spot was the huge quantity of supplies his troops had gathered up on their marches through Maryland and Pennsylvania. With those goods secured, the army could sustain itself for two or three months, which hopefully would be long enough to bring in the crucial fall harvest that would carry them through the lean winter months.[15]

The army's withdrawal began on July 4, the day after fighting had concluded at Gettysburg. Most impressive was the huge size of Ewell's retreating column, which required an immense number of wagons to haul off all the loot they had seized during their advance through the North. Asst. Quartermaster Charles S. Bahnson from Daniel's Brigade reported in a letter to his father that "our wagon train is tolerably extensive & consists of about 4000 wagons." He estimated that, "when stretched out on a road," the supply train was "about 40 miles long." Besides foodstuff-laden wagons, the column included huge numbers of livestock being driven south to Virginia.[16]

Although some of the vehicles began moving out in the morning on July 4, Ewell's supply train was so long that it took much of the day to get the entire column underway. "Wagons, horses, mules, and cattle captured in Pennsylvania, the solid advantages of this campaign, have been passing slowly along this road (Fairfield) all day," said Lt. Col. Arthur James L. Fremantle, an unofficial observer from the British Army. He grumbled that "so interminable was this train that it soon became evident that we should not be able to start till late at night."[17]

A correspondent attached to Lee's army was stunned by the huge number of cattle accompanying the retreating vehicles. He noted that "each wagon train seemed to have along with it quite large droves of beef cattle, which, we suppose, guarantees the subsistence question for a while at least, in the way of meat." All that was in addition to the many horses and cattle sent South prior to their departure. An observer from the Austrian army, who traveled with the troops on the retreat, estimated that "fifteen thousand cattle" had already "been driven to the rear for the use of the army."[18]

As it moved south, the column of wagons suffered heavily from the Federal cavalry under Brig. Gen. Judson Kilpatrick, who had been assigned to intercept the train. A gunner from the Ashby (Virginia) Horse Artillery noticed that "some of the wagons were chopped to pieces and others were burned." Maj. Eugene Blackford from O'Neal's Brigade especially complained that the enemy seized his "private wagon" filled with the "innumerable" goods he had procured on the way into the state. "All my clothes and entire cuisine are gone, and our mess, from being one of the most elegantly equipped in the Division, is now reduced to one tin cup," he lamented to his father.[19]

Although he inflicted some significant damage, Kilpatrick failed to destroy Ewell's wagon train. After making it safely across the Potomac, Capt. Reuben Pierson from Hays's Brigade gloated in a letter home that "thousands of cattle and horses and other valuable material" had arrived in Virginia without harm. Assistant Quartermaster Bahnson remained just as pleased with all the goods they had hauled back from Pennsylvania. "I think there is a scarcity of the following articles in that portion of the Keystone State which had the honor of receiving a visit from us, viz:—horses, mules, cattle, sheep, hogs, chickens, turkeys, onions & all kinds of garden truck, wagons, carriages, harness, & everything in fact that could be of use to us," he boasted to his father.[20]

Pvt. G. W. Nichols from Gordon's Brigade was dumbstruck by the sheer number of cattle and sheep that he spotted along the banks of the Shenandoah River following their return to Virginia. "The bend was about full," he recalled. "They were on both sides of the road for about two miles, and all were feeding about at will on the clover." One of the men guarding them informed him that the massive herd included about 22,000 head of cattle and 26,000 sheep. "I think we could see that many cattle, but I do not think we could see half that many sheep," the Georgian commented. "Most of them were brought from the great Cumberland Valley of Pennsylvania."[21]

Col. Clement Evans from the same brigade expressed his thoughts on the campaign in his diary on the day of his return to the south side of the Potomac. By all indications he remained far from devastated over the outcome. "The general results of the last 40 days are not all unsatisfactory," Evans argued. "We have drawn from the enemy subsistence stores for the whole army for two months. We have furnished our trains, cavalry & artillery with new & good horses—We have supplied ourselves with quite a thousand new wagons." He further pointed out that "the capture of ordnance & ordnance stores have been abundant."[22]

Another Georgian summed up his feelings about the outcome of their foraging activities in a letter to his hometown newspaper. He boasted that the Confederates had seized "immense numbers of horses, mules, and wagons, exchanging everything old and worthless for new and strong; driven many thousands of cattle out of the rich pastures of Pennsylvania; been for over a month at no expense to our Government; and given the Commissary Department in Richmond an opportunity to collect up stores for the future use of the army." While pleased with those results, nearly everyone who had suffered through the brutal fighting at Gettysburg knew that even their stunning success in gathering supplies hardly outweighed the crushing defeat that they had endured there.[23]

Notes

ABBREVIATIONS

ACWM   American Civil War Museum, White House and Museum of the Confederacy, Richmond, VA

ADAH   Alabama Department of Archives and History, Montgomery

Ammen   Tenth Paper—Second Series, Second Maryland Battalion, in S. Z. Ammen, "Maryland Troops in the Confederate Army," Thomas G. Clemens Collection, USAHEC

BC   George L. Mitchell Department of Special Collections and Archives, Hawthorn-Longfellow Library, Bowdoin College, Brunswick, ME

DaCol   Archives and Special Collections, Davidson College, Davidson, NC

DiCol   Archives and Special Collections, Waidner-Spahr Library, Dickinson College, Carlisle, PA

DU   William R. Perkins Library, Duke Univ., Durham, NC

EU   Stuart A. Rose Manuscripts, Archives and Rare Book Library, Emory Univ., Atlanta, GA

GAM   Georgia Archives, Morrow

GLIAH   Gilder Lehrman Collection, Gilder Lehrman Institute of American History, New York

GNMP   Library, Gettysburg National Military Park, Gettysburg, PA

HL   Etha Mayo Woodruff Memorial Collection of Family Papers, Manuscript Collections, Huntington Library, San Marino, CA

HRL   Stewart Bell Jr. Archives Room, Handley Regional Library, Winchester, VA

LOC   Manuscript Division, Library of Congress, Washington, DC

LOV   Archives, Library of Virginia, Richmond

MHS   Maryland Historical Society, Baltimore

NA   National Archives, Washington, DC

NCSA   North Carolina State Archives, North Carolina Office of Archives and History, Raleigh

OR   U.S. War Department. *The War of the Rebellion: A Compilation of the Official Records of the Union and Confederate Armies.* 70 vols. in 128 pts. Washington, DC: Government Printing Office, 1880–1901. All citations to ser. 1 unless otherwise noted,

PSA   Pennsylvania State Archives, Harrisburg

SHC   Southern Historical Collection, Wilson Library, Univ. of North Carolina at Chapel Hill

UGA   Special Collections Division, Hargrett Library, Univ. of Georgia, Athens

UNCW   Special Collections, William M. Randall Library, Univ. of North Carolina at Wilmington

USAHEC U.S. Army Heritage and Education Center, Carlisle, PA

UVA   Manuscripts Division, Alderman Library, Univ. of Virginia, Charlottesville

VHS   Virginia Historical Society, Richmond

VMI   Archives, Virginia Military Institute, Lexington

W&L   Special Collections and Archives, James G. Leyburn Library, Washington and Lee Univ., Lexington, VA

YCHC   Library and Archives, York County History Center, York, PA

YU   Manuscripts and Archives Library, Yale Univ., New Haven, CT

INTRODUCTION

1. William E. Ardrey Diary, May [2]9, 1863, William Erskine Ardrey Papers, DaCol; Jedediah Hotchkiss Journal, May 29, 1863, in McDonald, *Make Me a Map,* 149.

2. Warner, *Generals in Gray,* 84–85; Tagg, *Generals of Gettysburg,* 251–55.

3. Diary and Account Book of Col. John Lea, May 2, 1863, Record Group 109, NA.

4. Jedediah Hotchkiss to My Darling Wife, May 31, 1863, Jedediah Hotchkiss Papers, LOC; Alexander S. Pendleton to Kate Corbin, June 4, 1863, William Nelson Pendleton Papers, SHC.

5. Clement A. Evans to My Dearest Darling, June 7, 1863, in Stephens, *Intrepid Warrior,* 187; Sams, *With Unabated Trust,* 161.

6. "Gen. Jackson's Successor," May 29, 1863, *Richmond Daily Dispatch,* June 1, 1863.

7. Allie Clack to Dear Carrie, May 23, 1863, Carrie H. Clack Papers, SHC.

8. D. Pfanz, *Richard S. Ewell,* 166–67.

9. McKim, *Soldier's Recollections,* 134.

10. Henry W. Wingfield Diary, May 29, 1863, in W. Scott, "Two Confederate Items," 26; Thomas Henry Carter to My precious Wife, June 8, 1863, in Dozier, *Gunner in Lee's Army,* 193.

11. OR 25, pt. 2, 810; Gallagher, "Confederate Corps Leadership on the First Day at Gettysburg," 49.

12. Francis M. Parker to My Dear Wife, May 31, 1863, in Taylor, *To Drive the Enemy,* 283.

13. Charles C. Blacknall to Dear Bro. George, June 1, 1863, Oscar W. Blacknall Papers, Private Collections, NCSA.

1. "A FAIR OPPORTUNITY TO STRIKE A BLOW"

1. Tagg, *Generals of Gettysburg,* 257; Warner, *Generals in Gray,* 79.

2. J. A. Early, *Autobiographical Sketch,* vii.

3. Tagg, *Generals of Gettysburg,* 257.

4. J. A. Early, *Autobiographical Sketch,* 77.

5. Tagg, *Generals of Gettysburg,* 256–57; J. A. Early, *Autobiographical Sketch,* 121; Richard S. Ewell to Dear Gen'l, Jan. 7, 1863, in D. Pfanz, *Letters of General Richard S. Ewell,* 229; Richard S. Ewell to Dear Sir, Jan. 26, 1863, ibid., 231.

6. Sorrel, *Recollections,* 56; Wise, *End of an Era,* 228.

7. J. W. Baker, "War Reminiscences," *Clinch Valley News,* Apr. 22, 1921; Gordon, *Reminiscences,* 318; Wert, *Glorious Army,* 155.

8. Richard S. Ewell to Dear Lizinka, Aug. 17, 1862, in D. Pfanz, *Letters of General Richard S. Ewell,* 226–27; Richard S. Ewell to Dear General, Mar. 8, 1863, ibid., 235.

9. Tagg, *Generals of Gettysburg,* 260, 263, 266, 268.

10. Furgurson, *Chancellorsville 1863,* 253–72.

11. Clement A. Evans to My dear Darling, May 30, 1863, in Stephens, *Intrepid Warrior,* 173.

12. Warner, *Generals in Gray,* 158–59.

13. Clemmer, *Old Alleghany,* 318–24, 353–65.

14. "The Fight on the Allegheny," *Richmond Enquirer,* Dec. 20, 1861; *Macon Telegraph,* quoted in Clemmer, *Old Alleghany,* 367.

15. Robson, *How a One-Legged Rebel Lives,* 21.

16. W. H. Hull, "Some Recollections of the Civil War, Tenth Paper," *Pocahontas Times,* Apr. 22, 1909.

17. Bohannon, "Placed on the Pages of History," 11.

18. Dabney, *Life and Campaigns of Lieut.-Gen. Thomas J. Jackson,* 2:74.

19. Martin and Avery, *Diary from Dixie,* 232–35 (Sept. 7, 1863).

20. Thomas J. Jackson to James A. Seddon, Feb. 10, 1863, Hotchkiss Papers, LOC.

21. Tagg, *Generals at Gettysburg,* 269–71.

22. Ted Barclay to Dear Sister, May 26, 1863, Alexander Tedford Barclay Papers, W&L; Thomas F. Boatwright to My Darling Wife, June 1, 1863, Thomas F. Boatwright Papers, SHC; Wert, *Gettysburg, Day Three,* 58.

23. Tagg, *Generals of Gettysburg,* 284. For details on Rodes's career, see Krick, "We Have Never Suffered a Greater Loss," 117–43.

24. John Henry Cowin Diary, July 24, 1861, in Hubbs, *Voices from Company D,* 25.

25. "Letter from Virginia," Dec. 5, 1862, *Mobile Daily Advertiser and Register,* Dec. 14, 1862.

26. G. Campbell Brown to Rebecca Hubbard, Aug. 20, 1861, Polk, Brown, and Ewell Family Papers, SHC; Campbell Brown Journal, in Jones, *Campbell Brown's Civil War,* 45.

27. Warner, *Generals in Gray,* 263.

28. James Power Smith to My Dearest Sister, Jan. 21, 1863, quoted in Krick, "We Have Never Suffered a Greater Loss," 117; George Thomas Rust to Dear Beckie, May 1, 1863, Rust Papers, VIIS.

29. Eugene Blackford to Dear Father, Mar. 8, 1863, Robert L. Brake Collection, USAHEC.

30. Irby Goodwin Scott to Dear Father, Mar. 24, 1863, in Pearson, *Lee and Jackson's Bloody Twelfth,* 103.

31. Robert E. Rodes to Richard S. Ewell, Mar. 22, 1863, Polk, Brown, and Ewell Family Papers, SHC.

32. OR 25, pt. 1, 886; ibid., 33, 1134.

33. Eugene Blackford to My Dear Mary, May 21, 1863, in Ray, *Sharpshooter,* 172; W. Davies Tinsley to My Dear Mother, May 20, 1863, William Davies Tinsley Letters, GAM.

34. William B. Haygood to Mrs. and Miss Jackson, May 18, 1863, Edward Harden Papers, DU.

35. John H. Fain to My Dear Mother, May 8, 1863, Archibald Erskine Henderson Papers, ibid.

36. Berry Kinney to Dear Sir, May 14, 1863, in Watford, *Civil War in North Carolina,* 111.

37. Clack to Carrie, May 23, 1863, Clack Papers, SHC; Henry E. Handerson to Dear Father, May 13, 1863, in Cummer, *Yankee in Gray,* 103; Ted Barclay to Dear Sister, May 13, 1863, Barclay Papers, W&L.

38. Zebulon B. Vance to Jefferson Davis, May 13, 1863, in Mobley, *Papers of Zebulon Baird Vance,* 151–52.

39. Evans to Darling, May 30, 1863, in Stephens, *Intrepid Warrior,* 173; White, "Diary of the War," 181 (May 22, 1863).

40. Kinney to Sir, May 14, 1863, in Watford, *Civil War in North Carolina,* 111; John Thomas Traylor to My Dear Wife, May 14, 1863, John Thomas Traylor Collection, Troup County Archives, LaGrange, GA.

41. Warner, *Generals in Gray,* 58; Tagg, *Generals at Gettysburg,* 292–95.

42. William J. Lowery to "Dear Mother," May 26, 1863, Civil War Soldiers Letters and Diaries Archive, "Civil War Voices," *Soldier Studies,* http://www.soldierstudies.org/index.php?action=view_letter&Letter=508; Hugh M. Ingram to Dear Brother, May 30, 1863, H. M. Ingram Letters, LOV.

43. George W. Wills to My Dear Sister, May 25, 1863, George Whitaker Wills Letters, SHC; Thomas C. Land to Brother Hufham, May 31, 1863, *Biblical Recorder,* June 10, 1863; Edward H. Armstrong to Dear Pa, May 26, 1863, Thomas J. Armstrong Papers, UNCW.

44. Stephen Dodson Ramseur to My Heart's Darling, May 29, 1863, in Kundahl, *Bravest of the Brave,* 148.

45. Reuben Allen Pierson to Dear Father, May 8, 1863, in Cutrer and Parrish, *Brothers in Gray,* 189–90; Barclay to Sister, May 13, 1863, Barclay Papers, W&L.

46. "From the 4th North Carolina," May 27, 1863, *Carolina Watchman,* June 8, 1863, in Munson, *Confederate Correspondent,* 67.

47. James Z. Branscomb to Dear Sister, May 31, 1863, in Chappell, *Dear Sister,* 150; Francis M. Parker to My Dear Wife, May 25, 1863, in Taylor, *To Drive the Enemy,* 281.

48. Newsom Edward Jenkins Diary, June 3, 1863, in Garber, *Heart like a River,* 83; George P. Ring Diary, June 4, 1863, Louisiana Historical Association Collection, Special Collections, Howard-Tilton Memorial Library, Tulane Univ., New Orleans; Stephen Dodson Ramseur to My Heart's Precious Darling, June 3, 1863, in Kundahl, *Bravest of the Brave,* 149.

49. OR 27, pt. 2, 305.

50. Heth, "Causes of Lee's Defeat at Gettysburg," 153.

51. Gordon, *Reminiscences,* 138–39.

52. James I. Harris to Dear Friend Burton, Aug. 24, 1863, in Taylor, "Ramseur's Brigade in the Gettysburg Campaign," 28.

53. C. Hall, "The Army Is Moving," 14–16.

54. Hotchkiss Journal, June 7, 1863, in McDonald, *Make Me a Map,* 149.

55. "Letter from the Army of Virginia," June 16, 1863, *Mobile Daily Advertiser and Register,* June 30, 1863.

56. Ruffin Barnes to Dear Wife, June 8, 1863, in Johnston, "Confederate Letters of Ruffin Barnes," 81; Clement A. Evans Diary, June 8, 1863, in Stephens, *Intrepid Warrior,* 189; McKim, *Soldier's Recollections,* 138.

57. Alexander S. Pendleton to Kate Corbin, June 8, 1863, Pendleton Papers, SHC; Alexander S. Pendleton to Dear Mother, June 9, 1863, ibid.

58. Hotchkiss Journal, June 9, 1863, in McDonald, *Make Me a Map,* 150.

59. John T. Gay to Dear Pussie, June 10, 1863, Nix-Price Collection, Troup County Archives.

60. Smith, *Anson Guards,* 198; OR 27, pt. 2, 546.

61. C. Hall, "The Army Is Moving," 44; Dayton, *Diary of a Confederate Soldier: James E. Hall,* 81 (June 11, 1863).

62. Hotchkiss Journal, June 12, 1863, in McDonald, *Make Me a Map,* 150–51.

63. William E. Calder to Dear Mother, June 20, 1863, Calder Family Papers, SHC.

64. Lucy Rebecca Buck Diary, June 12, 1863, in Baer, *Shadows on My Heart,* 212.

65. Ashby, *The Valley Campaigns,* 240; Charles Eckhardt Diary, June 12, 1863, Warren Heritage Society, Front Royal, VA.

66. Edmund Stephens to Dear Parents, June 20, 1863, Edmund Stephens Collection, Cammie C. Henry Research Center, Watson Memorial Library, Northwestern State Univ. of Louisiana, Natchitoches; Robert Daniel Funkhouser, "Memoirs," in Hale and Phillips, *History of the Forty-Ninth Virginia Infantry,* 69.

67. Hotchkiss Journal, June 12, 1863, in McDonald, *Make Me a Map,* 152.

2. "A WORTHY SUCCESSOR OF JACKSON"

1. OR 27, pt. 2, 547.

2. Duncan, *Beleaguered Winchester,* 139–58; Stephens to Parents, June 20, 1863, Edmund Stephens Collection.

3. Noyalas, *My Will Is Absolute,* 79–116.

4. Quoted in Collins, "Grey Eagle," 61–62.

5. "The Victory at Winchester," June 16, 1863, *Augusta Weekly Chronicle and Sentinel,* June 28, 1863; Casler, *Four Years in the Stonewall Brigade,* 167.

6. Marcus Blakemore Buck Diary, June 12, 1863, Marcus Blakemore Buck Diary and Farm Journal, UVA.

7. OR 27, pt. 2, 440.

8. William James Kincheloe Diary, June 13, 1863, in Hale and Phillips, *History of the Forty-Ninth Virginia Infantry,* 69.

9. OR 27, pt. 2, 440, 500.

10. J. A. Early, *Autobiographical Sketch,* 241; OR 27, pt. 2, 460.

11. OR 27, pt. 2, 500.

12. Ibid., 460.

13. Ibid., 460, 477.

14. Ibid., 491; J. A. Early, *Autobiographical Sketch,* 242.

15. P. Johnson, *Under the Southern Cross,* 116; Mathews quoted in Wittenberg and Mingus, *Second Battle of Winchester,* 104.

16. Evans Diary, June 13, 1863, in Stephens, *Intrepid Warrior,* 189; "The Capture of Winchester," *Charleston Mercury,* June 27, 1863; OR 27, pt. 2, 491.

17. Kincheloe Diary, June 13, 1863, in Hale and Phillips, *History of the Forty-Ninth Virginia Infantry,* 70.

18. OR 27, pt. 2, 500.

19. John M. Steptoe to My Dear Carrie, June 15, 1863, Steptoe Family Papers, UVA.

20. OR 27, pt. 2, 440; Brown Journal, in Jones, *Campbell Brown's Civil War,* 193.

21. Samuel Angus Firebaugh Diary, June 14, 1863, SHC.

22. OR 27, pt. 2, 461.

23. Ibid., 440.

24. Ibid., 500; Randolph, *Gleanings from a Harvest of Memories,* 33.

25. OR 27, pt. 462.

26. Thomas Benton Reed Diary, June 14, 1863, in Reed, *Private in Gray,* 36.

27. Kincheloe Diary, June 14, 1863, in Hale and Phillips, *History of the Forty-Ninth Virginia Infantry,* 70; P. Johnson, *Under the Southern Cross,* 116; John K. Walker to Dear Father and Mother, June 17, 1863, John K. Walker Letters, Civil War Collection, EU.

28. Kate Sperry Diary, June 14, 1863, Kate Sperry Collection, HRL; Cornelia Peake McDonald Diary, June 14, 1863, in Gwin, *A Woman's Civil War,* 156.

29. William J. Seymour Journal, June 14, 1863, in Jones, *Civil War Memoirs of Captain William J. Seymour,* 61; James Calvin Zimmerman to Dear Wife, June 19, 1863, in Hartley and Zimmerman, *Fighting 57th North Carolina,* 111; "The Victory at Winchester," June 16, 1863, *Augusta Weekly Chronicle and Sentinel,* June 28, 1863.

30. Samuel H. Chisolm to Dear Brother, June 17, 1863, in Chisolm, "Forward, the Louisiana Brigade," 449.

31. J. Warren Jackson to My dear Brother, July 20, 1863, in M. Reed, "Gettysburg Campaign," 185; Reed Diary, June 14, 1863, in Reed, *Private in Gray,* 36.

32. Chisolm to Brother, June 17, 1863, in Chisolm, "Forward, the Louisiana Brigade," 449.

33. Reed Diary, June 14, 1863, in Reed, *Private in Gray,* 36; Buck, *With the Old Confeds,* 87–88; Seymour Journal, June 14, 1863, in Jones, *Civil War Memoirs of Captain William J. Seymour,* 62.

34. William Henry Mayo Diary, June 14, 1863, HL; Chisolm to Brother, June 17, 1863, in Chisolm, "Forward, the Louisiana Brigade," 449; Reed Diary, June 14, 1863, in Reed, *Private in Gray,* 36; Jackson to Brother, July 20, 1863, in M. Reed, "Gettysburg Campaign," 185.

35. Chisolm to Brother, June 17, 1863, in Chisolm, "Forward, the Louisiana Brigade," 449; Reed Diary, June 14, 1863, in Reed, *Private in Gray,* 36; Seymour Journal, June 14, 1863, in Jones, *Civil War Memoirs of Captain William J. Seymour,* 62; Mayo Diary, June 14, 1863, HL.

36. Henry H. Dedrick to My Dear Wife, June 14, 1863, Henry H. Dedrick Papers, VMI; Baker, "War Reminiscences," *Clinch Valley News,* Apr. 22, 1921; "John Lewis Poe's Account: The War of 1861 to 1865," 1926, List of Veteran Ancestors, Genealogy, Poeland, http://www.poeland.com/genealogy/auxdata/JLPoe_warDiary.html.

37. A. M. Riddle Diary, June 15, 1863, Confederate Miscellany, BC; Seymour Journal, June 14, 1863, in Jones, *Civil War Memoirs of Captain William J. Seymour,* 62.

38. OR 27, pt. 2, 473; Seymour Journal, June 14, 1863, in Jones, *Civil War Memoirs of Captain William J. Seymour,* 62.

39. Rivera, "Two Heroines of the Shenandoah Valley," 495.

40. Ackerd, "Early's Brigade at Winchester," 264; "The Capture of Winchester," *Charleston Mercury,* June 27, 1863.

41. OR 27, pt. 2, 47.

42. Gordon, *Reminiscences,* 68–69.

43. P. Johnson, *Under the Southern Cross,* 118.

44. William Beverley Pettit to My darling Wife, June 15, 1863, in Turner, *Civil War Letters,* 120.

45. OR 27, pt. 2, 501–2; Metts, "The Jordon Springs Battle," 105; Lauck, "Little Corporal's Story," 181.

46. McKim, *Soldier's Recollections,* 149–50; Owens, "Heroic Defense of Bridge," 43.

47. OR, 27, pt. 2, 517.

48. John Welsh to Dear Becky, June 15, 1863, in Bean, "House Divided," 417; James Peter Williams to Dear Sister, June 16, 1863, James Peter Williams Papers, UVA; Hayes, *Civil War Diary of Father James Sheeran,* 181 (June 15, 1863).

49. OR, 27, pt. 2, 53, 549; A. M. Riddle Diary, June 15, 1863, Confederate Miscellany, BC; John Garibaldi to Dear Wife, June 16, 1863, John Garibaldi Papers, VMI.

50. OR 27, pt. 2, 464; Henry W. Wingfield Diary, June 17, 1863, in W. Scott, "Two Confederate Items," 27.

51. Samuel Hoover to Dear Brother, June 16, 1863, Hoover Family Letters, James I. Robertson Jr. Civil War Sesquicentennial Legacy Collection, LOV; Daniel, "H. H. Harris Civil War Diary," 1769 (June 15, 1863); "The Capture of Winchester," *Charleston Mercury,* June 27, 1863; Leonard K. Sparrow to Dear Ma, June 16, 1863, Leonard K. Sparrow Papers, VHS.

52. George Bedinger to Dear Diddy, June 16, 1862 [1863], Bedinger-Dandridge Family Papers, DU; White, "Diary of the War," 189 (June 15, 1863).

53. "Correspondence of the Patriot: From the Sixth Regiment," June 17, 1863, *Greensboro Patriot,* July 2, 1863; Walker to Father and Mother, June 17, 1863, Civil War Collection, EU; William F. Wagner to Dear, June 17, 1863, in Hatley and Huffman, *Letters of William F. Wagner,* 54.

54. Hunter, "Thirteenth Virginia Infantry—Humor," 339; John Warwick Daniel to Dear Sister, June 20, 1863, in Sword, "Confederate Maj. John W. Daniel Describes the 2nd Battle of Winchester," 9.

55. OR 27, pt. 2, 549; William H. Lyons Diary, June 15, 1863, MHS.

56. H. Douglas, *I Rode with Stonewall,* 242; Walker to Father and Mother, June 17, 1863, Civil War Collection, EU; Chisolm to Brother, June 17, 1863, in Chisolm, "Forward, the Louisiana Brigade," 449.

57. Pettit to Wife, June 15, 1863, in Turner, *Civil War Letters,* 121.

58. Edgar, *My Reminiscences of the Stonewall Brigade,* 129.

3. "QUITE A BRILLIANT LITTLE AFFAIR"

1. OR 27, pt. 2, 547.

2. Ibid.; Gold, *History of Clarke County Virginia,* 226; Micajah Woods to My Dear Father, June 16, 1863, Micajah Woods Papers, UVA.

3. Warner, *Generals in Gray,* 154; Tagg, *Generals of Gettysburg,* 367.

4. OR 27, pt. 2, 547.

5. Samuel D. Pickens Diary, June 13, 1863, in Hubbs, *Voices from Company D,* 177; William W. Marston Diary, June 13, 1863, Civil War Collection, EU.

6. Gold, *History of Clarke County Virginia,* 13–14, 20, 30, 98.

7. Plater, "Civil War Diary of Miss Matella Page Harrison," 64 (June 13, 1863).

8. Pickens Diary, June 13, 1863, in Hubbs, *Voices of Company D,* 177.

9. Moore, "Through the Shadows," 2.

10. OR 27, pt. 2, 108–9, 547.

11. Lancelot M. Blackford to My Dear Father, June 28, 1863, Blackford Family Papers, UVA.

12. "Defense and Evacuation of Winchester," 483.

13. OR 27, pt. 2, 108–9, 547; "The Fight at Berryville, Va.: Captain Alexander's Baltimore Battery," *Baltimore Sun,* June 19, 1863; William H. Moffett to Dear Father, June 16, 1863, William H. Moffett Papers, MHS.

14. OR, 27, pt. 2, 547, 592.

15. Pickens Diary, June 13, 1863, in Hubbs, *Voices from Company D,* 177.

16. Wild, *Memoirs and History of Capt. F. W. Alexander's Baltimore Battery,* 50–52.

17. Calder to Mother, June 20, 1863, Calder Family Papers, SHC; Harris to Burton, Aug. 24, 1863, in Taylor, "Ramseur's Brigade in the Gettysburg Campaign," 28.

18. Calder to Mother, June 20, 1863, Calder Family Papers, SHC; John C. Gorman to Dear Friend Holden, June 22, 1863, *North Carolina Standard,* July 3, 1863.

19. Leon, *Diary of a Tar Heel,* 32 (June 13, 1863); OR 27, pt. 2, 565.

20. John F. Coghill to Dear Pappy, Ma and Mit, June 25, 1863, John Fuller Coghill Letters, SHC; John H. Harris Diary, June 13, 1863, in Hubbell, *Confederate Stamps,* app., 10; W. Davies Tinsley to My Dear Mother, June 26, 1863, Tinsley Letters, GAM.

21. Ardrey Diary, June 13, 1863, Ardrey Papers, DaCol; Smith, *Diary of the Civil War,* 9 (June 13, 1863).

22. Harris to Burton, Aug. 24, 1863, in Taylor, "Ramseur's Brigade in the Gettysburg Campaign," 28.

23. Gorman to Holden, June 22, 1863, *North Carolina Standard,* July 3, 1863; Ardrey Diary, June 13, 1863, Ardrey Papers, DaCol; Tinsley to Mother, June 26, 1863, Tinsley Letters, GAM.

24. Pickens Diary, June 13, 1863, in Hubbs, *Voices from Company D,* 177.

25. Calder to Mother, June 20, 1863, Calder Family Papers, SHC; John F. Shaffner to My Dearest Friend, June 23, 1863, John F. Shaffner Diary and Papers, Private Collections, NCSA; Eugene Blackford, "Memoirs," 221, Civil War Miscellaneous Collection, USAHEC.

26. Smith, *Anson Guards,* 198–99; Gorman to Holden, June 22, 1863, *North Carolina Standard,* July 3, 1863.

27. Purifoy, "With Jackson in the Valley," 383; W. Green, *Recollections and Reflections,* 172.

28. "Our Northern Campaign: Notes from the Diary of Capt. J. B. R—No. 1," *Countryman,* Sept. 22, 1863; Pickens Diary, June 13, 1863, in Hubbs, *Voices from Company D,* 177.

29. "Forty-Fourth Georgia Regiment, the Advance into Pennsylvania," June 23, 1863, *Augusta Weekly Chronicle and Sentinel,* July 7, 1863; OR 27, pt. 1, 193.

30. OR 27, pt. 2, 547–48; Gorman to Holden, June 22, 1863, *North Carolina Standard,* July 3, 1863.

31. Nye, *Here Come the Rebels!,* 87–88.

32. A. Smith, "Story of the Life and Trials of a Confederate Soldier," 266. Smithfield is known today as Middleway.

33. William J. Grant, "Letter from Lieut. W. J. Grant," *Cecil Whig,* June 27, 1863.

34. OR 27, pt. 2, 67; A. Smith, "Story of the Life and Trials of a Confederate Soldier," 266; Isaac Hamilton Brisco to Dear Father and Mother, Brothers and Sisters, Sept. 30, 1863, in Kesterson, *Campaigning with the 17th Virginia Cavalry,* 235.

35. W. K. to Messrs. Editors, June 19, 1863, *Richmond Enquirer,* July 3, 1863; Prowell, *History of the Eighty-Seventh Regiment, Pennsylvania Volunteers,* 67–69; OR 27, pt. 2, 67; Wildes, *Record of the One Hundred and Sixteenth Regiment Ohio Infantry,* 55.

36. Brisco to Father and Mother, Brothers and Sisters, Sept. 30, 1863, in Kesterson, *Campaigning with the 17th Virginia,* 235; OR 27, pt. 1, 193; W. K. to Editors, June 19, 1863, *Richmond Enquirer,* July 3, 1863.

37. Beach, *First New York (Lincoln) Cavalry,* 235; Stevenson, *Boots and Saddles,* 185.

38. A. Smith, "Story of the Life and Trials of a Confederate Soldier," 266; W. K. to Editors, June 19, 1863, *Richmond Enquirer,* July 3, 1863.

39. Nye, *Here Come the Rebels!,* 87–88.

40. Hodam, "The Hodam Manuscript," 285; A. Smith, "Story of the Life and Trials of a Confederate Soldier," 266.

41. Beach, *First New York (Lincoln) Cavalry,* 232–34; Stevenson, *Boots and Saddles,* 185; "General Milroy's Retreat: Story of It Told by the Late Col. Wm. A. McKellip," *Baltimore Sun,* Apr. 19, 1904.

42. William D. Hall, "Milroy at Winchester: A Fight of Thirty Minutes That Was One of the Most Desperate of the War," *Philadelphia Weekly Times,* Mar. 5, 1881; OR 27, pt. 2, 83.

43. Wild, *Memories and History of Capt. F. W. Alexander's Baltimore Battery,* 55.

44. Nye, *Here Come the Rebels!,* 128; Beach, *First New York (Lincoln) Cavalry,* 232–34; OR 27, pt. 2, 83.

45. OR 27, pt. 2, 83; Hall, "Milroy at Winchester"; "General Milroy's Retreat."

46. Henry Suydam to My Dearest Mother, June 16, 1863, in Black, *Lincoln Cavalryman,* 126–27; Beach, *First New York (Lincoln) Cavalry,* 232–34; "Letter from Captain Woodruff's Company," July 24, 1863, First New York (Lincoln) Cavalry, Civil War Newspaper Clipping Files, New York State Military Museum, Albany.

47. Hall, "Milroy at Winchester"; Scott, *36th and 37th Battalions Virginia Cavalry,* 3; OR 27, pt. 2, 83; ibid., pt. 1, 193.

48. OR 27, pt. 2, 548; Calder to Mother, June 20, 1863, Calder Family Papers, SHC.

49. Record of Events, 30th North Carolina Regiment, Field and Staff, June 10–13, 1863, in Hewitt, Trudeau, and Suderow, *Supplement to the Official Records,* 49(2):52.

4. "A THUNDERBOLT FROM A CLOUDLESS SKY"

1. Harris to Burton, Aug. 24, 1863, in Taylor, "Ramseur's Brigade in the Gettysburg Campaign," 28.

2. OR 27, pt. 2, 548.

3. Gorman to Holden, June 22, 1863, *North Carolina Standard,* July 3, 1863.

4. John S. Tucker Diary, June 14, 1863, ADAH; Ardrey Diary, June 14, 1863, Ardrey Papers, DaCol.

5. Norris, *History of the Lower Shenandoah Valley,* 242.

6. Myers, *Myers' History of West Virginia,* 2:139.

7. Voegle, "Chronology of the Civil War in Berkeley County," 3–4; Ted Barclay to Dear Mother, June 22, 1861, Ted Barclay Papers, LOV.

8. Aler, *History of Martinsburg and Berkeley County,* 286–87; Prock to Friend Greene, Mar. 10, 1862, in Landon, "14th Indiana Regiment in the Valley of Virginia," 286.

9. Calder to Mother, June 20, 1863, Calder Family Papers, SHC.

10. George W. Wills to My dear Mother, June 18, 1863, William H. Wills Papers, SHC; "From Williamsport, Maryland," June 17, 1863, *Macon Daily Telegraph,* July 1, 1863.

11. OR 27, pt. 2, 37–39.

12. Lewis H. Fuller Diary, June 14, 1863, James R. Droegemeyer Private Collection, Martinsburg, WV; W. K. to Editors, June 19, 1863, *Richmond Enquirer,* July 3, 1863.

13. Cordrey, "Life and Comments of a Common Soldier," 30, Munson, Underwood, Horn,

Fairfield, and Allied Families, http://brazoriaroots.com/acrobat/franms.pdf; Henry Gaddis to Dear Father, Mother, and Brother, June 16, 1863, in Bagley, "Letters Home Written by Henry Gaddis," Steve French Private Collection, Hedgesville, WV; J. Scott, "At Martinsburg, Va."

14. Gaddis to Father, Mother, and Brother, June 16, 1863, in Bagley, "Letters Home Written Home by Henry Gaddis," French Private Collection.

15. French, "Battle of Martinsburg," 11.

16. OR 27, pt. 2, 16–17, 38–39.

17. Ibid., 17–18, 548; Susan Nourse Riddle Diary, June 14, 1863, in Gardiner and Gardiner, *Chronicles of Old Berkeley*, 160.

18. OR 27, pt. 2, 548; W. K. to Editors, June 19, 1863, *Richmond Enquirer*, July 3, 1863.

19. Harris Diary, June 14, 1863, in Hubbell, *Confederate Stamps*, app., 10; James E. Green Diary, June 14, 1863, Private Collections, NCSA; OR 27, pt. 2, 548, 592.

20. OR 27, pt. 2, 548, 592; Krick, *Lee's Colonels*, 374; Meade, "Col. Thomas H. Carter," 41–42; Macaluso, *Morris, Orange, and King William Artillery*, 19.

21. Thomas Catesby Jones, "Civil War Reminiscences," 15, VHS; "From Williamsport, Maryland," June 17, 1863, *Macon Daily Telegraph*, July 1, 1863.

22. "Mr. F. G. Chapman Letter," June 19, 1863, *New York Herald*, June 27, 1863; Edward James to My Dear Mother, June 15, 1863, Civil War Manuscripts Collection, YU.

23. Henry Gaddis to Dear Father, Mother and Brother, June 22, 1863, in Bagley, "Letters Home Written by Henry Gaddis," French Private Collection; Darwin Sunderland to Home, June 21, 1863, Sunderland Family Correspondence, Special Collections, St. Lawrence Univ., Canton, NY; David Close to My Dear Aunt and Uncle, Aug. 24, 1863, in "The Civil War Letters of David Close to Rachel Close-Dunbar," ed. Don Close, "Letters, Accounts, Oral Histories," *The 126th Ohio Volunteer Infantry*, http://www.frontierfamilies.net/family/DCletters.htm.

24. Jonathan McCready letter, *Cadiz Republican*, July 15, 1863, quoted in Hall, *Appalachian Ohio and the Civil War*, 227; Cordrey, "Life and Comments of a Common Soldier," 30; William McVey to Lucy Henderson, June 1863, quoted in Porter, *A People Set Apart*, 227.

25. Skinner, *Surgeon's Story*, 3.

26. Lancelot Blackford to Father, June 28, 1863, Blackford Family Papers, UVA.

27. OR 27, pt. 2, 549, 565.

28. McCready letter, *Cadiz Republican*, July 15, 1863, quoted in Hall, *Appalachian Ohio and the Civil War*, 227.

29. OR 27, pt. 2, 549.

30. Gorman to Holden, June 22, 1863, *North Carolina Standard*, July 3, 1863; Calder to Mother, June 20, 1863, Calder Family Papers, SHC.

31. Bryan Grimes to My Dearest Little Darling, June 16, 1863, Bryan Grimes Papers, Private Collections, NCSA; Calder to Mother, June 20, 1863, Calder Family Papers; Norman, *Portion of My Life*, 183.

32. W. K. to Editors, June 19, 1863, *Richmond Enquirer*, July 3, 1863.

33. A. Smith, "Story of the Life and Trials of a Confederate Soldier," 267; Sunderland to Home, June 21, 1863, Sunderland Family Correspondence, Special Collections, St. Lawrence Univ.

34. Brisco to Father and Mother, Brothers and Sisters, Sept. 30, 1863, in Kesterson, *Campaigning with the 17th Virginia Cavalry*, 235; Hodam, *Journal of James H. Hodam*, 60.

35. Harris to Burton, Aug. 24, 1863, in Taylor, "Ramseur's Brigade in the Gettysburg Campaign," 28.

36. "Court of Inquiry Relative to the Evacuation of Martinsburg by the Command of Brig. Gen. Daniel Tyler," 11–13, Records of the Judge Advocate General's Office, Record Group 153, NA.

37. OR 27, pt. 2, 549.

38. W. K. to Messrs. Editors, July 18, 1863, *Rockingham Register,* July 24, 1863.

39. Jones, "Civil War Reminiscences," 15.

40. Leon, *Diary of a Tar Heel,* 31 (June 14, 1863).

41. "Forty-Fourth Georgia Regiment, the Advance into Pennsylvania," June 23, 1863, *Augusta Weekly Chronicle and Sentinel,* July 7, 1863; Jeremiah M. Tate to Dear Sister Mary, June 20, 1863, Jeremiah Tate Letters, GLIAH.

42. Leonidas Torrence to Dear Mother, June 17, 1863, in Monroe, "Road to Gettysburg," 508; Charles C. Blacknall to Dear Bro George, June 18, 1863, Blacknall Papers, Private Collections, NCSA.

43. Harris to Burton, Aug. 24, 1863, in Taylor, "Ramseur's Brigade in the Gettysburg Campaign," 28; Grimes to Little Darling, June 16, 1863, Grimes Papers, Private Collections, NCSA.

44. Bennett, "Fourteenth Regiment," 718.

45. Riddle Diary, June 14, 1863, in Gardiner and Gardiner, *Chronicles of Old Berkeley,* 160.

46. Calder to Mother, June 20, 1863, Calder Family Papers, SHC.

47. Marston Diary, June 14, 1863, Civil War Collection, EU; Tucker Diary, June 14, 1863, ADAH.

48. Blackford, "Memoirs," 223, Civil War Miscellaneous Papers, USAHEC; Tinsley to Mother, June 26, 1863, Tinsley Letters, GAM.

49. Bennett, "Fourteenth Regiment," 718.

50. Gorman to Holden, June 22, 1863, *North Carolina Standard,* July 3, 1863.

51. Blacknall to George, June 18, 1863, Blacknall Papers, Private Collections, NCSA.

52. Sidney J. Richardson to Dear Father and Mother, June 17, 1863, Sidney J. Richardson Papers, GAM; Grimes to Little Darling, June 16, 1863, Grimes Papers, Private Collections, NCSA.

53. A. Smith, "Story of the Life and Trials of a Confederate Soldier," 267.

54. Major Key, "Reminiscences of the Civil War: And Incidents Connected with the 44th Georgia and Other Regiments," *Jasper County News,* Jan. 5, 1899; "From Williamsport, Maryland," June 17, 1863, *Macon Daily Telegraph,* July 1, 1863; Bolling H. Hall to Dear Uncle, July 18, 1863, Bolling Hall Family Papers, ADAH.

55. John C. Key, "Memoirs," 41, GAM; Harris Diary, June 14, 1863, in Hubbell, *Confederate Stamps,* app., 10.

56. Charles Timothy Furlow Diary, June 14, 1863, in Charles T. Furlow, "Record of Current Events from the Time the 4th Ga Regt Left Camp Jackson, Va.," 42, Diaries Miscellaneous Collection (MS 181), YU; Key, "Reminiscences of the Civil War," *Jasper County News,* Jan. 5, 1899.

57. Blackford, "Memoirs," 224, Miscellaneous Civil War Collection, USAHEC.

58. OR 27, pt. 2, 549; Harris to Burton, Aug. 24, 1863, in Taylor, "Ramseur's Brigade in the Gettysburg Campaign," 28.

59. Purifoy, "With Jackson in the Valley," 384.

60. Tinsley to Mother, June 26, 1863, Tinsley Letters, GAM.

61. W. K. to Editors, June 19, 1863, *Richmond Enquirer,* July 3, 1863; Macaluso, *Morris, Orange, and King William Artillery,* 44; OR 27, pt. 2, 456; Jones, "Civil War Reminiscences," 15.

62. OR 27, pt. 2, 39; ibid., pt. 1, 193.

63. Ibid., pt. 2, 549.

64. Leon, *Diary of a Tar Heel,* 31–32 (June 15, 1863).

65. John Minnix to Dear Wife, June 16, 1863, Minnix-Tynes Family Papers, James I. Robertson Jr. Civil War Sesquicentennial Legacy Collection, LOV; Charles C. Blacknall to Dear Jinny, June 22, 1863, Blacknall Papers, Private Collections, NCSA; Charles C. Blacknall to Bro. George, June 23, 1863, ibid.

66. William Gaston Lewis to My Dear Mitte, June 18, 1863, W. G. Lewis Papers, SHC; Gorman to Holden, June 22, 1863, *North Carolina Standard,* July 3, 1863.

5. "COLD INDEED WAS OUR RECEPTION"

1. OR 27, pt. 2, 447; Thomas S. Taylor to Matilda Taylor, June 16, 1863, in Cross, *Letters Home,* 130.

2. W. Green, *Recollections and Reflections,* 171–72; William H. Hodnett Diary, June 15, 1863, in United Daughters of the Confederacy, Georgia Division, *Confederate Reminiscences and Letters,* 4:256; OR 27, pt. 2, 549.

3. Green Diary, June 15, 1863, Private Collections, NCSA.

4. Harris to Burton, Aug. 24, 1863, in Taylor, "Ramseur's Brigade in the Gettysburg Campaign," 28.

5. Furlow Diary, June 15, 1863, in Furlow, "Record of Current Events," 42, Diaries Miscellaneous Collection, YU; "Our Northern Campaign: Notes from the Diary of Capt. J. B. R—No. 1," *Countryman,* Sept. 22, 1863.

6. Tiffany, *Sketch of the Life and Services of Gen. Otho Holland Williams,* 29–30.

7. Ardrey Diary, June 15, 1863, Ardrey Papers, DaCol; Grimes to Little Darling, June 16, 1863, Grimes Papers, Private Collections, NCSA; Calder to Mother, June 20, 1863, Calder Family Papers, SHC; William E. Calder to Dear Mother, June 17, 1863, ibid.

8. "The Confederates in Maryland," June 17, 1863, *Richmond Daily Dispatch,* June 27, 1863.

9. "Forty-Fourth Georgia Regiment, the Advance into Pennsylvania," June 23, 1863, *Augusta Weekly Chronicle and Sentinel,* July 7, 1863.

10. Lucius T. C. Lovelace to Dear Father, June 17, 1863, in Davidson, *War Was the Place,* 88.

11. Richardson to Father and Mother, June 17, 1863, Richardson Papers, GAM.

12. OR 27, pt. 2, 550.

13. Henry B. Wood to Dear Parents and Sarah, June 22, 1863, in Wood, "From Montgomery to Gettysburg," 44; Watkins, *Notes on the Movement of the 14th North Carolina,* 13.

14. Blacknall to George, June 18, 1863, Blacknall Papers, Private Collections, NCSA.

15. For details on Lee's objectives in the campaign, see Brown, *Retreat from Gettysburg,* 11–20.

16. "The Confederates in Maryland," June 17, 1863, *Richmond Daily Dispatch,* June 27, 1863.

17. OR 27, pt. 2, 550.

18. Blacknall to George, June 18, 1863, Blacknall Papers, Private Collections, NCSA.

19. "The Confederates in Maryland," June 17, 1863, *Richmond Daily Dispatch,* June 27, 1863.

20. Ardrey Diary, June 16–17, 1863, Ardrey Papers, DaCol; Furlow Diary, June 17–29, 1863, in Furlow, "Record of Current Events," 43, Diaries Miscellaneous Collection, YU; Charles C. Blacknall to Dear Jinny, June 25, 1863, Blacknall Papers, Private Collections, NCSA.

21. Unrau, *Historic Resource Study: Chesapeake & Ohio Canal,* 751.

22. Blacknall to George, June 18, 1863, Blacknall Papers, Private Collections, NCSA; Shepherd G. Pryor to My Dearest Penelope, June [17], 1863, in Adams, *Post of Honor,* 368; Calder to Mother, June 17, 1863, Calder Family Papers, SHC.

23. Isaac V. Reynolds to Dear Wife, Aug. 9, 1863, Isaac V. Reynolds Papers, DU; A. Smith,

"Story of the Life and Trials of a Confederate Soldier," 267; W. K. to Editors, June 19, 1863, *Richmond Enquirer,* July 3, 1863.

24. Scott, *36th and 37th Battalions Virginia Cavalry,* 3; Hermann Schuricht Diary, June 15, 1863, in Schuricht, "Jenkins' Brigade," 339; W. K. to Editors, June 19, 1863, *Richmond Enquirer,* July 3, 1863.

25. "Jenkins' Raid into Pennsylvania," in F. Moore, *Rebellion Record,* 7:195; "Our Greencastle Correspondence," June 17, 1863, *New York Herald,* June 20, 1863; "Rebel Invasion of Pennsylvania," *Greencastle Pilot,* July 28, 1863.

26. Mohr, *Cormany Diaries,* 329 (June 16, 1863).

27. "Correspondence of the Express," June 17, 1863, *Lancaster Daily Express,* June 20, 1863; Hoke, *Great Invasion,* 103–4.

28. Hoke, *Great Invasion,* 101.

29. "Correspondence of the Express," June 17, 1863, *Lancaster Daily Express,* June 20, 1863; Mohr, *Cormany Diaries,* 329 (June 16, 1863).

30. E. E. Bouldin, "Lee's Advance into Pennsylvania: An Interesting Story by One of Virginia's Dashing Cavalrymen," *Richmond Times Dispatch,* Jan. 22, 1905; Hoke, *Great Invasion,* 101; "The Rebel Invasion," *Valley Spirit,* July 8, 1863.

31. Hoke, *Great Invasion,* 105–6.

32. "Correspondence of the Express," June 17, 1863, *Lancaster Daily Express,* June 20, 1863.

33. "The Rebel Invasion," *Valley Spirit,* July 8, 1863.

34. "Our Chambersburg Correspondence," June 17, 1863, *New York Herald,* June 20, 1863.

35. Jemima K. Cree to My Dear Husband, June 18, 1863, in Cree, "Jenkins' Raid," 95.

36. Mary Craig Eyster to Dear Jennie, June 21, 1863, Marianne Moore Papers, Rosenbach Museum and Library, Philadelphia.

37. "The Rebel Invasion," *Valley Spirit,* July 8, 1863; Hoke, *Reminiscences of the War,* 37.

38. Schuricht Diary, June 17, 1863, in Schuricht, "Jenkins' Brigade," 340.

39. "The Foray on Chambersburg," June 17, 1863, *New York Daily Tribune,* June 22, 1863.

40. Nye, *Here Come the Rebels!,* 146; Hoke, *Reminiscences of the War,* 39.

41. Amos Stouffer Diary, June 17, 1863, in Piston, "The Rebs Are Yet Thick about Us," 215; "Correspondence of the Express," June 17, 1863, *Lancaster Daily Express,* June 20, 1863.

42. "The Rebel Invasion," *Valley Spirit,* July 8, 1863.

43. Hoke, *Reminiscences of the War,* 38; "The Foray on Chambersburg," June 17, 1863, *New York Daily Tribune,* June 22, 1863. The *Tribune* letter is signed "J. H.," which stands for Jacob Hoke.

44. Henry Reeves to My Dear Sister Lizzie, July 4, 1863, Gregory A. Coco Collection, GNMP.

45. "Correspondence of the Express," June 17, 1863, *Lancaster Daily Express,* June 20, 1863; Cree to Husband, June 18, 1863, in Cree, "Jenkins' Raid," 94; Letter from Mr. Wallace to his Wife, June 17, 1863, *Lancaster Daily Express,* June 20, 1863.

46. Mohr, *Cormany Diaries,* 329–30 (June 16, 1863).

47. "Scenes at Chambersburg," *Times Picayune,* July 10, 1863. Although unsigned, the contents of the letter indicate that it was written by Reverend Reeves.

48. Hoke, *Reminiscences of the War,* 38.

49. W. K. to Editors, June 19, 1863, *Richmond Enquirer,* July 3, 1863; Reynolds to Wife, Aug. 9, 1863, Reynolds Papers, DU; Samuel William Newman Feamster to Dear Mother, June 23, 1863, Feamster Family Papers, LOC.

50. "Our Greencastle Correspondence," June 17, 1863, *New York Herald,* June 20, 1863.

51. "Police Affairs," *Harrisburg Daily Patriot and Union,* June 27, 1863.

52. Mary Clara Forney Diary, June 14–15, 1863, Wingard-Forney-Vaky Family Papers, Illinois History and Lincoln Collections, Univ. of Illinois at Urbana-Champaign.

53. "Rebel Invasion of Pennsylvania," *Greencastle Pilot,* July 28, 1863.

54. Hoke, *Great Invasion,* 111–12; Hoke, *Reminiscences of the War,* 39; Stouffer Diary, June 19, 1863, in Piston, "The Rebs Are Yet Thick about Us," 215.

55. *Fulton Democrat,* June 19, 1863, reprinted in "The Visit of Jenkins' Cavalry to McConnellsburg and Mercersburg," *Gettysburg Compiler,* June 29, 1863.

56. "The McConnellsburg Telegrams," June 19, 1863, *New York Herald,* June 21, 1863; Charlotte Lewis to Dear Mother-in-Law, June 19, 1863, in Gannett, "Twelve Letters from Altoona," 46.

57. *Fulton Democrat,* June 19, 1863, reprinted in "The Visit of Jenkins' Cavalry to McConnellsburg and Mercersburg," *Gettysburg Compiler,* June 29, 1863. Forney later turned himself in for trial and was acquitted of all charges. For details, see "Trial and Acquittal of Forney," *Valley Spirit,* Jan. 20, 1864; and Neal, "Civil War Draft Resistance in Fulton County," 5–32.

58. W. S. Fletcher Claim, in Cordell, "Civil War Damage Claims," 17; J. W. Greathead Claim, ibid., 20; "The McConnellsburg Telegrams," June 19, 1863, *New York Herald,* June 21, 1863; Hoke, *Great Invasion,* 111–12.

59. Adam Cook to Dear Son, June 23, 1863, in Patrick McCrary, *Private Cook and the College Company,* 31–32.

60. "War News," *Constitution,* June 27, 1863.

61. T. E. Patterson Account, Patterson Family Collection, Library, Fulton County Historical Society, McConnellsburg, PA.

62. William M. Patterson Claim, in Cordell, "Civil War Damage Claims," 32; David Hunter Patterson, "Memoirs of David Hunter Patterson," 1929, trans. and ed. William Remington Patterson Jr., 1991, chap. 9, Fulton County Pennsylvania Genealogy, http://www.rootsweb.ancestry.com/~pafulton/pathist/CH9.htm.

63. "Jenkins Cavalry at Mercersburg: Special Correspondence of the Press," June 20, 1863, *Philadelphia Daily Press,* June 24, 1863. The letter is signed "D.P.S.," which stands for Dr. Philip Schaff.

64. Philip Schaff Diary, June 19, 1863, in Schaff, "Gettysburg Week," 22; Thomas Creigh Diary, June 19, 1863, in Turner, "Civil War Days in Mercersburg," 34.

65. "War News," *Constitution,* June 27, 1863.

66. OR 27, pt. 2, 551.

67. Green Diary, June 17, 1863, Private Collections, NCSA; William Beavans Diary, June 17, 1863, William Beavans Diary and Letters, SHC.

68. Charles F. Bahnson to My Dear Father, June 19, 1863, in Chapman, *Bright and Gloomy Days,* 65; Pinckney Hatrick to Dear Bro and Sister, June 18, 1863, Hatrick Family Scrapbook, SHC.

69. OR 27, pt. 2, 555; Hotchkiss Journal, June 17, 1863, in McDonald, *Make Me a Map,* 153.

70. Blackford, "Memoirs," 225–26, Civil War Miscellaneous Collection, USAHEC.

71. "Third Alabama Infantry, Letter from Pennsylvania," June 28, 1863, *Mobile Daily Advertiser and Register,* July 20, 1863.

6. "WHEREVER EWELL LEADS, WE CAN FOLLOW"

1. Blackford, "Memoirs," 225–26, Civil War Miscellaneous Collection, USAHEC.

2. Preston H. Turner to My Dear Parents, June 28, 1863, Preston H. Turner Papers, SHC; Gorman to Holden, June 22, 1863, *North Carolina Standard,* July 3, 1863.

3. Shaffner to Friend, June 23, 1863, Shaffner Diary and Papers, Private Collections, NCSA; Pickens Diary, June 19, 1863, in Hubbs, *Voices from Company D,* 179; Ardrey Diary, June 16–17, 1863, Ardrey Papers, DaCol.

4. "Forty-Fourth Georgia Regiment, the Advance into Pennsylvania," June 23, 1863, *Augusta Weekly Chronicle and Sentinel,* July 7, 1863; Eugene Blackford to Dear Father, June 21, 1863, Lewis Leigh Collection, USAHEC.

5. Hoole, *History of the Third Alabama Regiment,* 40; "Extract from a private letter from one of the 3rd Ala. to a Mobile friend," June 21, 1863, *Macon Daily Telegraph,* July 3, 1863.

6. Shaffner to Friend, June 23, 1863, Shaffner Diary and Papers, Private Collections, NCSA.

7. Calder to Mother, June 20, 1863, Calder Family Papers, SHC.

8. Ardrey Diary, June 18, 1863, Ardrey Papers, DaCol; Tomlinson, "On the Advance into Maryland," 141.

9. Blackford, "Memoirs," 227, Civil War Miscellaneous Collection, USAHEC.

10. Pickens Diary, June 19, 1863, in Hubbs, *Voices from Company D,* 179.

11. Marston Diary, June 19, 1863, Civil War Collection, EU.

12. "Forty-Fourth Georgia Regiment, the Advance into Pennsylvania," June 23, 1863, *Augusta Weekly Chronicle and Sentinel,* July 7, 1863; "From the Forty-Third Reg't N.C.T.," July 20, 1863, *North Carolina Argus,* July 30, 1863.

13. Stephen Dodson Ramseur to My Precious Darling, June 28, 1863, in Kundahl, *Bravest of the Brave,* 151.

14. "Extract from a private letter from one of the 3rd Ala. to a Mobile friend," June 21, 1863, *Macon Daily Telegraph,* July 3, 1863.

15. Leon, *Diary of a Tar Heel,* 32 (June 19, 1863); John T. Nichols Diary, June 19, 1863, John Thomas Nichols Papers, DU; Blackford to Father, June 21, 1863, Leigh Collection, USAHEC; Ardrey Diary, June 16–17, 1863, Ardrey Papers, DaCol.

16. Blackford to Father, June 21, 1863, Leigh Collection, USAHEC; Park, "War Diary," 11 (June 20, 1863).

17. "Third Alabama Infantry: Letter from Pennsylvania," June 28, 1863, *Mobile Advertiser and Register,* July 20, 1863.

18. Pickens Diary, June 21, 1863, in Hubbs, *Voices from Company D,* 179.

19. Mary Louisa Kealhofer Diary, June 22, 1863, in Green, "A People at War," 255.

20. J. A. Stradley to Brother Hufham, June 29, 1863, *Biblical Recorder,* July 22, 1863; Thomas C. Land Diary, June 21, 1863, Howard Land Private Collection, Stafford, VA.

21. Bahnson to Father, June 19, 1863, in Chapman, *Bright and Gloomy Days,* 65.

22. David Ballenger to Dear Nancy, June 21, 1863, David Ballenger Letters, Schoff Civil War Collection, William L. Clements Library, Univ. of Michigan, Ann Arbor.

23. "Extract from a private letter from one of the 3rd Ala. to a Mobile friend," June 21, 1863, *Macon Daily Telegraph,* July 3, 1863.

24. Calder to Mother, June 20, 1863, Calder Family Papers, SHC; Ardrey Diary, June 19–21, 1863, Ardrey Papers, DaCol; Pickens Diary, June 21, 1863, in Hubbs, *Voices from Company D,* 179.

25. Charles F. Bahnson to My Dear Father, June 21, 1863, in Chapman, *Bright and Gloomy Days,* 66.

26. Reynolds to Wife, Aug. 9, 1863, Reynolds Papers, DU; Forney Diary, June 16–22, 1863, Wingard-Forney-Vaky Family Papers, Univ. of Illinois at Urbana-Champaign.

27. W. K. to Messrs. Editors, June 21, 1863, *Staunton Spectator,* July 21, 1863; Bender, "Civil War Memories," 296.

28. Hoke, *Reminiscences of the War*, 39; Jacobs, *Notes on the Rebel Invasion*, 11; Schuricht Diary, June 20, 1863, in Schuricht, "Jenkins' Brigade," 345.

29. Private Recruit, "Philadelphia City Cavalry," 283.

30. "Rebel Invasion of Pennsylvania," *Greencastle Pilot*, July 28, 1863.

31. Hege, "Civil War Unvarnished," 19; "Murder of Mr. Strite," *Franklin Repository*, July 15, 1863.

32. OR 27, pt. 2, 442; Hotchkiss Journal, June 19, 1863, in McDonald, *Make Me a Map*, 153.

33. Henrietta B. Lee to My precious Child, June 21, 1863, Goldsborough Family Papers, Special Collections, Library, Shepherd Univ., Shepherdstown, WV.

34. H. Douglas, *I Rode with Stonewall*, 243.

35. Charles A. Rollins, "Going to Gettysburg," *Lexington Gazette and Citizen*, Aug. 9, 1888; Harter, "Diary of John B. Sheets," 3 (June 18, 1863); McKim, *Soldier's Recollections*, 155.

36. Wood, *The War: "Stonewall" Jackson, His Campaigns, and Battles*, 137.

37. John William Ford Hatton, "Memoir, 1861–1865," June 19, 1863, LOC; Rollins, "Going to Gettysburg," *Lexington Gazette and Citizen*, Aug. 9, 1888; Clemens, "'Diary' of John H. Stone," 131 (June 19, 1863); McKim, *Soldier's Recollections*, 155.

38. Extracts from a Diary, June 18, 1863, in Ammen, 116; Extracts from the Diary of J. C. H., June 18, 1863, ibid., 113; Goldsborough, *Maryland Line*, 98; Samuel Thomas McCullough Diary, June 18, 1863, Hotchkiss Papers, LOC.

39. Casper C. Henkel to Dear Cousin, June 21, 1863, Henkel Family Correspondence, Modern Manuscript Collections, History of Medicine Division, U.S. National Library of Medicine, National Institutes of Health, Bethesda, MD.

40. Powell Benton Reynolds to Dear Mother, Aug. 7, 1863, in Dale Whitfield, "Private, Powell Benton Reynolds: Company 'K,' 50th Virginia Volunteer Infantry, C.S.A.," 2011, Lt. Gen. Wade Hampton Camp No. 273 SCV, http://www.wadehamptoncamp.org/aomo711-pbr.html; John Q. A. Nadenbousch to Dear Wife, June 22, 1863, Soldier Letters Collection, ACWM.

41. Brown Journal, in Jones, *Campbell Brown's Civil War*, 196; Hotchkiss Journal, June 19, 1863, in McDonald, *Make Me a Map*, 153.

42. Abram Schultz Miller to Dear Julia, June 19, 1863, James A. Miller Collection, HRL; Edward H. Armstrong to Dear Pa, June 19,1863, Armstrong Papers, UNCW.

43. Miller to Julia, June 19, 1863, Miller Collection, HRL; Alexander Tedford Barclay to Dear Sister, June 19, 1863, Barclay Papers, W&L.

44. Miller to Julia, June 19, 1863, Miller Collection, HRL.

45. Watkins Kearns Diary, June 20, 1863, VHS; Billie to Friend Lizzie, June 21, 1863, Terry Plank Collection, HRL; McCullough Diary, June 20, 1863, Hotchkiss Papers, LOC.

46. George Buswell to Dear Bro., June 24, 1863, Thirty-Third Virginia File, Confederate Regiments Files, GNMP; John M. Vermillion to Dear Kate, June 22, 1863, John D. Chapla Private Collection, Alexandria, VA.

47. Gabriel Shank Diary, June 20, 1863, in Weaver, "Gabriel Shank: Military Records, Articles, and Diary," http://www.rootsweb.ancestry.com/~varockin/shank/Gabriel_Shank.htm; Williams, *Stonewall's Prussian Mapmaker*, 83.

48. George Harlow to Dear Father, Mother, and Family, June 21, 1863, Harlow Family Papers, VHS.

49. Cowan and Metts, "Third Regiment," 194; McKim, *Soldier's Recollections*, 160.

50. Kearns Diary, June 21, 1863, VHS; William H. Proffit to Dear Father, June 22, 1863, Proffit Family Letters, SHC; Ferdinand J. Dunlap to Dear Sister, June 22, 1863, Ferdinand Dunlap Letters, Civil War Miscellaneous Collection, USAHEC.

51. Reed Diary, June 18, 1863, in Reed, *Private in Gray,* 39; Clement A. Evans to My dearest Darling, June 21, 1863, in Stephens, *Intrepid Warrior,* 209–10.

52. OR 27, pt. 2, 440; Jackson to Brother, July 20, 1863, in M. Reed, "Gettysburg Campaign," 186.

53. OR 27, pt. 3, 914; ibid., pt. 2, 550.

54. Goldsborough, *Maryland Line,* 284; Washington Hands, "Civil War Memoirs," 91, UVA; OR 27, pt. 2, 450, 455.

55. Tucker Diary, June 22, 1863, ADAH.

56. Marston Diary, June 22, 1863, Civil War Collection, EU.

57. Blackford to Father, June 22, 1863, Leigh Collection, USAHEC; "Third Alabama Infantry: Letter from Pennsylvania," June 28, 1863, *Mobile Advertiser and Register,* July 20, 1863.

7. "NO SIGNS OF SYMPATHY WITH THE REBELS"

1. Brumbaugh, "Confederate March through Greencastle," 14–15.

2. Charles Hartman Diary, June 22, 1863, Allison-Antrim Museum, Greencastle, PA, typescript; Wilson, "First Fighting in Pennsylvania," 70; "The Advance into Pennsylvania by Gen. Jenkins' Brigade," June 23, 1863, *Richmond Enquirer,* June 30, 1863.

3. Hartman Diary, June 22, 1863, Allison-Antrim Museum.

4. W. Reed, "Death of Corporal Rhial"; Hartman Diary, June 22, 1863, Allison-Antrim Museum; Wilson, "First Fighting in Pennsylvania," 70.

5. *History of Franklin County,* 363, 542–43.

6. OR 27, pt. 2, 551; Hotchkiss Journal, June 23, 1863, in McDonald, *Make Me a Map,* 154; Bond, "Company A, First Maryland Cavalry," 79.

7. W. Green, *Recollections and Reflections,* 173; Leon, *Diary of a Tar Heel,* 32 (June 22, 1863); Edwin R. Sharpe Diary, June 22, 1863, Edwin R. Sharpe Papers, Library and Archives Division, Georgia Historical Society, Savannah.

8. Wood to Parents and Sarah, June 22, 1863, in Wood, "From Montgomery to Gettysburg," 44; Lucius T. C. Lovelace to Dear Father, June 23, 1863, in Davidson, *War Was the Place,* 89; John T. Gay to Dear Pussie, June 23, 1863, Mary Barnard Nix Collection, UGA.

9. Marston Diary, June 22, 1863, Civil War Collection, EU; Blacknall to George, June 23, 1863, Blacknall Papers, Private Collections, NCSA.

10. *History of Franklin County,* 542–43.

11. "Rebel Invasion of Pennsylvania," *Greencastle Pilot,* July 28, 1863; Hoke, *Great Invasion,* 133; Hartman Diary, June 22, 1863, Allison-Antrim Museum; Reid, "Recollections of Lee's Invasion."

12. Lovelace to Father, June 23, 1863, in Davidson, *War Was the Place,* 89–90; Thomas M. Hightower to Dear Lou, June 22, 1863, Thomas M. Hightower Letters, GAM; Gay to Pussie, June 23, 1863, Nix Collection, UGA.

13. "P.W.A. in Maryland," June 27, 1863, in Styple, *Writing and Fighting the Confederate War,* 156.

14. McLachlan, "Civil War Diary of Joseph H. Coit," 252 (June 22, 1863).

15. For a detailed account of the army's slave-hunting policies, see D. Smith, "Race and Retaliation," 137–51.

16. Gorman to Holden, June 22, 1863, *North Carolina Standard,* July 3, 1863.

17. Hatton, "Memoir," June 23, 1863, LOC; William Robert Gwaltney Diary, June 23, 1863, W. R. Gwaltney Papers, SHC; Firebaugh Diary, June 23, 1863, SHC.

18. H. Douglas, *I Rode with Stonewall*, 244.

19. Samuel Thomas McCullough Diary, June 23, 1863, Hotchkiss Papers, LOC; Buswell to Bro., June 24, 1863, Thirty-Third Virginia File, Confederate Regiment Files, GNMP; Albion Martin to My dear Annie, June 23, 1863, "Dr. Albion Martin Letters," hometown.aol.com/Vir33rdreg/am.html (site discontinued; hardcopy in author's possession).

20. Hatton, "Memoir," June 23, 1863, LOC; Daniel, "H. H. Harris Civil War Diary," 1770 (June 23, 1863).

21. Gilmor, *Four Years in the Saddle*, 93–94.

22. "The Rebels in and out of Frederick," *Frederick Examiner*, June 17, 1863; Quynn, *Diary of Jacob Engelbrecht*, 971 (June 20, 1863); Catherine Susannah Thomas Markell Diary, June 20, 1863, Wallace, *Frederick Maryland in Peace and War*, 120. Although dated June 17, 1863, the newspaper issue actually was published sometime after June 23 and contained a detailed account of the attack on the town.

23. "Federal Dash into Frederick Maryland—Loyalty of the Women," June 22, 1863, *Sacramento Daily Union*, June 22, 1863; "The Rebels in and out of Frederick," *Frederick Examiner*, June 17, 1863.

24. Newcomer, *Cole's Cavalry* 51; "The Rebels in and out of Frederick," *Frederick Examiner*, June 17, 1863.

25. Gilmor, *Four Years in the Saddle*, 93–94.

26. Quynn, *Diary of Jacob Engelbrecht*, 971 (June 23, 1863).

27. Gilmor, *Four Years in the Saddle*, 94.

28. Nye, *Here Come the Rebels!*, 267–68; Schuricht Diary, June 21–23, 1863, in Schuricht, "Jenkins' Brigade," 345–46.

29. "The Invasion," *Franklin Repository*, July 15, 1863.

30. Nye, *Here Come the Rebels!*, 267–68; Schuricht Diary, June 21–23, 1863, in Schuricht, "Jenkins' Brigade," 345–46; Daniel D. Gitt, "An Incident of the Battle of Gettysburg," *Gettysburg Star and Sentinel*, July 29, 1883; Emmick, *Defending the Wilderness*, 120–22.

31. Firebaugh Diary, June 24, 1863, SHC; King, *My Experience in the Confederate Army*, 13.

32. OR 27, pt. 2, 503; Busey and Martin, *Regimental Strengths and Losses*, 152.

33. McKim, *Soldier's Recollections*, 163.

34. Gilmor, *Four Years in the Saddle*, 93–94.

35. Schaff Diary, June 24, 1863, in Schaff, "Gettysburg Week," 232; Goldsborough, *Maryland Line*, 101. For details on the town's history, see Woman's Club of Mercersburg, *Old Mercersburg*, 19–71.

36. McCullough Diary, June 24, 1863, Hotchkiss Papers, LOC; Firebaugh Diary, June 24, 1863, SHC; Edward H. Armstrong to Dear Pa, June 29, 1863, Armstrong Papers, UNCW; Gwaltney Diary, June 24, 1863, Gwaltney Papers, SHC.

37. Armstrong to Pa, June 29, 1863, Armstrong Papers, UNCW.

38. Waterman, Watkins, and Co., *History of Bedford, Somerset and Fulton Counties*, 627.

39. Nelson, *Confusion and Courage*, 12–14.

40. Samuel A. Steele to Editor Journal, Nov. 24, 1884, *Huntingdon Journal*, Nov. 28, 1884; Historical Comm. of the Old Home Week Assoc., *Historic Huntingdon*, 138.

41. Regimental Committee, *History of the One Hundred and Twenty-Fifth Regiment Pennsylvania Volunteers*, 196.

42. Extracts from a Diary, June 24, 1863, in Ammen, 116.

43. Steele to Editor, Nov. 24, 1884, *Huntingdon Journal*, Nov. 28, 1884.

44. James Pott letter, reprinted in Albert M. Rung, "Confusion and Courage at North Mountain," *Huntingdon Daily News,* Aug. 31, 1963.

45. Steele to Editor, Nov. 24, 1884, *Huntingdon Journal,* Nov. 28, 1884.

46. Gilmor, *Four Years in the Saddle,* 94; Whitfield Kisling to Dear Cousin, June 25, 1863, Whitield Kisling Letters, Soldier Letters Collection, ACWM; J. William Thomas Diary, June 24, 1863, Library, Fredericksburg and Spotsylvania National Military Park, Fredericksburg, VA; Steele to Editor, Nov. 24, 1884, *Huntingdon (PA) Journal,* Nov. 28, 1884.

47. John H. Black to Dear Jennie, July 1, 1863, in Coles and Engle, *Yankee Horseman in the Shenandoah Valley,* 46.

48. Steele to Editor, Nov. 24, 1884, *Huntingdon (PA) Journal,* Nov. 28, 1884.

49. Koonce, *Doctor to the Front,* 97.

50. Gilmor, *Four Years in the Saddle,* 94.

51. "McConnellsburg Taken," *Fulton Democrat,* July 10, 1863.

52. Extracts from a Diary, June 24, 1863, in Ammen, 116; Lyons Diary, June 24, 1863, MHS; Kisling to Cousin, June 25, 1863, Soldier Letters Collection, ACWM.

53. Extracts from a Diary, June 24, 1863, in Ammen, 116; Extracts from the Diary of J. C. H., June 18, 1863, ibid., 113.

54. Gilmor, *Four Years in the Saddle,* 94; "McConnellsburg Taken," *Fulton Democrat,* July 10, 1863.

55. T. and J. Greathead Claim, in Cordell, "Civil War Damage Claims," 20; W. S. Fletcher Claim, ibid., 17; S. E. Duffield Claim, ibid., 15; Henry M. Hoke Claim, ibid., 23.

56. Kisling to Cousin, June 25, 1863, Soldier Letters Collection, ACWM; Extracts from a Diary, June 24, 1863, in Ammen, 116; Firebaugh Diary, June 25, 1863, SHC.

57. Kisling to Cousin, June 25, 1863, Soldier Letters Collection, ACWM; Casper Henkel to Dear Cousin, July 12, 1863, in Henkel, "Letter Delivered after Many Years," 407.

58. Gilmor, *Four Years in the Saddle,* 94; George Finiff Claim, in Cordell, "Civil War Damage Claims," 16; John B. Patterson Claim, ibid., 30.

59. John Futch to My Dear & loving Wife, June 29, 1863, Futch Papers, Private Collections, NCSA; Gabriel Shank to Dear Annie, June 29, 1863, in Weaver, "Gabriel Shank: Military Records, Articles, Letters, and Diary," http://www.rootsweb.ancestry.com/~varockin/shank /Gabriel_Shank.htm.

60. Hiram Kibler to unknown "Miss," July 18, 1863, Hiram Kibler Letter, Pearce Museum, Navarro College, Corsicana, TX; Casper Henkel to Dear Cousin Maggie, July 21, 1863, Henkel Family Correspondence, U.S. National Library of Medicine.

61. Kisling to Cousin, June 25, 1863, Soldier Letters Collection, ACWM.

62. Extracts from a Diary, June 25, 1863, in Ammen, 116.

63. Gilmor, *Four Years in the Saddle,* 95; Hoke, *Great Invasion,* 152, 178; McKim, *Soldier's Recollections,* 165.

64. Hoke, *Great Invasion,* 179; Hoke, *Reminiscences of the War,* 57.

65. William McCandlish Diary, June 27–29, 1863, in William McCandlish, "Newville in War Times: From a Boy's Journal," Reed Scrapbook, Newville Historical Society, Newville, PA; Zenas J. Gray, "Camp Curtin Then, Camp Curtin Now: Reminiscences of War Time as Seen by a Boy," ibid.; Martha B. Munn to My Dear Granddaughter Martha Jane, Mar. 1929, in Martha B. Munn, "Civil War Days," Civil War Collection Files, Cumberland County Historical Society, Carlisle, PA; John Lefever Diary, June 29, 1863, ibid.

66. Hoke, *Great Invasion,* 179; Hoke, *Reminiscences of the War,* 57; Gilmor, *Four Years in the Saddle,* 95.

8. "GOING BACK INTO THE UNION"

1. Hudgins, "With the 38th Georgia Regiment," 161.

2. Kincheloe Diary, June 22, 1863, in Hale and Phillips, *History of the Forty-Ninth Virginia Infantry*, 72; White, "Diary of the War," 195 (June 22, 1863).

3. Clement A. Evans to My dearest Darling, June 23, 1863, in Stephens, *Intrepid Warrior*, 210; Seymour Journal, June 23, 1863, in Jones, *Civil War Memoirs of Captain William J. Seymour*, 64.

4. Hudgins, "With the 38th Georgia Regiment," 161; Agee, "Battle of Gettysburg."

5. Robert Sherrard Bell Diary, June 22, 1863, Old Courthouse Civil War Museum, Winchester, VA; John Henry Vest Diary, June 22, 1863, Soldier Diaries Collection, ACWM; J. A. Early, *Autobiographical Sketch*, 254.

6. OR 27, pt. 2, 463; Jubal A. Early to Henry B. McClellan, Feb. 2, 1878, Jubal A. Early Papers, LOC.

7. Krick, *Lee's Colonels*, 145; James H. Hodam, "Biographical Sketches," in Kesterson, *Campaigning with the 17th Virginia Cavalry*, 307.

8. Jackson to Brother, July 20, 1863, in M. Reed, "Gettysburg Campaign," 186.

9. William Britton Bailey Diary, June 22, 1863, Harrisburg Civil War Round Table Collection, USAHEC; Osborne Wilson Diary, June 23, 1863, in Morton, *History of Highland County Virginia*, 137.

10. Evans Diary, June 22, 1863, in Stephens, *Intrepid Warrior*, 204; Kincheloe Diary, June 22, 1863, in Hale and Phillips, *History of the Forty-Ninth Virginia Infantry*, 72–73; Hotchkiss Diary, June 22, 1863, in McDonald, *Make Me a Map*, 154.

11. P. Johnson, *Under the Southern Cross*, 120.

12. Joseph H. Truitt to Dear Parents, June 22, 1863, quoted in White, *History of the 31st Georgia Volunteer Infantry*, 84.

13. Kincheloe Diary, June 23, 1863, in Hale and Phillips, *History of the Forty-Ninth Virginia Infantry*, 72; Pierson, "Diary of Bartlett Yancey Malone," 36 (June 23, 1863).

14. Samuel W. Eaton Diary, June 23, 1863, Samuel W. Eaton Papers, SHC.

15. Pierson, "Diary of Bartlett Yancey Malone," 36 (June 23, 1863); Jackson to Brother, July 20, 1863, in M. Reed, "Gettysburg Campaign," 186.

16. For details on the town's history, see Dorsett, *Waynesboro as We Knew It*, 1–92.

17. Stoner, *Historical Papers*, 370.

18. Mayo Diary, June 23, 1863, HL; Agee, "Battle of Gettysburg."

19. Bender, "Civil War Memories," 297.

20. Evans Diary, June 23, 1863, in Stephens, *Intrepid Warrior*, 204; Kincheloe Diary, June 24, 1863, in Hale and Phillips, *History of the Forty-Ninth Virginia Infantry*, 73.

21. J. Arthur Taylor to My Dear Father, July 9, 1863, *Richmond Daily Whig*, July 23, 1863.

22. Bender, "Civil War Memories," 297.

23. Stoner, *Historical Papers*, 370–71.

24. Seymour Journal, June 23, 1863, in Jones, *Civil War Memoirs of Captain William J. Seymour*, 64; Mayo Diary, June 23, 1863, HL.

25. Stoner, *Historical Papers*, 369.

26. Bender, "Civil War Memories," 297.

27. "Our Army in Pennsylvania," July 19, 1863, *Mobile Advertiser and Register*, Aug. 9, 1863; William D. Lyon to Dear Brother George, July 18, 1863, William D. Lyon Papers, Pearce Museum, Navarro College, Corsicana, TX.

28. Bailey Diary, June 23, 1863, Harrisburg Civil War Round Table Collection, USAHEC; "Our Army in Pennsylvania," July 19, 1863, *Mobile Advertiser and Register,* Aug. 9, 1863; Dietrich, "Waynesboro in Civil War Days," 18; Forney Diary, June 23, 1863, Wingard-Forney-Vaky Family Papers, Univ. of Illinois at Urbana-Champaign.

29. Dietrich, "Waynesboro in Civil War Days," 13–14; Stoner, *Historical Papers, 375.*

30. Dietrich, "Waynesboro in Civil War Days," 32; Stoner, *Historical Papers,* 369.

31. Stoner, *Historical Papers,* 372.

32. Hodam, "From Potomac to Susquehanna," 78; Seymour Journal, June 23, 1863, in Jones, *Civil War Memoirs of Captain William J. Seymour,* 64.

33. Stoner, *Historical Papers,* 371.

34. Taylor to Father, July 9, 1863, *Richmond Daily Whig,* July 23, 1863.

35. Clement A. Evans to My dear Darling, June 25, 1863, in Stephens, *Intrepid Warrior,* 218; John Brown Gordon to My Own Precious Wife, June 23, 1863, John Brown Gordon Family Papers, UGA.

36. Jackson to Brother, July 20, 1863, in M. Reed, "Gettysburg Campaign," 186; Truitt to Parents, June 22, 1863, quoted in White, *History of the 31st Georgia Volunteer Infantry,* 84; Stoner, *Historical Papers,* 371. Although dated June 22, the Truitt letter contains details indicating that he finished writing it several days later.

37. Bender, "Civil War Memories," 298.

38. Jackson to Brother, July 20, 1863, in M. Reed, "Gettysburg Campaign," 186–87.

39. Stoner, *Historical Papers,* 369–70.

40. Dietrich, "Waynesboro in Civil War Days," 18.

41. "Letter from Ewell's Corps," June 25, 1863, *Savanah Republican,* July 6, 1863.

42. Bailey Diary, June 23, 1863, Harrisburg Civil War Round Table Collection, USAHEC.

43. Cartland, *Southern Heroes,* 236–37.

44. Stoner, *Historical Papers,* 370; Bender, "Civil War Memories," 298.

45. Evans to Darling, June 23, 1863, in Stephens, *Intrepid Warrior,* 212.

9. "THESE PEOPLE CERTAINLY MUST HAVE LIVED LIKE LORDS"

1. Francis M. Parker to My dear Wife, June 23, 1863, in Taylor, *To Drive the Enemy,* 289; David R. E. Winn to My Darling Wife, June 26, 1863, David Read Evans Winn Papers, EU.

2. Lovelace to Father, June 23, 1863, in Davidson, *War Was the Place,* 89.

3. Daniel, "H. H. Harris Civil War Diary," 1770 (June 24, 1863); Henry Roach to My Dear Sue, July 22, 1863, Almira Sue Browning Harvey Letters, LOV; William A. Smith to My Dear Loved Sunshine, June 24, 1863, William Adolphus Smith Papers, Littlefield Southern History Collection, Dolph Briscoe Center for American History, Univ. of Texas at Austin, John Garibaldi to Dear Wife, July 19, 1863, Garibaldi Papers, VMI.

4. OR 27, pt. 3, 912–13.

5. For discussions of Lee's motives for the orders, see Woodward, *Under a Northern Sky,* 27–28; Guelzo, *Gettysburg,* 74–75; Freeman, *Robert E. Lee,* 3:54–57.

6. Park, "War Diary," 12 (June 24, 1863).

7. John A. Stikeleather, "Memoirs," 38, Military Collections, NCSA; Jeremiah Tate to Dear Ma, June 28, 1863, Tate Letters, GLIAH.

8. Eugene Blackford to Dear Mother, June 28, 1863, Leigh Collection, USAHEC; Gorman to Holden, June 22, 1863, *North Carolina Standard,* July 3, 1863.

9. Sidney J. Richardson to Dear Mother and Father, June 23, 1863, Richardson Papers, GAM; Hightower to Lou, June 22, 1863, Hightower Letters, ibid.; Oliver E. Mercer to Dear Brother, June 26, 1863, in Wyatt, *Reeves, Mercer, Newkirk Families,* 273.

10. Fleming Saunders to My Dear Mother, [June 25, 1863], Saunders Family Papers, VHS; Sheetz to Brother, June 28, 1863, Second Virginia File, Confederate Regiment Files, GNMP; Buswell to Bro., June 24, 1863, Thirty-Third Virginia File, ibid.

11. John L. Hubbard to Uncle, July 19, 1863, Allan Tischler Collection, HRL.

12. J. B. Oliver, "My Recollections of the Battle of Gettysburg," 1, Military Collections, NCSA.

13. "The Destruction of Darien, Georgia," *Athens Enquirer,* June 23, 1863.

14. Asbury Hull Jackson to Dear Sister, June 23, 1863, Harden Papers, DU.

15. Thomas Henry Carter to My precious Wife, June 25, 1863, in Dozier, *Gunner in Lee's Army,* 196.

16. James Garland Pollard to Dear Brother, Sept. 5, 1863, John Garland Pollard Papers, Special Collections, Earl Greg Swem Library, College of William and Mary, Williamsburg, VA.

17. Winn to Wife, June 26, 1863, Winn Papers, EU.

18. Abram Schultz Miller to Dear Julia, June 25, 1863, Miller Collection, HRL.

19. Garibaldi to Wife, July 19, 1863, Garibaldi Papers, VMI.

20. Pettit to Wife, June 25, 1863, in Turner, *Civil War Letters,* 126.

21. Kearns Diary, June 24, 1863, VHS.

22. Gorman to Holden, June 22, 1863, *North Carolina Standard,* July 3, 1863; Gorman to Wife and Mother, July 8, 1863, *Raleigh Daily Progress,* July 22, 1863.

23. Blackford to Mother, June 28, 1863, Leigh Collection, USAHEC; G. Campbell Brown to Dear Sister and Mother, June 25, 1863, in Jones, *Campbell Brown's Civil War,* 229.

24. OR 27, pt. 2, 550–51; Richard S. Ewell to Dear Lizzie, June 24, 1863, in D. Pfanz, *Letters of General Richard S. Ewell,* 245.

25. Hayes, *Civil War Diary of Father James Sheeran,* 187 (June 27, 1863).

26. Alexander S. Pendleton to Kate Corbin, June 23, 1863, Pendleton Papers, SHC; Alexander S. Pendleton to Dear Mother, June 25, 1863, ibid.

27. Hoke, *Great Invasion,* 138–43; OR 27, pt. 3, 912–13.

28. White, "Diary of the War," 198 (June 26, 1863); Kearns Diary, June 28, 1863, VHS.

29. Blackford to Mother, June 28, 1863, Leigh Collection, USAHEC; Tate to Ma, June 28, 1863, Tate Letters, GLIAH.

30. A North Carolinian to Mr. Editor, July 10, 1863, *Wilmington Daily Journal,* July 17, 1863.

31. Coddington and Coddington, "Prelude to Gettysburg," 124–27.

32. "From the Forty-Third Reg't N.C.T.," July 20, 1863, *North Carolina Argus,* July 30, 1863.

33. J. W. B. to Editor, Aug. 12, 1863, *Augusta Weekly Chronicle and Sentinel,* Sept. 5, 1863; OR 27, pt. 2, 443, 550.

34. Williams, *Stonewall's Prussian Mapmaker,* 84.

35. Medicus M. Ward to Dear Ma and Pa, July 7, 1863, *Raleigh Weekly State Journal,* July 22, 1863; Isaac Reynolds to Dear Wife, July 20, 1863, Reynolds Papers, DU.

36. Harris, *Autobiography,* 91–92; W. P. Snakenberg, "The Civil War Memoirs of Private W. P. Snakenberg, Company K, 14th Louisiana Infantry Regiment," pt. 5, *Amite News Digest,* Oct. 3, 1984; "From the Fourth North Carolina," July 8, 1863, *Carolina Watchman,* July 27, 1863, in Munson, *Confederate Correspondent,* 89.

37. Charles S. Batchelor to My Dear Father, Oct, 18, 1863, Second Louisiana File, Confederate Regiment Files, GNMP; "The Invasion of Pennsylvania," *Macon Daily Telegraph,* July

21, 1863. For similar comments, see Thomas G. Read to Dear Wife, July 11, 1863, Read Family Correspondence, Rare Books and Special Collections, Univ. of Notre Dame, Notre Dame, IN; Algernon Joyner to Parents, July 30, 1863, Joyner Family Papers, SHC; and Oliver, "My Recollections," 1, Military Collections, NCSA.

38. Hufham, "Gettysburg," 451–52.

39. Watkins, *Notes on the Movement of the 14th North Carolina,* 14; Smith, *Anson Guards,* 200.

40. Brown to Sister and Mother, June 25, 1863, in Jones, *Campbell Brown's Civil War,* 229; Joseph J. Felder to Dear Pa, June 28, 1863, Lavender R. Ray Papers, GAM.

41. Seaton Gales to Dear Wife, July 8, 1863, Gales Papers, Private Collections, NCSA.

42. Eugene Blackford to Dear Father, June 28, 1863, Leigh Collection, USAHEC.

43. George Whitaker Wills to My Dear Sister, June 28, 1863, Wills Letters, SHC; John F. Christian to Mother, June 24, 1863, *Alabama Beacon,* July 10, 1863.

44. Gay to Pussie, June 23, 1863, Nix Collection, UGA.

45. Leon, *Diary of a Tar Heel,* 32 (June 23, 1863).

46. Blackford to Mother, June 28, 1863, Leigh Collection, USAHEC.

47. Abner E. McGarity to Dearest Tinie, July 16, 1863, in Burnett, "Letters of a Confederate Surgeon," 162; Addison Smith to Dear Sister, Sept. 8, 1863, in Kesterson, *Campaigning with the 17th Virginia Cavalry,* 270.

48. White, "Diary of the War," 198 (June 26, 1863); Hightower to Lou, June 22, 1863, Hightower Letters, GAM; "Our Northern Campaign: Notes from the Diary of Capt. J. B. R—No. 3," *Countryman,* Nov. 10, 1863.

49. William Gaston Lewis to My Dear Mitte, June 28, 1863, Lewis Papers, SHC; Pickens Diary, June 26, 1863, in Hubbs, *Voices from Company D,* 180; William E. Calder to Dear Mother, June 26, 1863, Calder Family Papers, SHC.

50. McGarity to Tinie, July 16, 1863, in Burnett, "Letters of a Confederate Surgeon," 162.

51. Carter to Wife, June 25, 1863, in Dozier, *Gunner in Lee's Army,* 195.

52. "From the Forty-Third Reg't. N.C.T.," July 20, 1863, *North Carolina Argus,* July 30, 1863; Leonidas L. Polk to Dear Wife, June 28, 1863, L. L. Polk Papers, SHC.

53. Gorman to Holden, June 22, 1863, *North Carolina Standard,* July 3, 1863.

54. Guelzo, *Gettysburg,* 78–79; Isaac Trimble to John Bachelder, Feb. 8, 1883, in Ladd and Ladd, *Bachelder Papers,* 2:925–26.

10. "NO ARMY EVER FARED BETTER"

1. Mohr, *Cormany Diaries,* 333–34 (June 23, 1863); Bowers, "William Heyser's Diary," 76 (June 23, 1863).

2. Nye, *Here Come the Rebels!,* 250.

3. Hoke, *Reminiscences of the War,* 46.

4. "The Rebel Invasion," *Valley Spirit,* July 8, 1863.

5. Reeves to Lizzie, July 4, 1863, Coco Collection, GNMP.

6. Hoke, *Great Invasion,* 132–33.

7. Mohr, *Cormany Diaries,* 333–34 (June 23, 1863).

8. Bowers, "William Heyser's Diary," 76 (June 23, 1863).

9. Thomas, *History of the Doles-Cook Brigade,* 7; "The Rebel Invasion," *Valley Spirit,* July 8, 1863.

10. *History of Franklin County,* 451–52.

11. Furlow Diary, June 17–29, 1863, in Furlow, "Record of Current Events," 44, Diaries Miscellaneous Collection, YU; J. W. B. to Editor, Aug. 12, 1863, *Augusta Weekly Chronicle and Sentinel,* Sept. 5, 1863.

12. Reeves to Lizzie, July 4, 1863, Coco Collection, GNMP.

13. John S. Apperson Diary, June 25, 1863, in Roper, *Repairing the "March of Mars,"* 477.

14. Purifoy, "With Ewell and Rodes in Pennsylvania," 463.

15. Leon, *Diary of a Tar Heel,* 33 (June 24, 1863); Furlow Diary, June 17–29, 1863, in Furlow, "Record of Current Events," 44, Diaries Miscellaneous Collection, YU; John C. Gorman to Dear Mother, June 25, 1863, Gorman Family Collection, North Carolina Collection, Durham County Library, Durham, NC; Gorman to Mother and Wife, July 8, 1863, *Raleigh Daily Progress,* July 22, 1863.

16. J. W. B. to Editor, Aug. 12, 1863, *Augusta Weekly Chronicle and Sentinel,* Sept. 5, 1863; Furlow Diary, June 17–29, 1863, in Furlow, "Record of Current Events," 44, Diaries Miscellaneous Collection, YU; Apperson Diary, June 25, 1863, in Roper, *Repairing the "March of Mars,"* 477.

17. Bowers, "William Heyser's Diary," 77 (June 24, 1863).

18. Reeves to Lizzie, July 4, 1863, Coco Collection, GNMP; Hoke, *Reminiscences of the War,* 54.

19. Love, "War as a Girl Saw It."

20. "The Rebel Invasion," *Valley Spirit,* July 8, 1863.

21. Hoke, *Great Invasion,* 136.

22. Nye, *Here Come the Rebels!,* 267–68; Jacob Shirk to Dear Cosen, July 8, 1863, "Jacob Shirk Letter after the Battle of Gettysburg," Letters from the Civil War, Shippensburg Digital History Museum, http://webspace.ship.edu/jqbao/ShipMuseum/page26/page29/page59/page59.html.

23. Kearns Diary, June 24, 1863, VHS; Williams to Pa, June 28, 1863, Williams Papers, UVA.

24. Robert W. Hunter to My Precious Sister, June 24, 1863, Second Virginia File, Confederate Regiment Files, GNMP; Vest Diary, June 24, 1863, Soldier Diaries Collection, ACWM.

25. Hoke, *Reminiscences of the War,* 47–48; Beck, *Third Alabama!,* 80–81.

26. "The Rebel Invasion," *Valley Spirit,* July 8, 1863.

27. Calder to Mother, June 26, 1863, Calder Family Papers, SHC; Brown Journal, in Jones, *Campbell Brown's Civil War,* 200.

28. Hoke, *Reminiscences of the War,* 49.

29. "The Rebel Invasion," *Valley Spirit,* July 8, 1863.

30. Bowers, "William Heyser's Diary," 77–78 (June 24, 25, 1863).

31. Hoke, *Reminiscences of the War,* 49; "The Rebel Invasion," *Valley Spirit,* July 8, 1863.

32. Reeves to Lizzie, July 4, 1863, Coco Collection, GNMP.

33. Jedediah Hotchkiss to Dear Wife, June 24, 1863, Hotchkiss Papers, LOC.

34. Foltz, "Notable Publication House in Chambersburg," 191.

35. Hoke, *Reminiscences of the War,* 50.

36. Hotchkiss to Wife, June 24, 1863, Hotchkiss Papers, LOC.

37. Williams to Pa, June 28, 1868, Williams Papers, UVA; Saunders to Mother, [June 25, 1863], Saunders Family Papers, VHS.

38. "Third Alabama Infantry, Letter from Pennsylvania," June 28, 1863, *Mobile Daily Advertiser and Register,* July 20, 1863.

39. "The Rebel Invasion," *Valley Spirit,* July 8, 1863; Bowers, "William Heyser's Diary," 78 (June 24, 1863).

NOTES TO PAGES 156–163

40. Hoke, *Great Invasion,* 156.

41. "The Invasion," *Franklin Repository,* July 15, 1863.

42. Bowers, "William Heyser's Diary," 78 (June 25, 1863); Mohr, *Cormany Diaries,* 334 (June 25, 1863).

43. Apperson Diary, June 25, 1863, in Roper, *Repairing the "March of Mars,"* 475–76.

44. Hotchkiss to Wife, June 24, 1863, Hotchkiss Papers, LOC.

45. Hoke, *Reminiscences of the War,* 49.

46. Harris to Burton, Aug. 24, 1863, in Taylor, "Ramseur's Brigade in the Gettysburg Campaign," 32; Ardrey Diary, June 25, 1863, Ardrey Papers, DaCol; Ewell to Lizzie, June 24, 1863, in D. Pfanz, *Letters of General Richard S. Ewell,* 245.

47. Hege, "Civil War Unvarnished," 19.

48. Hunsecker, "Civil War Reminiscences," 406–7.

49. Jacob Stouffer to Mary R. Stouffer, July 5, 1863, in H. Green, *Pages from a Diary,* 19.

50. J. A. Rohrer to Benjamin A. Hoover, Jan. 21, 1928, Benjamin Hoover II Private Collection, York, PA.

51. Greenwalt S. Barr Claim, Pennsylvania Civil War Border Claims, PSA; Jacob Hargbroad Claim, ibid.

52. Jacob Stouffer to Mary R. Stouffer, July 5, 1863, in H. Green, *Pages from a Diary,* 19; Christian Bitner Claim, Pennsylvania Civil War Border Claims, PSA; Reeves to Lizzie, July 4, 1863, Coco Collection, GNMP.

53. "The Rebel Invasion," *Valley Spirit,* July 8, 1863.

54. Eunice Stewart to Dear Parents, June 24, 1863, quoted in Bartek, "Rhetoric of Destruction," 62 (http://uknowledge.uky.edu/gradschool_diss/110/).

55. Quoted in Daihl, "Shippensburg, 1863," 369–70.

56. "Excerpts from the Diary of J. C. Atticks, Shippensburg, Penna.; during June and July 1863," June 24, 1863, Civil War Times Illustrated Collection, USAHEC. This is a reference to Shippensburg druggist John C. Altick.

57. Sharpe, "A Boy's Experience," 164.

58. OR 27, pt. 2, 565–66; Hands, "Civil War Memoirs," 93, UVA.

59. Leon, *Diary of a Tar Heel,* 33 (June 24, 1863); OR 27, pt. 2, 566; Green Diary, June 25, 1863, Private Collections, NCSA.

60. Eunice Stewart to Dear Parents, June 26, 1863, quoted in Bartek, "Rhetoric of Destruction," 62–63. Indian Spring is modern Dykeman Spring.

61. *History of Cumberland and Adams Counties,* 257–62; Pickens Diary, June 26, 1863, in Hubbs, *Voices from Company D,* 180.

62. "The Situation," *Harrisburg Daily Patriot and Union,* June 29, 1863; "A Scouting Party from Carlisle Captured," *Philadelphia Daily Press,* June 29, 1863.

63. Stewart to Parents, June 26, 1863, quoted in Bartek, "Rhetoric of Destruction," 62–63.

64. John Stumbaugh to My Dear Son, July 9, 1863, Harrisburg Civil War Round Table Collection, USAHEC.

65. "Excerpts from the Diary of J. C. Atticks," June 25–26, 1863, Civil War Times Illustrated Collection, ibid.; Daihl, "Shippensburg, 1863," 370–71.

66. Burkhardt, *Shippensburg, Pennsylvania in the Civil War,* 19, 25–27; Nye, *Here Come the Rebels!,* 302.

67. George Eyster to Dear John, July 8, 1863, Moore Papers, Rosenbach Museum and Library.

68. Hugh Craig to Dear Jennie, July 13, 1863, ibid.

69. "Our Northern Campaign: Notes from the Diary of J. B. R.—No. 3," *Countryman,* Nov. 10, 1863; Pickens Diary, June 26, 1863, in Hubbs, *Voices from Company D,* 180; Marston Diary, June 26, 1863, Civil War Collection, EU; Daniel, "H. H. Harris Civil War Diary," 1770 (June 26, 1863).

70. Green Diary, June 26, 1863, Private Collections, NCSA; Ardrey Diary, June 27, 1863, Ardrey Papers, DaCol; Apperson Diary, June 27, 1863, in Roper, *Repairing the "March of Mars,"* 479.

71. Mercer to Brother, June 26, 1863, in Wyatt, *Reeves, Mercer, Newkirk Families,* 273.

11. "ENOUGH TO FRIGHTEN US ALL TO DEATH"

1. OR 27, pt. 2, 464; Bender, "Civil War Memories," 298.

2. Bailey Diary, June 24, 1863, Harrisburg Civil War Round Table Collection, USAHEC.

3. John J. English to Dear Aunt and Uncle, July 9, 1863, in Julia Spicer, comp., "Aftermath of Gettysburg: Letters of John J. English," 1999, 6th North Carolina State Troops, Morrisville Civil War Battlefield Preservation, http://www.mindspring.com/~nixnox/english html (site discontinued; hardcopy in author's possession); Truitt to Parents, June 22, 1863, quoted in White, *History of the 31st Georgia Volunteer Infantry,* 84.

4. Evans Diary, June 24, 1863, in Stephens, *Intrepid Warrior,* 214–15.

5. Kincheloe Diary, June 23, 1863, in Hale and Phillips, *History of the Forty-Ninth Virginia Infantry,* 72; Nichols, *Soldier's Story,* 115.

6. Marcus Hefner to Dear Wife, July 19, 1863, Marcus Hefner Papers, Private Collections, NCSA; Reuben Allen Pierson to Dear Father, July 19, 1863, in Cutrer and Parrish, *Brothers in Gray,* 202–3.

7. Gordon, *Reminiscences,* 141; Eaton Diary, June 24, 1863, Eaton Papers, SHC.

8. Hefner to Wife, July 19, 1863, Hefner Papers, Private Collections, NCSA.

9. "Gordon's Brigade in the Late Campaign," July 20, 1863, *Savannah Republican,* Aug. 6, 1863.

10. J. A. Early, *Autobiographical Sketch,* 254–55.

11. Evans to Darling, June 25, 1863, in Stephens, *Intrepid Warrior,* 218; Seymour Journal, June 25, 1863, in Jones, *Civil War Memoirs of Captain William J. Seymour,* 65.

12. Joseph C. Snider Diary, June 23–25, 1863, "Joseph C. Snider's Journal of the Civil War, 1861–1864," Personal Papers Collection, LOC.

13. OR 27, pt. 2, 307, 464–65; J. A. Early, *Autobiographical Sketch,* 254–55.

14. Myers, *The Comanches,* 192; Joseph H. Trundle to Dear Sister, July 7, 1863, in Trundle, "Gettysburg Described in Two Letters," 211.

15. OR 27, pt. 2, 465; J. A. Early, *Autobiographical Sketch,* 255.

16. Hoke, *Great Invasion,* 170–71.

17. "Burning of Steven's Furnace," *Franklin Repository,* July 15, 1863; Nye, *Here Come the Rebels!,* 270.

18. Seymour Journal, June 24, 1863, in Jones, *Civil War Memoirs of Captain William J. Seymour,* 64–65; P. Johnson, *Under the Southern Cross,* 122; Hodam, "From Potomac to Susquehanna," 78.

19. J. A. Early, *Autobiographical Sketch,* 256; Hoke, *Great Invasion,* 170–71; Seymour Journal, June 24, 1863, in Jones, *Civil War Memoirs of Captain William J. Seymour,* 65.

20. J. A. Early, *Autobiographical Sketch,* 256.

21. Hoke, *Great Invasion,* 92.

22. Wingert, *Emergency Men!*, 60–98.

23. Quoted in ibid., 70; Myers, *The Comanches*, 192–93; J. A. Early, *Autobiographical Sketch*, 257–58.

24. "Diary of Abraham Essick (1849–1864; 1883; 1888), June 26, 1863, Franklin County Personal Papers, *The Valley of the Shadow,* Univ. of Virginia Library, http://valley.lib.virginia.edu/papers/FD1005.

25. Alleman, *At Gettysburg,* 22; Jacobs, *Notes on the Rebel Invasion,* 15.

26. Broadhead, *Diary of a Lady,* 3; Gates D. Fahnestock, "Speech before the National Arts Club of New York, February 14, 1934," Adams County Historical Society, Gettysburg, PA.

27. Neely, "John Charles Wills: Reminiscences," 29.

28. Mingus, *Flames beyond Gettysburg,* 118–19.

29. Eizabeth Thorn, "Woman, Keeper of Cemetery in 1863, Describes Battle," *Gettysburg Times,* July 2, 1938.

30. Wingert, *Emergency Men!,* 96; Private Recruit, "Philadelphia City Cavalry," 286.

31. OR 27, pt. 2, 465.

32. Hodam, "From Potomac to Susquehanna," 79; Hodam, *Journal of James H. Hodam,* 69.

33. Seymour Journal, June 26, 1863, in Jones, *Civil War Memoirs of Captain William J. Seymour,* 65; Sue King Black to Bell Miller Willard, n.d., Adams County Historical Society, Gettysburg, PA.

34. Hodam, "From Potomac to Susquehanna," 79; Hodam, "The Hodam Manuscript," 288.

35. Seymour Journal, June 26, 1863, in Jones, *Civil War Memoirs of Captain William J. Seymour,* 65.

36. P. Johnson, *Under the Southern Cross,* 122; Margaretta Kendlehart McCartney, "A Story of Early's Raid: When the Confederates First Arrived in Gettysburg, the Experiences of a Young Girl on the Night of June 26, 1863," *Gettysburg Compiler,* June 30, 1923; Buehler, *Recollections of the Rebel Invasion,* 10.

37. P. Johnson, *Under the Southern Cross,* 122–23.

38. David Kendlehart to General Early, June 26, 1863, in *History of Cumberland and Adams Counties,* 358.

39. J. A. Early, *Autobiographical Sketch,* 258; McCreary, "Gettysburg: A Boy's Experience," 244; Murdoch, "Catherine Mary White Foster's Eyewitness Account of the Battle of Gettysburg," 48.

40. Buehler, *Recollections of the Rebel Invasion,* 11.

41. Jackson to Brother, July 20, 1863, in M. Reed, "Gettysburg Campaign," 185; Bradwell, "Burning of Wrightsville," 300.

42. "The Rebels in Gettysburg," *Gettysburg Compiler,* June 29, 1863; Alleman, *At Gettysburg,* 22; "Diary of Abraham Essick," June 26, 1863, http://valley.lib.virginia.cdu/papers/FD1005.

43. "The Rebels in Gettysburg," *Gettysburg Compiler,* June 29, 1863; Evans Diary, June 26, 1863, in Stephens, *Intrepid Warrior,* 220; Clement Evans to My Dear darling, July 4, 1863, ibid.

44. Jordan, "'Remembrance Will Cling to Us through Life,'" 6.

45. Thorn, "Woman, Keeper of Cemetery in 1863, Describes Battle," *Gettysburg Times,* July 2, 1938.

46. Salome Myers Diary, June 26, 1863, Rodgers, *Ties of the Past,* 161; Buehler, *Recollections of the Rebel Invasion,* 12.

47. Herbert, "In Occupied Pennsylvania," 104–5.

48. Fastnacht, *Memories of the Battle of Gettysburg,* 3.

49. Broadhead, *Diary of a Lady*, 9.

50. J. A. Early, *Autobiographical Sketch*, 257–58; Nye, "First Battle of Gettysburg," 16.

51. Lydia Catherine Ziegler Clare, "A Gettysburg Girl's Story of the Great Battle," Adams County Historical Society, Gettysburg, PA.

52. C. Johnson, *Battleground Adventures*, 192.

53. Neely, "John Charles Wills: Reminiscences," 32.

54. OR 27, pt. 2, 465.

55. "The Rebels in Gettysburg," *Gettysburg Compiler*, June 29, 1863; Aaron Sheely, "The Battle of Gettysburg," ibid., Jan. 23, 1900.

56. Thorn, "Woman, Keeper of Cemetery in 1863, Describes Battle," *Gettysburg Times*, July 2, 1938; Horn, *Memoirs of Henry Eyster Jacobs*, 52; Buehler, *Recollections of the Rebel Invasion*, 13.

57. Sarah Barrett King, "Battle Days in 1863," *Gettysburg Compiler*, July 4, 1906.

58. Broadhead, *Diary of a Lady*, 9; McCreary, "Gettysburg: A Boy's Experience," 244.

12. "OUR ARMY LEFT A MARK EVERYWHERE IT WENT"

1. Seymour Journal, June 27, 1863, in Jones, *Civil War Memoirs of Captain William J. Seymour*, 65.

2. Jackson to Brother, July 20, 1863, in M. Reed, "Gettysburg Campaign," 187.

3. Mingus *Flames beyond Gettysburg*, 152–53.

4. "Our Army in Pennsylvania," July 18, 1863, *Mobile Advertiser and Register*, Aug. 9, 1863; Pierson to Father, July 19, 1863, in Cutrer and Parrish, *Brothers in Gray*, 204.

5. Lyon to George, July 18, 1863, Lyon Papers, Navarro College; Mathews, "'Wright's Legion.'"

6. Stiles, *Four Years under Marse Robert*, 200.

7. John A. McPherson to Dear Sir, Aug. 3, 1863, Avery Family of North Carolina Papers, SHC.

8. Joseph H. Hilton to Dear Cousin, July 18, 1863, Hilton Family Papers, Library and Archives Division, Georgia Historical Society, Savannah.

9. "Gordon's Brigade in the Late Campaign," July 20, 1863, *Savannah Republican*, Aug. 6, 1863.

10. "Our Army in Pennsylvania," July 19, 1863, *Mobile Advertiser and Register*, Aug. 9, 1863.

11. John Hundley to Dear Wife, July 19, 1863, Hundley Family Papers, SHC; John Cleek to Dear Father July 19, 1863, John Cleek Papers, DU.

12. Seymour Journal, June 29, 1863, Jones, *Civil War Memoirs of Captain William J. Seymour*, 69.

13. Cassandra Small to Oh my dear Lissie, July 8, 1863, Civil War Files, YCHC.

14. *Portland Daily Advertiser*, July 9, 1863, quoted in Mingus and McClure, *Echoing Still*, 65.

15. Charles F. Himes to Dear Rood, Oct. 2, 1863, Charles Francis Himes Family Papers, DiCol.

16. Farquhar, *First Million*, 69–72; Cassandra Small to My dear Lissie, June 30, 1863, Civil War Files, YCHC.

17. Mingus, *Flames beyond Gettysburg*, 163–65; Evans Diary, June 28, 1863, in Stephens, *Intrepid Warrior*, 220.

18. Farquhar, *First Million*, 77–78; James W. Latimer to Dear Bart, July 8, 1863, Civil War Files, YCHC; Small to Lissie, June 30, 1863, ibid.

19. Gibson, *History of York County*, 486; Charles Moore Jr. Account, Brake Collection, USAHEC.

20. Kincheloe Diary, June 28, 1863, in Hale and Phillips, *History of the Forty-Ninth Virginia Infantry,* 74.

21. J. A. Early, *Autobiographical Sketch,* 258–59.

22. "Resident Shared Memories of the Battle of Hanover," *York Daily,* July 12, 1905.

23. Reily and Sneeringer Claim, Pennsylvania Civil War Border Claims, PSA.

24. *York Daily,* Mar. 22, 1875, quoted in Mingus, "Whew! That Was Close," *Cannonball* (blog), Aug. 25, 2016, http://www.yorkblog.com/cannonball/2016/08/25/whew-that-was-close/.

25. *Hanover Spectator,* July 17, 1863, quoted in Mingus, "White's Comanches on the Warpath," 11; Prowell, *History of York County Pennsylvania,* 1:405–6.

26. Skelly, *Boy's Experiences,* 9.

27. "Holland's Store Robbed by Rebels: York Man Recalls Events of 1863 at Hanover," *York Daily,* July 12, 1905.

28. Mingus, *Flames beyond Gettysburg,* 175.

29. McClure, *East of Gettysburg,* 45.

30. Prowell, *History of York County Pennsylvania,* 1:406.

31. Skelly, *Boy's Experiences,* 9; Elijah V. White to Hon. John H. Alexander, Apr. 17, 1908, in Mosby, *Stuart's Cavalry in the Gettysburg Campaign,* 156; Mingus, "White's Comanches on the Warpath," 13.

32. Trundle to Sister, July 7, 1863, in Trundle, "Gettysburg Described in Two Letters," 212.

33. Mingus, "White's Comanches on the Warpath," 15–16; Mingus, *Flames beyond Gettysburg,* 183; Myers, *The Comanches,* 194.

34. "Little Stories of the Civil War Related by a York Survivor," *York Daily,* July 15, 1904.

35. Prowell, *History of York County Pennsylvania,* 1:406–7; Joseph Wible Claim, Pennsylvania Civil War Border Claims, PSA; Mingus, "White's Comanches on the Warpath," 18.

36. Henry Bott Claim, Scott Mingus Database of York County Civil War Damage Claims, YCHC; Botts and Hartman Damage Claim, ibid.

37. Henry Fishel Claim, ibid.

38. Mingus, *Flames beyond Gettysburg,* 188.

39. Prowell, *History of York County Pennsylvania,* 1:887.

13. "I WANT MY REQUISITIONS FILLED AT ONCE"

1. Jubal A. Early to George R. Prowell, June 4, 1885, Jubal A. Early File, YCHC.

2. Ibid.; "Manchester Resident Recalled Rebel Invasion," *York Daily,* July 21, 1903.

3. George W. Finlaw to W. P. Finlaw, July 1, 1863, in Mingus and McClure, *Echoing Still,* 65; Mingus, *Flames beyond Gettysburg,* 238.

4. For a detailed history of the town, see Gibson, *History of York County,* 13 179.

5. Evans to Darling, July 4, 1863, in Stephens, *Intrepid Warrior,* 221; *Columbia Spy,* Jan. 16, 1886, quoted in Mingus, *Flames beyond Gettysburg,* 202.

6. Gordon, *Reminiscences,* 142.

7. Prowell, *History of York County Pennsylvania,* 407–8.

8. Agee, "Battle of Gettysburg"; Evans to Darling, July 4, 1863, in Stephens, *Intrepid Warrior,* 221; P. Johnson, *Under the Southern Cross,* 123.

9. Small to Lissie, June 30, 1863, Civil War Files, YCHC.

10. M. L. Van Baman, "Confederate Invasion of York," *York Gazette,* June 28, 1913.

11. Evans to Darling, July 4, 1863, in Stephens, *Intrepid Warrior,* 221.

12. Small to Lissie, June 30, 1863, Civil War Files, YCHC; James W. Latimer to Dear Bart, July 8, 1863, Latimer Family Files, ibid.

13. Small to Lissie, June 30, 1863, Civil War Files, ibid.

14. Latimer to Bart, July 8, 1863, Latimer Family Files, ibid.

15. Gordon, *Reminiscences,* 143; *Atlanta Journal,* Sept. 16, 1888, quoted in Mingus, *Flames beyond Gettysburg,* 205–6.

16. Small to Lissie, June 30, 1863, Civil War Files, YCHC.

17. Jones, "Fifty-Seventh Regiment," 412.

18. Early to Prowell, June 4, 1885, Early File, YCHC; Prowell, *History of York County Pennsylvania,* 1:1072.

19. "The Occupation of York, PA," *York Gazette,* June 29, 1863; Prowell, *History of York County Pennsylvania,* 1:410.

20. Latimer to Bart, July 8, 1863, Latimer Family Files, YCHC; Kincheloe Diary, June 29, 1863, in Hale and Phillips, *History of the Forty-Ninth Virginia Infantry,* 76.

21. J. A. Early, *Autobiographical Sketch,* 259.

22. "The Occupation of York, PA," *York Gazette,* June 29, 1863.

23. Gordon, *Reminiscences,* 144; Bradwell, "Burning of Wrightsville," 300–301.

24. OR 27, pt. 2, 278.

25. Gordon, *Reminiscences,* 144.

26. Bradwell, "Burning of Wrightsville," 301.

27. "The Skirmish beyond Wrightsville," *Columbia Spy,* July 11, 1863.

28. Bradwell, "Burning of Wrightsville," 301.

29. Hodam, "The Hodam Manuscript," 288; "Our Army in Pennsylvania," July 18, 1863, *Mobile Advertiser and Register,* Aug. 9, 1863.

30. Evans to Darling, July 4, 1863, in Stephens, *Intrepid Warrior,* 221.

31. OR 27, pt. 3, 410–411; Robert Crane Deposition, July 20, 1863, Columbia Historical Preservation Society, Columbia, PA; Wray, *History of the Twenty Third Pennsylvania Volunteer Infantry,* 153.

32. Wister, *Reminiscences,* 163; Isaac Harris Diary, June 28, 1863, DiCol; .J. R. W. Adams to Dear Gazette, June 30, 1863, *Pittston Gazette,* July 9, 1863.

33. Bradwell, "Burning of Wrightsville," 301.

34. Gordon, *Reminiscences,* 148.

35. Bradwell, "Burning of Wrightsville," 301.

36. Mingus, "One of Gordon's Men Discusses the Rebels Saving Wrightsville, Pa. from Burning," *Cannonball* (blog), Jan. 25, 2014, http://www.yorkblog.com/cannonball/2014/01/25/one-of-gordons-men-discusses-the-rebels-saving-wrightsville-pa-from-burning/.

37. Evans to Darling, July 4, 1863, in Stephens, *Intrepid Warrior,* 221.

38. "Our Army in Pennsylvania," July 18, 1863, *Mobile Advertiser and Register,* Aug. 9, 1863; Hilton to Cousin, July 18, 1863, Hilton Family Papers, Georgia Historical Society.

39. Hodam, "The Hodam Manuscript," 288.

40. Mingus, "One of Gordon's Men Discusses the Rebels Saving Wrightsville," *Cannonball.*

41. J. A. Early, *Autobiographical Sketch,* 260–61.

42. Bradwell, "Burning of Wrightsville," 301; Henry Hantz Claim, Mingus Database of York County Civil War Damage Claims; Hodam, "The Hodam Manuscript," 288.

43. Jacob G. Leber Claim, Mingus Database of York County Civil War Damage Claims, YCHC.

44. *Columbia Spy,* Jan. 16, 1886, quoted in Mingus, *Flames beyond Gettysburg,* 286.

45. Rachel Bahn to Nephew, July 14, 1863, in Mingus and McClure, *Echoing Still,* 75.

46. Yeary, *Reminiscences of the Boys in Gray,* 579.

47. Gordon, *Reminiscences,* 148.

48. Latimer to Bart, July 8, 1863, Latimer Family Files, YCHC.

49. Prowell, *History of York County Pennsylvania,* 1:412.

50. J. A. Early, *Autobiographical Sketch,* 258–59.

51. Gibson, *History of York County,* 209–10.

52. Eaton Diary, June 28, 29, 1863, Eaton Papers, SHC; Hefner to Wife, July 19, 1863, Hefner Private Collections, Papers, NCSA.

53. Seymour Journal, June 29, 1863, in Jones, *Civil War Memoirs of Captain William J. Seymour,* 68.

54. Jackson to Brother, July 20, 1863, in M. Reed, "Gettysburg Campaign," 187; Kincheloe Diary, June 29, 1863, in Hale and Phillips, *History of the Forty-Ninth Virginia Infantry,* 76.

55. Nathan Lehmayer and Brothers Damage Claim, Mingus Database of York County Civil War Border Claims, YCHC; Jacob A. Sechrist Damage Claim, ibid.; Charles Spangler Damage Claim, ibid.

56. "The Occupation of York, PA," *York Gazette,* June 29, 1863; Zachariah K. Louck Claim, Mingus Database of York County Civil War Border Claims, YCHC; Josiah Myers Claim, ibid.

57. Mingus, "New Account of Louisiana Tigers in York County Surfaces," *Cannonball* (blog), May 11, 2016, http://www.yorkblog.com/cannonball/2016/05/11/new-account-of-louisiana-tigers-in-york-county-surfaces/#more-6081.

58. Seymour Journal, June 28, 1863, in Jones, *Civil War Memoirs of Captain William J. Seymour,* 67.

59. Mayo Diary, June 29, 1863, HL; Reed Diary, June 28, 1863, in Reed, *Private in Gray,* 41.

60. Gibson, *History of York County,* 209.

61. Snider Diary, June 26–28, 1863, "Joseph C. Snider's Journal of the Civil War," Personal Papers Collection, LOC; Kincheloe Diary, June 29, 1863, in Hale and Phillips, *History of the Forty-Ninth Virginia Infantry,* 76; Joseph French Harding, "Battle of Gettysburg," 43, Roy Bird Cook Collection, West Virginia and Regional History Center and Special Collections, West Virginia Univ., Morgantown.

62. Reed Diary, June 29, 1863, in Reed, *Private in Gray,* 41.

63. Hodam, "The Hodam Manuscript," 288; Jacob Brillinger Claim, Mingus Database of York County Damage Claims, YCHC.

64. J. Douglas, *Report of the Operations of the Sanitary Commission,* 8.

65. P. Johnson, *Under the Southern Cross,* 124; Agee, "Battle of Gettysburg"; Kincheloe Diary, June 29, 1863, in Hale and Phillips, *History of the Forty-Ninth Virginia Infantry,* 76.

66. Carrington, "First Day on Left at Gettysburg," 328; P. Johnson, *Under the Southern Cross,* 123; Jackson to Brother, July 20, 1863, in M. Reed, "Gettysburg Campaign," 187.

14. "WE DID NOT COME HERE FOR NOTHING"

1. Goldsborough, *Maryland Line,* 285; Hands, "Civil War Memoirs," 93, UVA.

2. Nye, *Here Come the Rebels!,* 299; Charles F. Himes Pocket Diary, June 25, 1863, DiCol; Himes to Rood, Oct. 2, 1863, Himes Family Papers, ibid.

3. Schuricht Diary, June 27, 1863, in Schuricht, "Jenkins' Brigade," 345.

4. Colwell, *Bitter Fruits,* 3, 13.

5. "The Invasion," *Carlisle American Volunteer,* July 9, 1863; Sullivan, *Boyhood Memories,* 13; Mary Matilda Loudon Diary, June 27, 1863, Civil War Collection Files, Cumberland County Historical Society, Carlisle, PA.

6. "The Invasion," *Carlisle American Volunteer,* July 9, 1863.

7. "The Rebel Occupation of Carlisle," *Christian Advocate and Journal,* July 16, 1863, in Wingert, *Rare and Unseen,* 40.

8. "The Invasion," *Carlisle American Volunteer,* July 9, 1863.

9. William E. Calder to Dear Mother, June 29, 1863, Calder Family Papers, SHC; Pickens Diary, June 27, 1863, in Hubbs, *Voices from Company D,* 181.

10. "The Invasion," *Carlisle American Volunteer,* July 9, 1863; R. K. Hitner to My Dear Friend, July 6, 1863, Carlisle Barracks Collection, USAHEC.

11. Unknown to Sidney Boden, July 11, 1863, Burgett-Irey Family Papers, Special Collections and Univ. Archives, Univ. Libraries, Univ. of Massachusetts–Amherst.

12. Sullivan, *Boyhood Memories,* 14; Hanna Culver to Dear Brother, July 9, 1863, Joseph Franklin Culver Collection, Special Collections Department, Library, Univ. of Iowa, Iowa City.

13. Brenner, "Confederates Found Food Plentiful throughout Cumberland Valley."

14. Pickens Diary, June 27, 1863, in Hubbs, *Voices from Company D,* 181; "Third Alabama Infantry, Letter from Pennsylvania," June 28, 1863, *Mobile Daily Advertiser and Register,* July 20, 1863; Nye, *Here Come the Rebels!,* 304.

15. Jedediah Hotchkiss to My Darling Sara, June 28, 1863, Hotchkiss Papers, LOC; Hightower to Lou, June 28, 1863, Hightower Letters, GAM; Wing, *History of Cumberland County,* 103–6; J. W. B. to Editor, Aug. 12, 1863, *Augusta Weekly Chronicle and Sentinel,* Sept. 5, 1863.

16. George D. Chenoweth to James W. Marshall, July 15, 1863, George D. Chenoweth Letter, DiCol; Conway Hillman to Dear Morgan, Sept. 9, 1930, James Henry Morgan Presidential Papers, ibid.

17. "Member of Class of '73 Here on Visit: Theodore Johnson Tells of Civil War Days in Carlisle," *Carlisle Evening Sentinel,* June 24, 1924.

18. Beetem, "Experiences of a West Ward Boy," 7.

19. Frank Bond, "Memoir," 166, Confederate States Army Bound Volumes, ACWM; Swank, *Courier for Lee and Jackson,* 41.

20. OR 27, pt. 2, 443; Wood to Parents, June 29, 1863, in Koonce, *Doctor to the Front,* 101–2.

21. White, "Diary of the War," 200 (June 27, 1863); Henry R. Berkeley Diary, June 27, 1863, in Runge, *Four Years in the Confederate Artillery,* 49.

22. Extracts from a Diary, June 27, 1863, in Ammen, 116.

23. McKim, *Soldier's Recollections,* 166; Firebaugh Diary, June 28, 1863, SHC.

24. Wharton, "First Battalion," 219; A. A. Anderson to Dear Brother, July 8, 1863, Patrick H. Cain Papers, DU; Green Diary, June 27, 1863, Private Collections, NCSA.

25. "The Invasion," *Carlisle American Volunteer,* July 9, 1863; Thomas Miller Griffith to Dear Bro. and Sister, July 3, 1863, Thomas Miller Griffith Papers, DiCol.

26. "The Invasion," *Carlisle American Volunteer,* July 9, 1863.

27. Tucker Diary, June 28, 1863, ADAH.

28. Apperson Diary, June 28, 1863, in Roper, *Repairing the "March of Mars,"* 481.

29. "The Invasion," *Carlisle American Volunteer,* July 9, 1863; Tousey, *Military History of Carlisle,* 229.

30. OR 27, pt. 2, 443, 551.

31. Griffith to Bro. and Sister, July 3, 1863, Griffith Papers, DiCol; "Evacuation of Carlisle by the Rebels," July 1, 1863, *New York Herald,* July 2, 1863; Hotchkiss to Sara, June 28, 1863, Hotchkiss Papers, LOC.

32. Gorman to Mother and Wife, July 8, 1863, *Raleigh Daily Progress,* July 22, 1863.

33. "The Invasion," *Carlisle American Volunteer,* July 9, 1863.

34. Sullivan, *Boyhood Memories,* 19; Gorman to Mother and Wife, July 8, 1863, *Raleigh Daily Progress,* July 22, 1863.

35. Leon, *Diary of a Tar Heel,* 33 (June 25–30, 1863); Apperson Diary, June 28, 1863, in Roper, *Repairing the "March of Mars,"* 480; Blackford to Father, June 28, 1863, Leigh Collection, USAHEC.

36. *History of Cumberland and Adams Counties,* 109. For a detailed history of the barracks, see Tousey, *Military History of Carlisle,* 1–230.

37. Ramseur to Darling, June 28, 1863, in Kundahl, *Bravest of the Brave,* 151.

38. Wills to Sister, June 28, 1863, Wills Letters, SHC; Weldon Davis to Dear Ma, June 28, 1863, in Eaton, *Rebecca's Letters,* 63.

39. Turner and Wall, "Twenty-Third Regiment," 233.

40. Blackford to Father, June 28, 1863, Leigh Collection, USAHEC. Both Blackford and Halsey lived in Lynchburg, Virginia, prior to the war.

41. D. Pfanz, *Richard S. Ewell,* 60–61; Brown Journal, in Jones, *Campbell Brown's Civil War,* 202.

42. Calder to Mother, June 29, 1863, Calder Family Papers, SHC; Gorman to Mother and Wife, July 8, 1863, *Raleigh Daily Progress,* July 22, 1863; Tucker Diary, June 27, 1863, ADAH.

43. Hotchkiss to Sara, June 28, 1863, Hotchkiss Papers, LOC; Eugene Blackford to William M. Blackford, July 16, 1863, quoted in Blackford, *Mine Eyes Have Seen the Glory,* 221.

44. J. W. B. to Editor, Aug. 12, 1863, *Augusta Weekly Chronicle and Sentinel,* Sept. 5, 1863.

45. Freeman, "Not Like 'Dumb Driven Cattle'"; William Jackson Underwood to My Dear Little Brothers, June 28, 1863, Underwood, Key Families Papers, Kenan Research Center, Atlanta History Center, Atlanta, GA. Thomas L. Elmore provided details on the two Dickinson graduates.

46. Morgan, *Dickinson College,* 316. For details on the visit to his son's camp prior to the invasion, see Charles Force Deems Journal, June 4, 1863, in Deems and Deems, *Autobiography of Charles Force Deems and Memoir by His Sons,* 184; and "An Interesting Letter," *Spirit of the Age,* June 22, 1863.

47. Marston Diary, June 29, 1863, Civil War Collection, EU; Clement Daniel Fishburne, "Memoirs," 2:87, UVA; Alexander D. Betts Diary, June 29, 1863, in Betts, *Experience of a Confederate Chaplain,* 38–39.

48. Alexander S. Pendleton to Kate Corbin, June 28, 1863, Pendleton Papers, SHC; S. D. Hillman, "A Few Days under Rebel Rule," *Carlisle American Volunteer,* Aug. 5, 1863.

49. Apperson Diary, June 29, 1863, in Roper, *Repairing the "March of Mars,"* 481.

50. Elihu Wesley Watson to My Dear Brothers, July 10, 1863, Watson Family Papers, Manuscripts Division, South Caroliniana Library, Univ. of South Carolina, Columbia; Furlow Diary, June 17–29, 1863, in Furlow, "Record of Current Events," 45, Diaries Miscellaneous Collection, YU.

51. Brown Journal, in Jones, *Campbell Brown's Civil War,* 201; Tagg, *Generals of Gettysburg,* 238; Myers, "Civil War Diary of Isaac Ridgeway Trimble," 10 (June 28, 1863); Trimble, "Battle and Campaign of Gettysburg," 122.

52. Tate to Ma, June 28, 1863, Tate Letters, GLIAH; Ramseur to Darling, June 28, 1863, in Kundahl, *Bravest of the Brave,* 151; Thomas Cleveland to My Dear Bettie, June 29, 1863, in Miyagawa, "Boys Who Wore the Gray," 63; Samuel H. Pendleton Diary, June 29, 1863, UVA.

53. Pickens Diary, June 29, 1863, in Hubbs, *Voices from Company D,* 181; Park, "War Diary," 12 (June 28, 1863).

54. Major Key, "Reminiscences of the Civil War: And Incidents Connected with the 44th Georgia and Other Regiments," *Jasper County News,* Jan. 5, 1899.

55. Pendleton to Corbin, June 28, 1863, Pendleton Papers, SHC; Wills to Sister, June 28, 1863, Wills Letters, SHC; John T. Gay to Dear Pussie, June 27, 1863, Nix Collection, UGA.

56. Apperson Diary, June 28, 1863, in Roper, *Repairing the "March of Mars,"* 481; Pendleton Diary, June 29, 1863, UVA; Leon, *Diary of a Tar Heel,* 32 (June 25–30, 1863).

57. Marston Diary, June 28, 1863, Civil War Collection, EU; Polk to Wife, June 28, 1863, Polk Papers, SHC; Record of Events, 30th North Carolina Regiment, Field and Staff, June 27, 1863, in Hewitt, Trudeau, and Suderow, *Supplement to the Official Records,* 4(2):693–94; Joseph J. Cowand to Dear Cousin Winaford, June 28, 1863, Winifred A. Cowand Papers, DU.

58. Jones, "Civil War Reminiscences," 16, VHS; Alexander S. Murdock to My Dear Nephew, July 19, 1863, Alexander Murdock Papers, Pearce Museum, Navarro College, Corsicana, TX.

59. B. Frank Hall, "Account of the Battle of Gettysburg, 1913," Lower Cape Fear Historical Society, Wilmington, NC.

60. Betts Diary, June 28, 1863, in Betts, *Experience of a Confederate Chaplain,* 38; Stradley to Hufham, June 29, 1863, *Biblical Recorder,* July 22, 1863.

61. Griffith to Bro. and Sister, July 3, 1863, Griffith Papers, DiCol; Hayes, *Civil War Diary of Father James Sheeran,* 188 (June 28, 1863).

62. Hotchkiss to Sara, June 28, 1863, Hotchkiss Papers, LOC.

63. Fishburne, "Memoirs," 2:89. Bliss was born in Florence, Alabama, in 1836. He had assumed the position as pastor at Carlisle only a month before the arrival of Confederate troops. For additional details on his career, see "Dr. Bliss Dies of Paralysis," *New York Times,* Apr. 12, 1909.

64. Civic Club of Carlisle, *Carlisle Old and New,* 57; Hotchkiss to Sara, June 28, 1863, Hotchkiss Papers, LOC. Fry took over as head of the church at Carlisle in 1854. For details on his career, see Leonard, *Who's Who in Pennsylvania,* 280–81.

65. Griffith to Bro. and Sister, July 3, 1863, Griffith Papers, DiCol.

66. Bennett, "Fourteenth Regiment," 719; Marston Diary, June 28, 1863, Civil War Collection, EU; Pendleton Diary, June 28, 1863, UVA.

67. Furlow Diary, June 17–29, 1863, in Furlow, "Record of Current Events," 45, Diaries Miscellaneous Collection, YU; Beavans Diary, n.d., Beavans Diary and Letters, SHC; William W. Sillers to Dear Sister, Aug. 7, 1863, Sillers-Holmes Family Correspondence, Rare Books and Special Collections, Univ. of Notre Dame, Notre Dame, IN.

68. Blacknall, "Memoirs," Blacknall Papers, Private Collections, NCSA.

69. Hufham, "Gettysburg," 452; Blackford, "Memoirs," 235, Civil War Miscellaneous Collection, USAHEC.

70. "From the Forty-Third Reg't N. C. T.," July 20, 1863, *North Carolina Argus,* July 30, 1863.

71. J. C. Early, "Southern Boy's Experience at Gettysburg," 416–17.

72. Leon, *Diary of a Tar Heel,* 32 (June 25–30, 1863); Turner and Wall, "Twenty-Third Regiment," 233.

73. Quoted in Lowry, *Story the Soldiers Wouldn't Tell,* 28.

74. Brown Journal, in Jones, *Campbell Brown's Civil War,* 201.

75. Stradley to Hufham, June 29, 1863, *Biblical Recorder,* July 22, 1863.

76. Brown Journal, in Jones, *Campbell Brown's Civil War,* 201. There appears to be no basis for the often-repeated story that this "elegant new flag" had been sent by the ladies of Richmond to General Lee "for him to present to the regiment most worthy of receiving and carrying it." For details on the claim of this honor for the Thirty-Second North Carolina, see London, "Thirty-Second Regiment," 525; F. A. Boyle, "The 32nd N.C. Regiment: How It Carried Its New Flag at Gettysburg," *Richmond Dispatch,* Aug. 11, 1895; and Henry T. Bahnson, "It was the New Confederate Flag of the Whole Army," *Raleigh News and Observer,* June 12, 1895.

77. Hall to Uncle, July 18, 1863, Bolling Hall Family Papers, ADAH.

78. W. Green, *Recollections and Reflections,* 174.

79. Marston Diary, June 28, 1863, Civil War Collection, EU; Hotchkiss Journal, June 28, 1863, in McDonald, *Make Me a Map,* 155; Ardrey Diary, June 29, 1863, Ardrey Papers, DaCol.

80. Turner to Parents, June 28, 1863, Turner Papers, SHC; Wills to Sister, June 28, 1863, Wills Letters, SHC.

81. Calder to Mother, June 29, 1863, Calder Family Papers, SHC.

15. "THE GENERAL WAS QUITE TESTY"

1. Guelzo, *Gettysburg,* 77–78.

2. Crist, *Confederate Invasion of the West Shore,* 7.

3. OR 27, pt. 2, 219–21.

4. Nye, *Here Come the Rebels!,* 327.

5. Brunhouse, *Miniatures of Mechanicsburg,* 17–20.

6. Hands, "Civil War Memoirs," 93, UVA; "The Rebel Invasion," *Cumberland Valley Journal,* July 23, 1863; Nye, *Here Come the Rebels!,* 331–32; Hauck, *Centennial Directory of the Borough of Mechanicsburg,* 13.

7. "The Rebel Invasion," *Cumberland Valley Journal,* July 23, 1863; Ellie D. to Dear Jennie, July 23, 1863, "Gettysburg Campaign: Graphic Descriptions of the Rebel Invasion of Mechanicsburg, Pa., Written by a Terrorized Civilian Lady," G168, Museum Quality Americana, http://www.mqamericana.com/Gett_Campgn_Rebel_Invasion.html (auction-item transcription).

8. Schuricht Diary, June 28, 1863, in Schuricht, "Jenkins' Brigade," 345; C. B. Niesley to Dear Parents, July 1, 1863, Harrisburg Civil War Round Table Collection, USAHEC.

9. "The Rebel Invasion," *Cumberland Valley Journal,* July 23, 1863; "The Rebels Retiring," July 1, 1863, *New York Times,* July 3, 1863.

10. "The Rebel Invasion," *Cumberland Valley Journal,* July 23, 1863; L. Brown to John B. Lingle, July 9, 1863, Harrisburg Civil War Round Table Collection, USAHEC.

11. Ellie D. to Jennie, July 23, 1863, "Gettysburg Campaign."

12. Nye, *Here Come the Rebels!,* 333.

13. "The Rebel Invasion," *Cumberland Valley Journal,* July 23, 1863.

14. Donehoo, *History of the Cumberland Valley,* 1:244. This area is known today as Camp Hill.

15. Wing, *History of Cumberland County,* 228; Nye, *Here Come the Rebels!,* 333.

16. Schuricht Diary, June 28, 1863, in Schuricht, "Jenkins' Brigade," 345.

17. Statement of Mrs. Lawrence Landis, Wilbur S. Nye Collection, GNMP; Nye, *Here Come the Rebels!,* 336; Schuricht Diary, June 28, 1863, in Schuricht, "Jenkins' Brigade," 345.

18. Harris, *Autobiography,* 71.

19. Eslinger, *Local History of Dillsburg,* 28; Prowell, *History of York County Pennsylvania,* 1:868–70; James J. Moore Claim, Mingus Database of York County Civil War Damage Claims, YCHC; A. N. Eslinger Claim, ibid.

20. William P. Smith Claim, York County Civil War Damage Claims, YCHC.

21. Culver to Brother, July 9, 1863, Culver Collection, Univ. of Iowa.

22. "Reminiscences of Nettie Jane Blair, August 1934," 7, Civil War Collection Files, Cumberland County Historical Society, Carlisle, PA.

23. Josiah S. Carothers Claim, Pennsylvania Civil War Border Claims, PSA.

24. Unknown to Boden, July 11, 1863, Burgett-Irey Family Papers, Univ. of Massachusetts–Amherst.

25. Bond, "Memoir," 166–67, Confederate States Army Bound Volumes, ACWM.

26. "Tablet Unveiled at Spot Where Rebels Turned," *Carlisle Evening Sentinel,* Oct. 26, 1929.

27. Hain, *History of Perry County,* 548; William McCandlish Diary, June 27, 1863, Reed Scrapbook, Newville Historical Society; Hocker, *Noble 300,* 161.

28. "One of the Heroes" to Editor, *Perry County Freeman,* Aug. 10, 1892; "The Rebels Moving on Havre de Grace," *Philadelphia Inquirer,* June 29, 1863.

29. Deppen, "Tales That Were Told in Lower Northumberland County," 173–74; "The Heroine of Herndon," *Selinsgrove Times,* Nov. 29, 1940. Trevorton Junction is known today as Herndon.

30. Micajah Woods to My Dear Father, May 3, 1863, Woods Papers, UVA; Micajah Woods to Dear Mother, June 30, 1863, ibid.; "The Rebel Invasion," *Cumberland Valley Journal,* July 23, 1863; Niesley to Parents, July 1, 1863, Harrisburg Civil War Round Table Collection, USAHEC.

31. Woods to Mother, June 30, 1863, Woods Papers, UVA.

32. Nye, *Here Come the Rebels!,* 341; Vincent A. Witcher to John W. Daniel, Mar. 22, 1906, John Warwick Daniel Papers, UVA; W. K. to Messrs. Editors, June 30, 1863, *Richmond Daily Dispatch,* Apr. 1, 1896; Crist, "Highwater 1863," 178.

33. OR 27, pt. 2, 443; Hotchkiss Journal, June 29, 1863, in McDonald, *Make Me a Map,* 156.

34. Schuricht Diary, June 29, 1863, in Schuricht, "Jenkins' Brigade," 345; W. K. to Editors, June 30, 1863, *Richmond (VA) Daily Dispatch,* Apr. 1, 1896.

35. Quoted in Crist, "Highwater 1863," 178.

36. OR 27, pt. 2, 552; Hotchkiss Journal, June 29, 1863, in McDonald, *Make Me a Map,* 156; Brown Journal, in Jones, *Campbell Brown's Civil War,* 203; Nye, *Here Come the Rebels!,* 336–37.

37. William C. Ousby to Dear Brother, June 28, 1863, William Clark Ousby Papers, Private Collections, NCSA; Thomas S. Taylor to My Dear Wife, June 28, 1863, Thomas S. Taylor Papers, ADAH; William A. Heirs to dear Cousin, June 28, 1863, William A. Heirs Letters, GLIAH.

38. Gay to Pussie, June 27, 1863, Nix Collection, UGA; Shepherd G. Pryor to My Dear Penelope, June 28, 1863, in Adams, *Post of Honor,* 370.

39. William Beverley Pettit to My darling Wife, June 25, 1863, in Turner, *Civil War Letters,* 126.

40. Felder to Pa, June 28, 1863, Ray Papers, GAM; James P. Garrison to Dear Wife, June 28, 1863, James P. Garrison Papers, EU; Polk to Wife, June 28, 1863, Polk Papers, SHC.

41. For details on the spying activities that led to the change in Lee's orders, see J. Hall, "Modern Hunt for Fabled Agent," 18–25.

42. Firebaugh Diary, June 28, 1863, SHC; John Goldsborough White, "A 'Rebel's' Recollections of Bloody Days That Led to Gettysburg," *Baltimore Sun,* May 26, 1929.

43. OR 27, pt. 2, 443, 552; ibid., pt. 3, 943; Extracts from a Diary, June 29, 1863, in Ammen, 116; White, "Diary of the War," 200 (June 29, 1863).

44. Sharpe, "A Boy's Experience," 166.

45. OR 27, pt. 3, 943.

46. Richard Albert Clarkson to Dear Mrs. Falconer, n.d., in "Richard Albert Clarkson: The Civil War," http://pamgarrett.com/features/clarra006_gettysburg.pdf.

47. Hotchkiss Journal, June 29, 1863, in McDonald, *Make Me a Map*, 155.

48. John F. Coghill to Dear Pappy, Ma and Mit, July 17, 1863, James O. Coghill Papers, DU.

16. "WE HAD NO IDEA OF OUR DESTINATION"

1. Sarah E. Motts, *Personal Experiences of a House That Stood on the Road* (Carlisle, PA: Hamilton Library Association, 1941), 8–9.

2. Nye, *Here Come the Rebels!*, 358–59; Blackford, "Memoirs," 236, Civil War Miscellaneous Collection, USAHEC; Hotchkiss Journal, June 30, 1863, in McDonald, *Make Me a Map*, 156.

3. Wing, *History of Cumberland County*, 224; Hotchkiss Journal, June 30, 1863, in McDonald, *Make Me a Map*, 156; Gorman to Mother and Wife, July 8, 1863, *Raleigh Daily Progress*, July 22, 1863.

4. Harris to Burton, Aug. 24, 1863, in Taylor, "Ramseur's Brigade in the Gettysburg Campaign," 31.

5. Abe Adams to Dear Father & Sisters, July 19, 1863, Adams Family Papers, James I. Robertson Jr. Civil War Sesquicentennial Legacy Collection, LOV; J. C. Early, "Southern Boy's Experience," 420.

6. Purifoy, "With Ewell and Rodes in Pennsylvania," 464; J. C. Early, "Southern Boy's Experience," 420.

7. Spectator to Mr. Editor, July 8, 1863, *Gettysburg Compiler*, Aug. 3, 1863; Jacob A. Gardner Claim in Kathleen Georg Harrison, ed., "Summary of Damage Claims from the Battle of Gettysburg for Adams County, PA," GNMP.

8. Nye, *Here Come the Rebels!*, 359; Grace, "Rodes's Division at Gettysburg," 614.

9. Leon, *Diary of a Tar Heel*, 34 (June 25–30, 1863); "Letter from the 3rd Ala from a member of the Gulf City Guards," July 9, 1863, *Mobile Daily Advertiser and Register*, July 24, 1863.

10. Bond, "Company A, First Maryland Cavalry," 78.

11. Wharton, "First Battalion," 238.

12. Hatton, "Memoir," June 29, 1863, LOC.

13. Kearns Diary, June 29, 1863, VHS; Casler, *Four Years in the Stonewall Brigade*, 173; Charles A. Rollins, "Going to Gettysburg," *Lexington Gazette and Citizen*, Aug. 9, 1888; E. Moore, *Story of a Cannoneer*, 191.

14. Bond, "Memoir," 169, Confederate States Army Bound Volumes, ACWM.

15. Bond, "Company A, First Maryland Cavalry," 78.

16. Bond, "Memoir," 169, Confederate States Army Bound Volumes, ACWM.

17. "The Invasion," *Carlisle American Volunteer*, July 9, 1863; Culver to Brother, July 9, 1863, Culver Collection, Univ. of Iowa.

18. "Respecting Private Property," *Carlisle Herald*, July 17, 1863.

19. Nye, *Here Come the Rebels!*, 349; Schuricht Diary, June 30, 1863, in Schuricht, "Jenkins' Brigade," 345.

20. "The Invasion," *Carlisle American Volunteer,* July 9, 1863; Beetem, "Experiences of a West Ward Boy," 10.

21. Herman Haupt, *Reminiscences of General Herman Haupt* (Milwaukee, WI: Wright and Joys Company, 1901), 211.

22. Nye, *Here Come the Rebels!,* 353–54, OR 27, pt. 2, 235.

23. OR 27, pt. 2, 232–33.

24. George W. Wingate, *History of the Twenty-Second Regiment of the National Guard of the State of New York from Its Organization to 1895* (New York: Edwin W. Dayton Publishers, 1896), 194–96.

25. Woods to Father, July 16, 1863, Woods Papers, UVA; OR 27, pt. 1, 193; Nye, *Here Come the Rebels!,* 354.

26. Schuricht Diary, June 30, 1863, in Schuricht, "Jenkins' Brigade," 345.

27. Vincent A. Witcher to John W. Daniel, Mar. 1, 1906, Daniel Papers, UVA.

28. "The Invasion," *Carlisle American Volunteer,* July 9, 1863; Schuricht Diary, June 30, 1863, in Schuricht, "Jenkins' Brigade," 345.

29. Wittenberg and Petruzzi, *Plenty of Blame to Go Around,* 120–39.

30. OR 27, pt. 2, 467–68.

31. Prowell, *History of York County Pennsylvania,* 1:965.

32. OR 27, pt. 2, 467–68; Myers, *The Comanches,* 194–95.

33. *Commemorative Biographical Record of Washington County, Pennsylvania* (Chicago: J. H. Beers and Company, 1893), 390.

34. OR 27, pt. 2, 467–68.

35. Hatton, "Memoirs," June 30, 1863, LOC; Extracts from a Diary, June 30, 1863, in Ammen, 116.

36. I. H. M'Cauley, *Historical Sketch of Franklin County, Pennsylvania* (Chambersburg, PA: John M. Pomeroy, 1878), 151; Daniel, "H. H. Harris Civil War Diary," 1771 (June 30, 1863); White, "Diary of the War," 201 (June 30, 1863); Hayes, *Civil War Diary of Father James Sheeran,* 192 (June 30, 1863).

37. Witcher to Daniel, Mar. 1, 1906, Daniel Papers, UVA; Spectator to Editor, July 8, 1863, *Gettysburg Compiler,* Aug. 3, 1863.

38. Gardner, *Sunset Memories,* 69; Hoke, *Great Invasion,* 229–31.

39. H. Pfanz, *Gettysburg: The First Day,* 24–29.

40. Bond, "Company A, First Maryland Cavalry," 79; Bond, "Memoir," 170–71, Confederate States Army Bound Volumes, ACWM.

41. OR 27, pt. 2, 444.

42. Trimble to Bachelder, Feb. 8, 1883, in Ladd and Ladd, *Bachelder Papers,* 2:927; Trimble, "Battle and Campaign of Gettysburg," 122.

43. OR 27, pt. 2, 444. Middletown is known today as Biglerville.

EPILOGUE

1. OR 27, pt. 2, 444; J. A. Early, *Autobiographical Sketch,* 267.

2. For detailed accounts of the fighting on the morning of July 1, see Martin, *Gettysburg July 1,* 59–202; and H. Pfanz, *Gettysburg: The First Day,* 51–130.

3. OR 27, pt. 2, 553.

4. Ibid., 554.

5. Ibid., 555. For details on the decision not to attack Cemetery Hill, see H. Pfanz, *Gettysburg: Culp's Hill and Cemetery Hill*, 76–80.

6. Gorman, "Memoirs of a Rebel," 24. The Gettysburg portion of Gorman's memoirs is based on a letter to his mother that was originally published as "Battles of Gettysburg," *North Carolina Standard*, Aug. 4, 1863.

7. Krick, "Three Confederate Disasters on Oak Ridge," 138–39.

8. OR 27, pt. 2, 446–47.

9. J. A. Early, *Autobiographical Sketch*, 273.

10. OR 27, pt. 2, 588.

11. "Copy of a portion of Capt. Turner's Memoranda relating to Gettysburg written before Col. Walter Taylors book—either in '76 or '77," in Jones, *Campbell Brown's Civil War*, 322; OR 27, pt. 2, 470; J. A. Early, "Leading Confederates on the Battlefield," 280.

12. OR 27, pt. 2, 447; G. Campbell Brown to Henry Jackson Hunt, May 7, 1885, in Jones, *Campbell Brown's Civil War*, 329.

13. Collins, *Major General Robert E. Rodes*, 280, 284; J. C. Early, "Southern Boy's Experience," 417.

14. Tagg, *Generals of Gettysburg*, 272; Ted Barclay to Dear Sister, July 8, 1863, Barclay Papers, W&L.

15. Brown, *Retreat from Gettysburg*, 389–90.

16. Charles F. Bahnson to Dear Father, July 15, 1863, in Chapman, *Bright and Gloomy Days*, 70.

17. Lord, *Fremantle Diary*, 220 (July 4, 1863).

18. *Richmond Daily Examiner*, July 21, 1863, quoted in Brown, *Retreat from Gettysburg*, 331; Ross, *A Visit to the Cities and Camps of the Confederate States*, 76.

19. Neese, *Three Years in the Confederate Horse Artillery*, 192; Eugene Blackford to William M. Blackford, July 16, 1863, quoted in Blackford, *Mine Eyes Have Seen the Glory*, 219.

20. Pierson to Father, July 19, 1863, in Cutrer and Parrish, *Brothers in Gray*, 202–3; Bahnson to Father, July 15, 1863, in Chapman, *Bright and Gloomy Days*, 70.

21. Nichols, *Soldier's Story*, 123.

22. Evans Diary, July 14, 1863, in Stephens, *Intrepid Warrior*, 238.

23. "Letter from Lee's Army," July 15, 1863, *Augusta Weekly Chronicle and Sentinel*, Aug. 4, 1863.

Bibliography

NEWSPAPERS

Alabama Beacon (Greensboro)
Amite (LA) News Digest
Athens (GA) Enquirer
Augusta (GA) Weekly Chronicle and Sentinel
Baltimore Sun
Biblical Recorder (Raleigh, NC)
Cadiz (OH) Republican
Carlisle (PA) American Volunteer
Carlisle (PA) Evening Sentinel
Carlisle (PA) Herald
Carolina Watchman (Salisbury, NC)
Cecil Whig (Elkton, MD)
Charleston (SC) Mercury
Christian Advocate and Journal (New York City)
Clinch Valley News (Jeffersonville, VA)
Columbia (PA) Spy
The Constitution (Keokuk, IA)
The Countryman (Turnwold, GA)
Cumberland Valley Journal (Mechanicsburg, PA)
Franklin Repository (Chambersburg, PA)
Frederick (MD) Examiner
Fulton Democrat (McConnellsburg, PA)
Gettysburg (PA) Compiler
Gettysburg (PA) Star and Sentinel
Gettysburg (PA) Times
Greencastle (PA) Pilot
Greensboro (NC) Patriot
Hanover (PA) Spectator
Harrisburg (PA) Daily Patriot and Union

Huntingdon (PA) Daily News
Huntingdon (PA) Journal
Jasper County News (Monticello, GA)
Lancaster (PA) Daily Express
Lexington (VA) Gazette and Citizen
Macon (GA) Daily Telegraph
Mobile (AL) Daily Advertiser and Register
Mobile (AL) Evening News
New York Daily Tribune
New York Herald
New York Times
North Carolina Argus (Wadesboro)
North Carolina Standard (Raleigh)
Perry County Freeman (Bloomfield, PA)
Philadelphia Daily Press
Philadelphia Inquirer
Philadelphia Weekly Times
Pittston (PA) Gazette
Pocahontas Times (Marlington, WV)
Portland (ME) Daily Advertiser
Raleigh (NC) Daily Progress
Raleigh (NC) News and Observer
Raleigh (NC) Weekly State Journal
Richmond (VA) Daily Dispatch
Richmond (VA) Daily Examiner
Richmond (VA) Daily Whig
Richmond (VA) Enquirer
Richmond (VA) Times Dispatch
Rockingham (VA) Register
Sacramento (CA) Daily Union
Savannah (GA) Republican
Selinsgrove (PA) Times
Spirit of the Age (Raleigh, NC)
Staunton (VA) Spectator
Times Picayune (New Orleans)
Valley Spirit (Chambersburg, PA)
Wilmington (NC) Daily Journal
York (PA) Daily
York (PA) Gazette

MANUSCRIPT SOURCES

Adams County Historical Society, Gettysburg, PA
    Sue King Black Letter
    Lydia Catherine Ziegler Clare, "A Gettysburg Girl's Story of the Great Battle"
    Gates D. Fahnestock, "Speech before the National Arts Club of New York, February 14, 1934"

Alabama Department of Archives and History, Montgomery
   Bolling Hall Family Papers
   Thomas S. Taylor Papers
   John S. Tucker Diary

Allison-Antrim Museum, Greencastle, PA
   Charles Hartman Diary. Typescript

American Civil War Museum, White House and Museum of the Confederacy, Richmond, VA
   Confederate States Army Bound Volumes
   Soldier Diaries Collection
   Soldier Letters Collection

Atlanta History Center, Kenan Research Center, Atlanta, GA
   Underwood, Key Families Papers

Bowdoin College, George L. Mitchell Department of Special Collections and Archives, Hawthorn-Longfellow Library, Brunswick, ME
   Confederate Miscellany

John D. Chapla Private Collection, Alexandria, VA
   John M. Vermillion Letter

College of William and Mary, Special Collections, Earl Greg Swem Library, Williamsburg, VA
   John Garland Pollard Papers

Columbia Historical Preservation Society, Columbia, PA
   Robert Crane Deposition

Cumberland County Historical Society, Carlisle, PA
   Civil War Collection Files

Davidson College, Archives and Special Collections, Davidson, NC
   William Erskine Ardrey Papers

Dickinson College, Archives and Special Collections, Waidner-Spahr Library, Carlisle, PA
   George D. Chenoweth Letter
   Thomas Miller Griffith Papers
   Isaac Harris Diary
   Charles Francis Himes Family Papers
   Charles Francis Himes Pocket Diary
   James Henry Morgan Presidential Papers

James R. Droegemeyer Private Collection, Martinsburg, WV
   Lewis H. Fuller Diary

Duke Univ., William R. Perkins Library, Durham, NC
   Bedinger-Dandridge Family Papers
   Patrick H. Cain Papers
   John Cleek Papers
   James O. Coghill Papers
   Winifred A. Cowand Papers

Edward Harden Papers
Archibald Erskine Henderson Papers
John Thomas Nichols Papers
Isaac V. Reynolds Papers

Durham County Library, North Carolina Collection, Durham, NC
Gorman Family Collection

Emory Univ., Stuart A. Rose Manuscripts, Archives and Rare Book Library, Atlanta, GA
Civil War Collection
James P. Garrison Papers
David Read Evans Winn Papers

Fredericksburg and Spotsylvania National Military Park, Library, Fredericksburg, VA
J. William Thomas Diary

Steve French Private Collection, Hedgesville, WV
Rachel McFerran Bagley, ed., "Letters Home Written by Henry Gaddis during the Civil War, 1862–1865"

Fulton County Historical Society, Library, McConnellsburg, PA
Patterson Family Collection

Georgia Archives, Morrow
Thomas M. Hightower Letters
John C. Key, "Memoirs"
Lavender R. Ray Papers
Sidney J. Richardson Papers
William Davies Tinsley Letters

Georgia Historical Society, Library and Archives Division, Savannah
Hilton Family Papers
Edwin R. Sharpe Papers

Gettysburg National Military Park, Library, Gettysburg, PA
Gregory A. Coco Collection
Confederate Regiment Files
Kathleen Georg Harrison, ed., "Summary of Damage Claims from the Battle of Gettysburg for Adams County, PA"
Wilbur S. Nye Collection

Gilder Lehrman Institute of American History, Gilder Lehrman Collection, New York
William A. Heirs Letters
Jeremiah Tate Letters

Handley Regional Library, Stewart Bell Jr. Archives Room, Winchester, VA
James A. Miller Collection
Terry Plank Collection
Kate Sperry Collection
Allan Tischler Collection

Benjamin Hoover II Private Collection, York, PA
   J. A. Rohrer Letter

Huntington Library, Manuscript Collections, San Marino, CA
   Etha Mayo Woodruff Memorial Collection of Family Papers

Howard Land Private Collection, Stafford, VA
   Thomas C. Land Diary

Library of Congress, Manuscript Division, Washington, DC
   Jubal A. Early Papers
   Feamster Family Papers
   John William Ford Hatton, "Memoir, 1861–1865"
   Jedediah Hotchkiss Papers
   Personal Papers Collection

Library of Virginia, Archives, Richmond
   Ted Barclay Papers
   Almira Sue Browning Harvey Letters
   H. M. Ingram Letters
   James I. Robertson Jr. Civil War Sesquicentennial Legacy Collection

Lower Cape Fear Historical Society, Wilmington, NC
   B. Frank Hall, "Account of the Battle of Gettysburg, 1913"

Maryland Historical Society, Baltimore
   William H. Lyons Diary
   William H. Moffett Papers

National Archives, Washington, DC
   Diary and Account Book of Col. John Lea, Record Group 109
   Records of Judge Advocate General's Office, Record Group 153

Navarro College, Pearce Museum, Corsicana, TX
   Hiram Kibler Letter
   William D. Lyon Papers
   Alexander Murdock Papers

Newville Historical Society, Newville, PA
   Reed Scrapbook

New York State Military Museum, Albany
   New York Civil War Newspaper Clipping Files

North Carolina State Archives, North Carolina Office of Archives and History, , Raleigh
   Military Collections
         J. B. Oliver, "My Recollections of the Battle of Gettysburg"
         John A. Stikeleather, "Memoirs"
   Private Collections
         Oscar W. Blacknall Papers
         Futch Papers
         Gales Papers

James E. Green Diary
Bryan Grimes Papers
Marcus Hefner Papers
William Clark Ousby Papers
John F. Shaffner Diary and Papers

Northwestern State Univ. of Louisiana, Cammie C. Henry Research Center, Watson Memorial Library, Natchitoches
Edmund Stephens Collection

Old Courthouse Civil War Museum, Winchester, VA
Robert Sherrard Bell Diary

Pennsylvania State Archives, Harrisburg
Pennsylvania Civil War Border Claims, 1868–78

Rosenbach Museum and Library, Philadelphia
Marianne Moore Papers

Shepherd Univ., Library, Special Collections, Shepherdstown, WV
Goldsborough Family Papers

St. Lawrence Univ., Special Collections, Canton, NY
Sunderland Family Correspondence

Troup County Archives, LaGrange, GA
Nix-Price Collection
John Thomas Traylor Collection

Tulane Univ., Louisiana Historical Association Collection, Special Collections, Howard-
Tilton Memorial Library, New Orleans
George P. Ring Diary

U.S. Army Heritage and Education Center, Carlisle, PA
Robert L. Brake Collection
Carlisle Barracks Collection
Civil War Miscellaneous Collection
Civil War Times Illustrated Collection
Thomas G. Clemens Collection
Harrisburg Civil War Round Table Collection
Lewis Leigh Collection

U.S. National Library of Medicine, Modern Manuscript Collections, History of Medicine
Division, National Institutes of Health, Bethesda, MD
Henkel Family Correspondence

Univ. of Georgia, Special Collections Division, Hargrett Library, Athens
John Brown Gordon Family Papers
Mary Barnard Nix Collection

Univ. of Illinois at Urbana-Champaign, Illinois History and Lincoln Collections
Wingard-Forney-Vaky Family Papers

Univ. of Iowa, Library, Special Collections Department, Iowa City
Joseph Franklin Culver Collection

Univ. of Massachusetts–Amherst, Special Collections and Univ. Archives, Univ. Libraries, Amherst
Burgett-Irey Family Papers

Univ. of Michigan, Schoff Civil War Collection, William L. Clements Library, Ann Arbor
David Ballenger Letters

Univ. of North Carolina at Chapel Hill, Southern Historical Collection, Wilson Library
Avery Family of North Carolina Papers
William Beavans Diary and Letters
Thomas F. Boatwright Papers
Calder Family Papers
Carrie H. Clack Papers
John Fuller Coghill Letters
Samuel W. Eaton Papers
Samuel Angus Firebaugh Diary
W. R. Gwaltney Papers
Hatrick Family Scrapbook
Hundley Family Papers
Joyner Family Papers
W. G. Lewis Papers
William Nelson Pendleton Papers
Polk, Brown, and Ewell Family Papers
L. L. Polk Papers
Proffit Family Letters
Preston H. Turner Papers
George Whitaker Wills Letters
William H. Wills Papers

Univ. of North Carolina at Wilmington, William M. Randall Library, Special Collections
Thomas J. Armstrong Papers

Univ. of Notre Dame, Rare Books and Special Collections, Notre Dame, IN
Read Family Correspondence
Sillers-Holmes Family Correspondence

Univ. of South Carolina, Manuscripts Division, South Caroliniana Library, Columbia
Watson Family Papers

Univ. of Texas at Austin, Littlefield Southern History Collection, Dolph Briscoe Center for American History
William Adolphus Smith Papers

Univ. of Virginia, Manuscripts Division, Alderman Library, Charlottesville
Blackford Family Papers
Marcus Blakemore Buck Diary and Farm Journal
John Warwick Daniel Papers
Clement Daniel Fishburne, "Memoirs"

Washington Hands, "Civil War Memoirs"
Samuel H. Pendleton Diary
Steptoe Family Papers
James Peter Williams Papers
Micajah Woods Papers

Virginia Historical Society, Richmond
 Harlow Family Papers
 Thomas Catesby Jones, "Civil War Reminiscences"
 Watkins Kearns Diary
 Rust Papers
 Saunders Family Papers
 Leonard K. Sparrow Papers

Virginia Military Institute, Archives, Lexington
 Henry H. Dedrick Papers
 John Garibaldi Papers

Warren Heritage Society, Front Royal, VA
 Charles Eckhardt Diary

Washington and Lee Univ., Special Collections and Archives, Leyburn Library, Lexington, VA
 Alexander Tedford Barclay Papers

West Virginia Univ., West Virginia and Regional History Center and Special Collections, Morgantown
 Roy Bird Cook Collection

Yale Univ., Manuscripts and Archives Library, New Haven, CT
 Civil War Manuscripts Collection
 Diaries Miscellaneous Collection

York County History Center, Library and Archives, York, PA
 Civil War Files
 Jubal A. Early File
 Latimer Family Files
 Scott Mingus Database of York County Civil War Damage Claims

ARTICLES AND CHAPTERS

Ackerd, M. H. "Early's Brigade at Winchester." *Confederate Veteran* 29 (1921): 264.
Agee, George F. "The Battle of Gettysburg." *Sunny South,* July 20, 1901.
Bean, William G. "A House Divided: The Civil War Letters of a Virginia Family." *Virginia Magazine of History and Biography* 59 (1951): 397–422.
Beetem, Charles Gilbert, ed. "Experiences of a West Ward Boy." In *Civil War Miscellany: Essays on the Confederate Invasion, Occupation, and Bombardment of Carlisle, Pa., during the Gettysburg Campaign of 1863,* edited by Cumberland County Historical Society, 5–10. Carlisle, PA: Hamilton Library Association, 1963.
Bender, Lida Welsh. "Civil War Memories." *Outlook* 140 (June 24, 1925): 295–98.

Bennett, R. T. "Fourteenth Regiment." In Clark, *Histories of the Several Regiments and Battalions from North Carolina*, 1:704–32.

Bohannon, Keith S. "Placed on the Pages of History in Letters of Blood: Reporting on and Remembering the 12th Georgia Infantry in the 1862 Valley Campaign." In *The Shenandoah Valley Campaign of 1862*, edited by Gary W. Gallagher, 115–43. Chapel Hill: Univ. of North Carolina Press, 2003.

Bond, Frank A. "Company A, First Maryland Cavalry." *Confederate Veteran* 6 (1898): 78–80.

Bowers, William S., ed. "William Heyser's Diary." *Kittochtinny Historical Society Papers* 16 (1970–78): 1–88.

Bradwell, I. G. "The Burning of Wrightsville, Pa." *Confederate Veteran* 27 (1919): 300–301.

Brenner, W. O. "Confederates Found Food Plentiful throughout Cumberland Valley." Carlisle Civil War Centennial Supplement. *Carlisle (PA) Evening Sentinel,* June 21, 1963.

Brumbaugh, Thomas. "The Confederate March through Greencastle." *Valley of History* (Spring 1969): 13–17.

Burnett, Edmund Cody, ed. "Letters of a Confederate Surgeon: Dr. Abner Embry McGarity, 1862–1865." *Georgia Historical Quarterly* 29 (1945): 159–89.

Carrington, James McDowell. "First Day on Left at Gettysburg." *Southern Historical Society Papers* 37 (1909): 326–37.

Chisolm, Samuel H. "Forward, the Louisiana Brigade." *Confederate Veteran* 27 (1919): 449.

Clemens, Thomas G., ed. "The 'Diary' of John H. Stone, First Lieutenant, Company B, 2nd Maryland Infantry, CSA." *Maryland Historical Magazine* 85 (1990): 109–43.

Coddington, Edwin B., and Edwin P. Coddington. "Prelude to Gettysburg: The Confederates Plunder Pennsylvania." *Pennsylvania History* 30 (1963): 123–47.

Collins, Carrie C. "Grey Eagle: Major General Robert Huston Milroy and the Civil War." *Indiana Magazine of History* 90 (1994): 48–72.

Cordell, Glenn R., ed. "Civil War Damage Claims from Fulton County, Pennsylvania." *Fulton County Historical Society Publications* 22 (2001): 1–45.

Cowan, John, and James I. Metts. "Third Regiment." In Clark, *Histories of the Several Regiments and Battalions from North Carolina*, 1:178–214.

Cree, Jemima K. "Jenkins' Raid." *Kittochtinny Historical Society Papers* 5 (1905–8): 92–99.

Crist, Robert G. "Highwater 1863: The Confederate Approach to Harrisburg." *Pennsylvania History* 30 (1963): 158–83.

Cunningham, S. A. "Heroic Defense of Bridge at Stephenson's Depot." *Confederate Veteran* 29 (1921): 43.

Daihl, Samuel L. "Shippensburg, 1863." *Kittochtinny Historical Society Papers* 14 (1963): 367–72.

Daniel, W. Harrison, ed. "H. H. Harris Civil War Diary (1863–1865)." *Virginia Baptist Register* 35 (1996): 1766–86.

"The Defense and Evacuation of Winchester, on June 13th 1863." *Continental Monthly* 4 (1863): 483.

Deppen, George E. "Tales That Were Told in Lower Northumberland County." *Proceedings of the Northumberland County Historical Society* 8 (1936): 172–75.

Dietrich, Matilda Ripple. "Waynesboro in Civil War Days." In *Waynesboro during the Civil War*, edited by Todd Andrew Dorsett, 13–19, 32–33. Waynesboro, PA: Antietam Historical Association, 2011.

Early, John Cabell. "A Southern Boy's Experience at Gettysburg." *Journal of the Military Service Institution of the United States* 48 (1911): 415–23.

Early, Jubal A. "Leading Confederates on the Battlefield: A Review by General Early." *Southern Historical Society Papers* 4 (1877): 241–81.

Foltz, M. A. "A Notable Publication House in Chambersburg, 1835–1864." *Kittochtinny Historical Society Papers* 5 (1905–8): 183–99.

Freeman, R. W. "Not Like 'Dumb Driven Cattle.'" *Sunny South,* May 1, 1897.

French, Steve. "The Battle of Martinsburg." *Gettysburg Magazine* 34 (Jan. 2006): 7–25.

Gallagher, Gary W. "Confederate Corps Leadership on the First Day at Gettysburg, A. P. Hill and Richard S. Ewell in a Difficult Debut." In *The First Day at Gettysburg: Essays on Confederate and Union Leadership,* edited by Gary W. Gallagher, 3–56. Kent, OH: Kent State Univ. Press, 1992.

Gannett, Michael R., ed., "Twelve Letters from Altoona, June–July 1863." *Pennsylvania History* 46 (1980): 39–56.

Gorman, George, ed. "Memoirs of a Rebel: Being the Narratives of John Calvin Gorman, Captain, Company B, 2nd North Carolina Regiment, 1861–1865, Part II: Chancellorsville and Gettysburg." *Military Images* 3, no. 6 (May–June 1982): 21–25.

Grace, C. D. "Rodes's Division at Gettysburg." *Confederate Veteran* 5 (1897): 614–15.

Green, Fletcher M., ed. "A People at War: Hagerstown, Maryland, June 15–Aug. 31, 1863." *Maryland Historical Magazine* 40 (1940): 251–59.

Hall, Clark B. "The Army Is Moving: Lee's March to the Potomac, Rodes Spearheads the Way." *Blue and Gray Magazine* 21, no. 3 (Spring 2004): 6–22, 44–52.

Hall, James O. "A Modern Hunt for Fabled Agent: The Spy Harrison." *Civil War Times Illustrated* 24, no. 10 (1986): 18–25.

Harter, Dale, ed. "The Diary of John B. Sheets, of Mt. Crawford, Co. I, 33rd Virginia Infantry, C.S.A." *Harrisonburg-Rockingham Historical Society Newsletter* 31 (Winter 2009): 3, 7.

Hege, Henry B. "The Civil War Unvarnished—Henry B. Hege to Henry G. Hege, July 12, 1863." *Mennonite Research Journal* 5 (Apr. 1964): 19, 22.

Henkel, Casper C. "Letter Delivered after Many Years." *Confederate Veteran* 16 (1908): 407–8.

Herbert, T. W., ed. "In Occupied Pennsylvania." *Georgia Review* 4 (1950): 103–13.

Heth, Henry. "Causes of Lee's Defeat at Gettysburg." *Southern Historical Society Papers* 4 (1877): 151–60.

Hodam, James H. "From Potomac to Susquehanna." In *Under Both Flags: A Panorama of the Civil War,* edited by C. E. Graham, 78–81. Chicago: Monarch, 1896.

———. "The Hodam Manuscript: Reminiscences of a Confederate Soldier." In Kesterson, *Campaigning with the 17th Virginia Cavalry,* 274–305.

Hudgins, F. L. "With the 38th Georgia Regiment." *Confederate Veteran* 26 (1918): 161.

Hufham, J. D., Jr. "Gettysburg (Being an Account of the Experiences of a Veteran, Told by Himself)." *Wake Forest Student* 16 (1897): 451–56.

Hunsecker, Catharine. "Civil War Reminiscences." *Christian Monitor* 16 (1924): 406–7.

Hunter, Alexander. "Thirteenth Virginia Infantry—Humor." *Confederate Veteran* 16 (1908): 339–40.

Johnston, Hugh Buckner, Jr., ed. "The Confederate Letters of Ruffin Barnes of Wilson County." *North Carolina Historical Review* 31 (1954): 75–99.

Jones, Hamilton C. "Fifty-Seventh Regiment." In Clark, *Histories of the Several Regiments and Battalions from North Carolina,* 3:404–29.

Jordan, Brian Matthew, ed. "'Remembrance Will Cling to Us through Life:' Kate Bushman's Memoir of the Battle of Gettysburg." *Adams County History* 20 (2014): 4–21.

Krick, Robert K. "Three Confederate Disasters on Oak Ridge: Failures of Brigade Leadership on the First Day at Gettysburg." In *The First Day at Gettysburg: Essays on Confederate and Union Leadership*, edited by Gary W. Gallagher, 92–139. Kent, OH: Kent State Univ. Press, 1992.

———. "We Have Never Suffered a Greater Loss Save in the Great Jackson: Was Robert E. Rodes the Army's Best Division Commander?" In *The Smoothbore Volley That Doomed the Confederacy*, edited by Robert K. Krick, 117–43. Baton Rouge: Louisiana State Univ. Press, 2002.

Landon, William, ed. "The 14th Indiana Regiment in the Valley of Virginia." *Indiana Magazine of History* 30 (1934): 275–98.

Lauck, T. H. "The Little Corporal's Story." *Confederate Veteran* 29 (1921): 181.

London, Henry A. "Thirty-Second Regiment." In Clark, *Histories of the Several Regiments and Battalions from North Carolina*, 3:521–50.

Love, Jenny. "War as a Girl Saw It: A Graphic Picture of Chambersburg during the Invasion of Lee and Ewell into Pa." *National Tribune*, May 12, 1910.

Mathews, W. C. "'Wright's Legion,' afterwards Known as the Thirty-Eighth Georgia Regiment, C.S.A." *Sunny South*, Jan. 10, 1891.

McCreary, Albertus. "Gettysburg: A Boy's Experience of the Battle." *McClure's Magazine* 33 (1909): 243–53.

McLachlan, James, ed. "The Civil War Diary of Joseph H. Coit." *Maryland Historical Magazine* 60 (1965): 245–60.

Meade, Everard Kidder. "Col. Thomas H. Carter, C.S.A.—A Sketch." *Proceedings of the Clarke County Historical Association* 3 (1943): 41–42.

Metts, James I. "The Jordon Springs Battle." *Confederate Veteran* 29 (1921): 104–5.

Mingus, Scott L., Sr. "Jenkins' Cavalry Raid through Northwestern York County, Pennsylvania." *Gettysburg Magazine* 44 (Jan. 2011): 41–52.

———. "White's Comanches on the Warpath at Hanover Junction." *Gettysburg Magazine* 42 (Jan. 2010): 8–21.

Miyagawa, Ellen, ed. "The Boys Who Wore the Gray: A Collection of Letters and Articles Written by Members of the Fluvanna Artillery, 1861–1865, Part I." *Bulletin of the Fluvanna County Historical Society* 41 (Apr. 1986): 1–44.

Monroe, Haskell, ed. "The Road to Gettysburg: The Diary and Letters of Leonidas Torrence of the Gaston Guards." *North Carolina Historical Review* 36 (1959): 509–57.

Moore, Samuel Scollay. "Through the Shadows: A Boy's Memories of the Civil War in Clarke County." *Proceedings of the Clarke County Historical Association* 24 (1989–90): 1–98.

Murdoch, David A., ed. "Catherine Mary White Foster's Eyewitness Account of the Battle of Gettysburg." *Adams County History* 1 (1995): 45–67.

Myers, William Starr, ed. "The Civil War Diary of Isaac Ridgeway Trimble." *Maryland Historical Magazine* 17 (1922): 1–20.

Neal, Amanda Daniels. "Civil War Draft Resistance in Fulton County." *Fulton County Historical Society Publications* 33 (2012): 1–36.

Neely, Benjamin Kerr, ed. "John Charles Wills: Reminiscences of the Three Days Battle of Gettysburg at the Globe Hotel." *Adams County History* 13 (2007): 26–59.Nye, Wilbur S. "The First Battle of Gettysburg." *Civil War Times Illustrated* 4 (Aug. 1965): 12–19.

Owens J. W. "Heroic Defense of Bridge at Stephenson's Depot, Va." *Confederate Veteran* 29 (1921): 43.

Park, Robert E. "War Diary of Captain Robert Emory Park." *Southern Historical Society Papers* 26 (1898): 1–31.

Pierson, William Whatley, Jr., ed. "The Diary of Bartlett Yancey Malone." *James Sprunt Historical Publications* 16, no. 2 (North Carolina Historical Society, 1919): 1–59.

Piston, William Garrett, ed. "The Rebs Are Yet Thick about Us: The Civil War Diary of Amos Stouffer of Chambersburg." *Civil War History* 38 (1992): 210–31.

Plater, Richard C., Jr., ed. "Civil War Diary of Miss Mattella Page Harrison of Clarke County, Virginia, 1835–1898." *Proceedings of the Clarke County Historical Association* 22 (1982–83): 3–79.

A Private Recruit. "Philadelphia City Cavalry: Service of the First Troop Philadelphia City Cavalry during June and July, 1863." *Journal of the Military Service Institution of the United States* 43 (1908): 281–96.

Purifoy, John. "With Ewell and Rodes in Pennsylvania." *Confederate Veteran* 30 (1922): 462–64.

———. "With Jackson in the Valley." *Confederate Veteran* 30 (1922): 383–85.

Reed, Merl E., ed. "The Gettysburg Campaign—A Louisiana Lieutenant's Eye-Witness Account." *Pennsylvania History* 30 (1963): 184–91.

Reed, W. A. "Death of Corporal Rhial." *Kauffman's Progressive News,* June 22, 1886.

Reid, John W. P. "Recollections of Lee's Invasion." *Kauffman's Progressive News,* Apr. 11, 1919.

Rivera, John J. "The Two Heroines of the Shenandoah Valley." *Confederate Veteran* 8 (1900): 493–96.

Schaff, Philip. "The Gettysburg Week." *Scribner's Magazine* 16 (1894): 21–27.

Schuricht, Hermann. "Jenkins' Brigade in the Gettysburg Campaign: Extracts from the Diary of Lieutenant Hermann Schuricht, of the Fourteenth Virginia Cavalry." *Southern Historical Society Papers* 24 (1896): 339–51.

Scott, Josephus B. "At Martinsburg, Va." *National Tribune,* May 18, 1916.

Scott, W. W., ed. "Two Confederate Items." *Bulletin of the Virginia State Library* 16 (July 1927): 9–47.

Sharpe, John C. "A Boy's Experience during the Civil War." *Pennsylvania History* 6 (1939): 159–69.

Smith, Addison Austin. "A Story of the Life and Trials of a Confederate Soldier and the Great Loop He Made in Three Years." In Kesterson, *Campaigning with the 17th Virginia Cavalry,* 256–68.

Smith, David G. "Race and Retaliation: The Capture of African Americans during the Gettysburg Champaign." In *Virginia's Civil War,* edited by Peter Wallenstein and Bertram Wyatt-Brown, 137–51. Charlottesville: Univ. of Virginia Press, 2005.

Smith, James M. L. "How General Gordon Saved My Life." *Sunny South,* Sept. 23, 1904.

Sword, Wiley, ed. "Confederate Maj. John W. Daniel Describes the 2nd Battle of Winchester at the Beginning of the Gettysburg Campaign." *Gettysburg Magazine* 35 (2006): 7–9.

Taylor, Michael W., ed. "Ramseur's Brigade in the Gettysburg Campaign: A Newly Discovered Account by Capt. James I. Harris, Co. I, 30th Regt., N.C.T." *Gettysburg Magazine* 17 (July 1997): 26–40.

Tomlinson, A. R. "On the Advance into Maryland." *Confederate Veteran* 30 (1922): 141.

Trimble, Isaac R. "The Battle and Campaign of Gettysburg." *Southern Historical Society Papers* 26 (1898): 116–28.

Trundle, Joseph H. "Gettysburg Described in Two Letters from a Maryland Confederate." *Maryland Historical Magazine* 54 (1959): 210–12.

Turner, J. D. Edmiston, ed. "Civil War Days in Mercersburg as Related in the Diary of the Rev. Thomas Creigh, D.D., August 1, 1862–July 20, 1865." *Kittochtinny Historical Society Papers* 12 (1939–49): 29–40.

Turner, V. E., and H. C. Wall. "Twenty-Third Regiment." In Clark, *Histories of the Several Regiments and Battalions from North Carolina,* 2:180–268.

Voegle, Fred B. "Chronology of the Civil War in Berkeley County." *Berkeley Journal* 26 (2000): 1–26.

Wharton, R. W. "First Battalion." In Clark, *Histories of the Several Regiments and Battalions from North Carolina,* 4:225–42.

White, William S. "A Diary of the War, Or What I Saw of It." In *Contributions to a History of the Richmond Howitzer Battalion, Pamphlet No. 2,* edited by Carlton McCarthy, 84–285. Richmond, VA: Carlton McCarthy, 1883.

Wilson, George W. "First Fighting in Pennsylvania." *Confederate Veteran* 21 (1913): 70.

Wittenberg, Eric J. "This Was a Night Never to Be Forgotten: The Midnight Fight in the Monterey Pass, July 4–5, 1863." *North & South Magazine* 2, no. 6 (Aug. 1999): 44–54.

Wood, Wayne, ed. "From Montgomery to Gettysburg: War Letters from Alabama Soldier Henry B. Wood." *Alabama Heritage Magazine* 15 (1990): 26–45.

BOOKS

Adams, Charles R., Jr., ed. *A Post of Honor: The Pryor Letters, 1861–1863.* Fort Valley, GA: Garret, 1989.

Aler, F. Vernon. *Aler's History of Martinsburg and Berkeley County, West Virginia.* Hagerstown, MD: Mail, 1888.

Alleman, Matilda Pierce. *At Gettysburg; or, What a Girl Saw and Heard of the Battle, a True Narrative.* New York: W. Lake Borland, 1889.

Ashby, Thomas A. *The Valley Campaigns: Being the Reminiscences of a Non-Combatant While between the Lines in the Shenandoah Valley during the War of the States.* New York: Neale, 1914.

Baer, Elizabeth R., ed. *Shadows on My Heart: The Civil War Diary of Lucy Rebecca Buck of Virginia.* Athens: Univ. of Georgia Press, 1997.

Beach, William H. *The First New York (Lincoln) Cavalry: From April 19, 1861, to July 7, 1865.* New York: Lincoln Cavalry Association, 1902.

Beck, Brandon H., ed. *Third Alabama!: The Civil War Memoir of Brigadier General Cullen Andrews Battle, CSA.* Tuscaloosa: Univ. of Alabama Press, 2000.

Betts, A. D. *Experience of a Confederate Chaplain: 1861–1864.* Greenville, SC: N.p., 1907.

Black, Daniel P., ed. *A Lincoln Cavalryman: The Civil War Letters of Henry Suydam, 1st New York Lincoln Cavalry.* Hampstead, MD: Old Line, 2011.

Blackford, L. Minor. *Mine Eyes Have Seen the Glory.* Cambridge, MA: Harvard Univ. Press, 1954.

Broadhead, Sarah M. *The Diary of a Lady of Gettysburg, Pennsylvania, from June 15 to July 15, 1863.* Gettysburg, PA: N.p., n.d.

Brown, Kent Masterson. *Retreat from Gettysburg: Lee, Logistics, and the Pennsylvania Campaign.* Chapel Hill: Univ. of North Carolina Press, 2005.

Brunhouse, Robert L. *Miniatures of Mechanicsburg.* Mechanicsburg, PA: Mechanicsburg Museum Association, 1986.

Buck, Samuel D. *With the Old Confeds: Actual Experiences of a Captain in the Line.* Baltimore: H. E. Houck, 1925.

Buehler, Fannie J. *Recollections of the Rebel Invasion: And One Woman's Experience during the Battle of Gettysburg.* Hershey, PA: Gary T. Hawbaker, 1896.

Burkhardt, William H. *Shippensburg, Pennsylvania in the Civil War.* Shippensburg, PA: Shippensburg Historical Society, 1964.

Busey, John W., and David G. Martin. *Regimental Strengths and Losses at Gettysburg.* Hightstown, NJ: Longstreet House, 1986.

Cartland, Fernando G. *Southern Heroes or the Friends in War Time.* Cambridge, MA: Riverside, 1895.

Casler, John O. *Four Years in the Stonewall Brigade.* Girard, KS: Appeal, 1906.

Chapman, Sarah Bahnson, ed. *Bright and Gloomy Days: The Civil War Correspondence of Charles Frederic Bahnson, a Moravian Confederate.* Knoxville: Univ. of Tennessee Press, 2003.

Chappell, Frank Anderson, ed. *Dear Sister: Civil War Letters to a Sister in Alabama.* Huntsville, AL: Branch Springs, 2012.

Civic Club of Carlisle, Pennsylvania. *Carlisle Old and New.* Harrisburg, PA: J. Horace McFarland, 1907.

Clark, Walter, ed. *Histories of the Several Regiments and Battalions from North Carolina in the Great War 1861-'65: Written by Members of the Respective Commands.* 5 vols. Goldsboro, NC: Nash Brothers, 1901.

Clemmer, Gregg S. *Old Alleghany: The Life and Wars of General Ed Johnson.* Staunton, VA: Hearthside, 2004.

Coles, David J., and Stephen D. Engle, eds. *A Yankee Horseman in the Shenandoah Valley: The Civil War Letters of John H. Black, Twelfth Pennsylvania Cavalry.* Knoxville: Univ. of Tennessee Press, 2012.

Collins, Darrell L. *Major General Robert E. Rodes of the Army of Northern Virginia: A Biography.* Clarendon Hills, CA: Savas Beatie, 2008.

Colwell, David G. *The Bitter Fruits: The Civil War Comes to a Small Town in Pennsylvania.* Carlisle, PA: Cumberland County Historical Society, 1998.

Commemorative Biographical Record of Washington County, Pennsylvania. Chicago: J. H. Beers, 1893.

Crist, Robert G. *Confederate Invasion of the West Shore—1863.* Carlisle, PA: Cumberland County Historical Society, 1963.

Cross, Harlan Eugene, Jr. *Letters Home: Three Years under General Lee in the 6th Alabama.* Fairfax, VA: History4All, 2012.

Cummer, Clyde Lottridge, ed. *Yankee in Gray: The Civil War Memoirs of Henry E. Handerson with a Selection of His Wartime Letters.* Cleveland, OH: Press of Western Reserve Univ., 1962.

Cutrer, Thomas W., and T. Michael Parrish, eds. *Brothers in Gray: The Civil War Letters of the Pierson Family.* Baton Rouge: Louisiana State Univ. Press, 2004.

Dabney, R. L. *Life and Campaigns of Lieut.-Gen. Thomas J. Jackson (Stonewall Jackson).* 2 vols. London: James Nisbet, 1866.

Davidson, William H., ed. *War Was the Place: A Centennial Collection of Confederate Soldier Letters.* Chambers County, AL: Chattahoochee Valley Historical Society, 1961.

Dayton, Ruth Woods, ed. *The Diary of a Confederate Soldier: James E. Hall.* Lewisburg, WV: N.p., 1961.

Deems, Edward M., and Francis M. Deems, eds. *Autobiography of Charles Force Deems and Memoir by His Sons Rev. Edward M. Deems and Francis M. Deems.* New York: Fleming H. Revell, 1897.

Donehoo, George Patterson. *A History of the Cumberland Valley in Pennsylvania.* 2 vols. Harrisburg, PA: Susquehanna History Association, 1930.

Dorsett, Todd Andrew. *Waynesboro as We Knew It.* Waynesboro, PA: Antietam Historical Association, 2012.

Douglas, Henry Kyd. *I Rode with Stonewall.* Chapel Hill: Univ. of North Carolina Press, 1940.

Douglas, John Hancock, ed. *Report of the Operations of the Sanitary Commission during and after the Battles at Gettysburg, July 1st, 2nd and 3rd, 1863.* New York: W. C. Bryant, 1863.

Dozier, Graham, ed. *A Gunner in Lee's Army: The Civil War Letters of Thomas Henry Carter.* Chapel Hill: Univ. of North Carolina Press, 2014.

Duncan, Richard R. *Beleaguered Winchester: A Virginia Community at War.* Baton Rouge: Louisiana State Univ. Press, 2007.

Early, Jubal A. *Autobiographical Sketch and Narrative of the War between the States.* Philadelphia: J. B. Lippincott, 1912.

Eaton, Lafayette Claud, Jr., ed. *Rebecca's Letters: A Saga of a Confederate Family.* Vallejo, CA: N.p., 2000.

Edgar, Alfred M. *My Reminiscences of the Stonewall Brigade and the Immortal 600.* Charleston, WV: 35th Star, 2011.

Emmick, David J. *Defending the Wilderness: The Amick Family in the Fight.* Issaquah, WA: Flying A Books, 2007.

Eslinger, A. N. *Local History of Dillsburg, Pa.* Dillsburg, PA: Dillsburg Bulletin Printers, 1902.

Farquhar, A. B. *The First Million the Hardest: An Autobiography.* Garden City, NY: Doubleday, Page, 1922.

Fastnacht, Mary Warren. *Memories of the Battle of Gettysburg: Year 1863.* New York: Princely, 1941.

Freeman, Douglas Southall. *Robert E. Lee: A Biography.* 3 vols. New York: Charles Scribner's Sons, 1934.

Furgurson, Ernest B. *Chancellorsville 1863: The Souls of the Brave.* New York: Alfred A. Knopf, 2002.

Garber, Pat, ed. *Heart like a River: The Story of Sergeant-Major Newsom Edward Jenkins, 14th North Carolina Infantry, 1861–1865.* Lynchburg, VA: Schroeder, 2011.

Gardiner, Mabel Henshaw, and Ann Henshaw Gardiner, eds. *Chronicles of Old Berkeley: A Narrative History of a Virginia County from Its Beginning to 1926.* Durham, NC: Seeman, 1938.

Gardner, Leonard Marsden. *Sunset Memories: A Retrospect of a Life Lived during the Last Seventy-Five Years of the Nineteenth Century, 1831–1901.* Gettysburg, PA: Times and News, 1941.

Gibson, John. *History of York County Pennsylvania, from the Earliest Period to the Present Time.* Chicago: F. A. Battey, 1886.

Gilmor, Harry. *Four Years in the Saddle.* New York: Harper and Brothers, 1866.

Gold, Thomas D. *History of Clarke County Virginia and Its Connections with the War between the States.* Berryville, VA: Chesapeake, 1962.

Goldsborough, W. W. *The Maryland Line in the Confederate Army, 1861–1865.* Baltimore: Guggenheimer, Weil, 1900.

Gordon, John Brown. *Reminiscences of the War.* New York: Charles Scribner's Sons, 1904.

Green, Helen Binkley, ed. *Pages from a Diary, 1843–1880: Excerpts from the Diaries of Jacob Stouffer and Eliza Ryder Stouffer.* Hagerstown, MD: H. B. Green, 1966.

Green, Wharton Jackson. *Recollections and Reflections: An Auto of Half a Century and More.* Raleigh, NC: Edwards and Broughton Printing, 1906.

Guelzo, Allen C. *Gettysburg: The Last Invasion.* New York, Alfred A. Knopf, 2003.

Gwin, Minrose C., ed. *A Woman's Civil War: A Diary with Reminiscences of the War, from March 1862.* Madison: Univ. of Wisconsin Press, 1992.

Hain, Harry Harrison. *History of Perry County, Pennsylvania.* Harrisonburg, PA: Hain-Moore, 1929.

Hale, Laura Virginia, and Stanley S. Phillips. *History of the Forty-Ninth Virginia Infantry, C.S.A., "Extra Billy's Smith's Boy."* Lanham, MD: S. S. Phillips and Associates, 1981.

Hall, Susan G. *Appalachian Ohio and the Civil War, 1862–1863.* Jefferson, NC: McFarland, 2000.

Harris, Nathaniel E. *Autobiography: The Story of an Old Man's Life with Reminiscences of Seventy-Five Years.* Macon, GA: J. W. Burke, 1928.

Hartley, William R., III, and David J. Zimmerman, eds. *The Fighting 57th North Carolina: The Life and Letters of James Calvin Zimmerman.* Morrisville, NC: Lulu, 2006.

Hatley, Joe M., and Linda B. Huffman, eds. *Letters of William F. Wagner, Confederate Soldier.* Wendell, NC: Broadfoot's Bookmark, 1983.

Hauck, A. J. *Hauck's Centennial Directory of the Borough of Mechanicsburg.* Mechanicsburg, PA: N.p., 1876.

Haupt, Herman. *Reminiscences of General Herman Haupt.* Milwaukee: Wright and Joys, 1901.

Hayes, Patrick J., ed. *The Civil War Diary of Father James Sheeran: Confederate Chaplain and Redemptorist.* Washington, DC: Catholic Univ. of America Press, 2016.

Hewitt, Janet B., Noah Andre Trudeau, and Bryce A. Suderow, eds. *The Supplement to the Official Records of the Union and Confederate Armies.* 95 vols. Wilmington, NC: Broadfoot, 1995–2000.

Historical Committee of the Old Home Week Association. *Historic Huntingdon, 1709–1907.* Huntingdon, PA: Historical Committee, 1907.

History of Cumberland and Adams Counties, Pennsylvania. Chicago: Warner, Beers, 1886.

History of Franklin County, Pennsylvania. Chicago: Warner, Beers, 1887.

Hocker, Dennis J. *The Noble 300: The Untold Story of the Battle of Sterrett's Gap.* Las Vegas, NV: Genesis, 2014.

Hodam, Robert P., ed. *The Journal of James Hodam: Sketches and Personal Reminiscences of the Civil War as Experienced by a Confederate Soldier.* Eugene, OR: Western Printing, 1996.

Hoke, Jacob. *The Great Invasion of 1863.* Dayton, OH: W. J. Suey, 1887.

———. *Reminiscences of the War; or, Incidents Which Transpired in and about Chambersburg.* Chambersburg, PA: M. A. Foltz, 1884.

Hoole, William Stanley, ed. *History of the Third Alabama Regiment, C.S.A. by Col. Charles Forsyth.* University, AL: Confederate, 1991.

Horn, Henry E., ed. *Memoirs of Henry Eyster Jacobs: Notes on the Life of a Churchman.* 3 vols. Huntingdon, PA: Church Management Service, 1974.

Hubbell, Raynor. *Confederate Stamps, Old Letters and History.* Griffin, GA: N.p., 1959.

Hubbs, G. Ward, ed. *Voices from Company D: Diaries by the Greensboro Guards, Fifth Alabama Infantry Regiment, Army of Northern Virginia.* Athens: Univ. of Georgia Press, 2003.

Jacobs, Michael. *Notes on the Rebel Invasion of Maryland and Pennsylvania and the Battle of Gettysburg, July 1st, 2nd, and 3rd 1863.* Philadelphia: J. B. Lippincott, 1864.

Johnson, Clifton, ed. *Battleground Adventures: Stories of Dwellers on the Scenes of Conflict in Some of the Most Notable Battles of the Civil War.* Boston: Houghton Mifflin, 1915.

Johnson, Pharris Deloach, ed. *Under the Southern Cross: Soldier Life with Gordon Bradwell and the Army of Northern Virginia.* Macon, GA: Mercer Univ. Press, 1999.

Johnston, Frontis W., ed. *The Papers of Zebulon Baird Vance.* Vol. 1. Raleigh: North Carolina Division of Archives and History, 1963.

Jones, Terry L., ed. *Campbell Brown's Civil War: With Ewell and the Army of Northern Virginia.* Baton Rouge: Louisiana State Univ. Press, 2001.

———. *The Civil War Memoirs of Captain William J. Seymour: Reminiscences of a Louisiana Tiger.* Baton Rouge: Louisiana State Univ. Press, 1991.

Kesterson, Brian Stuart. *Campaigning with the 17th Virginia Cavalry: Night Hawks at Monocacy.* Washington, WV: Night Hawk, 2005.

King, John R. *My Experience in the Confederate Army and in Northern Prisons Written from Memory.* Clarksburg, WV: United Daughters of the Confederacy, 1917.

Koonce, Donald B., ed. *Doctor to the Front: The Recollections of Confederate Surgeon Thomas Fanning Wood, 1861–1865.* Knoxville: Univ. of Tennessee Press, 2000.

Krick, Robert K. *Lee's Colonels: A Biographical Register of the Field Officers of the Army of Northern Virginia.* Dayton, OH: Morningside, 1991.

Kundahl, George G., ed. *The Bravest of the Brave: The Correspondence of Stephen Dodson Ramseur.* Chapel Hill: Univ. of North Carolina Press, 2010.

Ladd, David L., and Aubrey J. Ladd, eds. *The Bachelder Papers: Gettysburg in Their Own Words.* 3 vols. Dayton, OH: Morningside House, 1994.

Leon, Louis. *Diary of a Tar Heel Confederate Soldier.* Charlotte, NC: Stone, 1913.

Leonard, John W., ed. *Who's Who in Pennsylvania: A Biographical Dictionary of Contemporaries.* New York: L. R. Hamersly, 1908.

Lord, Walter, ed. *The Fremantle Diary: Being the Journal of Lieutenant Colonel Arthur James Lyon Fremantle, Coldstream Guards, on His Three Months in the Southern States.* Short Hills, NJ: Burford Books, 1954.

Lowry, Thomas Power. *The Story the Soldiers Wouldn't Tell: Sex in the Civil War.* Mechanicsburg, PA: Stackpole Books, 1994.

Macaluso, Gregory J. *Morris, Orange, and King William Artillery.* Lynchburg, VA: H. E. Howard, 1991.

Martin, David G. *Gettysburg July 1.* Conshohocken, PA: Combined Books, 1995.

Martin, Isabella D., and Myrta Lockett Avery, eds. *A Diary from Dixie, as Written by Mary Boykin Chesnut.* New York: D. Appleton, 1905.

M'Cauley, I. H. *Historical Sketch of Franklin County, Pennsylvania.* Chambersburg, PA: John M. Pomeroy, 1878.

McClure, James. *East of Gettysburg: A Gray Shadow Crosses York County.* York, PA: York Daily Record, 2003.

McCrary, M. Patrick, ed. *Private Cook and the College Company at Gettysburg.* Anchorage, AK: NBF, 2013.

McDonald, Archie P., ed. *Make Me a Map of the Valley: The Civil War Journal of Stonewall Jackson's Topographer.* Dallas, TX: Southern Methodist Univ. Press, 1973.

McKim, Randolph H. *A Soldier's Recollections: Leaves from the Diary of a Young Confederate.* New York: Longman, Green, 1910.

Mingus, Scott L., Sr. *Flames beyond Gettysburg: The Confederate Expedition to the Susquehanna, June 1863.* Clarendon Hills, CA: Savas Beatie, 2011.

Mingus, Scott L., Sr., and James McClure. *Echoing Still: More Civil War Voices from York County, Pa.* Orrtanna.PA: Colecraft Books, 2013.

Mobley, Joe A., ed. *The Papers of Zebulon Baird Vance.* Vol. 2, *1863.* Raleigh: North Carolina Division of Archives and History, 1995.

Mohr, James C., ed. *The Cormany Diaries: A Northern Family in the Civil War.* Pittsburgh: Univ. of Pittsburgh Press, 1982.

Moore, Edward A. *The Story of a Cannoneer under Stonewall Jackson.* New York: Neale, 1907.

Moore, Frank E., ed. *The Rebellion Record: A Diary of American Events.* 12 vols. New York: D. Van Norstrand, 1863–65.

Morgan, James Henry. *Dickinson College: The History of One Hundred and Fifty Years, 1783–1933.* Carlisle, PA: Mount Pleasant, 1933.

Morton, Oren F. *A History of Highland County Virginia.* Roanoke, VA: Stone Printing and Manufacturing, 1911.

Mosby, John S. *Stuart's Cavalry in the Gettysburg Campaign.* New York: Moffat, Yard, 1908.

Motts, Sarah E. *Personal Experiences of a House That Stood on the Road.* Carlisle, PA: Hamilton Library Association, 1941.

Munson, E. B., ed. *Confederate Correspondent: The Civil War Reports of Jacob Nathaniel Raymer, Fourth North Carolina.* Jefferson, NC: McFarland, 2009.

Myers, Frank. *The Comanches: A History of White's Battalion, Virginia Cavalry.* Baltimore: Kelly, Piet, 1871.

Myers, Sylvester. *Myers' History of West Virginia.* 2 vols. Wheeling, WV: Wheeling News Lithography, 1915.

Neese, George M. *Three Years in the Confederate Horse Artillery.* New York: Neale, 1911.

Nelson, John H. *Confusion and Courage: The Civil War in Fulton County, Pa., June 1863.* McConnellsburg, PA: Fulton County Civil War Reenactment Advisory Committee, 1996.

Newcomer, C. Armour. *Cole's Cavalry; or, Three Years in the Saddle in the Shenandoah Valley.* Baltimore, MD: Pushing, 1895.

Nichols, G. W. *A Soldier's Story of His Regiment (61st Georgia) and Incidentally of the Lawton-Gordon-Evans Brigade, Army of Northern Virginia.* Jessup, GA: N.p., 1898.

Norman, William M. *A Portion of My Life: A Short & Imperfect History Written while a Prisoner of War Johnson's Island.* Winston-Salem, NC: John. F. Blair, 1959.

Norris, J. E. *History of the Lower Shenandoah Valley.* Chicago: A. Warner, 1890.

Noyalas, Jonathan A. *My Will Is Absolute: A Biography of Union General Robert H. Milroy.* Jefferson, NC: McFarland, 2006.

Nye, Wilbur Sturtevant. *Here Come the Rebels!* Dayton, OH: Morningside, 1988.

Pearson, Johnnie Perry, ed. *Lee and Jackson's Bloody Twelfth: The Letters of Irby Goodwin Scott, First Lieutenant, Company G, Putnam Light Infantry, Twelfth Georgia Volunteer Infantry.* Knoxville: Univ. of Tennessee Press, 2012.

Pfanz, Donald C., ed. *The Letters of General Richard S. Ewell: Stonewall's Successor.* Knoxville: Univ. of Tennessee Press, 2012.

———. *Richard S. Ewell: A Soldier's Life.* Chapel Hill: Univ. of North Carolina Press, 1998.

Pfanz, Harry W. *Gettysburg: Culp's Hill and Cemetery Hill.* Chapel Hill: Univ. of North Carolina Press, 1993.

———. *Gettysburg: The First Day.* 1987. Chapel Hill: Univ. of North Carolina Press, 2001.

Porter, Lorle. *A People Set Apart: Scotch-Irish in Eastern Ohio.* Zanesville, OH: New Concord, 1998.

Prowell, George R. *History of the Eighty-Seventh Regiment, Pennsylvania Volunteers.* York, PA: Press of the *York Daily,* 1903.

———. *History of York County Pennsylvania.* 2 vols. Chicago: J. H. Beers, 1907.

Quynn, William R., ed. *Diary of Jacob Engelbrecht, 1818–1882.* Frederick, MD: Publish America, 2006.

Randolph, Isham. *Gleanings from a Harvest of Memories.* Columbia, MO: E. W. Stevens, 1937.

Ray, Fred L., ed. *Sharpshooter: The Selected Letters and Papers of Maj. Eugene Blackford, C.S.A., Volume 1.* Asheville, NC: CSF, 2015.

Reed, Thomas Benton. *A Private in Gray.* Camden, AR: T. R. Reed, 1905.

The Regimental Committee. *History of the One Hundred and Twenty-Fifth Regiment Pennsylvania Volunteers, 1862–1863.* Philadelphia: J. B. Lippincott, 1906.

Robson, John S. *How a One-Legged Rebel Lives: Reminiscences of the Civil War.* Durham, NC: Educator Company Printers and Binders, 1898.

Rodgers, Sarah Sites, ed. *The Ties of the Past: The Gettysburg Diaries of Salome Myers Stewart, 1854–1922.* Gettysburg, PA: Thomas, 1996.

Roper, John Herbert, ed. *Repairing the "March of Mars": The Civil War Diaries of John Samuel Apperson, Hospital Steward in the Stonewall Brigade, 1861–1865.* Macon, GA: Mercer Univ. Press, 2001.

Ross, Fitzgerald. *A Visit to the Cities and Camps of the Confederate States.* London: William Blackwood and Sons, 1865.

Runge, William H., ed. *Four Years in the Confederate Artillery: The Diary of Private Henry Robinson Berkeley.* Chapel Hill: Univ. of North Carolina Press, 1961.

Sams, Anita B., ed. *With Unabated Trust: Major Henry McDaniel's Love Letters from Confederate Battlefields as Treasured in Hester McDaniel's Bonnet Box.* Monroe, GA: Historical Society of Walton County, 1977.

Scott, J. L. *36th and 37th Battalions Virginia Cavalry.* Lynchburg, VA: H. E. Howard, 1986.

Skelly, Daniel A. *A Boy's Experiences during the Battles of Gettysburg.* Gettysburg, PA: N.p., 1932.

Skinner, Calvin. *Surgeon's Story: Reminiscences by Dr. Calvin Skinner, July 10, 1894, a Paper Written to the W. D. Brennen Post, Grand Army of the Republic.* Albany: New York State Archives, 1894.

Smith, Treadwell. *Treadwell Smith's Diary of the Civil War, October 17, 1859–April 20, 1865.* Berryville, VA: Civil War Centennial Committee, Berryville and Clarke County Chamber of Commerce, 1965.

Smith, William Alexander. *The Anson Guards, Company C, Fourteenth Regiment North Carolina Volunteers, 1861–1865.* Charlotte, NC: Stone, 1914.

Sorrel, G. Moxley. *Recollections of a Confederate Staff Officer.* New York: Neale, 1905.

Stephens, Robert G., Jr., ed. *Intrepid Warrior: Clement Anselm Evans, Confederate General from Georgia.* Dayton, OH: Morningside Books, 1992.

Stevenson, James H. *Boots and Saddles: A History of the First Volunteer Cavalry of the War, Known as the First New York (Lincoln) Cavalry.* Harrisburg, PA: Patriot, 1879.

Stiles, Robert. *Four Years under Marse Robert.* New York: Neale, 1904.

Stoner, Jacob H. *Historical Papers: Franklin County and the Cumberland Valley, Pennsylvania.* Chambersburg, PA: Craft, 1947.

Styple, William B., ed. *Writing and Fighting the Confederate War: The Letters of Peter Wellington Alexander, Confederate Correspondent.* Kearny, NJ: Belle Grove, 2002.

Sullivan, James W. *Boyhood Memories of the Civil War, 1861–'65, Invasion of Carlisle.* Carlisle, PA: Hamilton Library Association, 1933.

Swank, Walbrook D., ed. *Courier for Lee and Jackson: 1861–1865 Memoirs.* Shippensburg, PA: Burd Street, 1993.

Tagg, Larry. *The Generals of Gettysburg: The Leaders of America's Greatest Battle*. Campbell, CA: Savas, 1998.

Taylor, Michael W., ed. *To Drive the Enemy from Southern Soil: The Letters of Col. Francis Marion Parker and the History of the 30th Regiment North Carolina Troops*. Dayton, OH: Morningside House, 1998.

Thomas, Henry Walter. *History of the Doles-Cook Brigade: Army of Northern Virginia, C.S.A.* Atlanta: Franklin Printing and Publishing, 1903.

Tiffany, Osmond. *A Sketch of the Life and Services of Gen. Otho Holland Williams*. Baltimore: John Murphy, 1851.

Tousey, Thomas G. *Military History of Carlisle and Carlisle Barracks*. Richmond, VA: Dietz, 1939.

Turner, Charles Wilson, ed. *Civil War Letters of Arabella Spears and William Beverley Pettit*. Roanoke: Virginia Lithograph and Graphics, 1988.

United Daughters of the Confederacy, Georgia Division. *Confederate Reminiscences and Letters, 1861–1865*. 18 vols. Atlanta: United Daughters of the Confederacy, 1995–2000.

U.S. War Department. *The War of the Rebellion: A Compilation of the Official Records of the Union and Confederate Armies*. 70 vols. in 128 parts. Washington, DC: Government Printing Office, 1880–1901.

Unrau, Harlan D. *Historic Resource Study: Chesapeake & Ohio Canal*. Hagerstown, MD: U.S. Department of the Interior, 2007.

Wallace, David H., ed. *Frederick Maryland in Peace and War, 1856–1864: Diary of Catherine Susannah Thomas Martell*. Frederick, MD: Frederick County Historical Society, 2006.

Warner, Ezra J. *Generals in Gray: Lives of the Confederate Commanders*. 1959. Baton Rouge: Louisiana State Univ. Press, 1988.

Waterman, Watkins, and Company. *History of Bedford, Somerset and Fulton Counties, Pennsylvania*. Chicago: Waterman, Watkins, 1884.

Watford, Christopher M., ed. *The Civil War in North Carolina: Soldiers' and Civilians' Letters and Diaries, 1861–1865*. Vol. 1, *The Piedmont*. Jefferson, NC: McFarland, 2003.

Watkins, Thomas J. *Notes on the Movement of the 14th North Carolina Regiment*. Wadesboro, NC: Anson County Historical Society, 1991.

Wert, Jeffrey D. *Gettysburg, Day Three*. New York: Simon and Schuster, 2001.

———. *A Glorious Army: Robert E. Lee's Triumph, 1862–1863*. New York: Simon and Schuster, 2011.

White, Gregory C. *A History of the 31st Georgia Volunteer Infantry: This Most Bloody and Cruel Drama*. Baltimore: Butternut and Blue, 1997.

Wild, Frederick W. *Memoirs and History of Capt. F. W. Alexander's Baltimore Battery of Light Artillery, U.S.V.* Baltimore: Press of the Maryland School for Boys, 1912.

Wildes, Thomas F. *Record of the One Hundred and Sixteenth Regiment Ohio Infantry Volunteers in the War of the Rebellion*. Sandusky, OH: I. F. Mack and Brother, 1884.

Williams, Richard Brady, ed. *Stonewall's Prussian Mapmaker: The Journals of Captain Oscar Hinrichs*. Chapel Hill: Univ. of North Carolina Press, 2014.

Wing, Conway P. *History of Cumberland County, Pennsylvania*. Philadelphia: James D. Scott, 1879.

Wingate, George W. *History of the Twenty-Second Regiment of the National Guard of the State of New York from Its Organization to 1895*. New York: Edwin W. Dayton, 1896.

Wingert, Cooper H. *Emergency Men! The 26th Pennsylvania Volunteer Militia and the Gettysburg Campaign*. Lynchburg, VA: Schroeder, 2013.

————, ed. *Rare and Unseen: Original Documents of Harrisburg and the Cumberland Valley in the Civil War.* Camp Hill, PA: N.p, 2013.

Wise, John S. *The End of an Era.* Boston: Houghton Mifflin, 1901.

Wister, Jones. *Jones Wister's Reminiscences.* Philadelphia: J. B. Lippincott, 1920.

Wittenberg, Eric J., and Scott L. Mingus. *The Second Battle of Winchester: The Confederate Victory That Opened the Door to Gettysburg.* Clarendon Hills, CA: Savas Beatie, 2016.

Wittenberg, Eric J., and J. David Petruzzi. *Plenty of Blame to Go Around: Jeb Stuart's Controversial Ride to Gettysburg.* Clarendon Hills, CA: Savas Beatie, 2006.

The Woman's Club of Mercersburg Pennsylvania. *Old Mercersburg.* Williamsport, PA: Grit, 1912.

Wood, James H. *The War: "Stonewall" Jackson, His Campaigns, and Battles, the Regiment as I Saw Them.* Cumberland, MD: Eddy, 1910.

Woodward, Steven E. *Under a Northern Sky: A Short History of the Gettysburg Campaign.* Wilmington, DE: Scholarly Resources Books, 2003.

Wray, W. J. *History of the Twenty Third Pennsylvania Volunteer Infantry: Birney's Zouaves.* Philadelphia: New York Public Library, 1904.

Wyatt, Lillian Reeves, ed. *The Reeves, Mercer, Newkirk Families: A Compilation.* Jacksonville, FL: Cooper, 1956.

Yeary, Mamie, ed. *Reminiscences of the Boys in Gray, 1861–1865.* Dallas, TX: Smith and Lamar, 1912.

ONLINE SOURCES

Bartek, James M. "The Rhetoric of Destruction: Racial Identity and Noncombatant Immunity in the Civil War." http://uknowledge.uky.edu/gradschool_diss/110/.

Cordrey, Francis. "Life and Comments of a Common Soldier." 1893. Transcribed by Laura M. Cooper. Munson, Underwood, Horn, Fairfield, and Allied Families. http://brazoriaroots.com/acrobat/franms.pdf.

"Diary of Abraham Essick (1849–1864; 1883; 1888)." Franklin County Personal Papers. *The Valley of the Shadow.* Univ. of Virginia Library. http://valley.lib.virginia.edu/papers/FD1005.

"John Lewis Poe's Account: The War of 1861 to 1865." 1926. List of Veteran Ancestors. Genealogy. Poeland. http://www.poeland.com/genealogy/auxdata/JLPoe_warDiary.html.

Mingus, Scott L., Sr. *Cannonball* (blog). http://www.yorkblog.com/cannonball/.

Patterson, David Hunter. "Memoirs of David Hunter Patterson." 1929. Transcribed and edited by William Remington Patterson Jr. 1991. Fulton County Pennsylvania Genealogy. http://fulton.pa-roots.com/pathist/toc.htm.

Weaver, Margaret S. Mohr, comp. "Gabriel Shank: Military Records, Articles, Letters, and Diary." 2003. Gabriel Shank and Aldine Kieffer Collection. http://www.rootsweb.ancestry.com/~varockin/shank/Gabriel_Shank.htm.

Index

Page numbers in italics refer to illustrations.